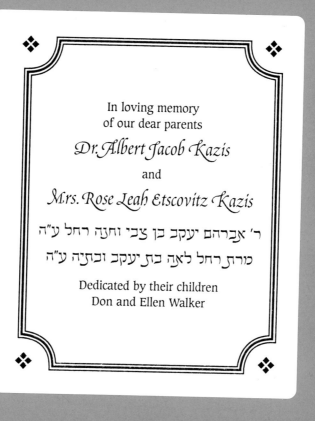

In loving memory
of our dear parents
Dr. Albert Jacob Kazis
and
Mrs. Rose Leah Etscovitz Kazis

ר' אַבְרהם יעקב בן צְבִי וחַנָּה רחל ע"ה

מרת רחל לאָה בת יעקב ובתָיה ע"ה

Dedicated by their children
Don and Ellen Walker

Dear Rebbi,

Please accept this small token of our appreciation for your devotion and dedication to our children, and for your family's commitment to your *avodas hakodesh.*

We know that it takes both work and sacrifice on your part, and we are hopeful that our children bring you much nachas and satisfaction. *"Kol hamelameid es ben chaveiro Torah k'ilo yoldo,"* we are grateful beyond words for your choosing to partner with us in the *chinuch* of our precious children. Your inspiration and the love for Yiddishkeit you instill in them will last the rest of their lives, and will carry on to their own children.

Realize that we don't take your efforts for granted, nor the support of your *mishpachah.* Thank you is simply inadequate.

This *sefer* focuses on the important mitzvah of *kibbud av v'eim.* We hope it provides you hours of inspirational reading for you and your family.

May you be *gebentched* with abundant health, nachas, and *hatzlachah* in every way.

Best wishes for a *chag kosher v'sameiach.*

Chasdei Lev

Chasdei Lev - POB 297257 Brooklyn, NY 11229 -- (718) 831-2500
www.chasdeilev.org

My Father

Sons and daughters
tell of their
devotion, challenges,
and successes
in honoring their parents

Published by

Mesorah Publications, ltd

My Mother and Me

By **Yehudis Samet**

author of the best-selling *The Other Side of the Story*

with **Aviva Rappaport**

Halachos by **Rabbi Yehuda Samet**

FIRST EDITION
Six Impressions ... January 2014 — June 2016
Seventh Impression ... February 2017

Published and Distributed by
MESORAH PUBLICATIONS, LTD.
4401 Second Avenue / Brooklyn, N.Y 11232

Distributed in Europe by
LEHMANNS
Unit E, Viking Business Park
Rolling Mill Road
Jarow, Tyne & Wear, NE32 3DP
England

Distributed in Australia and New Zealand
by **GOLDS WORLDS OF JUDAICA**
3-13 William Street
Balaclava, Melbourne 3183
Victoria, Australia

Distributed in Israel by
SIFRIATI / A. GITLER — BOOKS
POB 2351
Bnei Brak 51122

Distributed in South Africa by
KOLLEL BOOKSHOP
Northfield Centre, 17 Northfield Avenue
Glenhazel 2192, Johannesburg, South Africa

Please address any comments to:
Yehudis Samet 917-254-4444 (Israel)   MyFatherMyMotherandMe@gmail.com

ISBN 10: 1-4226-1454-9 / ISBN 13: 978-1-4226-1454-9

Typography by CompuScribe at ArtScroll Studios, Ltd.
Printed in the United States of America

כדי לקיים מצות עשה של כבד את אביך ואת אמך מדין מכבדו במותו,
הננו מקדישים חיבורנו זה לזכרון עולם ולעילוי נשמת הורינו היקרים

אבי מורי ר׳ אברהם זאב ב״ר יהודה ע״ה
נלב״ע י״ג אלול תשס״א

אמי מורתי מרת גיטל ב״ר יצחק דוד הלוי ע״ה
נלב״ע א׳ טבת תשנ״ב

אבי מורי ר׳ צבי הירש ב״ר שלמה ע״ה
נלב״ע י״ח אב תשס״ב

אמי מורתי מרת אסתר ב״ר חיים אפרים ע״ה
נלב״ע ו׳ תמוז תש״ע

תהא נשמתם צרורה בצרור החיים

Rabbi I. Scheiner

Dean *of Kamenitzer Yeshiva*

51 Zephania St., Jerusalem

Tel. (02) 532-2512

הרג יצחק שיינר

ראש ישיבת קמניץ

רחוב צפני' 51, ירושלים

טלפון 2512-532

בס"ד

מאד שמחתי לשמוע שידי"ן מאז, הרב יהודה סמט שליט"א, עומד להוציא לאור ספר חשוב פרי יגיעה ועמל רב, בשפה האנגלית, על מצות כיבוד אב ואם אשר התורה הק' כבר הבטיחה לנו, עבור קיומה, אורך ימים ושנות חיים בזה ובבא.

הספר כולל הלכות עיקריות, מעלת מצות כבוד ומורא וחומרת עון המצערם. מלוקט מדברי רבותינו והספרים הקדושים בשילוב של סיפורים נפלאים מחיי אנשי ונשי חיל שבימינו.

כפי שאנחנו רואים צריכים זירוז גדול בקיומה למעשה, אין ספק שמספר זה תצא תועלת לרבים, שיתעורר כל אחד לקיום המצוה כהלכתה ובהידור.

על כן אברכו שיזכה להמשיך לשקוד על דלתי התורה מתוך מנוחת הנפש והרחבת הדעת ובזכות מצות כאו"א נזכה להתקרבות הגאולה כמובא בחז"ל ובספרים הק' בביאת גואל צדק במהרה בימינו אמן.

יצחק שיינר

Table of Contents

In Addition

Preface

It began with a gift.

Browsing in a bookstore, my sister came across a book entitled *The Fifth Commandment* (ArtScroll/Mesorah 1998), a presentation of the halachos of *kibbud av va'eim*. She bought a copy for herself and presented one to each of us siblings. As soon as I opened it, I realized I was holding a treasure.

Eager to discover how far and wide the brilliance of this mitzvah radiated, I did some investigating.

The classes I was giving at the time provided the opportunity. Here was a cross section of women and girls of all ages, from many different countries, and of various educational backgrounds.

From a showing of hands, it became clear that these halachos were unfamiliar to most. How could such essential information, indispensable to everyday living, have been overlooked?

Yes, it was a treasure, but for many, a buried one. Shouldn't it be retrieved and shared with its rightful owners?

Therein began, with my husband's direction and guidance, an exploration of the intricacies of a child's obligations to his parents. We started with "the basics," and went on to explore nuances. Difficult questions were brought for clarification to *poskim*, until we were able to put together a curriculum whose goal was to present the letter of the law *and* the spirit of this mitzvah.

As this material was presented to communities the world over, from Miami to Montreal, Gateshead to Gibraltar, Baltimore to Beit Shemesh, Teaneck to Toronto…the response was almost heartbreaking. "Where has all this been hiding?" participants lamented. So many needless mistakes made, so much grief caused by not knowing these halachos in their fullest!

In high schools and seminaries, camps and bungalow colonies, lecture series and seminars, we explored the vast terrain of this mitzvah. Questions asked by participants necessitated further clarification of practical halachah, which gave us answers for sticky issues and tricky situations.

And then, of course, came the stories. In city after city, lecture after lecture, people shared their personal stories as well as those of others who excelled in this mitzvah. It is their narratives that fill these pages.

My thanks to those who went out of their way not only to tell their stories but to put pen to paper so that we can experience their trials and triumphs in their own words. Understandably, many requested anonymity. Thus, with the exception of well-known Rabbinic personalities, names as well as other identifying features have been altered to respect this privacy.

Thanks as well — and apologies — to those whose stories regrettably were not able to be included. Though your story does not appear in these pages, you are truly an inspiration to those who see you living this mitzvah.

Hundreds and thousands of stories are waiting to be told, stories of sons and daughters whose dedication and sacrifice for their parents leave us in awe and humbled. Even more important, their stories, too, are no doubt being recorded in a celestial book, in an everlasting way.

Acknowledgments

We wish to express our thanks to the many people who played important roles in the publication of this book.

With everlasting appreciation to our beloved parents, *zichronam livrachah*, to whom this book is dedicated, for their bountiful love, support and guidance, and the rich legacy they bequeathed to us which is woven into these pages.

It has been my privilege to once again partner with Mrs. Aviva Rappaport, being the beneficiary of her writing, editing, and publishing expertise. Her ability to unravel complex material and present it in a clear, logical order, her keen observations and creativity have turned a raw manuscript into a beautifully crafted work. Her enthusiasm, encouragement, and delightful sense of humor kept us afloat during the many months we have worked together.

To Rabbi Yitzchak Breitowitz, senior lecturer at Yeshivas Ohr Somayach, previously Rav of Woodside Synagogue Ahavas Torah, Silver Spring, Maryland, who reviewed portions of the initial draft, contributing valuable comments, changes, and additions.

To Rabbi Yisrael Dovid Harfenes, *poseik* and author of *Vayevarech Dovid*, for clarifying difficult halachic issues. The *Shailos & Teshuvos, Cheilek* II of *Vayevarech Dovid*, bring to light a wealth of practical halachic applications pertaining to *kibbud av va'eim*.

To Rav Yaakov Reisman, Mara D'asra of Agudas Yisrael of Long Island, who made available the tape of his presentation "Who Says Children Are for Nachas?" and gave permission to include parts in the final chapter.

To Mrs. Rachel Grossman, for typing the manuscript from dictation. We greeted each other bright and early in the morning and yawned together during late night sessions. My words barely spoken, her quick grasp and agile hands had already placed them on the page. In addition to her professional typing skills, she assisted in translating, writing, and editing parts of the text, contributing substantially to its quality, and was a good sounding board throughout.

To Mrs. Leah Schuster, who taped and edited the series of lectures on *kibbud av va'eim*, which served as the basis for these chapters, making it available for reference and additionally for distribution to the public. And always with a smile.

To Mrs. Naomi Gefen, Mrs. Miriam Gitlin, Mrs. Tammy Gilden, Mrs. Rivka Gold, and Mrs. Chedva Chaimovitch, who all had a part in enhancing the manuscript.

To Rabbi and Rebbetzin Pliskin for their constant encouragement.

To Project Derech, a non-profit organization, dedicated to strengthening the mitzvah of *kibbud av va'eim*. Their program is used in hundreds of schools around the world. A *kuntres* compiled by this organization covers basic halachos of respect for parents and parents-in-law. We thank the founders for sending us their not-yet-published booklet entitled, "Life-Assurance."

Our thanks to Rav Nosson Scherman and Rav Meir Zlotowitz for undertaking the publication of this book.

To Rav Chaim Zev Malinowitz, who gave of his time and scholarship to read the entire manuscript and the extensive footnotes for halachic accuracy, offering helpful suggestions and providing important corrections and clarifications.

To Mr. Shmuel Blitz for his professional competence, for keeping things running smoothly.

To Mrs. Miriam Zakon, Senior Editor, who masterfully coordinated the multi-faceted stages of the book's completion, with all its details and deadlines. All chapters were enhanced by passing through her careful scrutiny and benefited from her trademark insightful revisions. Her patience in handling the many editorial changes is greatly appreciated. Well known for her exceptional devotion to her late mother, she brought a sensitivity and appreciation for the importance of this mitzvah to this volume.

To Mrs. Judi Dick, Senior ArtScroll Editor. These pages bear the stamp of her editorial skills. Questioning and verifying every word and nuance, her detailed, vital corrections and improvements have greatly enhanced the book's clarity.

Thank you Rabbi Moshe Rosenblum for reviewing the accuracy of the Hebrew text. To Eli Kroen for the beautiful cover design. To Rivky Plittman for the magnificent page design. To Mrs. Esther Feierstein for her meticulous proofreading and Mrs. Estie Dicker for entering the corrections to the manuscript.

And to the hundreds of "children" of all ages, around the world, who agreed to share their stories.

We offer our thanks to Hashem Yisborach for enabling us to complete this project, the culmination of many years of effort. From its inception, we have experienced a clear outpouring of *siyata d'Shmaya*. Our sincere hope is that nothing found in these pages be a source of error or misunderstanding, but rather will increase the *nachas* He has from His children and bring honor to His name.

––––––•·◆·•––––––

Although there are aspects of *kibbud av va'eim* not touched upon, our goal has been to arouse heightened awareness of some of the many treasures of this precious mitzvah, to define and refine the bond between parent and child. Aside from the obvious benefit to the family unit, honoring parents brings other far-reaching results, as we learn from the following *Midrash*.

כֵּן אָמְרוּ בְּאַגָּדָה, אָמַר רַב אֶלֶכְסַנְדְּרִי אָמַר רַבִּי
שִׁמְעוֹן בֶּן לָקִיש, בֹּא וּרְאֵה כַּמָּה גְּדוֹלָה הִיא זְכוּתוֹ
שֶׁל מְכַבֵּד אֲבוֹתָיו...הוּא מְקָרֵב גְּאוּלָה לְיִשְׂרָאֵל
שֶׁנֶּאֱמַר "הִנֵּה אָנֹכִי שֹׁלֵחַ לָכֶם אֶת אֵלִיָּה הַנָּבִיא
לִפְנֵי בּוֹא יוֹם ה' הַגָּדוֹל וְהַנּוֹרָא. וְהֵשִׁיב לֵב־אָבוֹת
עַל־בָּנִים וְלֵב בָּנִים עַל־אֲבוֹתָם."

The Midrash teaches: Rav Alexandri said in the
name of Shimon ben Lakish, "Look how great
is the merit of the child who honors his parents.
He is actually hastening the *Geulah*, as it states
(*Malachi* 3:23,24), 'Behold, I will send to you Eliyahu HaNavi in preparation for the great and
awesome day, when Hashem's glory will fill the
world. He will return the hearts of fathers with
[their] sons and the hearts of sons with their
fathers'" (*Meah Shearim, Shaar* 68).

Here is a clear affirmation that it is the Almighty's Will that
children and parents be united in peace and harmony, as a
prerequisite for the great *Geulah*.

And so, dear child, whatever your age — know that every act
of honor shown your parent brings our Final Redemption that
much closer.

My Father My Mother and Me

A Note to the Reader

This is a children's book. Or rather, this is a book for children.

No matter how old you are, you are someone's child; you have, or once had, a father and a mother. So this is a book for you.

———•◆•———

Every child is presented with preordained parents, a parcel packed especially for him or her stamped "HANDLE WITH CARE" — take care to honor your father and mother. *How can we know what that means*, we wonder. And then we see a note: "Further information for proper care can be found in the instruction manual."

That instruction manual is the *Shulchan Aruch*.

Shulchan Aruch, literally "Set Table" also known as *The Code of Jewish Law*, was authored by Rav Yosef Karo in Tzefas in the 16th century.

This vast, comprehensive, and monumental work, which gives a final ruling on Talmudic, Geonic, and major subsequent halachic authorities, incorporates almost the entire Rabbinic literature up to that time. Together with its commentaries, it is the most widely accepted compilation of Jewish Law ever written.

The *Shulchan Aruch* has four sections, each divided into chapters and paragraphs. The details of children's obligations to parents are found in the second section, *Yoreh Deah*, Chapters 240:1-25 and 241:1-9. (For an outline of these paragraphs see Appendix A.)

These chapters form the foundation for this book.

A Note to Every Parent

If you are a parent, please don't "throw the book" at your child — not this book, anyway.

Chinuch is not so much what we preach as who we are, and that is what speaks to our children, whatever their age.

The objective is to focus on ourselves, and our own obligations as a "child." Are we doing all we can to fulfill our many obligations to *our* parents, whether they are in this world or the Next?

Turn the pages and find out.

Introduction: The Fifth Commandment

When *Klal Yisrael* stood at Sinai and accepted the wisdom and yoke of Torah, we became a nation. At that unforgettable moment in history, we received the Ten Commandments, the Almighty's gift to His people.

1. "I am Hashem, your G-d…"
2. "You shall not recognize the gods of others…"
3. "You shall not swear with Hashem's Name in vain…"
4. "Remember the Sabbath day…"
5. "Honor your father and your mother…"
6. "You shall not kill…"
7. "You shall not commit adultery…"
8. "You shall not steal (i.e., kidnap)…"
9. "You shall not bear false witness…"
10. "You shall not covet…"

Mankind is familiar with the fifth commandment, "Honor your father and your mother," since the teachings of the Ten Commandments have continued to reverberate throughout the civilized world for millennia.

Yes, we all agree — honor your parents — but what exactly does that entail?

Many are hard put to answer. Some say, "Just use your common sense." Others don't think too much about the question and stumble along as best as they can. But we in *Klal Yisrael* know that for us the parent-child relationship is governed by explicit Torah directives.

Among the 613 mitzvos in the Torah are the many that define our responsibilities to others — mitzvos like not bearing a grudge, not taking revenge or causing pain with words, visiting the sick, hosting guests, providing for the needy, judging favorably, and not coveting possessions of others. Over and above these general responsibilities, in which parents are included, the Torah specifies additional obligations that apply exclusively to a father and mother.

כַּבֵּד אֶת אָבִיךָ וְאֶת אִמֶּךָ לְמַעַן יַאֲרִכוּן יָמֶיךָ...

Honor your father and your mother so that your days will be lengthened... (*Shemos* 20:12).

כַּבֵּד אֶת אָבִיךָ וְאֶת אִמֶּךָ, כַּאֲשֶׁר צִוְּךָ ה' אֱלֹקֶיךָ, לְמַעַן יַאֲרִיכֻן יָמֶיךָ, וּלְמַעַן יִיטַב לָךְ...

Honor your father and your mother as Hashem, your G-d, commanded you, so that your days will be lengthened and it will be good for you... (*Devarim* 5:16).

אִישׁ אִמּוֹ וְאָבִיו תִּירָאוּ...

Revere your mother and father... (*Vayikra* 19:3).

וּמַכֵּה אָבִיו וְאִמּוֹ...

[It is forbidden to] hit a father or mother... (*Shemos* 21:15).

וּמְקַלֵּל אָבִיו וְאִמּוֹ...

[It is forbidden to] curse a father or mother... (*Shemos* 21:17).

אָרוּר מַקְלֶה אָבִיו וְאִמּוֹ...

[It is forbidden to] belittle or demean a father or mother… (*Devarim* 27:16).

Heightening our awareness of the implications of these mitzvos and understanding the Torah approach to the parent-child bond will enable us to extirpate foreign ideas that have crept into our homes and negatively affected that connection. Aligning our minds to Torah thinking prepares us for success in our role as children to the parents who were especially chosen for us.

Join us on a magnificent tour of this mitzvah. Be amazed by the breathtaking scenery and enjoy meeting over 170 residents who will share their real-life stories with you.

Our packed itinerary follows the authentic map of the region, the *Shulchan Aruch*. At every stop, we'll listen to the voices of our Sages, who offer intriguing guidelines and advice. We'll linger a while at each scenic view — and then move on to other spots equally inspiring. Even travelers who have been here many times will find new activities and out-of-the-way, captivating spots to enjoy.

We will also take you to places designated "for advanced hikers only." It may be a steep incline, but the view is fabulous.

At times, you will find yourself in front of a towering edifice. As you peek through a window, you will see benches filled with some of our greatest Sages, deeply immersed in study and ruling on complex issues of *kibbud av va'eim* (honoring parents). Mark the spot. You can return at your leisure for a more careful examination.

Some spots are beyond the scope of our tour. Feel free to explore on your own.

This will be the journey of a lifetime. So let's begin…

HONOR

The mitzvah of honoring parents is all-encompassing and includes our actions, our speech, our thoughts, and our feelings.

It applies equally to sons and daughters, single or married — with some qualifications for a married woman. There is no difference between the obligation to a father and the obligation to a mother.

This mitzvah never ends. As long as *we* are alive, we have a responsibility to our parents.

HONOR
In Deed

Honoring parents **in deed** requires providing for a parent's physical needs and includes all preparations necessary to fill those needs.

❖ When parents, young or old, cannot care for themselves, this is mandatory (i.e., a *"chiyuv,"* Torah obligation).

❖ Even when parents are self-sufficient, *any* benefit given by a son or daughter is a fulfillment of the mitzvah, "Honor your father and mother."

❖ When we extend ourselves in an extraordinary way, we beautify this mitzvah (i.e., *hiddur mitzvah*).

Chapter 1

Honoring In Deed

אֵיזֶהוּ כִּבּוּד? מַאֲכִיל וּמַשְׁקֶה, מַלְבִּישׁ וּמְכַסֶּה,
מַכְנִיס וּמוֹצִיא...

What is honor? Providing food and drink,
clothing and covering, bringing in and
escorting out… (*Shulchan Aruch* 240:4).

The Sages chose six words to define honoring parents in
deed:

1. מַאֲכִיל — providing food
2. מַשְׁקֶה — providing drink
3. מַלְבִּישׁ — providing clothing
4. מְכַסֶּה — providing covering
5. מַכְנִיס — bringing in
6. מוֹצִיא — escorting out

Our Sages didn't mean to exclude actions other than the six
examples given, but since listing all parental needs is impossible,
they gave these six general categories.

These general categories branch out into thousands and tens
of thousands of examples, dependent upon and determined
by each individual situation. With thought and imagination,

creative sons and daughters can add their own original ideas. The opportunities are innumerable.[1]

Each one of the heart-warming stories you will read in this chapter is taken from the lives of sons and daughters who make these six words come alive.

"Providing food and drink..."

Direct physical benefit includes all preparatory actions.[2] Here are just a few examples: grocery shopping or standing on line to buy takeout / transporting the purchases / carrying in the bundles / putting groceries away / peeling, cutting, frying, baking/ catering to particular dietary needs and preferences[3] / setting the table / serving / cleaning up / offering snacks and drinks. When necessary, blending, grinding, and chopping food to make it palatable, and actually feeding. If parents are nourished by a feeding tube, continually checking that it is operating properly or assigning someone to do so.

Each act of assistance is, in and of itself, a fulfillment of "honoring in deed."[4]

Even when there is a live-in, an aide, a helper, a caregiver, or a sibling providing these services, sons and daughters should participate in any way they can.[5]

> **WHENEVER I SEE A FEDEX TRUCK** drive by, I smile. The purple-and-orange logo on the side always brings back memories of a time when I was able to honor my father and, in a small way, follow in the footsteps of my very special mother, a"h.
>
> After my parents were able to leave Shanghai, they moved to the Telshe campus in Cleveland. My mother was a dedicated wife and a longtime educator. She taught for forty-two years in the same first grade classroom. As you might imagine, she taught second generations. When the children filed in on the first day of school, my mother was able to say to them, "This is the seat your Abba sat in."
>
> Growing up, I saw from my mother just how dedicated a woman could be to her husband. She took care of my father completely — and he, in turn, relied on her for everything,

especially when it came to anything food related. Honestly, I don't think my father ever made himself a cup of coffee.

When my mother died suddenly in her sleep, it came as a terrible shock. So many people felt the pain of her loss — friends, neighbors and students who were touched by this remarkable woman — but most of all, my father. It was so hard to lose his most precious partner.

My father was now alone in his home. No question that the wonderful friends and neighbors on campus would (and did) do whatever it took to ensure that my father had what he needed. But I, as a daughter, felt I must contribute to my father's care. My dilemma was that I lived 500 miles away. With small children and a job, I couldn't be running back and forth to Cleveland, and my father wasn't ready to pick up and undergo another major change.

I needed a plan. After throwing around and discarding a few possibilities and discussing it with my husband, we came up with something we felt might work. You could call it "nurturing and nourishing long distance."

The first thing I did was go out and buy some oversized pots, plenty of containers, and a packet of labels. Once a week, I stood in my kitchen and cooked and cooked for hours. I prepared a full week's worth of hearty, well-spiced and flavored dishes, with an eye to my father's old-time favorites, just the way my mother would have done. I packed everything in clearly labeled containers, and froze it all.

FedEx was my first partner in this plan, and I had a special arrangement with them. Back in the days before 24/7 drop-off points, they'd come to my house at 7 p.m., the last stop of the day. Well-frozen, the food was shipped overnight. Bright and early, at eight in the morning, the package would arrive at my father's door, still frozen, and he would put the whole box in the fridge.

My other partner was a neighbor of my father's, and I'd made special arrangements with her as well. She would unpack the carton and separate everything according to my directions. Then she'd return each day to warm up a meal just before my father came home.

I did this every single week for six months. At that point my father moved, first to an apartment near us, and then to our home, and I was finally able to preside over every aspect of his care, and serve him his meals myself for ten years.

But I'll never forget those six months. There was something truly special about those times when I FedExed those meals. As I packed them up and sent them off, I knew that when my father sat down to a warm supper, knowing that so much love and planning had gone into it, not only would his hunger be assuaged, but some of his grief as well.

MAYBE IT'S BECAUSE I'M THE OLDEST. *Or maybe it's my nature and I'd be like this no matter where I was in the family. But when I see something that doesn't seem quite right, I just have to do something about it.*

That's exactly how it was with Mommy coming home. She opens the door to the house, and boom! All us kids run out and jump on her.

"Wad'ya bring me?"

"Did you buy me new markers?"

"I'm hungry. What's for supper?"

"Dovi hit me!"

"My bag broke — I need it fixed now!"

"Did you get potato chips?"

This scene has been playing out for years now, and though I'm embarrassed to admit it, I used to be part of it. But yesterday, when Mommy came home, I sort of hung back and just watched. And I realized that the whole picture was very, very wrong.

And I knew just what I was going to do about it.

"Isn't that what all kids do?" one brother asked.

I finally got my brother Pinny to see reason, though. And then I told him my plan.

"So don't you think it would be very nice if the first thing we did when Mommy comes home is to see what we can do for her, instead of the other way around? Like, 'Mommy, could I take your coat or briefcase? Could I put away your packages?'"

After more coaxing, he agreed it was doable.

With that under my belt, I made the rounds of the rest of my siblings. In the end, they were all convinced, and agreed that they would each come up — on their own — with something to do for Mommy when she came home.

As my mother's usual arrival time drew near, I stood at the window looking out at the street. I saw the car's headlights as she pulled into the driveway, and then flicker off when she parked. I couldn't wait for her to get out of the car and come inside so that we could all surprise her. I was also looking forward to seeing what each of my siblings had come up with.

When Mommy walked in the door and said, "Hi, kids! I'm home!," there was the usual sound of feet pounding on the floor as we hurried to greet our mother — each with his own original surprise.

But this time, instead of pouncing on Mommy with our usual demands, each one of us presented Mommy with his or her own original surprise. Amid giggling and clapping, and a tear or two that appeared at the corner of Mommy's eyes, Pinny handed Mommy a cup of coffee just like she likes. Michali shyly gave her a chocolate bar filled with nougat- Mommy's favirote. Yocheved bought Mommy her cozy slippers....

Should I continue? Because as delightful as these details are, that's not really what I want to tell you. Most remarkable- and simply amazing to watch-was the major shift that happened in our house that afternoon.

While we, as children, will continue to be "takers," our goal should be to develop ourselves as "givers." This wisdom is the basis of all successful relationships— looking beyond ourselves to discover the needs of others. Exercising this "giving muscle" begins at home with our parents as worthy recipients. It should be learned early on, with many years to practice and perfect.

"...clothing..."

You've just returned home, your hands still smarting from the cold. As your father gets ready to leave, you hurry to bring him his scarf, knowing he would have taken it himself had he realized the wind velocity.

That's thoughtful of you. It's also a specific fulfillment of the mitzvah of "clothing."

Providing clothing can include purchasing necessary garments/ laundering/ ironing/ drop-off and pick-up from the cleaners[6] / all clothing repairs, whether done by yourself or by a seamstress or tailor / searching for a misplaced item of clothing / accompanying a parent to choose a garment / dressing assistance such as closing buttons and snaps, fastening jewelry, and zippering.

> *GRANDMA HAS HAD TROUBLE* *with her back for many years. Even as a younger woman, she was always grateful when someone helped her with her coat. Grandpa usually did this, but if my father were present, he would always hurry to offer, saying, "Let me help you, Ma."*
>
> *Now that she is older and things are even harder for her, my father does more than this. As Grandma prepares to leave the house, he will offer the familiar, "Let me help you, Ma." Then he will help her on with her sweater and overcoat and button her up.*
>
> *"Button it until the top, dear. All the way up," instructs Grandma. "Don't be afraid. It won't hurt me." She stretches her neck, lifting her chin upward, so that my father can button the very top button. He hesitates. It certainly does look like that would be uncomfortable! Ever so gently, he closes the button.*
>
> *"Good!" declares Grandma, nodding her approval.*
>
> *My father then places her woolen hat snugly on her head, and ties her favorite brown-and-blue scarf on top of that. Then he gently places her large sunglasses on her face, so that the wind won't hurt her eyes.*
>
> *All bundled up, Grandma smiles at him lovingly. We cannot see the grateful twinkle in her eyes from behind the dark glasses, but we can hear it in her voice.*
>
> *"Thank you, dear," she says. "Let me give you a kiss."*
>
> *And my father bends his head to receive that gesture of her appreciation.*

Footwear needs is part of clothing needs.[7] This can include buying shoes, bringing them in for repair, putting them on, tying laces, and polishing.

> *THREE-YEAR-OLD FRUMI is sitting on the floor playing. Nearby sits father, a sefer in his hands.*
>
> *For a minute, Frumi is confused. She just heard her father telling her to bring him his slippers.* This can't be, *thinks Frumi,* because the slippers are right there near Papa's chair!
>
> *"But Papa," Frumi ventures, "all you have to do is bend down and you can get them yourself."*
>
> *"Yes, I could," says Frumi's father, Harav Chaim Pinchas Scheinberg. "But if I bend down to get them, you won't get the mitzvah."*

"...and covering..."

"He must clothe them as is befitting, covering them from winter's cold, in a wrap befitting them, and give them proper beds" (*Menoras HaMaor*).

Ensuring adequate heating[8] and cooling, bringing a sweater, covering with a blanket, and seeing that a parent has a comfortable bed and bedding are all part of the mitzvah of "covering."

The broad lesson is to be concerned about a parent's general physical comfort.

> *ALTHOUGH WE MOVED to the southeastern coast, I haven't forgotten the Chicago winters of my youth. My sister still lives in our old hometown, not far from my father, who recently became a widower. My warmhearted sibling thinks of unique ways to radiate that warmth and love to our father. Here's one case in point. Every morning in the frigid winter, at 7 a.m., she comes over to warm up his car, so that by 7:10, when he leaves for work, the car is nice and toasty warm.*

> *MY MOTHER IS STILL in her own home. That's where she wants to be, in her familiar surroundings. This can only work because she has a full-time aide. Otherwise, her weakened mobility and fading memory would make this a dangerous choice.*

Mommy comes to one of us siblings for a Shabbos or Yom Tov. Otherwise, we go there — at least one of us every day.

It's a long day for our mother, made even longer because there is not much to fill it. I do my best to see that, if she's up to it, we get out for a few hours.

In the warm seasons, we sit for hours by a lake or in a park holding hands. On sunny days, we always have to remember to take a parasol. Due to a skin condition, Mommy can't be exposed to the sun, but the doctor said that as long as I keep the parasol at a protective angle, it's fine to be outdoors.

Once in a while, Rosetta, my mother's aide, will say to me, "Isn't that heavy for you, honey? Why don't you let me hold that umbrella so that you can rest your arm?"

I look at my mother's hands intertwined in mine... Thoughts come to my mind of what those hands did for me... a cool hand on my burning forehead...her hands rushing to finish a repair on my favorite skirt so that I could wear it that very day...the hands that gave my baby his first bath.

I thank Rosetta, but decline her offer.

I put my free arm around my mother, and we exchange a smile. Could my mother read my thoughts? How good it is for me to be able to use my hands to give back, in some small way, to my beloved mother, whose hands did so much for me.

"...bringing in..."

"Bringing in" — a short phrase that covers a lot of ground. The following illustrates the breadth of this aspect of the mitzvah:

❖ Preparing the house for a parent's arrival by stocking it with basic food supplies and adjusting the heating or air conditioning.

❖ Welcoming parents.[9]

❖ Assisting them *into* their home. This can include: letting a parent lean on us for support; providing a ramp, a walker, or a cane; shoveling snow to make a path. Also assisting parents *within* their home.

❖ Ensuring that parents have proper lodgings:[10] locating a suitable home for rent or purchase; a place to stay when they visit you; finding a suitable assisted living facility.

❖ Equipping a home: ensuring that parents have appropriate furnishings and appliances, or helping parents design a new home or remodel.

❖ Maintaining a home: keeping the house clean and organized when parents need or ask.[11]

❖ Hosting parents in our *own* home is part of "bringing in" (see Chapter 4: "Hosting").

When parents return from a trip, it's a mitzvah to welcome them home,[12] particularly when parents are infrequent travelers and any trip is a special occasion. If they need help with luggage, it is part of a child's mitzvah of "bringing in" to be as close to the arrival point as possible.

> *MY IN-LAWS WERE RETURNING from a trip abroad, and were scheduled to arrive at JFK at 6:20 a.m. My husband, Aaron, or one of his brothers, is always there to greet them when they land and to help them with their luggage. This time it was Aaron's turn.*
>
> *We live in New Jersey, about an hour-and-a-half drive from the airport, so Aaron left the house at 5:30 that morning. He got to the airport in plenty of time, but due to a delay, he had to wait several hours until they passed through customs and collected their suitcases.*
>
> *I've accompanied him on previous pickups, so I can tell you how it goes.*
>
> *Greeting them as only a son can, he takes the luggage cart and maneuvers it through the crowd, tsk-ing as they relay details of a delay or some other glitch in the trip as he escorts them to his car.*
>
> *Luggage in the trunk, my in-laws comfortably relaxing in the back seat, Aaron chauffeurs them to their home in Brooklyn. On arrival, he carries in their suitcases, places them at a comfortable height for unpacking, bids them farewell, and then drives back to New Jersey.*
>
> *The trip my husband made from New Jersey to the airport to Brooklyn and then back to New Jersey normally takes four and a quarter hours, more with traffic. If you add on the extra*

time waiting for a delayed flight, and also add in twenty-five
dollars in tolls and at least twenty dollars in gas, wouldn't a
taxi have been a more reasonable choice? A taxi from JFK to
Brooklyn takes only forty-five minutes and costs about forty
dollars.

What makes more sense? To my husband and his brothers,
it's not even a question. To me, this speaks volumes about
my husband's special family.

Though our logic would say, "A taxi is a more reasonable
choice," part of the mitzvah of honoring parents is the personal
touch.

Those who can't be at the arrival point should at least call to
welcome their parents and ask about the trip.

Among the obligations of "bringing in" is making sure
that parents have suitable housing when they need or ask for
assistance. This would include finding the right assisted living
facility.

IMA HAD BEEN HOSPITALIZED *for excruciating head-*
aches, a turn for the worse in her Parkinson's disease, and
general difficulty in day-to-day functioning. After testing and
prescribing the appropriate medication, the doctor explained
to us that they had done what they could.

"Your mother is ready for discharge," he told us, "on
condition that she has 24-hour care. Someone must be with
her at all times to assist her with all of her needs."

Together with our father, we siblings discussed the options
and decided that, as a temporary measure, we would find
a facility for Ima. With Hashem's help, the medications and
physical therapy she would receive there would allow for
her rehabilitation to the point where she could return home.
Most important was that both Abba and Ima thought this
was a good idea.

Now which nursing home should we choose?

In our area, there are quite a few homes. My job was to go
look at the different facilities, speak to the staff, and get a
feeling for the place. Then the family would make a decision.

And so the search began.

First and foremost, we agreed that any facility had to be nearby, so that everyone, including the grandchildren, could visit Ima regularly. The more distant homes were therefore out of the question.

I went to the first nursing home on my list. The director perused Ima's medical file and said that she was not suitable for their facility.

The second facility on my list was very close to our home, but we hadn't heard the best things about it.

The search continued.

In the third place, the residents I saw were all in wheelchairs, many of them with IVs, and some were even continually connected to oxygen. I couldn't see my mother fitting in there.

I headed to a fourth facility. The people sitting in the main room barely spoke. This place was definitely out of the question for my mother, who, baruch Hashem, *had her wits about her, and wanted and needed to speak to the people around her.*

A fifth nursing home was newly renovated and beautiful, but we were not happy with the staff. There went that one!

The sixth home was a large facility. My sister and I know the supervisor well, and we felt that this would be beneficial, that she would take good care of our mother. But when we presented the idea to Abba, he was adamantly opposed. He had once visited an acquaintance in this home who had complained. Whether or not his claim was true, it gave my father a very bad feeling about the place. Though we had heard wonderful things about this nursing home, we felt that Abba's comfort with the situation was of utmost importance. So this one too was vetoed.

Finally, upon visiting our seventh option, we found the right place, and brought Ima there.

The beginning went well. Ima was happy.

Unfortunately, though, it didn't last long. Ima's roommate was awake at night, talking to herself and making noise, and it disturbed Ima.

We asked if she could be switched to a different room. This was easier said than done, as there were two patients to a room, and their medical conditions had to be compatible. In the end, to our relief, it worked out, and they found a suitable room.

In the new room, another difficulty arose. Ima's roommate refused to turn on the air conditioner. It was the peak of the summer, and Ima was suffering from the oppressive heat.

At first, there seemed to be no solution, but we persisted, and Ima was moved to a private room.

All in all, it was a wonderful setup.

Except…

With all the benefits of her own private room, Ima was bored and lonely.

Our mother is a very sociable person. She needs to talk to people and to hear their stories. The moment she was alone in her own room for most of the day, she desperately missed having people to talk to (despite the fact that we visited often). So we ordered a private phone line. The idea was excellent, and allowed Ima the social interaction that she so needed.

But even the best ideas have their drawbacks. With a listening ear always a mere phone call away, Ima would call to tell us about each and every thing that bothered her.

"There's no place like home," she would say despondently. "Can you get me out of here already?"

We gently explained all the benefits of remaining, at least for the present. She insisted, however, that home was the best, that she wanted to be home, and that she was capable of handling it.

The primary difficulty was that she still could not walk very much, and she could not go up stairs. My parents live one flight up, with no elevator.

That left us with one alternative: to bring her home — to our home. I am the only daughter whose home wouldn't involve steps. I could also give Ima her own room. Still, it was not exactly ideal. I have a large family, including small, mischievous children. There is plenty of noise and a lot *going on, things that are usually difficult for Ima to tolerate. To add to that, it was the beginning of summer vacation, and everyone was home.*

Still, Ima said she preferred coming "home" to me rather than staying in the nursing home. She said she knew I would be busy, but she didn't need anything.

"I won't ask anything of you," she told me. "Even a little bit of bread and water would be enough for me to eat and drink. The main thing is for me to get out of this place."

One afternoon when I went to visit, all she did was beg me to pack her things because she was leaving. I told her that she couldn't just "run away" like that. Paperwork needed to be taken care of in the office. She would need a discharge summary from the doctor, and the nurse would have to give her all of her medicines with a detailed explanation of how many to take of each pill and when.

But Ima was insistent — now! "If we wait for the morning, it will be another day…and then another!"

I left the room and called my husband to ask if I could bring Ima home. My wonderful, understanding husband said that it was fine, and that I should do whatever I felt best.

It did take another day to take care of all the arrangements. Meanwhile, I asked the children to help me prepare the house for Savta. I will never forget their joy and excitement when they heard that Savta was coming to live with us.

Ima lived with us for several months. She was so happy in our home. The children were constantly around her. And did we pamper her!

During this time, my mother's health improved and she reclaimed some of her mobility. She was now able to use steps, though still with difficulty. At the same time, we renovated her apartment, making it more user-friendly.

After two months, Ima's dream was realized. What a happy day that was for my mother when she was able to return with Abba to their own home.

Children who are still living at home have many opportunities to help their parents maintain the home: straightening their room before they leave for school / putting their belongings in their place / clearing the table and washing up/ taking out the trash / keeping up with chores / participating in Shabbos preparations.

With the additional effort of proper intent, a son or daughter can transform a tedious job, sluggishly performed, to an act with inestimable reward.

Even children who are married and no longer living in their parents' home have opportunities for helping their parents maintain the home, for instance, by helping to keep the house clean and organized.

> **FROM THE TIME MY MOTHER** first married, she's always had a live-in maid. My mother loves to cook and entertain, and we kids keep her plenty busy. She leaves all the housekeeping to the maid.
>
> Our Gramma, my mother's mother, lives nearby. Gramma has always done her own cleaning. She's never wanted household help. When it became harder for her to clean everything by herself, my mother went over and did the cleaning for her.
>
> That said a lot to us kids. Imagine — while the maid was cleaning our home, my mother was over at Gramma's cleaning her home.
>
> My mother would surely have hired help, but Gramma couldn't accept having a stranger in her home.
>
> **ACTUALLY, IT WAS MY** brother-in-law's idea, so I'll give credit where credit is due. He is the youngest of the ten Becker children. When my sister-in-law, who is number nine, got married, he found himself an only child in that once-teeming home.
>
> With winter almost behind him, my ever-responsible brother-in-law's mind went into high gear. Everyone's married, he thought. Who's going to help with Pesach cleaning this year?
>
> Necessity being the mother of invention, he picked up the

phone and started dialing his siblings. Each got a personal invitation to a family meeting to discuss the upcoming Yom Tov.

They all showed up on the given day, and the problem was laid out on the table.

By the end of the meeting, the children had devised a strategy that they proposed to their parents. On Rosh Chodesh Nissan, they would come for the day and continue the next day, dividing up the work. With team effort, they could finish cleaning the whole house in these two days (exclusive of the parents' bedroom, as per their mother's request).

My in-laws didn't say no, so the plan went into effect.

Part of the plan was that Mommy and Tatty would leave for those two days. (Of course, Mommy would not hear of not providing lunch for her workers.)

All of the siblings arrived early on Rosh Chodesh and dived in, two siblings to a room. The daughters got the detailed work, and the sons were assigned to the heavier jobs.

The next day, they returned to finish up whatever remained undone. Finally, they lined the fridge and unloaded dishes.

When the parents returned, the house was all set for Tatty to kasher the counters. Then Mommy got to work.

And that's how this Erev Pesach custom began.

Last year, some grandchildren were already of age to chip in and join the Becker siblings on Rosh Chodesh, and to help Savta with the cooking.

Can't the Beckers hire professionals to do what the children do?

Yes.

But who could be counted on to clean better than they, having been trained over the years to do it just like Mommy taught them?

The children unanimously feel this is the right and proper thing to do to express their appreciation for all that they received and are still receiving. It is their pleasure to take something off her shoulders.

And truth be told — it really is a pleasure. With everyone immersed in a busy life, the brothers and sisters get two days, between all the washing and scrubbing that they're doing, to have one grand time together.

"...and escorting out..."

If a parent has difficulty entering or leaving the premises, a son or daughter must help them.

Escorting out includes:

❖ Physically assisting parents to enable them to leave the house

> **DUE TO ACUTE DIABETES,** *my father had to take early retirement. Though his diet was strictly maintained, it seemed too late to reverse the nerve damage already there. He suffered excruciating pain in his feet. My father described it as "sharp needles" pricking his feet. Numerous vascular transplants didn't help. Over time, his feet developed open wounds which then ulcerated. The pain was so intense that even a sheet covering the feet was intolerable. A big hole was cut in the front of my father's shoes, exposing the toes, to offer some relief. By now, my father could not walk or even stand.*
>
> *All this time, my brother, Meyer, was by his side: before work, after, between, whenever he could. Meyer regulated our father's meals and his insulin, according to the blood test results. Doctors, hospitals, medicines, hospital beds, special mattresses — you name it, Meyer was on top of it all.*
>
> *Despite the constant care, gangrene set in. To save my father's life, the doctors amputated his leg at the knee, and soon after, the second leg.*
>
> *Meyer did everything: research on the doctors and conferring with them, acting as our liaison with rabbanim, setting up the house for a double amputee. You can understand what this meant for my mother. Besides allowing her to keep her job, Meyer alleviated the pressures of daily life.*
>
> *The diabetes also affected my father's heart (he had a triple bypass) and kidneys. The kidneys got worse and worse until there was no kidney function. In addition to doctors' appointments and emergency hospital visits, my father now needed dialysis three times a week. Since sitting proved*

to be way too painful, he needed to lie in a slightly raised position and would have to be transported on a gurney.

My parents' home, on the second floor of a two-family house, boasted a unique, horseshoe-shaped staircase, with a sharp U-turn. There was simply no way to manipulate a gurney around that turn. The best bet would have been to move, but after fifty years in that home, my parents weren't budging. My father couldn't, and my mother wouldn't. So that was out.

There was also no place to install an internal elevator. So that was out too.

Meyer, who works in construction, came up with an ingenious solution. He built an elevator for my father on the outside of the house, alongside my father's bedroom porch. A "hydraulic fork lift" was its official name.

Two pieces of steel extended from the forklift, to which he welded steel beams. To these, he welded a steel deck, and surrounded the whole thing with a steel gate and two hinged doors to serve as an entrance and exit.

He created an opening in the porch that matched the door of the "elevator." Three sets of switches activated the lift. The whole base of the lift was buried in 2,000 pounds of concrete. It has a 3,000-pound capacity, and is large enough to accommodate two paramedics and a gurney.

My father is taken in a gurney from his bed out to the adjacent porch, onto the elevator, then lowered and taken into a waiting ambulance.

It may not be a conventional elevator, but it sure does the job.

❖ Accompanying parents to any place they want to go

❖ Encouraging parents who are homebound, due to physical or emotional reasons, to get dressed and go out

I'VE OFTEN MET MY NEIGHBOR, Chaviva, on the Avenue with her mother. One time, they were going together to get facials. Another time, I bumped into them sharing a Danish in a coffee shop, laughing like two schoolgirls.

That's what I happened to see myself, but from conversations with Chaviva, I know that there are days and

months full of such shared moments. She is giving her mother a reason to get up, dressed, and out.

"How do you have time?" I once asked Chaviva.

"I am crazy busy," Chaviva admitted. "But we all have priorities," she added with her winning smile, before she hurried off.

❖ Respectfully escorting parents as they leave

> **MY HUSBAND** *and I are visiting our daughter Nechami and her family. We are getting ready to leave.*
>
> *"Yaeli," calls Nechami, "Saba and Savta are leaving!"*
>
> *Out runs little pajamed Yaeli, who jumps into our arms for a kiss.*
>
> *While our son-in-law is leading the 3-year-old, an 8-year-old skips over to the door where we're standing, and shyly plants two kisses, one for my husband and one for me.*
>
> *Nechami lifts the baby, who is not to be excluded. By this time, the whole family is present.*
>
> *With wishes of "thanks for coming" and "come again," we are escorted down the stairs to our car. They wave good-bye until they can't see us anymore.*
>
> *We never tire of this send-off and beautiful display of affection.*
>
> *Even if we are in a hurry, this is one thing we don't want to miss!*

❖ When parents leave for an extended trip, it's proper to help them, arriving early to assist with packing when appropriate, locking up, taking care of leftover food, carrying their luggage, and so on, and finally to wish them a safe trip.

❖ Providing transportation for parents is part of the mitzvah of escorting out.[13] When getting to their destination requires traveling, and parents require (for example, wheelchair bound) or request assistance, a son or daughter is obligated to provide that assistance or see to it that it is available.

When parents *can* manage alone, we are still fulfilling the mitzvah of "escorting out," any time we assist them in their travel needs.

———•◦•——

Think about it: The *Shulchan Aruch* has chosen six words — food and drink, clothing and warmth, bringing in and out… What should that bring to mind?

Isn't this what our parents did for us all the years we were growing up? They fed us, they dressed us, they chauffeured us. We can never repay, but at least we should try to reciprocate — in every possible way.[14]

In every possible way

"These six words [of the *Shulchan Aruch*, and, originally, of the *Gemara*] are examples of our more comprehensive goal…to supply all their needs" (*Sefer Chareidim*).[15]

We find this thought expressed by the Rambam when he tells us that "the obligations of sons and daughters to their parents are more than can be listed and warrant a lengthy discussion. *Chazal* list these six, but the intention is anything…that benefits our parents."[16]

As the *Sefer Chinuch* (33) states: ...כָּל תּוֹעֶלֶת וְכָבוֹד שֶׁיּוּכַל, "any benefit and honor possible…"

"…any benefit…"

Anything we can do for our parents' convenience, anything that helps make life easier for them is considered part of "all their needs."[17]

> *I WAS WITH MY ISRAELI SISTER-IN-LAW*, Ora, and her teenage daughter, Talia. Anxious to spend some time together, we met to do a tour of the Old City.
>
> We wound our way through alleys and byways. Descending some steps, it was touching to see Talia slip her hand into her mother's. What a lovely gesture! While we might expect that from a small child, it's probably not all that common for an

18-year-old.

As we strolled, I commented to Ora on this lovely display of affection between mother and daughter.

Ora smiled in Talia's direction. "Yes, she's a sweetie, our Talia. And also very helpful."

Helpful? That wasn't the word I would have chosen to describe that scene.

Noting my puzzlement, Ora hurried to explain. "I guess I never told you that I have acrophobia. My kids know that I don't do well with heights or steep steps. So, when we're out together and headed for the stairs, they're right at my side to offer a hand."

❖ Business needs are included.[18]

> **ONE OF MY STRONGEST** *childhood memories is of my father working hard at many different jobs to support the family. As busy as he was, family — and above all, his parents — came first.*
>
> *Grandpa owned a busy butcher shop. As my grandfather aged, it became hard for him to lift the carcasses and cut the meat. But he persisted, because this was his livelihood and customers depended on him.*
>
> *My father had always helped out in the store at busy times or whenever he had a chance, but now he made sure to be there every single day. At the end of his own long workday, my father would travel to his father's butcher shop to help him prepare all the cuts of meat for the next day.[18] Sometimes I went along. I'd stand there watching as my father lifted, sawed, chopped, sliced, and packaged alongside his father.*
>
> *As a child, it was the enormity of the carcasses that caught my attention. Today, looking back, it's the enormity of other things that strikes me.*
>
> *I'm sure my father was exhausted from his own long workday, but then to volunteer for more hours of exhausting labor with never a word of complaint…!*
>
> *It was so natural, so matter of fact. Although he never said these words, his actions announced "My father could use my help. I have two hands and a few available hours."*

CHAPTER 1: HONORING IN DEED

So totally obvious.

❖ Medical care is certainly "any benefit," and includes arranging doctors' appointments; driving to and from appointments; arranging hospitalization and insurance; taking care of pharmaceutical needs, labs, and tests.

> **DR. GLENDALL'S EXPRESSION** *was impassive. "We'll just have to open it up again and hope it heals correctly this time."*
>
> *My mother squeezed my hand as he told a nurse, "Get Mrs. Ellis settled in pre-op."*
>
> *"But there are no beds, doctor. We're full right now. Overfull, in fact. There won't be an opening till," she flipped through some papers, "tomorrow afternoon, at two-thirty."*
>
> *"Fine. It can wait till then." The doctor turned back to my mother. "We'll see you tomorrow afternoon, Mrs. Ellis. Arrive an hour early for admission." As he swung around to leave the room, I slipped my hand out of my mother's and raced after him.*
>
> *"Dr. Glendall, isn't there anything that can be done to avoid surgery?"*
>
> *He shook his head as he hurried down the hall. "If a scar heals from the outside in, it must be reopened. Right now, toxic pus is seeping into your mother's body, filling her with infection. It has to be let out."*
>
> *"But is there any way to do that without operating?"*
>
> *We'd arrived at the elevators. He turned to face me. I guess he was evaluating the type of explanation an 18-year-old required. "Once a scar heals, only surgery can open it," he said and then added, "Maybe if it was soaked in hot water for twenty-four hours it would open — but that's, of course, not feasible."*
>
> *The elevator arrived and he stepped inside. "Surgery is the only option," he told me as the doors closed.*
>
> *I quickly turned and raced back to the room where my mother sat waiting.*
>
> *"What happened?" she asked, her face drawn from pain and fear.*
>
> *"I just wanted to ask him if there was any other option.*

And, baruch Hashem, *there's hope," I told her.*

Dr. Glendall may have brushed off the soaking option, but I wasn't going to let my mother go into another surgery without doing everything I could to prevent it. Not after everything she had been through. And definitely not given how much she feared going under the knife.

She has good reason for her fears, *I mused as we rode back to the small apartment in Queens she'd moved into after my father's death. The past decade had been one long trauma of surgical errors and surgeries to fix those errors. Each time my mother entered the hospital, she was paralyzed with fear.*

When we arrived home, I set to work.

"Come lay on your bed, Mommy, where you'll be comfortable," I said, helping her into her room. I raced to the kitchen to prepare some boiling water. Then I gathered towels and set myself up at my mother's side.

The afternoon faded into the night, a long, blurry stretch of constant motion. Soaking the wound was tedious work. I would take each towel from the pot of hot water, squeeze it out, wait till it had cooled a little before laying it carefully on my mother. Then I would place another towel in the pot so it would be ready when I needed it, and turn back to the current compress, running to the kitchen every now and then to heat more water. With every compress, I davened that Hashem bless my efforts with success.

Dip, squeeze, soak…dip, squeeze, soak, run and make food for Mommy…dip, squeeze, soak, boil more water…dip, squeeze, soak, Mommy's thirsty, bring a drink of water…dip, squeeze, soak…

Fatigue was not long in coming. My back ached from bending over to hold the compresses in position and keep watch on the temperature, the muscles in my arms screamed in protest as I carried yet another pot heavy with hot water, and my eyelids drooped, begging for sleep. But I pushed myself to keep going.

And I didn't stop, not when the first pastels of dawn appeared across the sky, not when the sounds of honking cars and city bustle flitted in through the window — I couldn't stop, I wouldn't stop, I would do everything I could to spare my mother from this dreaded surgery.

And finally, just as afternoon began, the scar opened. I wept as the wound began to drain.

"It worked, Mommy!" I cried. "It opened!"

My mother struggled to sit up, and we embraced, our tears mingling — tears of relief and gratitude that she would not need another operation, topped by my gratitude to the One Above Who helped me give my mother twenty-four hours of non-stop care, commitment, and love.

"Any benefit possible." It can include so much: Paying bills, running errands, making purchases, handling issues of medical insurance, taxes, credit cards. Making those tiresome phone calls to clarify when problems arise. Handling bank accounts and paperwork.

"...and any honor possible..."

"One should honor his parents in every way possible..." (*Meiri, Kiddushin* 31).[19]

This refers to any expression of respect and every demonstration of honor — individualized to the taste of the parent.

Some examples: Allowing a parent to enter first; preferential seating; respectful greetings and farewell; not keeping a parent waiting; showing regard and concern for parents' close friends and associates.[20]

❖ Allowing a parent to enter first

When entering a room or coming into the house together with a parent, it is a sign of respect to allow the parent to enter first.[21]

THE YEAR WAS 1935. *Mama, Papa, my little sister, Rivky, and I were on a boat, on our way back from Europe. Papa and Mama [Rav and Rebbetzin Chaim Pinchas Scheinberg] had been in Mir for five years. If you read my Aunt Ruchoma's book "All for the Boss," you will know that that was not a small undertaking. We might have stayed on, except that Papa's status was in question. Since Papa was born in Poland, he would lose his American citizenship if he remained in*

Europe for more than five consecutive years.

When we arrived in the States, we moved in with Zeidy and Bubby Herman until Papa got on his feet financially. The Hermans said to Papa and Mama, "The whole world we let in, and not you?" [Reb Yaakov Yosef Herman was renowned for his hachnassas orchim.]

We lived with Zeidy and Bubby for about a year. As little as I was, Zeidy had no compunction about disciplining me. I will tell you now about one such incident.

My mother and I were coming home from an outing, and I, a typical, lively 4-year-old, bounded up the three flights of stairs and walked into the house, only to be met by my imposing Zeidy Herman.

"Fruma'leh, vu iz de Mama?" *(Where is Mama?)*

"Mama's on her way up," I replied happily.

"You came in before your Mama? You didn't wait for your Mama?"

I started to sense that all was not right. Nonetheless, I answered truthfully, "Yes."

Zeidy looked at me sternly. "Where's your kibbud eim? *Which child walks into the house before a Mama?"*

I didn't answer the question. Of course, I ran up first. Which mother can run up as fast as a 4-year-old? I thought logically.

"Now," said my Zeidy, "you go down all three flights — all the way to the bottom (and those were very steep steps!) — and feel bad that you went in before Mama. Then you'll remember not to go in before your Mama again."

My Bubby Herman heard my Zeidy reprimanding me. My Bubby, who was the "softy," came to see what was going on.

"Yaakov Yosef," she said, "what are you telling Fruma'leh?"

"She went in before Bash'ke. How could she go in before her Mama?"

"I think," said my wise Bubby, "better she should go down one flight and feel very, very bad, and then come up." She shot a look that told Zeidy he should remember I was only 4.

"Nu," said Zeidy. "Your Bubby is always right."

So it was decided. I went down one flight. I stayed there

for a while, because my Bubby said I should feel "very, very bad," and I wasn't sure how much "very, very bad" was supposed to feel.

When I came up, my Zeidy called me over. "Come sit down, Fruma'leh, and I'll tell you why I sent you down.

"Du veist vos iz a mama? (Do you realize what a mother is?)" Zeidy began seriously.

I was big enough to realize that he didn't want an answer.

"A mama is kodesh kedoshim. *I grew up without a mother. No one told me when to go to sleep or when to get up. No one told me to put on a sweater because it was cold, and no one told me to take off my sweater when it was warm."**

"I can't forget this scene," says Rebbetzin Frumie Altusky. "I can't forget it, because my Zeidy had tears in his eyes as he spoke. And my Zeidy almost never cried.

"Zeidy said, 'A mama. Ah! A mama. A mama is worth her weight in gold. You have to carry a mama on a golden tray.'

"My Zeidy ended with the words — and remember, they were said over seventy years ago, but I hear them as if they were just said now, 'Mir darf shanaven a mama' — a mother is to be cherished and treasured."

Of course, when parents are uncomfortable with this gesture of allowing them to enter first, we honor them by allowing them their preference.

❖ Preferential seating

When there is a head table or dais at a *simchah*, a parent should be seated, when appropriate and appreciated, toward the center, which is considered the most important place. At a family *simchah*, for example a wedding, *sheva berachos*, or *bar mitzvah*, parents (unless they object) should be seated as close as possible to the *baal simchah*.

❖ Respectful greeting and farewell

---

* His parents had returned to Europe. With no money for an additional ticket, 13-year-old Yaakov Yosef remained in America until his parents could find the means to bring him home. Not only wasn't he resentful, he worked to send his parents money (*All For the Boss*, Feldheim, 1984, p. 35).

It is proper to greet a parent when we visit in their home or meet them elsewhere,[22] as well as offer a farewell when we leave.[23] Accepted greetings would be based on family or community practice (handshake, kiss, etc.). In some communities, it is the custom to kiss a father's hand when greeting him or offering mazel tov, and upon leaving.[24] In others, this custom is practiced only on Shabbos and Yom Tov. [25] Still others have the custom to kiss the mother's right hand on Shabbos eve.[26] In some communities, it is accepted for a son who is called up to the Torah to kiss his father's hand upon ascending. When returning after the *aliyah*, the son honors his father by again kissing his hand. Where these customs are practiced, it would be considered a slight to refrain.[27]

I CAN'T SAY I NEVER HEARD about the custom, but I rarely, if ever, saw it practiced. Don't get me wrong. I, personally, think it's a beautiful thing. Just, in our circles, we don't do it.

So when my oldest son, Azriel, got engaged, he was in for quite a shock.

When the kallah's grandfather walked into the engagement celebration, of course everyone stood up, Azriel together with everyone else. But then he saw all the children and grandchildren get up, one by one, go over to the saba, and kiss his hand!

No one had given him advance notice. I guess, to the other side it was so basic, not even worthy of mention.

"Ima," he said to me afterward, "I was standing there, not sure what to do. It was sort of obvious what I'd better do. I had just never done it before."

It was a little awkward for Azriel, but he moved over to join the line. He wasn't going to embarrass his kallah, the saba, or himself.

I was proud of him when he told me the story, thankful he had had the sense to start off on the right foot.

❖ Showing concern for parents' close friends and associates

MY FATHER-IN-LAW USES A LAWYER, Mr. Ringel, who has been very helpful to him in his business dealings. Over the years, they have developed a close relationship. As a matter of fact, when our baby was born, Mr. Ringel sent us a stunning baby gift.

So, last month, when Mr. Ringel's daughter got married, it was not surprising that my father-in-law asked us to make sure to attend the wedding.

My husband has a very tight schedule, and the night of the wedding was particularly inconvenient, but there was no question that this meant a lot to his father, and that it was unthinkable not to make the effort.

Not only did we go, but the week before the wedding we dressed the baby in the outfit Mr. Ringel had given us, took pictures, and sent them to him together with a cute note.

At the wedding, Mr. Ringel thanked my husband for his originality and thoughtfulness, and complimented my father-in-law on his charming son.

The indispensable "how"

...וְיִתְּנֶנּוּ לוֹ בְּסֵבֶר פָּנִים יָפוֹת...

...and it must be given *b'seiver panim yafos*...

(*Shulchan Aruch* 240:4).

In this chapter we explored the six directives of honoring parents in deed, as discussed in the *Shulchan Aruch*. That was *what* we have to do.

Immediately, the *Shulchan Aruch* follows with *how* we have to do it: "It must be given *b'seiver panim yafos*."

Harav Avigdor Miller explains:[28]

סֵבֶר, *seiver* (expression), is akin to the word *s'vara*, which denotes thought and interest;

פָּנִים, *panim* (face), the least one can do is turn his face when his father or mother enters the room [connoting attention and involvement];

יָפוֹת, *yafos*: In addition, our face should have a pleasant expression.

How? An interested, attentive, and pleasant

demonstration of filial devotion. To express externally what we feel internally — that these actions and this service are not a burden, but a privilege.

IT WAS MY FIRST SHABBOS experience. *Some fellow in a black suit approached me at the Western Wall and asked if I wanted to go with some other guys for a Friday night meal. I wasn't doing too much (actually, nothing at all), so I figured I didn't have much to lose.*

Little did I know that I had a lot to lose. Luckily, I lost it.

Slowly but surely over the years, I left behind a lot of baggage. It's been a long journey, and it all started that Friday night.

You understand, this Shabbos thing was a first for me, and it hit me hard.

I don't want to underplay the food, which was awesome and abundant. The singing — well, in my crowd, men didn't do too much singing, but I could see how they were really caught up in it. A lot of philosophical discussion...and with it all, it was amazing that every kid got a chance to talk. And then they told me that they do this every week!

Mostly, I was impressed with the kids, and the parent-kid connection — real quality time. But of all the things that got me that night, I'll tell you which one did it. It happened so quickly. The family didn't even seem to notice. But for me, it turned my life around.

She was just a little girl. Not being into kids, I can't really give you an age, but I suppose if we round it off to 10 or 11, we'll be somewhere close. They called her Racheli.

Little Racheli did something that made her minute-before-smiley father very serious. Father and mother conferred. Racheli was in the dock, tearful. Judgment was passed: Racheli was informed that she would miss her turn to wash the dishes after the meal.

Racheli pouted. The family continued their meal.

I was speechless. The whole thing blew my mind.

I guess everyone has his own story of what turned him on to his Jewish genes. For me, it was Racheli's "punishment."

From where I was coming, it was like landing on a different planet, where they were speaking a language I had never heard, behaving in a way I had never seen.

I had the rest of the meal to chew this over. Dessert was served, and I was still clueless. So, after the meal, I cornered my host.

He smiled at my question. "To our kids, helping out is a privilege."

Was this for real?

I realized that there was something special going on in that house, and that I had better find out about it — fast.

Chapter 2

When It's *Their* Will, *That's* the Way!

R' YISHMAEL'S MOTHER came to the Sages to complain about her son. "Rebuke my son, Yishmael," she said, "for he does not show me honor."

The Sages were dismayed. How could that be? "Is it possible that R' Yishmael does not show honor to his mother? What has he done to you?"

"When he returns from the beis medrash," she said, "I want to wash his feet and drink the water, but he will not permit it."

The Sages ruled, "If this is her wish, this is the way to honor her." *

"His will is his honor" (רְצוֹנוֹ שֶׁל אָדָם זֶהוּ כְּבוֹדוֹ) is a Torah principle.[1] It is a directive for a child to be attuned to his parents' preferences.

---

* Except when it involves a transgression, which would include endangering health. Apparently this water was not considered a health risk.

As we have seen, we have a mitzvah to honor our parents in deed. But whatever we do for parents is only a mitzvah if it's *what* they want and *the way* they want it.

A daughter would like to serve her parents dinner. The parents want the daughter to rest instead. What should she do?

The daughter might think that she's losing out on the mitzvah of honoring her parents that she would have by serving them dinner. But, in fact, respecting her parents' wishes *is* the mitzvah.

One side of a story...and another

The right way is their way

◀ "You know Mom and I have so much free time now. Why don't you call more often? And put the grandkids on the phone — even the little ones. We like the babbling too."

▶ My father doesn't like to speak to my children on the phone. He claims that he can't understand what they're saying. We live so far away from them — how can he deny my children the right to have a connection with their grandfather? And how can he deny himself that joy?

Parents are entitled to do it the way they prefer. You are "entitled" to go along.

◀ I hired someone to take care of my finances now that I'm alone. The man is an accountant. He was a close friend of my late husband, a long-time family friend, and I know I can trust him. I know my children will offer their "good" advice and insist they know better but I certainly wouldn't want to involve them.

▶ "The only people I would trust with my personal records are my children."

------◆·◆·◆------

◀ We always seat our parents at the dais at every *simchah*, whether it's a *bris*, a *bar mitzvah,* or a wedding.

▶ My parents won't sit at the head table. They say it's their pleasure at a *simchah* to sit with their family, whom they rarely see.

———————

◀ My parents were preparing for their 50th wedding anniversary for months — and discussing it for almost a decade. And why not? Isn't it a milestone that few reach?

With a heart full of thanks to the Almighty for allowing them to reach this day, my parents wanted to share this momentous occasion with every last family member and friend, business acquaintance, and neighbor.

▶ My parents never allowed us to make them a celebration for their golden wedding anniversary. They certainly wouldn't make one for themselves. It wasn't a financial consideration. Not at all.

We were well aware of our parents' views on this subject. If any of us ever brought it up, just to check to see if they had changed their minds, my mother would remind us in no uncertain terms, "You know Aunt Becky lost her husband. You haven't forgotten, have you, that Uncle Abe has no wife! Do you expect us to flaunt our marriage in front of them?"

There was no point in making a big bash if the guests of honor didn't want that honor. So, to mark the date, the immediate family just went out to dinner at a quiet spot.

———————

◀ Both my parents and in-laws do a lot of traveling. Whenever my parents return from a trip, I'm there to greet them. No matter when, I make it my business to pick them up. I know they would be quite disappointed, and even hurt, if I wasn't there.

▶ My in-laws would never hear of me or my husband driving a distance to meet them. They take a cab. There is no room for discussion on this matter.

———————

◄ My mother's greatest pleasure is to be surrounded by all her children and grandchildren. The more the merrier. We are all always invited.

▶ My mother is a warm and loving grandmother, and loves to see us. At the same time, she cannot handle noise or commotion over a certain limit. She likes to host only one child and family at a time.

This mother has let her preference be known. But that's not always the case. Keep your antenna up and actively listen for how this mitzvah of honoring parents is going to play out in your life.

What is said and what is meant

"No! No! No! No! Absolutely not!" is what a parent might say. But what does he mean?

A common concern of parents is being a burden on children. This is one reason parents may reject an offer of help even when it is in their best interests to accept.

What they might really want is a little assurance that the help you've offered is truly not an imposition. They would like to hear that you sincerely mean it and are happy to do it. Your job is to do the convincing.

> *"I DON'T NEED IT. I don't want it. I'll just end up giving it away anyway."*
>
> *"But why, Dad? You always love my food when you visit us."*
>
> *"You're a great cook, Laya. But I'm doing just fine with what I have."*
>
> *Why is he saying that? I wondered as we ended the conversation and I put down the phone. I knew that since my mother had passed away, he was eating only cold food. With no cooking skills to speak of, Dad claims that herring, sardines, and crackers are all he needs.*
>
> *"Nonsense," I said aloud, standing there next to the phone. "He's not eating properly, and I just can't neglect him."*
>
> *But he wasn't letting anyone help!*

With my husband's encouragement, I cooked up a storm and made a trip to my father's home early Friday afternoon. Who wouldn't prefer chicken soup with kneidelach, roasted chicken, and kugel to sardines?

Ever gracious, Dad welcomed me and thanked me for my efforts, but warned me that I should never do this again.

Next week, my husband made the trip with two bags full of food and an expensive wine.

I got a call thanking me, telling me how delicious everything was, and asking me — please — not to send anything anymore. "I don't need it. I don't want it."

I'm not sure how much more we would have pushed, except that by the third week, we got a call from my brother.

"Dad is telling the whole family how much he enjoys your food. He says he has so much, it lasts him the whole week."

Next week, Dad still told me, "Laya, you really don't have to send anything. I don't need it. But if you really want, just send…"

You may hear a no and wonder if it's a final no. How can you be sure whether to proceed or desist?

While children usually know their parents well, we have to ask Hashem for the understanding and Heavenly assistance to know when to push ahead and when to back down.

MY FATHER HAD TO *go to the doctor this week. I feel that it's better for him not to drive alone, lately more than ever.*

However, Abba never wants us to do anything for him. Whenever we ask him if we can accompany him anywhere, and particularly now to the doctor, the answer is always a clear no. Then of course we can't go.

I decided that this time I wouldn't ask him.

I am in touch with my parents every day, and I knew that Abba would be leaving at 4 p.m. to be at his appointment on time. I live about a ten-minute walk from my parents, so I planned to leave the house at a quarter to four, giving myself plenty of time to get there. I hoped that if I were already there, he would let me come along.

At 3:30, I called my mother about something else, and

while we were talking, she told me that Abba was getting ready to leave. I bid my mother a quick good-bye, rushed down the stairs, and ran the whole way. When I got to my parents' house, out of breath, I saw that Abba's car was not in the driveway.

Did he guess that one of us would show up? Did he leave early so he wouldn't have to inconvenience anyone?

I'm sure we don't give him that impression, because we truly don't feel that way.

Standing there in the hot sun, I was so bothered that my carefully planned strategy hadn't worked. I was very thirsty (after that run), and would have wanted to go in for a cold drink, but I knew I shouldn't. If I did, my mother would immediately call my father and say, "Why did you leave early? Sruly came over specially, and would have wanted to go with you." Then my mother and father would both be aggravated. Instead of doing something good for them, what would I have accomplished?

So I turned and slowly walked home.

I had time on my way home to think the same thoughts that have been going through my mind lately: "How do we balance what we are sure is good for our parents, with what they want for themselves?"

We don't have to make these decisions ourselves. And at times we shouldn't. Some of these issues should be decided by medical authorities and/or a Rav.

As parents get older, we must pray for the wisdom and sensitivity not to encroach on our parents' right to make their own decisions while at the same time doing our part to ensure their safety and optimal health.

THE MINUTE SHAVUOS *was over, the phone rang. I was closest to the phone, so I picked up. It was my mother-in-law.*

"Tell Mordy to come right away. I can't get Dad out of the chair. Something must have happened to his back," she said, sounding perfectly miserable. "He can't lift himself, and I'm having no luck helping him."

I motioned to our son, Uri, to run across to shul, while I continued to speak to my mother-in-law, assuring her that Mordy would leave immediately. Of course he would. It's a twenty-minute ride that Mordy makes daily in the best of times, so I knew his mother could count on him in this fix, no matter what else was on his agenda.

In a minute, Mordy was rushing into the house, with Uri at his heels. He grabbed the car keys, waved good-bye, and made a dash for the car.

Mind you, this was no ordinary night. The sky was ablaze with lightning, and the thunder boomed overhead as I watched my husband drive away.

He returned home about three hours later, totally wiped out. He described for us the long and arduous drive — and the surprising events of that evening.

"Honestly, I felt like the thunder was just on top of me," he told us. "With Shavuos fresh in my mind, I was thinking, What a finale. Is this what Maamad Har Sinai sounded like?

"Clutching the wheel, I drove for about ten minutes. Just then, the rain started pouring down. I could barely see the road. This isn't good, I said to myself and decided to pull over before attempting the highway.

"After about twenty minutes, it looked safe to continue. I drove slowly...but really slowly. What usually takes me twenty minutes to drive, now took well over an hour.

"I arrived in Riverdale to see Mom wringing her hands, never dreaming it would take me so long, and Dad sitting forlorn in his armchair.

"What was this all about? Was it my father's chronic back pain, or was it just that he had sat too many hours in one position?

"With a thumbs up to my mother, I went straight over to my father. Slowly and carefully, I helped him stand up and waited until he steadied himself. Then, with the help of his walker, I maneuvered him into bed.

"'Thanks so much for coming, dear,' Mom said, 'and have a safe trip home.'

"'So soon? I just came. Tell me what else I can do for you.'

"But Mom and Dad both insisted that everything else was under control. I could go, and in the morning, the aide would assist them.

"'Ma, I think — ' I tried protesting again.

"'Don't think, just go home. Go home. We're fine.'

"'Are you sure you're okay? I don't mind staying.'

"'We're fine. Really. Go home. It's late.'

"I kissed them good-night, ending this five-minute visit.

"I walked down the steps, got into my car, turned on the windshield wipers, gripped the wheel, and prepared for a slow ride home. A three-hour ride for a five-minute visit."

We spoke about this evening many times. I remember it because of the storm winds and torrential rains. Mostly, I remember it because it was the night my amazing husband taught me the real meaning of kibbud av va'eim.

Chapter 3

Whether Near or Far

Proximity offers a broad range of opportunities that distance denies. The ideal situation is for children to be on hand to care for parents' needs, even non-urgent ones. Living close by enables us to drop in from time to time to see if we can lend a hand, and, when care is not needed, simply to be there so that our parents can have the pleasure of seeing us and spending time together.

HOW CAN I DESCRIBE MY BROTHER, HESHY? Would the words "caring," "devoted," and "dedicated" do him justice?

Even if Heshy had lived on the other side of the globe, I'm sure my parents would be first and foremost in his thoughts. The fact that he lives ten minutes from our parents keeps them front and center in his life.

He will do anything and everything, at any time and at any cost — rain or shine, requested or not — for them. Nothing is too difficult or too time consuming when it comes to helping our parents, directly or indirectly, in any area. You think I'm exaggerating? Judge for yourself.

He is there to make all their medical appointments and consultations, and is by their side when the time comes to accompany them. This isn't uncommon — I have plenty of friends who do this for their parents.

But how many sons would think of arranging fresh challah for their parents close to Shabbos? You might think that Heshy brings challah once — late Friday afternoon. Oh, no! Friday, mid-morning, Heshy comes in with fresh, warm challah he just picked up from the bakery. Good enough. Very good enough. But not for Heshy. On long Fridays, there is a second, afternoon, delivery. There is Heshy, carrying challah from a later baking — even fresher, warmer, softer, easier for Dad to eat. (The morning challah was delivered to make sure that there would be some in the house just in case he missed the afternoon delivery.)

It's not that we siblings don't pitch in. Our neighbors have always commented that the entrance to my parents' home is like a revolving door. We all come — sometimes from great distances — for long visits. But competing with Heshy is something else.

It was always important to Dad to daven three tefillos in shul. When he was able to get to a minyan — but not on his own — Heshy arranged a ride. If Heshy couldn't be there on the spot to help Dad into the car, he arranged for someone else to be there, and also made sure that there was someone to accompany Dad home.

Later, when our father had difficulty getting out of the house, a minyan was brought to him. I remember one Simchas Torah when our house was alive with singing and dancing to best any shul.

When Dad became incapacitated, Heshy found even more things to do to alleviate the strain on our devoted mom. If any of the siblings would suggest something that could ease Mommy's load or make life more pleasant for Dad, Heshy immediately urged, "Okay, okay — just order it." Or, for example, when he saw Dad reading in a poor light, quick as a wink, "lighting" was marked on his "to do" list. No sooner said than done. In no time, Dad had more and better lighting to facilitate learning and reading.

Heshy's morning begins with Modeh Ani, immediately

*followed by a good morning call to our parents. "Good
night" for Heshy means calling home to see if all is well.
Making sure, for instance, that our ailing father, who counts
on Heshy to be his calendar, remembered to count the
Omer.*

*My brother's thoughts are everywhere, spanning
continents. Once, there was a critical medical problem. He
arranged for and hired a minyan to daven at* kivrei tzaddikim
in Eretz Yisrael.

*Let me stop here to say that my sister-in-law, Rena, Heshy's
wife, supports all the varied responsibilities and activities
of her husband's* kibbud horim, *as multifaceted, original,
creative, and time-consuming as they are. Our family knows
that much of the credit for our parents' superlative care goes
to her.*

*When our father was hospitalized for a few months, Heshy
visited every day to put on Dad's tefillin. The hospital is an
hour's drive each way.*

*At one point, the nurses refused to move my father to sit
on a chair, as the doctors recommended. They said that a
raised bed was sufficient. But my brother never settles for
second best when caring for our father. He was determined
to have our father sit upright on a chair. My brother hired an
aide, drove him to the hospital, helped him move our father
from bed to chair, waited an hour, helped move our father
back to the bed, and then drove back home! He paid the
aide for his services for all those hours (a three-hour salary
for basically ten minutes of work) "just" so that our father
could have the preferred benefit of a chair over a raised bed.*

*Soon after, the hospital informed us that there was nothing
more they could do, and Dad would have to be transferred to
another facility, and that we should start looking around. Well,
when Heshy heard that, he was adamant — "No facility for our
father," he said firmly. "We are going to bring Dad home."*

*"Home?!" all of the siblings echoed. "With the imminent
deadline the hospital gave us?"*

*Besides, our father was very sick. The doctors said that
wherever he would go, it wouldn't be for too long.*

This made absolutely no difference to Heshy. He rolled up his sleeves and got to work. This meant finding 24-hour help in the house, getting a hospital bed, hiring an electrician to make sure that the house was wired to accommodate all the electrical equipment Dad would need, and then finding a carpenter. Doorways needed to be widened so the wheelchair could go through.

Meanwhile, the hospital was pressuring us. They said they weren't going to be able to wait too much longer. Heshy begged them to hold on a little bit longer until the construction was finished. Between rushing the workers, pleading with the hospital, and equipping the house, Heshy was running in circles, even with our help.

Finally, much to Heshy's joy, and of course, to ours too, my father did come home — to his own renovated house, fully equipped with all his medical apparatus. All the conveniences made especially to suit his needs, beckoning to him, calling out, "Welcome home."

Ten days later Dad passed away, surrounded by people who loved him and doted on him constantly. Of course, even then, Heshy took charge of every detail.

We are witness that, to Heshy's everlasting credit, he gave new dimensions to the words, "caring," "devoted," and "dedicated." But if we would compliment my brother Heshy on what he did, he would just brush us off.

That's Heshy.

"YOUR PARENTS ARE UNUSUAL…"

"Such special people…"

"It's amazing what they do…"

I hear this all the time. But you know how it is. You live in your house — your own world — and you think, "Isn't this the way it's supposed to be? Isn't that what all people do?" Even the extraordinary becomes ordinary, if it happens all the time.

Immediately after Grandma Weiss passed away, my parents evaluated the situation and made their decision: Grandpa Weiss should not be left alone for a whole day. So every afternoon, after we kids came home from school, we'd pack up the van and go to Grandpa's house. We brought along supper, spent the evening together, and then slept over so Grandpa would have company.

This whole process began long before the afternoon. Our mom first shopped for Grandpa's favorite foods, cooked them just the way he liked, and then packed it all up, including enough for the next day's lunch. Neighbors caught a glimpse of our daily exodus every day at about the same time. Our response to their inquiries usually elicited a lot of "wow"s and "amazing"s. No matter what was going on, we piled into the van with our cooler, assorted bags, pajamas, school bags, and anything else we needed for the next morning.

As the weeks went by, my parents saw that this was not going to be a practical long-term arrangement. They also realized that they needed a solution for the daytime hours. Weighing the options, they made a second major decision. We would move near Grandpa.

To us kids, this decision totally defied logic. Didn't it make more sense to uproot one person than to move a whole family? Though the move was close enough so that we could all stay in our schools, still, we all had friends on the block. Who wants to start all over again with new neighbors?

My parents, though, said that we were more flexible and would adjust, whereas Grandpa needed his familiar surroundings.

In one month, our house was sold and we'd rented a new place big enough for Grandpa to move in with us.

I'm sure the move wasn't easy for my father, since he is the Rav of a small shul in our old neighborhood, which is a long walk away, especially in the winter. But we never heard a peep from him. All of us followed his lead and settled into a routine that was anything but routine, if you know what I mean.

Before our eyes unfolded a drama — not a short skit, not a sketch, but a real production. The principal actors were my grandfather and his son and daughter-in-law (my parents).

We kids played minor, but essential, roles. Some of us were the stuntmen (just kidding).

SCENE 1

The sun is peeking over the horizon. There is Dad, jumping out of bed. Grandpa likes to go to an early minyan, and Dad is right there to escort him. After davening, they stay for the Daf.

SCENE 2

There is Mrs. Weiss (my mother) bustling around the kitchen. Actually, I think you could call my mother the star of the show. She definitely has a leading role.

Mom is there to greet Grandpa when he comes home from the shiur.

"Hi, Dad. How would you like your eggs today?" she greets Grandpa. This is usually followed by, "I left your mail on the table."

If you're thinking the rest of the day's meals are self-service, you'd be wrong. Three times a day, Grandpa gets a full spread.

Sit back and relax, because this is a long scene.

Mom is always making sure that Grandpa looks tip-top, is well nourished, and is engaged in enjoyable activities.

SCENE 3

Scene 3 opens with my father at his desk in his office. He is on the phone, very likely returning a call from a professional relating to Grandpa, or interrupting a meeting to take a call from a doctor. Maybe it's his father's test results...or the need to discuss a new plan of action. At any point in his day, business might grind to a halt when Dad leaves to accompany Grandpa to an appointment or pop into the house to give his father a good word.

SCENE 4

Dad's home from work. The whole family sits down to dinner. Dad goes through Grandpa's bills, and then they learn together.

Tonight is a family bar mitzvah. *Before they leave together for the event, Dad, Grandpa's social secretary, books Grandpa's ticket for next week to an out-of-town wedding that Grandpa would like to attend. Of course, Dad will accompany him.*

And now, if you were to call my parents to the stage for a round of applause, they would most likely respond, "What did we do? We know plenty of people who do the same, and even much more."

You'll never have to ask them for an encore. Every day — day in, day out, week in, week out, month after month — they offer us a perfect repeat performance.

You will notice that we kids are in some of these scenes you are watching of this family saga, taking a cue from our parents, learning up close a thing or two about devotion. I hope you will say that our performance is also pretty good.

I'm sure you will agree, though, that my folks are a hard act to follow.

WE RECENTLY MOVED *to an area outside of Jerusalem. The natural reaction of people was, "Why did you move?" Moving would mean packing, unpacking, readjustment to new areas and new people. So what prompted us to move?*

We loved our neighbors and neighborhood, especially that it was around the corner from our son, Asher, and his family. Somehow, though, that wasn't close enough for Asher's liking. Next door was what he wanted.

The search began for two apartments side by side: one large enough for a family of seven children bli ayin hara, *and one small enough for Grandma and Grandpa. We saw new apartments, plans for apartments not-yet-built, and older apartments. We looked at neighborhoods developing into religious areas, and those not developing. We talked to real estate agents, private owners, and made all kinds of contacts. Asher did the groundwork, and we looked and discussed and discussed and discussed. There was no end to the conversations.*

Asher was determined to find apartments for us that were not 101 steps to walk up on Shabbos, which, I think, was the major consideration for this move. My son and his family lived on the 5th floor. He was looking toward the future. True, my husband and I can walk those steps, but if they ever became an obstacle and a cause for us to think twice about coming for Shabbos, that wouldn't suit our son.

After much investigation and negotiation, it seemed the only reasonable option was for us to move to a less-developed suburb of Jerusalem. Asher literally led us step by step through the whole process.

A year and a half later, we were both settled in. Chol HaMoed Succos we were all together — children, grandchildren, and great-grandchildren — for a seudah, a dream come true. We are living side by side, one large house for our son and his family, and a honeymoon cottage for us.

In the devar Torah *that Asher gave, he talked about Yaakov Avinu being told by Hashem to take with him three generations, and said that we, like Yaakov Avinu, now had three generations together. He told everyone how much we, as grandparents, had given to him and his family.*

It was the words he said then that I will never forget: "When we first thought of this move, we were mainly thinking about how good this would be for Grampa and Gramma. Now, we see how very good this has been for us. It's we who are the lucky ones."

We can't sufficiently express our gratitude to him and our daughter-in-law for their continuing concern for our wellbeing and their everyday contact with us. They have given more than anyone can ask for.

What is striking about this special story is Gramma's reaction. One would think that making the effort to find adjacent homes was such a warm, loving gesture that nothing could top it. But when she recounts the story, she emphasizes, "What I will never forget were my son's words in the succah."

Had Asher gone to this tremendous effort, but along the way left a message that "my elderly parents need watching," he might have marred his entire endeavor. That Gramma and Grampa were able to retain their dignity and were considered "givers" was what made her heart soar.

It is preferable and desirable for a child to live near parents. How can we serve them completely and properly otherwise?

> **WHEN MY PARENTS STARTED** *their married life, they lived near my father's parents. At first finances were a big struggle, but slowly, over the years, they built up their business, until it was quite a thriving enterprise.*
>
> *My parents could now well afford to buy a bigger, nicer home, and my father was looking into other communities.*
>
> *For my mother, my father's word was law. But we kids can all attest to our mother's reaction each time Dad broached this topic. With a shake of her head, a slight wave of her hand, and just a touch of a frown on her face, my mother would say with conviction, "You just don't move away from parents."*

That said, nearness is not always feasible.

For instance, the price of renting or purchasing a home near parents is more than children can afford.

When parents facilitate a move to a distant location by agreeing to participate in costs, or agree to the move even without financial assistance, they are thereby waivering the honor (kibbud) and forgoing the service (shimush) which is their due (see Ch 17 for further discussion on "the waiver"-mechila).

Legitimate considerations for relocating

A child has obligations to himself that may require relocation. Therefore, though he will lose the opportunity to provide the care that proximity affords, he is justified in moving away, even without parental consent, for several halachically condoned reasons:[1]

1. If a son cannot financially provide for himself and his family while living near his parents[2]

2. If health issues mandate a move, e.g., to obtain superior medical care or to live in a climate better suited to his or his family's health needs[3]

3. If he feels the move will enhance his (or his family's) growth in Torah through better mentors, teachers, study partners, or a more spiritually elevating atmosphere[4]

4. For the educational needs of his children[5]

5. If living near parents puts an unmanageable strain on the marriage, regardless of where the blame lies, a couple should consult with a Rabbinic authority in order to accurately and objectively assess the situation.[6]

In addition, within each of the above, their are scenarios that call for clarification. One example—the halacha differentiates between a son who cannot make a suffcient living to support his family there and a son who can't support his family as well as he would want.

When a child feels he must relocate at a distance from his parents, it would be proper, and wise, to clarify the halacha, enabling him to align his will with the Will of the Almighty.

If parents require physical care, a child may not leave unless he has arranged a suitable substitute (a sibling or hired help) that pleases the parents, and returns when feasible to check on parents' wellbeing.[7]

We may have to leave our parents' locale, thus forgoing opportunities for mitzvos that proximity affords, but distance does not exempt us from what we *are* able to do. This thought should accompany us: I know that I'm depriving you of the opportunities for assistance and the *nachas* that proximity brings, so I'm going to bend over backward to do whatever I can for you to bring you *nachas* from afar.

Out of sight, but not out of mind

Living at a distance necessitates that thought and effort be put into keeping the parent-child connection close.[8]

Connecting

DURING MY FIRST THIRTEEN YEARS in Eretz Yisrael, *my parents lived in the States. In those days, telephone calls were expensive, so we kept in touch mainly through letters, mostly from my mother to me.*

When my parents came to live here, they were in a different city, so I kept in touch by calling twice a week.

At that time Rav Nisson Alpert (the son-in-law of Rav Chaim Pinchas Scheinberg, ztz"l,) passed away. When he was buried in Eretz Yisrael, the family brought along a little notebook with the Rav's personal commitments, which they read at the funeral. Of course, it was all very inspiring, but one commitment in particular struck me. Rav Alpert took it upon himself to call his parents every single day.

From that time on, I did the same.

At the shivah for my mother, a"h, I told this story. One of the people present at the time told me afterward that he was so inspired, he started calling his parents every day.

Parents whose children live at a distance pine — as in "yearn intensely" — for their presence. Imagine the joy these parents had at receiving a call from their son every single day.

I LIVE IN NEW YORK. My parents live in Florida. One morning, I called my mother, and the phone rang and rang. Eventually I hung up before the answering machine clicked on and got busy around the house.

In the evening, I tried again, and this time, my mother picked up.

"Hi, Mommy. I'm so glad to get you in. I tried this morning but no one answered."

"You did? I'm so sorry I missed you. Why didn't you leave a message?"

"Well, I didn't think about it. I knew I was going to call back in a few hours."

"Shuli, if I don't answer, always leave a message. Even if I can't speak to you, I just love to hear your voice."

A few seconds more can make Mom's day.

A call to a parent is like no other call we'll make. All the respect and reverence required of us must somehow be conveyed without the richness of a personal encounter, and in a much shorter time frame.

The thought foremost in our mind when we call a parent should be, *This call is for him.*

Basic courtesy brings us to ask the party we are calling, "Is this a good time for you?" For a parent, we upgrade this to finding out in advance when they want us to call.

"When is a convenient time to call, Dad?"

It doesn't hurt to double check at the outset of the call, either.

"Am I interrupting something, Mom?"

Parents want to hear the news, so fill them in.

"The lawyer said it looks like we'll be able to build soon."
"I went to that lecture I told you about. Would you like to hear a few of the main points?"
"You'll never believe what Riki did this morning. It's hard to believe she's only 4. Listen to this…"

Parents want to feel valued.

"Your suggestion worked, Dad. I spoke to my supervisor and he said…"
"Mom, I renegotiated my contract. Just like you said, I was able to convince them to let me leave earlier."

Parents want to hear you appreciate them.

"Dad, I can't tell you how thrilled Shlomo was with the tickets you and Mom sent. We're so excited about flying in for Shira's wedding. Thanks tons."

Parents need to hear that you respect them.

"I see someone's trying to get me, Mom. It may be the delivery we're expecting. Do you mind if I pick up to see who it is?"
"I hear what you're saying, Dad. I'll give it some thought."

"A virtual shared life"

What would you say about a busy mom who has been sending an email newsletter — with pictures — for *over nine years*? (A sample, complete with a photo, appears on the facing page.) Here are her thoughts:

Hoffman Highlights

Vol. II, Issue 33

To Our Dear Family,

Here's the news from this week...

Shoshana News

One morning, instead of the usual, "Mommy, I don't want to go to Gan," Shoshana said, "Mommy, why do we have to go to Gan anyway?" Mommy explained, "Well, you see, you need to learn a lot of things to be an adult in this world — you need to learn how to read so that you can read signs and know where you are going, and know what to buy. We need to learn math so that we can add up numbers and figure out how much things cost. We need to learn about science so that we understand how the world works..." Shoshana paused and then reflected, "We don't do any of that stuff in Gan!"

Rivka News

Two cute Rivka stories this week:

Rivka was asking Totty how to know which shoe goes on which foot. Totty explained, "the Velcro always goes away from your body." Rivka added, "also, if it hurts, it's the wrong foot."

Mommy has a campaign with Rivka to "listen the FIRST time" (she even has a star chart when she listened the first time and Mommy doesn't have to repeat herself). This week, Rivka was jumping on the bed and Mommy said, "Stop jumping." Mommy had to say it twice before Rivka listened. Mommy reminded Rivka,

"You listened the second time. I want you to listen the first time." Rivka explained, "I tried to listen the

first time, but I was jumping so fast that my body couldn't stop when I told it to."

Shaindy News

Shaindy spotted Chaim picking up a stray coin. As he held the coin in his hand, she said, "Oh, no, Chaim! That's very chas veshalom."

Chaim News

Chaim is enjoying his new sneakers (thank you, Bubby!). His favorite word is no, and he likes to use it when it's appropriate — and when it isn't.

Chaim went to shul with Totty for the first time last Friday night! He was so excited to experience this privilege. Boy, did he feel special! Totty reported that Chaim sat quietly the whole time.

Binyamin News

On our way home from the park, Binyamin was amazed that the moon kept following us. He asked so many good questions like, "How does the moon move?" and "How come there's only one?" Best of all, he wanted to know why the moon was only following us and not the people who were walking in the opposite direction!

IF YOU ASK OLIM what the hardest part of moving to Eretz Yisrael *is, many will say "family."*

When we moved, we left all of our siblings and parents behind in the States. Though I missed them, the hardest part for me was knowing that I had packed up their nachas *and moved it 6000 miles away.*

I wanted to do something to soften the blow. I decided to send an email newsletter with photos of the kids. After my first issue, I got such great feedback that I decided to make it a weekly project.

I found that especially when the children were younger and not particularly good phone conversationalists, it was a great way to keep everyone in touch with our lives. The grandparents appreciated it greatly, and my mother-in-law prints them out every week on glossy stock paper and keeps binders (now nine years' worth) on display. My mother prints the newsletters, keeping one copy for Shabbos reading around the house and to show friends.

I wasn't sure how often I would be able to write, but I managed to keep it up weekly for the first five years. After that, with a house full of children (who were older and stayed up later at night), I had to settle for monthly updates — but by then, the kids could keep up conversations on the phone.

"Hoffman Highlights" have become such a part of our lives that when something funny or memorable happens, one of the kids will usually remind me to jot it down for the Highlights. The greatest benefit of the entire endeavor was enabling my parents and in-laws to feel like they knew their grandchildren, even when we were living so far away.

Nothing compares with time shared in person, but our newsletters went a long way in bridging continents and creating a virtual shared life.

Put your parents in the picture

Family photos. Parents hang them on the fridge, display them proudly on a breakfront, on their office desk or on their computer screen...and *kvell.*

"Our son sent us a digital picture frame. He had uploaded his family pictures onto a memory card that is inserted in the frame. This displays a slideshow of everything inserted. We enjoyed it for months. Then he sent us updated pictures, and we changed the show for more weeks of happy viewing."

"One of the nicest gifts we received from our daughter and her family is the talking album lying here on my coffee table. It works like this: Every page has a place for a photo and a button to press, which allows you to record a message. Imagine! We can look at a child's or grandchild's picture, press a button, and hear the message they recorded especially for us. And we can enjoy hearing this as often as we want!

"I think my parents flipped when they received a package from my sister living on the West Coast. It was a bunch of pillows. Each one had a picture of one of her children. The pillow colors matched the décor of the den. They bring joy to the room, and continue to be a conversation piece for any visitor."

Gifts

Can we count, or simply remember, even a portion of the gifts we have received from our parents, from the practical to the extravagant, and some just for fun?

From early on, we want to consider: **What can I give back?**

The following are voices from around the globe, sending their love from across land and sea:

"We mailed our father, who is a chazzan, an oversized siddur for a *shaliach tzibbur* with large print, and a *tehillim* with large print for our mother."

"I thought my hardworking mother could use some pampering, so I gave her a gift certificate to a local day spa. Was she excited!"

"The World's Best Balabuste" is what we had embroidered on the apron we sent to Mom. It wasn't expensive, but much appreciated. Especially meaningful was the accompanying card lauding her culinary talents and thanking her for the thousands of gourmet meals, served so lavishly over the years."

Gifts needn't be costly to be appreciated. Personalized mugs are in most budgets.

And don't forget magnets!

Least costly, but certainly not least enjoyed, might be a poem, full of praise and abundant appreciation.

Not only material, tangible gifts can be given. One way we can honor parents from afar is through baby naming. To some parents, this is the most meaningful and appreciated gift of all.*

Occasions

It is helpful to mark occasions on a calendar at the beginning of a new year. Acknowledge these events — birthdays, anniversaries, promotions, awards — with a call, card, flowers, or something your parent would enjoy.

> *"I sent my mother a very authentic looking talking rose for her birthday. Squeeze its stem and it says, 'I love you.'"*
>
> *"We kids all chipped in and bought Mom a string of pearls for her birthday, thanking her for the 'pearls of wisdom' she shares with us."*

When we are far away, there is a lot that we can't do. But there is still plenty that can be done.

And, of course, davening for parents can be done from all over the world.

---

* See Chapter 13, "And His Name Shall Be Called..."

Chapter 4

Hosting

כְּשֶׁיִּכָּנֵס הָאָב אוֹ הָאֵם לְבֵיתוֹ שֶׁל בֵּן
יִשְׂמַח בָּהֶם וִיקַבְּלֵן בְּסֵבֶר פָּנִים יָפוֹת...
When a father or mother enter a child's
home, it should be a happy occasion,
and they should be received pleasantly…
(*Menoras HaMaor*).[1]

"I THOUGHT WE'D DO pickled tongue with an apricot sauce. Dad's going to love that. He said it was his absolute favorite last year. Wad'ya think about that?"

I was on the phone with my mother, discussing the menu for the upcoming Yom Tov.

"Ma, what do you think about tongue?" I repeated when she didn't respond the first time.

Again, there was silence on the other end.

"Ma, are you there…?"

"Yes, I'm here," came the stiff reply.

"Ma, what's the matter? I was just saying how much Daddy is gonna love…"

"Daddy and I weren't invited."

I winced. Oh no! How did this happen? I try so hard to be careful. Did I really forget to officially invite my mother, when I know how important this formality is to her?

I could have tried saying, "Ma, you and Daddy come every Yom Tov," but I knew that was the wrong direction. Oh, Hashem, help me fix this!

It turned out that I didn't get a chance to say anything, because my mother was getting a call on her second line. This worked to my benefit, because meanwhile I had an inspiration.

An hour later, I was at her doorstep with a very professional-looking invitation.

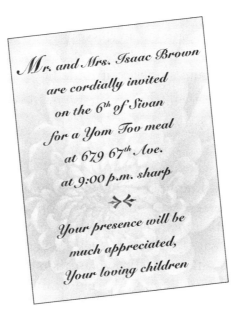

Mr. and Mrs. Isaac Brown
are cordially invited
on the 6th of Sivan
for a Yom Tov meal
at 679 67th Ave.
at 9:00 p.m. sharp
❋
Your presence will be
much appreciated,
Your loving children

You might think, "Come on, isn't that childish? Is your mother really going to go for this? Isn't it just a bit patronizing?

Well, let me tell you, I delivered this invitation with a flourish, my mother smiled, and we had two happy guests for Yom Tov.

Now, if you ask me why it worked, I would say, first, because Hashem helped. Second, because I care about pleasing my mother, especially when it's such a small, easily doable thing. If this is important to my mother, who cares why? It doesn't matter if I wouldn't do it that way, or if most people wouldn't, or if all my friends wouldn't. My formal invitation meant, "I know you like it this way. Sorry for my oversight. Please come."

If my attitude had been, "Ma, give me a break. We both know you have a standing invitation," that would have left both me and my mother unhappy.

She's a terrific daughter, isn't she? She's a creative and a caring daughter — but best of all, she cared enough to do it the way it pleased her mother. And that's our GPS for this chapter — and for this mitzvah.

———◆———

Inviting parents to visit us and hosting them is an aspect of the mitzvah of "bringing in." In classes I've given over the years, we've brainstormed on this topic. I'd like to share with you a sampling of ideas and stories contributed by participants.

Your parents are coming for a visit. Where do you start? With…

The invitation

"You know, Dad, I'm here whenever you'd like to come. Just pick up the phone." That might work for some parents, who don't mind inviting themselves. They have no problem picking up the phone to say, "Hi, is next week convenient?"

Other parents, like Mrs. Brown in the story above, want a warm, personal invitation, and some want it each and every time.

On time.

> **"THAT'S WHAT HE SAID?"**
> *"Yes, by Motza'ei Shabbos."*
> *"Really?"*
> *"Really."*
> *I was speaking with my brother, Yitzy. Since my father became a widower, the two of us plus another sister take turns hosting him for Shabbos. I guess we weren't doing as good a job as I thought.*

Yitzy had just hung up from speaking with Dad. It's not that Dad was complaining. It's just that he was asking that we make up our minds immediately after Shabbos as to what "his plans" were for the following week.

Until now, it had been a random order based on whichever one of us was most available that week, which meant that Dad was in limbo until we all managed to make up our minds.

Now that I think about it, how unsettling not to know until the last minute where you will be for Shabbos.

How come we didn't get this on our own?

Once you've extended the invitation, consider if your parents need...

Travel assistance

"I helped book my father's flight to us. I got him a really good deal."

"My parents-in-law came to us for a *bar mitzvah*. We reserved seats for them on the direct bus to Toronto."

"I printed out directions to our house for my mother to give to the taxi driver."

Hosting parents is an art. It goes a step beyond regular hosting because of our additional obligations to these special guests. Thinking through the visit ahead of time gives us a better chance of fulfilling the mitzvah properly.

Getting ready

THOUGH WE COME OFTEN, my daughter still calls before every visit for our "request list." My husband has gastrointestinal issues, and we are always trying new diets.

Our conversations go something like this:

"Hi, Mommy," Bracha says to me.

After we check in about the kids, I hear, "OK, Mommy.

My pencil is poised. What's up this week? Really? No more
potatoes? So tell me, what do I do about cholent?
"It's fine. I'll make a separate one for Dad."

It's a good idea to get to know your parents' needs and
preferences: "Zeidy likes Diet. Make sure it's on the list. And
make sure to buy a sugarless cake."

When you buy your mother's special brand of coffee or
your father's favorite cut of meat for their enjoyment, you are
beautifying this mitzvah.

Think through the visit in advance. Are stairs difficult for
your parents? Would they prefer a downstairs room? The master
bedroom? A separate apartment?

What more can you do to make their visit as comfortable as
possible for them? Do they need a heater or an air conditioner?
Reading material? How can you upgrade the usual refreshments
and gift basket you set out for guests to show your parents how
special they are to you?

It's time to take out gifts that your parents have given you.
That pretty dish your mother gave you, the jewelry she hopes
you like. Can you dress the children in some of the outfits they've
been sending or give the pleasure of seeing grandkids reading
the books and playing with the toys that they have given them?

How about creating a big sign for the front door and/or a
warm welcome sign for their room?

Before you know it…

They're here!

❖ The moment of arrival sets the tone. Make it count. Begin with
a warm welcome.

> **WHEN SAVTA CAME TO THE STATES** *for a visit, after not*
> *having been there for a while, she was welcomed like a*
> *visiting dignitary.*
>
> *Imagine this scene. Savta is exiting Customs, wheeling her*
> *luggage cart. Suddenly, she is surrounded by about fifty (!)*
> *descendants, three generations, who have come to greet her.*

Balloons are flying and signs pop up like daisies on a field, saying, "Welcome to Our Beloved Savta." Some are carrying bouquets. I see a few wet eyes from onlookers who can't help but be touched by this moving display of affection.

Now, picture this. Savta is ushered into a waiting car, buckled up, and, amid great fanfare, escorted to her destination by a "presidential" motorcade, each car manned by a loving relative.

Not everyone can get to the airport or orchestrate such a regal welcome, and not every parent wants or expects it. No matter. It's not a competition. The point is, what would *your* parent appreciate?

Here's a basic welcome everyone can give: "Dad, call me when you're ten minutes away from the house, and I'll come out and help you bring in your stuff."

Carrying in a parent's luggage is part of the mitzvah of "bringing in." As is offering them refreshments:

❖ Next, show them where they will sleep.

WE ARRIVED AT OUR CHILDREN'S *apartment late Friday afternoon. Our son immediately took our bags, and we followed him in. Next thing we knew, he deposited our belongings in the master bedroom.*

My first thoughts were, I can't displace my daughter-in-law. She'll have to take out everything she needs. What if she forgets something and needs it late at night or early in the morning? She'll surely be embarrassed to knock.

I was about to protest, when I heard my son say, "Mommy, until now, Gila and I haven't been able to host you the way we would have liked. Now that we finally have a bigger apartment and the pleasure of having you come, both of us want you to take the master bedroom suite."

When I continued protesting, he added, "Otherwise, how are our children going to learn the proper way to honor parents?"

Was he saying that just to convince us?

I'll never know, but who am I to argue with better chinuch for our grandchildren?

❖ Here's some **food** for thought.

> *HARAV AVRAHAM TCHECHNOV, the* Tzelusa d'Avraham, *was very careful to keep the instruction of the* Gemara Yerushalmi *that a* talmid chacham *should not eat delicacies at a meal that is not a* seudas mitzvah. *He was, therefore, careful not to eat fish, which was a very special dish for him, unless it was a* seudas mitzvah.
>
> *Once when he came to visit his son, the Rav of Strikov, he was surprised to see that his son had prepared a meal of fish for him, though he was aware of his father's custom. When Rav Avraham questioned his son, he answered, "And is a meal to honor your father not considered a* seudas mitzvah?"[2]

❖ When parents will be with us for a meal, halachos of Torah etiquette come into play regarding the seating.

> *AS WE SAT DOWN TO DINNER, my son-in-law directed my husband to one head of the table and me to the other.*
>
> *We hadn't visited our children recently, mostly hosting them in our more spacious home.*
>
> *Surrounded by our lively grandchildren, I was just getting ready to sit, when 3-year-old Chavi rushed over to me.*
>
> *"Grandma, we can't sit in that chair! It's Mommy's chair."**
>
> *My son-in-law, smiling at his clever daughter, gave her cheek a pinch, and said, "You're right, Chavi — you don't, but Grandma's allowed. Besides, Grandpas and Grandmas get special seats."*

It is proper, though not obligatory, to seat a father and mother (and father-in-law and mother-in-law) in the most prestigious places at the table.[3]** In many families, the visiting father and mother are automatically seated at the two heads of the table, or the father at the head and the mother beside him. No one asks, because it is self-understood. It's also fine if a parent prefers a different seat for whatever reason.

---

* See Chapter 18.

** However, if other siblings seat the parents at the head of the table in their home, a son or son-in-law should weigh the pros and cons of deciding otherwise, to ensure that it would not be considered a slight.

❖ Serve 'em right!

> *IN OUR HOME, it was a given that grandparents were served first. It made no difference whether it was parents or in-laws, whether it was a Shabbos meal, a weekday meal, or just a snack — if Grandma and Grandpa were visiting, and we children offered something to our parents, we were sure to hear them say, "Did you offer some to Grandpa yet?" or "Make sure Grandma has a drink first."*
>
> *If we mistakenly served our father first, as we were used to doing on a regular basis, he would not just pass the plate to his father or mother, but would gently, yet audibly, tell us so that both we and our grandparents heard, "Please serve Grandpa/Grandma first. You can bring mine afterward."*

A wife's obligation: When her parents are guests in her home and they are seated at a meal, even though a wife should serve her husband first and then her parents, nevertheless, a husband preferably should tell his wife to serve her parents first,[4] unless it is self-understood.

A child's obligation: A child is obligated to serve his father first, before he serves a grandparent. In some homes, a child serves the parent and the parent then passes the food to the grandparent. In other homes, the father makes it clear to everyone that he forgoes the privilege and wants the grandparents to be served first.

Some of the "firsts" that should be offered to a parent at a Shabbos meal:[5] *Kiddush*, washing hands, *Hamotzi*, when a serving dish is passed the parent should be offered first, leading *Bircas HaMazon* and *zemiros*.

Farewells

> **"Escorting out"** — how is this to be done? The child should accompany his father and mother and not turn his back until they are out of sight (*Menoras HaMaor*).[6]

AS I WAS PASSING BY 2 PANIM MEIROT ST., home of Harav Chaim Pinchas Scheinberg zt"l, I beheld a most beautiful sight.

Rav Scheinberg (then in his late 90s) was sitting in the front passenger seat of Reb Asa Wittow's car. R' Asa, a long time talmid of the Rosh Yeshiva was seated behind the wheel, ready to take Rav Scheinberg to the airport for one of his many trips abroad on behalf of Yeshivas Torah Ore. The car's motor was running, and it seemed that they were ready to pull out. Were they waiting for something...or someone?

Just then, Rebbetzin Fruma Altusky, Rav Scheinberg's daughter, who lives in the apartment below her parents and was always by her father's side, hurried down the building's ramp toward the car.

From where I was standing, I watched the scene that was playing out before my eyes.

Rebbetzin Altusky bent her head down near the car's open window. Rav Scheinberg stretched out his hands above her head and gave her a berachah. Then Rebbetzin Altusky gently took her father's hand in hers...and kissed it.

"Lechaim u'leshalom, Papa," I heard her say. The car slowly pulled out.

I turned to go, tears in my eyes. How privileged I had been that morning...to witness the farewell of this gadol hador and his daughter...

Not long after this story was shared with me, I met Rebbetzin Altusky. I related the incident and asked, "May we include this story in the book on honoring parents? Is it accurate?"

"Yes," she confirmed, "but something very important is missing. You left out that when my parents drove away, I always walked after the car. I *always* escorted my parents whenever they were leaving."

Escorting any guest is a mitzvah. How much more so for parents. Included is: packing up food for the trip home, if that would be appreciated / bringing their bags to the car / walking them out to the car / driving them to the airport, train, or bus, if possible personally, and if not, arranging for it / waving until they are out of sight.

Our virtual visit is over. We hope you enjoyed it. We know your parents did!

Hosting frequently

When a son or daughter is able to have parents as weekly or frequent Shabbos guests, different questions arise for consideration:

❖ Will the son relinquish his place at the head of the table every Shabbos?

❖ Will the son defer to his father or father-in-law for *Kiddush* every week?

❖ Will the son never lead the *zemiros*?

❖ How will this arrangement affect the children?

❖ What if parents are critical or intrusive and this is on a regular basis and/or in front of the children?

❖ What if one's spouse opposes an "every-week" situation?

What is manageable on occasion may require different consideration when visits are frequent. These questions and others like them should be brought to the attention of your Rabbinic authority who knows your family situation well. The Rav can help clarify and prioritize according to Torah guidelines.

Hosting parents long-term

Whether young or elderly, for a variety of reasons, parents might move into the homes of their children.
Sometimes for a month at a time…

MY PARENTS HAD A FIRE in their home that caused extensive damage. The repairs would take half a year. It was so disturbing for them to be displaced, along with the loss of most of their possessions accumulated over a lifetime. We invited them to live with us in the interim, feeling that being surrounded by loving family would buoy their spirits.

Or even years…

YOU, OF COURSE, would never know it. No one did. But I knew that my beautiful mother had an unusually shaped head.

I also knew she wasn't born that way. It was one of the many souvenirs of Auschwitz that she carried with her wherever she went.

How did it happen? One icy day when she and her sister were being force-marched in the snow, my mother whispered to her sister, "Look down! We're walking on bodies!" This little distraction bothered the Nazi guard, who raised his whip and with tremendous force brought it down on my mother's head. She survived, but neither she nor we can understand how.

The dent in her skull also survived, leaving her head almost heart-shaped. Later, when we lived in New York, and Germany was compensating victims, people had to be examined by a German doctor to see who qualified. Initially, the doctor decided that my mother wasn't maimed enough to be compensated. Then he saw her head.

My mother was 18 years old when she was liberated from Auschwitz. She and her older sister were what was left of their illustrious family. They walked out with nothing but the ugly scars and terrifying memories.

The frightening question then arose: Where would they go?

My mother left the misery of Europe, wandering first to Paris, eventually making her way to Brazil. In the Jewish community of Rio de Janeiro, she met my father, a single man of 42, twenty-two years her senior. There I was born, their only child.

We lived in Brazil for eight years. After a while, my parents were able to find a sponsor, and we moved to New York.

I had a wonderful childhood. My parents showered me with all that any girl could wish for.

In time, my parents saw me marry and move to Eretz Yisrael. *In those early years, my mother was very busy, and she and my father were satisfied to know I was happy.*

All that changed when my father died at the age of 67, leaving my mother a young widow in her 40s. With my father gone and me living so far away, my mother was really alone.

During the final stages of my father's illness, my mother had been diagnosed with her own illness. After his passing, her condition worsened. The doctors concluded she needed an operation to save her life.

By now, I was the mother of two small children. My husband and I decided that we wanted my mother to come live with us. I went back to New York to be with my mother for her surgery, then settled all that needed to be sold, tied up loose ends, and made the final plans for the move.

I knew my mother would need to recuperate. What I didn't know was what a transformation would be taking place in her life.

We came back to Yerushalayim to my 75-meter apartment: two bedrooms, a living room with an adjacent balcony, a small kitchen with an eating area, and a porch off the kitchen, which we enclosed for additional sleeping space.

My mother slept in the second bedroom with my oldest daughter, Suri, then a toddler. I would have given her her own private room, but she told me that she liked having the baby with her.

There were many good years. My mother cooked and baked delicious challahs and her Hungarian specialties. She read the children stories and played with them, listened to them, and had nachas watching them grow and flourish.

For me, the most difficult challenge was that my mother refused to go outside. Though the operation was considered a success, it left my mother both weak physically and unsteady emotionally. The war years, which seemed to have been dormant as I was growing up, again became alive to her. She told me she heard the screaming, saw the flames, and heard the shooting. She was petrified that the Nazis were outside.

So here was my mother, living with us, but staying indoors twenty-four hours a day, seven days a week.

"I know I put myself in prison," she used to say, "but I don't care. I'm too frightened to go out. I'm comfortable here, and this is where I want to stay."

The only fresh air she allowed herself was on our quiet balcony. There she enjoyed many restful hours surrounded by family. Neighbors visited to drink in her wisdom, which reflected her deep piety and love of Hashem.

The second hardest part was the screaming at night. My mother would wake up many times in the night. The dreams were so real to her, the horror so jolting that it ripped through her. Suri, who had slept with my mother since she was a baby, mostly slept through it. We all got used to it...if one ever really could.

The light was on in my mother's room for the full fourteen years she lived with us, day and night. Somehow that light was comforting to her, and Suri got used to it.

Twelve years after the operation, my mother's illness came back. Our lives were turned upside down. We ran from one difficult treatment to another, and were in and out of the hospital, sometimes for a blood transfusion, other times, for a complication from one of the treatments. She was very, very frightened. I didn't leave her for a minute. I spoke to her constantly, trying to calm her fears.

When I couldn't accompany my mother, my husband went with her. Actually, I think she preferred his company to mine. He was calmer and a great conversationalist. He told her divrei Torah, which she loved. In fact, my husband handled most of the medical issues. He researched the doctors, made the appointments, and made sure the necessary medicines were always on hand. They were like mother and son. When my husband came home, the first thing he did was to look for my mother. Then he'd give her the warmest, "Hello, Ma." He fought for her life, running with her to any doctor he felt might possibly help.

As the sickness worsened, my mother became increasingly incapacitated. The illness was literally eating away her body. I took care of all her needs, including personal ones. Eventually, she needed to be bathed, dressed, and fed.

It was not easy. In one room, my mother was dying. In the other, my children were busy singing and playing. Life and death under one roof.

To see my mother withering away was very painful for me, but we did what had to be done. In our small apartment, the children did whatever they could to give Bobby her comfort and privacy.

When I think back on those years growing up with my beloved parents, and then the later years when my mother shared the growing-up years with my children, I am so glad that I was able to be there for her when she needed me.

Whatever I did in those fourteen years, I did with a feeling of deep appreciation and love. I am an only child. There was never a question, not for me and not for my devoted husband and children that this was the proper thing to do.

My daughter Suri, who shared a room with my mother all those years, married an exceptional man from a distinguished family, and they are blessed with outstanding children.

Subsequently, my husband and our family were offered a great opportunity. We were able to sell our apartment and move into a spacious home.

I see these as Hashem's special blessings to our family.

Inviting parents to live with children no doubt presents challenges. But we are told, "According to the difficulty is the measure of the reward."

"Ma, come live with us." Not everyone can say those words, but when you can say them and mean it sincerely, and when the family is able to pull together to make it work, then it is considered the highest level of "bringing in." It gives us the most opportunity to fulfill this mitzvah continuously.[7]

Fortunate are the children who see this mitzvah in practice. Both the *zechus* of the mitzvah and the hands-on experience will go a long way to ensure that this mitzvah is passed down from generation to generation.

Chapter 5

Visiting Days

Did you go to camp when you were young? Remember Visiting Day? Kids eagerly anticipating a visit from their family?

Were you a parent of a camper? Do *you* remember Visiting Day? You had it circled in red on the calendar, planned your summer around that day, came with armloads full of expected goodies. If it was bumper-to-bumper with your gang in the back crying most of the way, didn't you still greet your camper with a warm hug and kiss, and paste a smile on your face — despite all this?

What don't we do for our kids' happiness!

What *shouldn't* we do for our parents' happiness![1]

Visiting parents is yet another aspect of *kibbud av va'eim*.[2]

In *Parashas Vayigash*, we are told of the historic encounter between father and son after twenty-two years of separation:

> וַיֶּאְסֹר יוֹסֵף מֶרְכַּבְתּוֹ וַיַּעַל לִקְרַאת יִשְׂרָאֵל אָבִיו גֹּשְׁנָה וַיֵּרָא אֵלָיו
>
> Yosef harnessed his chariot and went up toward his father, Yisrael, to Goshen, and appeared before him... (*Bereishis* 46:29).

Yosef harnessed his chariot… Rashi comments: Yosef himself harnessed the horses (he didn't allow anyone to help him), because he was eager to show honor to his father.

Yosef…appeared before him… Rashi tells us that part of the joy of a visit is simply seeing a child.[3]

Rav Shmuel Houminer in his *sefer Eved HaMelech* comments on this:

> It is a great joy for a father and mother to see their children, especially if a considerable length of time has elapsed since they last saw them. Therefore, it is proper for children who are visiting parents to have in mind to appear before them so their parents can enjoy them and so that they can fulfill their parents' wishes in an appropriate manner.[4]

"…to appear before them…": For a parent, just seeing a child is a pleasure in and of itself. "Wait — stand back, dear. Let me just look at you a minute!"

"…can enjoy them…": The purpose of the visit is to bring parents pleasure.

"…so they can fulfill their parents' wishes…": Coming to visit in order to do things that you know will please them, the way they prefer.

Even if we're not specifically asked, if we know that our parents will enjoy seeing us, we fulfill the mitzvah of honoring them each and every time we visit. Even when there will be no assistance involved[5] — no cooking, serving meals, or fixing things around the house — every visit brings pleasure to our parents and therefore is a mitzvah for the child.* This includes weekdays as well as Shabbos and Yom Tov.

When a parent specifically asks, or tells us how much we are missed, the level of obligation changes.[6]

Sons and daughters should make an effort to visit parents, even if they are married and live at a distance.[7]

---

* But not a Torah obligation

ME, SPONTANEOUS? No one would use that word to describe me. I'm the deliberate, cautious, plan-in-advance type. That's why this whole impromptu trip was so outrageous.

My parents are very active in their suburban community where they have lived for several decades. It's where I grew up. They have generously endowed institutions and various programs. They do a lot of volunteering and open their homes for community events. I was, therefore, not surprised when I received a call one spring day that they would be honored at a dinner for one of the local organizations. There would be a big-name speaker and an elegantly catered dinner. My parents were the honorees of the evening.

My mother's excitement on a one-to-ten hit top number. Soon, we received a gold-embossed invitation to this gala affair, accompanied by a form, enabling us to either place an ad or dedicate good wishes to the honorees that would appear in the journal to be distributed the evening of the event.

I knew the first thing all honorees do is to open the journal to see which friends and family responded. My parents would be no different, so I knew we had to do this in a grand way.

This was certainly an easy opportunity, handed to me on a silver platter, to give my mother public recognition. I put the form with the other bills that needed attention on a shelf and then (really inexcusable, I know) just let it slip my mind.

That Wednesday, my husband Eli and I were taken by surprise when we received in the mail a sizeable sum of money that had been owed to us for quite some time.

The following Sunday, I sat down with that pile of "to do" papers. I was determined to make it all disappear that day, my parents' journal entry included.

Though I like to pride myself on my efficiency, a quick look at the form revealed that I had been asleep at the wheel. The final date for responding was the previous day!

I quickly called my husband. Eli told me to call the number on the form. Maybe they could still push this under the wire. No such luck.

This wasn't going to be good. My parents, particularly my mother, were not going to be happy to find nothing from me in "her" journal. It was a slap in the face, topping a relationship that wasn't too great to begin with.

When Eli came home, he found one forlorn wife. "What can you do now to make up to your parents?" he asked, as I served supper.

"Probably call her the day of the dinner...maybe a box of chocolates sent to her door," I answered flatly.

Eli looked up, and caught my eye. "I have a better idea. Why don't you just go?"

I was speechless. But it didn't take me long to find my tongue. "Are you serious? Smack dab in the middle of everything? Are you remembering that we have kids? Who will take care of them? And how can we afford this extravagance? And what about my job," I spluttered.

"Whoa, hold on," Eli said, laughing. "No need to press the panic button. Let's first call a travel agent and see how much we're talking about."

Still in a state of shock, I poured myself a cold drink as Eli punched in the number.

By the end of the conversation, we had found a reasonably priced flight with suitable flying options. My very supportive husband booked the ticket. He and a few neighbors would watch two of our kids; I would bring the youngest two with me. My boss was accommodating.

Everything was falling into place. It looked like any obstacles were slowly being cleared away.

The clincher for my husband was the serendipitous arrival of that unexpected check. The Almighty had given us His nod.

"I'm letting you go, and even encouraging you, but you have to keep these rules," my husband warned me the day before the flight. "You have to allow your mother to spend as much time as possible with the kids, even if it means they don't sleep as much as you'd like and even if it's hard for you. And you must be willing to let your mother show you off as much as she wants."

All went according to plan. I flew in the next day. I spoke to my father when I booked the ticket to get his okay on the surprise I was planning for my mother. He was thrilled to be part of it and gladly picked me up from the airport.

After a half-hour drive, we pulled into the driveway, locked the car, and walked to the front door. We rang the bell, and amid excited exclamations of disbelief, tears and laughter, I was enveloped in my mother's embrace.

This time, my trip wasn't for a Pesach visit or a family vacation. I was coming for a special event for my parents. And, on top of that, it was a surprise! People would be coming from all over to honor them at the dinner. But I had come the greatest distance. I knew people would make a fuss over my thoughtfulness and the gorgeous grandchildren.

When we walked into the hall, jaws dropped. That evening, I kept repeating to everyone, "I flew in to honor my parents. I knew they would enjoy having me and two of my kids here."

Do you think my mother looked at the journal for one minute? She was so busy showing off me and my kids and kvelling.

"Your daughter really came in especially for this dinner? Aw, come on...really? Wow!"

I stayed ten days. Every day we did something else memorable. My mother couldn't get enough of the children, especially the baby. If Zevi was up in the middle of the night, my mother was right there beside him. Zevi was now fed, bathed, changed, and smothered with love by Savta.

The night before we left, my mother and I shared a quiet moment.

"Mommy, I hope we made your day special by sharing it with you."

I wasn't prepared for her response. I knew it had been really over the top for me to jump on a plane with so little forethought. I also knew my mother would flip out...and she did. With it all, I still didn't imagine how much this was going to mean to her.

At my words, "I hope we made your day special," her whole

demeanor changed. The light mood of a moment before passed. When my mother finally spoke, they were words I think I will never, ever forget.

"This is the nicest thing anyone ever did for me," my mother said with a tremor in her voice. "You not only made my day, you made my week. You made my life."

While all agree that visiting parents is proper, there is no set frequency required. It depends on many variables.

1. Distance

2. Finances

3. Other responsibilities, such as family, learning, work

4. The number of siblings

5. The nature of the parents: Some parents feel slighted if children do not visit often. Sons and daughters in that situation should make decisions in light of the above factors with emphasis on this last factor.[8]

Parents in need

A child is obligated to visit and care for parents who are elderly or ill and need care. This should be done on a daily basis. Even if the child lives at a distance, he can either make an arrangement with siblings or hire an aide or find another suitable plan. Under no circumstances is a child allowed to leave a parent without proper care.[9]

> *MY HUSBAND IS A BUSY PERSON. He is the Rav of a shul, has a demanding teaching position and many community and professional responsibilities. Nevertheless, he travels half an hour every morning to his parents' home to help them with basics they cannot do for themselves.*
>
> *I think he's amazing for doing this. When I told him, he countered, "Do you think I'm amazing for wearing tzitzis?"*

If a child can't visit, he must find a substitute. When proper supervision is medically indicated, it is forbidden to leave parents without this supervision.[10]

Leaving well enough alone?

A parent may be physically well, but alone or lonely. He may spend most of his time at home (retired, not employed, or lost a spouse). Most likely he would enjoy company, especially that of a child. Then, it is a mitzvah for a child to go as often as possible, finding interesting topics of conversation or activities that will engage his parent.[11] Phone calls are a second-best option when visiting is not possible.

For some parents, this visit is so essential, it could be as obligating as a parent who needs physical care.[12]

> **WHEN MY HUSBAND'S FATHER** passed away, my young mother-in-law still had small children at home, so her day was full.
>
> But her heart was broken.
>
> My husband's sister, Naomi, the oldest daughter, is married with a family of her own. After everyone is asleep and her husband has left for his evening shiur, Naomi welcomes the babysitter and then drives over to spend an hour or so with her mother. Sometimes, they go for a walk. Usually, they just sit and schmooze.
>
> "Some people like their privacy," Naomi explained to me one day. "My mother is not like that. She is a very sociable person. When the kids go to sleep, I know those are the hardest hours for her. My father, a"h, isn't going to walk through the door as he always did. At least I can give my mother something to look forward to. She knows that when everything has quieted down, the bell will ring and the house will come to life again. We sit and talk, review our day. Sometimes I can make some calls or take care of something for her, but it's really the company more than anything else.
>
> "Don't think that I don't look forward to this time together also, and my mother knows it. I think that's what really makes this work. Being with a daughter who loves her makes the difference."

A requested visit

When a parent asks a child to visit, this becomes an obligation. Nonetheless, there is a difference between a request for assistance and a visit that is solely for a child's company.

Physical assistance vs. social visits

When a parent, young or old, requires physical assistance, whether it's requested or not, whether daily or occasionally, it is the child's responsibility to make sure that his parent is cared for. When a child cannot be there in person for legitimate reasons (as defined by halachah and mentioned above, i.e. distance, finances, other responsibilities), he must provide a satisfactory replacement.[13]

When a son or daughter is asked to visit solely for social reasons, it is surely a mitzvah to "appear." However, when there are conflicting demands on a son's or daughter's time, or a loss involved (family, learning, or work obligations), the visit may need to be brief, and sometimes the child won't be able to come at all. Here, of course, a replacement can't "take over."* Unavoidably, he is unable to fulfill this mitzvah.

That said, surely chapters can be filled with stories of sons and daughters who have zero extra time and many pressing obligations, yet — even when not requested — will not deny themselves this mitzvah or their parents this pleasure.

EVER SINCE I GOT MARRIED, I am careful to call my parents each day.

I do this because I am the youngest in my family and when I got married, I left my parents with an empty house. They are both people on the go, both with full-time jobs. So the purpose of my calls was not to make sure they weren't bored, but just to show them that I hadn't "run away." I would call even just for a moment, to say good night, so as not to miss a day of being in touch. Eventually, my father

---

* See Chapter 9: "A Winning Presentation," doing the mitzvah personally.

retired, but was still busy with shiurim *and* chavrusas.

Occasionally I dropped in during the week, and I kept this up even when, three years after our marriage, we moved to another city, not far from my parents' home.

One day, while I was visiting my mother, one of the many guests who frequent my mother's home asked me why I didn't come to visit more often. I answered that I call every day, and added that my mother did not want to disturb my learning by having me travel between cities to visit her.

The conversation ended on that note. But the question continued to bother me. Maybe I really should come to visit more often. On the other hand, I knew that my parents wouldn't want me to come especially for them. I tried to figure out how I could come without them objecting.

Not long after, I heard that my Rosh Yeshivah from my younger years gave a shiur *for* yungeleit *every Tuesday not far from my parents' home. I told my parents that I was coming for the Rosh Yeshivah's* shiur, *and that I would also stop in to visit them, although more truthful was that I was coming for them and also had the advantage of catching a good class.*

This is how I got into the routine of coming to visit every Tuesday between 9:30 and 10:30 at night, a time when both of my parents were home. Every week, I would prepare topics of interest to speak about. Every Tuesday, I would glance over the newspaper so I'd be up-to-date on what was going on. As time went on, my sisters and brothers began to visit more frequently, after hearing from my parents how much they anticipated and enjoyed my weekly visit.

I still kept up the daily phone calls. It was clear from our conversations that my parents waited for Tuesday. I heard it from my mother's voice and from comments like, "See you on Tuesday," or "We'll discuss it further when you come." This was enough of an incentive to continue my visits.

This year, I was offered a position as a maggid shiur *in a prominent yeshivah. By the nature of the job, I was burning the midnight oil, but I did not give up the weekly visits. Now I came only for my parents, and did not even have time to attend the* shiur. *Of course, I did not tell this to my parents, not wanting them to be upset that I was going so much out of my way for them. In a similar vein, I would always make an effort to look very relaxed when I visited, so that they would not feel that I was under pressure.*

One week — it was Parashas Vayigash — I felt that I simply had too much to do. It was the time for chazarah in the yeshivah, and I had nearly one hundred tests to grade, aside from shiurim to prepare. I decided that this week, for the first time, I would not go to visit my parents.

On Tuesday morning, I opened the Sefer Ralbag written in the 14th century on Chumash, and I saw that in Parashas Vayigash, he writes in the "toali'ot" (the practical applications that he derives from the parashah):

Although Yosef was a king in Mitzrayim, and was overtaxed with very important communal matters (since he was mishneh l'melech, and these were years of famine during which Yosef was in charge of providing food for all of Mitzrayim), still, he left everything to go out to greet his father, Yaakov. This is to teach you that even if one has a prestigious position, he should not be mevater on his parents' honor.

When I saw these words, I felt that they were a Heaven-sent message. Instead of giving up my visit, as I had wanted to, I packed a lot into the time that I had, and went to visit my parents.

The next week, I thought that since I was even more swamped with work, I certainly would not make my weekly trip. On Tuesday, however, I opened the Ralbag — this time to Parashas Vayechi — and I saw that once again, he stressed a similar idea.

Since then, I do not give up my Tuesday visit, no matter how busy I am.

The greater the sacrifice...

SINCE MY HUSBAND'S PASSING, I've spent the past several years helping my mother make Pesach. It means a long trip to my mother's hometown, where I know hardly anyone. Not that it matters. I rarely leave my mother's home for the three weeks I'm there. I spend the time cleaning and organizing and taking care of things that have waited for me, and getting the house ready for Yom Tov.

Only the two of us sit together at the Seder. It's a far cry from what I've left behind. What enjoyment it would be for me to spend the holiday with my children — seeing my grandchildren in their Yom Tov finery, hearing them say the "Ma Nishtana" and sing the Haggadah, and enjoying a festive Shulchan Orech.

My mother can't travel, so she can't come to us. There are many reasons why we can't bring the family to her.

It's true that this is a sacrifice, but when Yom Tov comes, I smile at my mother from across the table, and she returns a smile full of love. We read the Haggadah together, and I'm at peace with my decision.

I'm thankful that I can be helpful and give her nachas. *I'm hanging on to each day because I know this mitzvah won't last forever.*

Chazal tell us, "The greater the sacrifice, the greater the difficulties, the greater the reward."[14] A mitzvah that entails sacrifice and involves complications and frustrations is worth a hundred times more than the "easier" ones.

Parents away from home

Visiting parents who are living with siblings

IN HER LATER YEARS, the mother of the Chazon Ish lived in Bnei Brak with her daughter, Rebbetzin Pesha Miriam Kanievsky, the wife of the Steipler Gaon and mother of Harav Chaim Kanievsky, shlita.

The Chazon Ish lived in Givat Rokeach, which was a distance from his mother. There was no paved road between their homes, just a dust and gravel path. Even though his mother was not ill, the Chazon Ish went every day to visit her, to see how she was, and to engage in pleasant conversation. In the sefer *Orchos Rabbeinu, it relates, in the name of Rav Chaim Kanievsky, her grandson, that during the time she lived in the Steipler's home, the Chazon Ish, who famously never stopped learning for a moment (rather than going to sleep, sleep overcame him) and carried all of Klal Yisrael on his shoulders, came every day and spent a half hour or more visiting with his mother, discussing topics that would be of interest to her.*[15]

This is the living psak *of the Chazon Ish.*

Visiting parents in a facility

THE FIRST SIGN that something was amiss with Daddy was when he started asking everyone what the time was, even though he had a watch. And then, a minute later, he would ask again and then say, "Did I just ask you that?"

Daddy's forgetfulness started extending to the day of the week. He would be shocked to see Mommy cooking on what he thought was Shabbos, though it was actually Tuesday.

After numerous medical tests and consultations, we were devastated to learn that Daddy had vascular dementia.

Daddy's condition, though, was just the first challenge. With hindsight and knowledge accumulated over the years, my siblings and I realized that Mommy was in a slowly worsening situation long before Daddy started developing symptoms.

Now, everything makes sense: Mommy's strange habit of wrapping certain items and then hiding them; her firing virtually every cleaning lady she had because she thought they were stealing... Now we are no longer puzzled by or embarrassed by Mommy's behavior because we know it wasn't our sweet, gentle, refined Mommy reacting: it was the Alzheimer's that was slowly taking over her mind.

For a while, we considered bringing my parents to live with us. They had been with my sister abroad for three and a half years, with round-the-clock help by an exceptional aide who actually managed on her own to help both Mommy and

Daddy. But now it was my turn to take the responsibility. We considered enlarging and renovating our apartment to bring them to live with us under the same roof.

But it wouldn't work. Mommy and Daddy are not just an aging, elderly couple who can no longer live on their own. They need to be lifted, dressed, bathed, fed, and (this is so hard to write) diapered. They can no longer say, "I'm thirsty-hungry-hot-cold-something hurts me…"

The cost of enlarging our apartment to house my parents and an aide/aides, plus the necessary renovations to accommodate all the required equipment, would have been prohibitively expensive. Not to mention that finding good, reliable help to care for one person is hard enough, let alone for two! So the idea was dropped.

And I have a family too.

When my parents first moved into the nursing home, my hope and my plan was that I would visit them several times a week (my sibling lives too far away for frequent visits). But it didn't work out that way at all. Their first Shabbos in the nursing home found me staying with them, to help them get adjusted to their new surroundings.

Then one week of daily visits turned into two weeks and then three. I realized that the correct thing for me to do was to indeed come see them daily and feed them supper. Now, whatever my daily activities, they all come to a halt at 5:45 p.m. when I leave for the nursing home.

Some people say I'm such a tzaddeikes, to go night after night, and on Erev Shabbos in the summer and Motza'ei Shabbos in the winter. I tell them not to fool themselves. There are days that I have real fights with my yetzer hara, like when it's too cold or too hot. Days when my feet hurt or I feel that a headache is coming on. Days when all I want to do is stay in the comfort of my home and cook or clean or iron or even do nothing other than being home with the family. But I nevertheless go.

Sometimes I can also feel so bone tired as I make my way to the nursing home. Yet it's not a choice, because I know how important it is for my parents to see/hear/feel me, even if it's only for a short time each day.

Leaving them each night is the worst part. An aide comes to wheel my mother back to her room, and then I accompany my father to his. I stay with him until he wants to go to sleep. We sit together. He is hardly able to keep his head up. His eyes are closing, and he's fighting sleep because...he doesn't want me to leave.

He puts his hand on mine and holds me tight, screaming soundlessly, "Don't go!" So I stay a bit more because...how can I walk out?

When I know that finally I must leave, I hug and kiss Daddy and apologize over and over that now I have to go. Then my father turns his head away from me. It seems that he can't bear to see me go. This is such a hard moment for both of us. Is he frightened? Lonely? What other thoughts does he have that he is not able to express?

I have been asked if I feel resentful. To whom? There is no direction at which to aim resentment. I wish my parents could have grown old gracefully. But I'm not running the world. I try to internalize as much as possible that Hashem Yisbarach *knows exactly what He's doing and everything is running according to His plan.*

I usually come home drained from my visits, more emotionally than physically, because even though I know that this is our reality, and it has been so for years, it is nevertheless so difficult for me to witness my parents' "shells" night after night. At the same time, I know their essences are buried somewhere in their dementias. Once in a while, on a "good day," I get a glimpse of what was. With every spoonful of food I give them, I know Mommy and Daddy are enabling me to do one of the most difficult mitzvos to fulfill properly.

I try not to complain, but there are days that all I can do when I get home is cry from frustration, grief, and exhaustion. I feed, talk to, hug and kiss two of the most precious and beloved people in my life who can no longer reciprocate in any way. My parents are completely dependent on others for absolutely everything. Once upon a time, they were the most altruistic givers. Today, through no choice of their own, they have become complete "takers." But in that "taking," they have given me the most amazing gift of all: enabling me to pay back, on some level, what they gave me — my life and the most cherished and treasured memories a child could ask for.

This exceptional daughter is moving from "obligation" to *"hiddur mitzvah"* — and gaining so much in the process!

Visiting parents who are hospitalized

If a parent is hospitalized, any help given is the mitzvah of providing "all their needs." Though the hospital staff is primarily responsible for patient care, and even if a private nurse is provided, it is a benefit and encouragement to an ill person to see caring family members.

WHEN OUR FATHER was brought to the ICU after open heart surgery, my brother, Tzvi, and I were by his side. Our father was heavily sedated and didn't wake up until the second day, but that didn't stop us from talking to him. Though he didn't respond, we'd heard enough stories to be convinced that on some level he heard us. We repeated the names of his children and grandchildren, saying how much they loved him and couldn't wait to see him.

If you've ever spent time near a loved one in an ICU, you know what a disconcerting and disorienting place it is. Machines are beeping, lights are flashing, staff rushes in and out for emergencies you can't understand, and your overriding concern is, "Will my loved one make it?"

We were there continuously. No way did I want my father to wake up and find himself alone, with no one from the family by his side. When he woke up, he needed to know that he was well and the operation was successful.

Sure enough, the first question my father asked was, "Am I still alive?" How gratifying for us to be able to show him pictures of his grandchildren and reassure him that yes, he was alive and well, and recovering.

Tzvi and I had left our families and jobs and flown halfway

across the country to be with our father.
But that's what it's all about, isn't it?

Even parents in a coma...

If a parent is hospitalized in a coma, where expert medical knowledge says there is no hope for reversal, it is a mitzvah of *kibbud av va'eim* for a child to visit the parent,[16] even if a private nurse is in attendance, for these reasons:

1. For the child: This obligation is primarily directed toward the child. While he may have positive feelings in his heart, it is not sufficient. The Torah also requires this visit as an outward expression of respect.

2. For the parent: It will most likely positively affect the type of care a parent receives.

3. For others: It adds to our parent's prestige in the eyes of those who see this act of honor, regardless of the parent's awareness.

I STOOD IN THE CORNER of the elevator, nestled behind a middle-aged man with a rolling IV stand and beside a young couple cradling their baby, the pink plastic ID tag still wrapped around that tiny new wrist. The elevator stopped at each floor, the doors rolling open, then closing, bringing in the smell of antiseptic, and a churning stream of people. Somewhere in this huge medical center lay my friend Ilinka, comatose and unconscious, in a world all her own.

I'd known Ilinka since we were girls in Hungary before the war. We were close then, neighbors and friends, and while we'd kept in touch over the years, it was still that young face I pictured as I davened each morning for the recovery of Rivka Chana bas Chaya.

Although I'd never called her Rivka Chana, saying her full name seemed so right, so fitting. Because Rivka Chana bas Chaya was who she was — Ilinka, yes, but the daughter of Chaya. That was, after all, how she had defined herself, when she sacrificed her youth, devoting herself entirely to caring for her paralyzed mother.

We — her friends and classmates — seized each stage of

life that greeted us. We married, had children, built lives for ourselves. Ilinka refused to give any thought to marriage. "Who will be there for my mother?" she'd ask when people tried to suggest a match.

Her mother needed total care. And so single she remained: Ilinka, the devoted daughter.

When the Nazis marched into Hungary, and evil turned our world on its head, Ilinka, who was already 35 years old, was taken to the camps.

With war's end, those of us who survived attempted to build a new life. The Nazis had murdered Ilinka's family — her parents and siblings, nieces and nephews. Her brother-in-law, Reb Yitzchok, who had been sent to Siberia, had survived. After the war, he was on a train, traveling home, when a landsman gave him startling news — "Ilinka is alive." He searched for her, and with great Divine providence, they met and eventually married.

They had two sons, and then a third after they came to America. It was in the years that followed that we were reunited. She was still the same Ilinka I knew from Hungary: regal and refined. Her family attested to her greatness of stature on more than one occasion. "It was impossible to speak to our mother in anything less than a respectful manner," they would say. "She carried herself with such nobility that we had to speak to her in a dignified way."

I was jolted back to the present as the elevator doors slid open again, and I saw I'd reached her floor. My heartbeat quickened as I followed the arrows and walked toward her room.

When her son, Ezriel, had called to tell me about the aneurysm, he'd said she was in a coma and intubated. The doctors claimed she couldn't hear or respond to anyone, and that the chances she'd ever wake up were bleak. But her children felt that she was aware on some level, and they were determined to make sure that she was not alone, and had family and friends around her.

I saw her room number at the end of the hall, and began to slow my gait. I wanted to see her, yes, but at the same time,

I was anxious, fearful. What would I see when I entered the room? Could I handle the pain of seeing my dear old friend in such a state?

But here I was, standing just a few steps away from her room. I took a deep breath and peeked in.

There was Ezriel, sitting beside her bed. A monitor of some sort, flashing lights and emitting a steady stream of beeps, blocked my view of Ilinka's face, but I could see the gentle way Ezriel held her hand in his own, the raw emotion that squeezed his brows together, the attentive tilt of his head. He was speaking to her, his words low and steady, his eyes locked on her face.

After nearly a minute his features relaxed, and he looked up and saw me in the doorway.

He rose in greeting, showing me to a chair beside his mother. She was so pale, so frail looking, lying there in the hospital bed, her eyes closed.

"You can speak to her, tell her you're here," Ezriel said.

I nodded, and Ezriel stepped away to give me some privacy. He sat in the far corner of the room, murmuring Tehillim, while I stroked Ilinka's hand. I spoke to her about our years in Hungary, hoping that she would hear and remember. I told her I was davening for her, and how moved I was by the love and respect her sons showed for her. She had, I said, raised truly exemplary sons.

And indeed, she had. When I left the hospital that day, instead of feeling depressed, I was uplifted, inspired. The dedication and kavod that radiated from that room was like a beacon of holiness, and I felt something pulling at me, urging me to return.

And return I did, many times, over the course of her hospitalization. The reverence her sons afforded their mother was a splendid thing — something I wanted to be a part of. The hospital staff, it seemed, felt the same way. The way they cared for her! They saw the way Ilinka's sons treated her, and their own attitude toward her mirrored that.

The family's constant presence helped, too, I'm sure. Ilinka's sons were there a good ten hours a day, every day, and even when night fell and visitors faded away.

It blew me away. I've seen many families that extend themselves for a parent, but for three sons to come sit by their mother's side daily for six months? Other family members filled in gaps, giving the sons and families some respite, but still, the days that these men dedicated, men with weighty obligations on their shoulders — it was really something extraordinary.

I thought about it often, and particularly so the last time I went to visit Ilinka before she passed away. When I entered the room, Leib, her youngest son, was sitting by her side, holding her hand and singing her a song.

I clearly remember Ezriel's words, echoing those of his brothers: We staunchly believe that our mother deserves to have returned to her that dedicated care she selflessly showered on her own mother.

How heartwarming...how appropriate...and how very well deserved.

Parents hosting children

"My husband is going away for a week..."
"We had major flooding in the house..."
"I just had a baby..."
"I'm so excited to come for Yom Tov..."
...are just some of the reasons a child is asking to be hosted by parents.

Parents enjoy hosting their children, but they have **no obligation** to do so. The mitzvah of honoring through visiting and hosting belongs to children.

Does this mean that we can't visit our parents to fulfill our own needs? To rest, relax, and enjoy great cooking? Not at all. And parents certainly want that. But our main intention should be to bring joy and be enjoyed, fulfilling the mitzvah of *kavod* and *yirah* by helping out and behaving in a way that will not cause parents distress.

In general, the idea is to be sensitive to a parent's particular needs.

A son or daughter might consider prior to his visit: What can I prepare that would be appreciated or make it easier for my parents or in-laws?

Here's a daughter who found a unique way of making herself available to her mother before an upcoming visit: "Mom, tell me things you like to do the least, and I'll do them for you."

Once there, a child can consider what can be done now. A sure winner is to steer clear of arguing or contradicting, or complaining about food and accommodations. Some things, like expressing appreciation, just take a little bit of thought.

Parents, for their part, should be concerned about their obligation not to "trip" their adult children. Even dedicated sons and daughters have conflicting obligations. Though we enjoy seeing our children, there is usually another side in the picture: the in-laws. Constant demands that children visit, to the exclusion of the other set of parents, will put your sons and daughters in a very difficult position.

Think if the situation were reversed…

Rather than press them to the wall and tighten the screws, put on a cheerful face and encourage time sharing.

Our challenge as parents is to keep our antennae up, listen to signals, and not jeopardize our married children's *shalom bayis* by insisting on visits.

———

Visiting parents is a great opportunity for teaching the mitzvah of *kibbud av va'eim* to children.

When children see that visiting parents isn't easy — the tumult of packing up…the inconvenience of being away from home… cramped, unfamiliar, or uncomfortable sleeping space… having to lower the decibel level… the obligations that are forfeited to make this trip — they notice whether we complain and grumble, or zip our lip, aim to be cooperative, and smile, although at times it is obvious the situation is challenging for us.

This "picture" is worth a thousand lectures on *kibbud av va'eim*.

Chapter 6

Who Pays?

Is a child only required to buy, prepare, and serve the food to his parent, or is he also obligated to pay the grocery bill?*

Is he only required to help his parents dress, or must he also pay for their clothing?

When it's necessary to find suitable housing, who has to pay the rent?

The answer is... it depends. It depends on the parent's financial status and the child's financial status.[1]

Parents who are self-sufficient

A child is **not responsible** to contribute to the expenses of a self-sufficient parent.

> *MY FATHER'S NATURE is to manage with whatever he has — and not because he's stingy. As a matter of fact, he would give the shirt off his back to anyone. He just never*

---

* In the context of children's financial obligation to parents, "child" refers to a son, or an unmarried, divorced, or widowed daughter. A married daughter's obligation is included in the obligation of the son-in-law. Where questions of a married daughter's financial obligation to her parents arise, Rabbinic guidance should be sought.

seems to care whether he has those "shirts." Even when my mother pressures him and insists that he needs something for himself, he demurs.

Last year, at the beginning of the winter, my parents visited us for a few days. One morning, as we were all sitting around the breakfast table, my husband got up to leave. As I watched him put on a sweater, it struck me that I hadn't seen my father put on a sweater the whole time he was here. I realized, Hey! My father probably doesn't even have a sweater for the winter. It would be just like him to tell Mommy he doesn't need one.

I knew if I asked him if he could use one, he would change the subject.

After conferring with my mother, I went to a neighbor who has a basement clothing store. She gave me several new men's sweaters in different sizes, colors, and patterns, so that my father could choose.

I came home with the sweaters and I brought them over to my father. At first, he pushed me off. I knew he would. But I persisted. He did me a favor and looked them over, chose one, and then wrote out a check. He handed it to me with a warm smile.

This daughter fulfilled the mitzvah of *kibbud av va'eim*. How? By showing her concern and putting in the effort to make the purchase. The father, who could well afford it, paid.

Parents who are not self-sufficient

When parents are not self-sufficient, the extent of the child's obligation will depend on his own financial situation.

A prosperous child

A child who has sufficient income **is responsible** to support a parent who is unable to provide for himself.[2]

If a son has been blessed by Hashem with wealth and his parents are needy, it is the son's responsibility to provide for his parents' needs in a pleasant manner.[3]

A "needy parent" is one who does not have sufficient income for food, clothing, and shelter. If Hashem blesses the children with abundant resources, what a perfect opportunity to give something back.

MY PARENTS WERE ALWAYS supportive of my brother and me in every way, even after I married. When my husband and I were facing financial difficulty, my parents volunteered to pay our mortgage and cover other expenses until we could get back on our feet. Eventually, I was able to become very successful in a new career.

Fifteen years ago, my mother, a"h, passed away. Part of our heartache was hearing a court confirm that there was medical negligence. As a result, my father was awarded a large financial settlement.

A short time before this, my brother, Dovid, started a new business venture with a unique product. Everyone was very excited about its potential. Just as my father was always there for me, he came through for my brother now with the same generosity. Over the course of fifteen years, my father invested funds from the settlement in Dovid's business. Despite the many potential customers with large contracts, many of the deals never closed. The business was just scraping by. Yet though the overall picture didn't look good, Dovid was optimistic, and so my father kept investing to keep the business afloat.

As a widower, my father managed quite well. He was healthy and financially independent, still working as a marketing consultant for a Japanese semiconductor company. He had a personal bookkeeping system to keep track of all his bills, which he paid on a timely basis.

And then came the call.

My brother, Dovid, was killed in a tragic accident. My dear father, who had pulled himself together after my mother's death, was felled by the loss of his son, in the prime of life. He was barely able to function, let alone continue his consulting. To add to his grief, it was discovered that Dovid's business was deeply in the red. In effect, my father had lost his complete investment.

Due to his emotional turmoil, which affected his work capacity, coupled with the economic downturn, my father eventually lost his job. With no work to fill his days, no wife, no only son, no savings, and no income, we felt it was like watching a sinking ship.

My husband and I discussed my father's situation. We agreed that we had to throw out a lifeline — and fast. We came to a mutual decision. We could not bring back my mother or my brother, but we would not despair of saving my father from going under.

Even though this entailed a healthy chunk of our overall income, my generous husband agreed to this plan: we paid off my father's outstanding debts, which had accumulated since he had stopped receiving a salary. In addition, we offered him a job at the same salary he was getting before he was let go.

Because my father was technologically savvy, I could give him a niche in my work. True, I had been doing that work myself. Never mind. My father now had a stimulating job and a well-paying salary.

And I had a father.

A child with limited resources

A "child with limited resources" is one whose income can cover only his and his family's needs but not his parents' needs as well. In what way can he still contribute to his needy parents?

When he tithes 10 percent of what he earns, he should give from that. (A wealthy child should not use *tzedakah* funds, as it would demean his parents in his eyes. Using money from *maaser* applies only to someone who has no other choice.)[4]

We can shape and sharpen our understanding of the Torah position on a child's unique and overriding obligations to parents from the following:

A person must first provide for himself, his wife and children who are part of his household. His charity contributions should then be in this order (*Shulchan Aruch*):[5]

1. Needy parents

2. Needy independent children

3. Needy brothers and sisters

4. Other relatives who are needy

5. Needy neighbors

6. Needy people who dwell in his city

7. Needy residents of other cities

Notice the parents' place on the list!

❖ A child may not give *tzedakah* to other needy people before he takes care of his parents' needs.[6]

❖ Though we are cautioned not to give all our *maaser* to one needy person, parents are an exception. We give to our parents what they need, even if it means we won't have enough left to give to other needy people.[7]

❖ Though there may be other people in more dire circumstances, parents come first.[8]

❖ Preferably, we should provide parents with all their needs. (People differ in their "needs." When a question arises, a Rav should be consulted.) With other needy people, we provide for their basic needs and then go on to provide for a different needy person. This is not so with parents.[9]

A child who is needy

A child who does not have enough for his own basic needs and the needs of his household is exempt from sacrificing the little he has to give to parents.

Nonetheless, when a son and his family sacrifice in order to share the little they have, though it is surely not an obligation, it is a great mitzvah.

> *I KNEW MY PARENTS NEEDED ME. There was no question that I'd have to go. But how?*
>
> *"By hook or by crook, I'll get there," I told myself, and then added wryly, "Well, Libby, since you're not a crook, it'll have to be by hook."*

"Quite funny you are today, Madam," I said to my mirror image as I passed her on my way out of the house that morning.

I had no way of knowing that what I was saying wasn't going to be far from the truth.

I'm sure our situation is like a lot of other families. My father's memory was slowly going, along with a lot of other things. My parents were finding it hard to manage finances, shopping, cooking. My mother, who was declining at a faster pace, could barely take care of her own personal needs.

My siblings called a meeting. I'm the only one out of the country, so I participated in a conference call. The conclusion was: divide and conquer. Two sisters would divide the weekdays, and all that entailed: appointments, doctors, meds, shopping, laundry, outings. One brother and his family would take the weekends and pay for cleaning help. Two sisters-in-law would send over food. By the end of the conversation, it was all sorted out.

Where did I fit in? I got the summer.

My sisters and their families run a camp. They needed the time and the revenue, and I needed to replace them. It was the least I could do to pitch in while they carried responsibility the other ten months. My husband, the good sport and dedicated son-in-law that he has always been, agreed that he and our two teenage daughters would hold down the fort.

And that's what happened for the last three years.

I knew already months in advance that this year would be different. Some bad investments threw us into heavy debt. My husband and I cut corners on extras and necessities too. There wasn't a dime available this year for a ticket. My parents couldn't give us anything toward plane fare, either, since they had no income and their savings were used up. My siblings were already contributing heavily in every way. I couldn't disappoint them, and I couldn't press my husband. That's when I had this hook or crook conversation with myself, and started praying even harder that some solution would come up.

One morning, I found myself behind my friend, Sima, in a line inching its way toward the checkout. This gave Sima ample time to describe her recent trip.

Her grandson was being bar mitzvah *— in Australia no less. Sima had just made a wedding, so there was no extra cash available. On the other hand, she said, she didn't want to miss this event. "So, Libby, I sold my jewelry. It was worth it. I was there. I flew in and I had such* nachas.*"*

Later that day, as I was scrubbing dirty collars, I brightened. That's it! *I thought.* If Sima could do it for a bar mitzvah, I could surely do it for kibbud av va'eim. Besides, didn't righteous women over the generations sell their precious possessions for some greater good?

I wiped my hands and headed for the jewelry box. Never much the jewelry person, I wondered skeptically, "What could I sell?"

As I opened the box, my heart gave a little lurch. "Calm down," I said. "This is the right thing to do."

First, I touched my gold necklace. I lifted it out. With one last look, I placed it on the side. Next was a gold bracelet. I added this, plus my gold watch, to the modest collection. In another corner of my jewelry box was the pin from my in-laws, semiprecious stones set in gold. "Do you want to be included?" I asked the earrings with the diamond chips, unostentatiously twinkling up at me.

And then I noticed them — the little hooks. There were about a dozen inexpensive necklaces, but the hooks — the clasps — were gold. And then I saw more hooks, actually clip-on earrings — a bunch of them that I had had from the time I was a girl. Some were without a pair and weren't worth much, but the hooks were all gold. I gathered them all together, and I had a good laugh over my prophetic words.

I headed for a jeweler. The first store I went into said they would only give me jewelry for jewelry. The second store was willing to give me cash for my gold. I put my collection on the scale. My heart was racing. In the end, I was quite short of my goal. I went home and took out my box again, hoping there was something I had overlooked. But there wasn't.

The only thing left was my diamond ring.

Libby, don't even think in that direction. Dov would be so hurt if you sold that.

"Okay, okay. Not nice," I admitted to myself.

Still, I decided to ask my son, Ari, if he knew anyone reliable who evaluated diamonds. I figured if I could get a really great price, I just might consider the possibility of approaching my husband.

Ari wasn't overly enthused.

"Ma, are you sure you want to go ahead?"

I had gone over this in my mind many times, so my answer was on the tip of my tongue. "You can't take diamonds with you, but this ticket is going to go with me straight to the Kisei HaKavod — a mitzvah earned the hard way — and that's going to sparkle for me for eternity."

In the end, I never had to ask my husband, because I never sold my diamond. Nor the gold. Nor the hooks. Because a few days later, Ari called.

"Ma," and I could hear the smile in his voice. "You can stop worrying. I bought you a ticket. It won't be easy to pay for it, but I'll work something out."

He quickly added, "Don't worry, Ma. It's not by hook and surely not by crook, but you're good to go."

Here are a few key issues that arise in a discussion of "who pays?"

Q In a family of several children, how is the cost of providing for parents divided?

A Costs should be divided equally among all the children. However, if some are wealthy and others have less, support should be proportional according to their ability to pay.[10] *

Q Does a wealthy son-in-law have an obligation to help his needy in-laws?

---

* Some say that personal attention to the needs of parents is the responsibility of the prosperous child alone (since needy children must be occupied with earning a living). It might be advantageous for a prosperous son to hire his needy brother to take care of parents, allowing his parents to be attended to by their own son. In that way, the prosperous son fulfills his obligation and at the same time gives his sibling a source of income.

A In-laws are among the family members who take precedence in *maaser* obligations ("Don't ignore your own flesh and blood"[11]) over nonfamily members.[12]

Q If parents ask a child to assist them in a way that requires traveling for the child, who pays?

A If a child prefers to use transportation because it's more *convenient* for him, then the son pays. The rule is, anything that a child does to make it easier for *himself* to honor his parents is the son's expense.

However, if the son *must* use transportation, the parent pays. Similarly, if getting to his parents' home more quickly so as not to cause distress requires transportation, the parent pays. All this is for the parent's direct benefit.[13]

If a child is allowed according to halachah to be reimbursed for travel expenses, and the parent has the means to give but hasn't offered, it's permitted to ask for reimbursement — but in a sensitive way. It's important for the child to avoid giving the impression that he's not willing to put out money for his parent. He might say, "Sorry that I have to ask you for travel expenses. I'd cover the cost myself if I could."

Q If a father has resources but is so frugal that he refuses to buy himself a warm winter coat, turn on the heat on cold winter days, or pay for medicines that he needs, is a child required to pay?

A It's not an obligation, but it is surely a mitzvah.[14]

Q When a child calls a parent, mails a letter for his parent, or incurs any other minor expense in connection with his parent, who pays?

A Minimal expenses such as these are the child's responsibility. Asking parents to pay back such small amounts is tantamount to saying, "You're not worth very much to me."[15]

Other questions that can arise in this area…

Q If a child has a minimal salary and can't help his parents financially, should he be making efforts to garner funds from other sources?

Q Is a child required to pay his parents' debts?

Q If a parent can work but chooses not to, is the child obligated to support him?

Most important is that we don't decide on our own, but consult with a Rabbinic authority conversant with the intricacies of these halachos, who will rule in accordance with each individual's circumstances.

A bill for services rendered

Were you charged for the services your parents performed for you, even for just the first two years of your life?

Diaper changes 5 times a day, 7 days a week, 52 weeks of the year.

No days off, and remember — night rates are more.

Bottles — were you charged for the formula or the labor? Do you know how much it would have cost to hire a night nurse to care for fussy you?

And later, did you ever tally up how much your parents invested in your education — from nursery school on?

What about your clothing? Shoes? Toys? Were you presented with a bill for any of these?

Were you treated to (the luxury of) camp? Did your parents cover your medical expenses? Were your teeth fixed? Were your feet fixed? Were you given lessons? Piano? Swimming? Were you ever driven to rehearsals, play dates, or for a haircut? Were you billed for the gas? Did you save the receipts?

The cost of raising a child for a family earning $65,000 and up, including expenses for: housing, food, transportation, clothing, health, education, and miscellaneous totals approximately a quarter of a million dollars for the first seventeen years of a child's life.[16]* Did you ever think how hard your parents must have worked to pay for all that?

---

* According to one survey, half of the children in the world live in poverty. These children are raised on an average of $16,500 total for the first 17 years of their life. Camp? A cell phone? Let's just talk about three meals a day.

And what about all the perks you got living at home? Think about the staffing you would have needed to get to where you are today: cook, dish washer, laundress, valet or maid, chauffeur, recreation coordinator, shopper, personal secretary. Imagine if you had to attract and retain a candidate to fill all these roles.

According to the US Bureau of Labor Statistics, the cost of hiring someone to do all these jobs would be $115,000 annually. Multiply that by 17 years, and it's close to $2,000,000. How many summer jobs would you have to take to pay Mom and Dad for services rendered?

This, of course, does not factor in spiritual training and mentoring and davening, which a hired hand would never do.

And how much is a parent's love worth?

Be appreciative, and just be glad that your parents never sent you an invoice.

> *RAV ELIYAHU ELIEZER DESSLER,* author of Michtav MeEliyahu, *living in London, had been sending financial assistance to his father, Rav Reuven Dessler, who was living, at that time, in Lithuania. Rav Reuven was reluctant to accept this assistance and wrote to say that his son should not feel obliged.*
>
> *The following is part of a response written in 1929 by Rav E. E. Dessler:*
>
> *…Why do you think that I don't owe anything to you? Is there anyone in the world to whom I owe more than you? What of the tremendous amounts of money that you have spent on me from the time I was born? (And that takes into account only the monetary aspect of what I was given)…*
>
> *Who could give such a distorted verdict as to claim that only loans from strangers need to be paid back? … Does it say anywhere in the Shas that a parent is obligated to spend anywhere near the amounts that parents spend on their children's education? Is there no obligation for a son to return this? [Especially if a father has lost his money and could benefit from this small offer.]*[17]
>
> *Please, my esteemed and honored father, forgive me for these words. It is just that they come from a heart filled with*

pain. If I could pay back even a little bit of the money that you spent so liberally to provide me with every comfort and beyond, you would not be lacking anything and could live a comfortable life in Eretz Yisrael, as is your desire. Unfortunately, I am unable to do so at this time. But is there any room for even the slightest thought that the small amount [I am sending you which] you now spend on your expenses is not absolutely yours without any doubt at all...?

Your son..., who worries about your well-being and anxiously waits to hear from you,
E. E.[18]

Which parent doesn't want and hope always to be independent in every way? It follows that when parents are needy, not only must children be there to assist, but equally important, they must be extremely sensitive in the way that assistance is given.

From Rav Eliyahu Dessler's letter to his father, the message conveyed was that R' Reuven, his father, was doing him a favor by accepting this money, which was just a small part of what was "owed."

And he was.

Chapter 7

Rise to the Occasion

חַיָּיב אָדָם לַעֲמוֹד מִפְּנֵי אָבִיו

Children are obligated to stand for parents

(Shulchan Aruch 240:7).

We heard this story from our neighbor. He was so excited about it that he didn't wait until he returned home, but called specially from the States to share it.

I WAS AT A FUNDRAISING DINNER for Yeshivas Torah Ore. There were many familiar faces, but as it turned out, seated next to me at the table was someone I had never met before. Yitzchak Goodman introduced himself, and in the course of our conversation, he mentioned that he was scheduled to speak the next night at an NCSY convention, where he'd been asked to give an inspirational talk on overcoming disabilities.

It was a long evening, and we had plenty of time to talk. It was an unforgettable one, because that night Yitzchak, a double amputee, told me his story.

"In 2005, I was in a horrific car crash. I was driving my Mitsubishi, and was hit head on. My car was thrown off the road into a ditch.

"I was knocked unconscious. I had to be cut out of the car. I was rushed to the hospital, fighting for my life. Much later when the police showed us pictures of the wreck, it was impossible to imagine anyone surviving. Miraculously, I did survive, but my legs didn't.

"I spent six weeks in the ICU and then another eight months in the hospital for continued treatment. It was a long haul.

"A year after the accident, I was fitted for prosthetics. It wasn't going well. There were infections, chafing, and I almost gave up. At first, I didn't want them. I knew I would be spending most of my time in a wheelchair, since the effort to walk was sapping my strength. In the end, I reconsidered and took the prosthetics."

I'm sitting next to Yitzchak, and there were no prosthetics in sight. I guess he must have read my thoughts, because he said to me, "They're in the car. I only use them occasionally."

When is that? I was thinking.

"I need them for only one thing. I use them to stand up for my parents."

It should be apparent that it's your parent

Picture this not uncommon scene: A son or daughter is lying on the bed, reading. A parent walks into the room. What happens?

Does he stand?

Does she at least sit up?

Does he at least turn his head in the direction of the parent and grunt a hello?

Does she even notice that anyone has entered?

The mitzvah of standing for a parent is so discredited nowadays that were we to see someone standing for his parents, we would tend to think that he is an exceptionally pious person, taking on himself extra stringencies.

But in fact, standing for a parent is a halachah found in the *Shulchan Aruch*. When we read in the Torah, "Honor your father and mother," one defining aspect is "standing up."

If we want to give honor to someone, one of the ways to do so, the Torah tells us, is by standing. We stand for a king, we stand for the elderly, we stand for the learned, and we stand for our teacher. We stand for the Torah itself.

And we stand for our parents. We learn this from the Gemara, where we are told of Rav Yosef, who heard his mother's footsteps and stood up for her.[1]

YESTERDAY, I ATTENDED A CLASS. The subject was "The Torah Obligation to Stand for Parents." I am 40 years old, and I have never yet stood for my parents. Though I did learn about this mitzvah in school, I thought it was just a nice thing to do if you wanted to. I had no idea that I would be fulfilling a positive mitzvah of the Torah every time I stand.

A son and daughter are obligated to stand up for their father and mother. Though there are leniencies and stringencies within the halachah, the following are accepted guidelines:

Take a stand!

Who? The obligation is the same for sons and daughters, single or married.

When and where? We should stand as soon as we see our parent entering the room we're in.*

THE CHASSIDIM OF VIZHNITZ are gathered, awaiting the Rebbe's entrance. Someone announces that the Rebbe, Harav Moshe Yehoshua, will be arriving momentarily. The assembly comes to attention, erect on their feet. The singing begins in anticipation.

One lone figure remains seated.

An onlooker might think, "What happened here? Shouldn't the loyal chassidim, witnessing this disrespect, give him a nudge, a reminder? A shtikel kavod for the Rebbe, if you will!"

But no one says a word to defend the Rebbe's honor.

Soon, the door opens and the Rebbe appears on the thresh-

---

* Some say that we need to stand only when they come close (within *four amos*).

old. That lone chassid, Reb Yisrael, Reb Moshe Yehoshua's son, jumps to his feet to fulfill the mitzvah of the Torah of standing for a parent "as soon as they come into sight."

Today, Reb Yisrael Hager is the Vizhnitzer Rebbe, teaching and guiding his kehillah. But long before he succeeded his father at the helm of Vizhnitz, he was teaching in a large forum, in a very public way, the obligation of a child to a parent.

How much? We should stand to our full height.[2]

How long must we remain standing? Until

(a) the parent leaves the room or is no longer within our sight;

(b) the parent reaches his destination (and either sits down or remains standing).[3]

Then we may sit down.[4]

How often? For those who follow the Ashkenazic tradition, the obligation is to stand once during the morning and once during the evening.[5] Though twice is the minimum, there is no maximum.[6]

In the Sephardic tradition, one stands up every time a parent walks into the room.[7] Likewise, the custom is to stand when one's father is called for an *aliyah*. The son stands until the father reaches the *bimah* and also when the father descends. Many stand during the *leining* as well.[8]

Every parent?

Some people may feel: My parents are just "regular" people. They have no special position in the community, no title. My father's not a scholar. My parents are still young people.

Notwithstanding, they are *your* parents. We are standing up for the parents that Hashem has chosen for us. We are standing up not because our parents asked us to do so, but because Hashem has asked us to do so. We stand up as if we are declaring, "I, your son/daughter, am at your service."

The case for not standing

Today, most parents are not particular about children standing for them. Because of the great familiarity that exists between parents and children, many fathers and mothers are not comfortable with this gesture. They neither expect nor desire this form of honor.

One reason is because they don't view standing as an honor bestowed on them by the child, but rather as a burden to the child. That kind of honor is not welcome.[9]

Two halachic principles address this concern:

1. A parent may forgo honor for himself, particularly when he sees that the child finds the mitzvah too difficult (אָב שֶׁמָּחַל עַל כְּבוֹדוֹ כְּבוֹדוֹ מָחוּל).

2. We honor a parent in the way that he prefers (רְצוֹנוֹ שֶׁל אָדָם הוּא כְּבוֹדוֹ).

Based on this, when a parent prefers, but does not insist, that his child refrain from rising, then the child defers to his parent's will.

However, even if a parent exempts his child from standing, a son or daughter — including married children — may not ignore his parent's entrance. Some gesture is required: there is an obligation to rise a bit (הִידוּר). This, too, affords a parent respect.[10]

What happens if a parent objects even to this slight gesture of respect and deference and will not allow any standing at all? In that case, the way to honor the parent is by not standing. Since a child's hands (and feet) are tied, a verbal greeting would be a reasonable substitute.

The case for standing

> Abba HaKohen, the son of Rav Papa, said: "When I saw a group of people, I would take a different path so as not to burden them, that they should not see me and stand for me. When I told this to R' Yose, the son of Zevida, he said to me: 'You must pass by them, so that they see you and stand for you. You will thus cause them to have yiras Shamayim, as it says, "You shall arise before an elderly person...and you will fear Hashem, your G-d."'"[11]

While a parent may excuse his child from standing, it is not advisable to do so on a long-term basis.

While a child may ask a parent to be excused on occasion, it should be only that. There are many reasons. Most important is that Hashem, in His wisdom, gave us His mitzvos to be kept, not discarded.[12]

In the words of Harav Moshe Sternbuch:

It is proper to train a child from when he is small to stand [for his parents] — once in the morning and once at night. Training children in this [mitzvah], thus establishing the proper relationship between child and parent according to the Torah, brings about reverence and respect for parents from the time that children are small.

When parents decline this honor, they nullify the yoke of honor and respect toward them [that their children carry].

On the contrary, it is a favor to children to allow them to fulfill a *mitzvas aseh* twice a day for their father and mother.

It is appropriate for a mother to train a child to stand for his father from the time he is small, before 5 years old. She should explain to him that each time, he fulfills a *mitzvas aseh*. So, too, should the father train the child to stand for his mother, so that he has a feeling of respect and reverence toward both of them. *This way, the standing will not be a burden, but will be done with awe, reverence, and* **derech eretz.**[13]

Whenever a son/daughter is able to do this mitzvah, he should grab this opportunity to fulfill a mitzvah that carries with it the promise of lengthened years and well-being with one swift movement.

The halachos of standing offer a wealth of insight into the extent of honor the Almighty desires that we extend to our parents.

A son or daughter is obligated to stand even if the parent does not realize what the child is doing![14] For instance, if…

...a father walks into the room while engaged in a complex discussion, and he doesn't notice his child sitting unobtrusively in the corner;

...a parent is blind;

...a parent does not recognize his son (for example, due to dementia);

...and even if a parent is unconscious or in a coma (for example, you are present when he is brought into the room)...

...the child still has to stand up for him!

Just as we are required to stand for a *Nasi* or king , even if he is not aware of the honor we are giving him, similarly, we give honor to parents even when they are unaware.[15]*

How do we understand this?

Standing serves more than one purpose:

❖ We stand primarily to fulfill Hashem's will.

❖ We stand to give honor to our parents.

❖ When we stand, it gives our parents dignity in the eyes of onlookers. The message we send is that we consider our parents worthy of this honor.

❖ When we stand it is a quick reminder (minimally) two times a day of the deference we are required to show toward our parents.

❖ When we stand, it is a great praise of our nation and our Torah.

❖ Standing sends a subliminal message to parents: You are being honored. Remember to be an honorable person, worthy of that honor.

I DIDN'T USUALLY STAND UP when my parents entered the room, but I did go to welcome them when they came into the house. Now that I understood the importance of this mitzvah from class discussions, I decided I would like to start doing this mitzvah when I come back home from seminary.

I think that when a son or daughter brings home "new" mitzvos, new at least to parents who have not practiced them, a natural feeling of suspicion and maybe awkwardness surfaces,

---

* In addition, others see that though the parent is disadvantaged, we always treat him respectfully.

a feeling that something foreign has entered their home.

Though my parents know about this mitzvah, part of what makes this so tricky is that they were not sitting in class with me while I was being supplied with halachic sources and inspired by stories. There is now such a big gap — that big ocean — between where they are and where I have been.

I think the way I will succeed will be to make standing more than a technical action, more than a mechanical knee jerk, but the result of a whole new style of respect. I believe opposition is more likely to occur when parents see the standing as artificial and superficial, without much meaning, not reflective of a deeper understanding of parenthood and the proper response to parents.

My mother might not say it, but she might be thinking, "You'll stand up and then slap me with a refusal to hang up the phone when I need it."

Or my father might think, "Fine that you're standing, but when I ask you to call Savta to thank her for the Chanukah gift, you say you have no time. It's true that standing doesn't take much effort, but how long will it take to call Savta?"

The most important thing, I think, is to be as consistent as possible, and to make the action of standing only one thing among all the other opportunities to be mechabed *parents.*

That's why I think I won't ask my parents beforehand or warn them that I'm going to take this halachah upon myself. It has to be natural, and we don't even have to speak about it, because they will see that this is part of a big picture.

I think that if they see this as an additional expression of kibbud av va'eim, it will pass well.

It costs no money, takes almost no time, and needs minimal effort.

Be the first in your neighborhood!

Be the first in your family!

Some people are busy saving the whales. As Jews, we have to be particularly concerned about saving mitzvos that are in danger of extinction.

Chapter 8

Married Children's Obligations

Even after marriage, both men and women remain obligated in the mitzvah of honoring their parents.

A married man: A married man remains fully obligated in all three aspects of **HONOR**: in deed, in thought, and in speech.

When a man marries, he doesn't leave behind these obligations. He retains these responsibilities to his parents even as he takes on new overriding commitments to his wife. His challenge is to arrange his life and schedule to accommodate both marital and filial obligations, just as he has to balance and integrate davening, learning, and work responsibilities.

If caring for his parents upsets the tranquility in the home, *shalom bayis* comes first. He may not overlook his obligations to his wife and children to better care for his parents' physical needs.* This should be decided in consultation with a halachic authority who knows the family situation.

---

* Though he may not be able to personally provide care, he would be obligated to find a replacement so that his parents' needs are not neglected.

A husband should make every effort to have his wife partner with him in this mitzvah. The reasons are many: (1) he has a mitzvah to honor his parents, and it's her *zechus* to help him fulfill that obligation, the same way she would want to help him in his other spiritual endeavors; (2) a married woman has an obligation to honor her in-laws; (3) this mitzvah is a *zechus* for the family; and (4) it's important for the children's *chinuch*.

His obligation of **REVERENCE** — to refrain from demeaning and offensive behavior and contradictory speech — also remains the same.

A married woman: When a daughter becomes a wife, the focus of her responsibility shifts from her parents to her husband, children, and home. The Torah lifts some of her filial obligations because of her new marital and domestic responsibilities, but does not release her from obligations that are within her ability to perform.[1] An example would be rising in her parents' honor.[2]

A married woman is obligated fully in two aspects of **HONOR**:

in *thought*, proper attitude
in *speech*, speaking respectfully to and about parents

But *deeds*, service and personal care, comes with a qualifier. She's exempt when giving assistance that would clash or conflict with her responsibilities as a married woman.

Her obligation of **REVERENCE** — to refrain from demeaning and offensive behavior and contradictory speech — remains the same.

Partners in peace

A husband should not object to his wife assisting her parents or just bringing them *nachas*, unless he has a legitimate reason.

A clever wife is one who knows how to balance her obligations. She will make an effort to honor her parents without disrupting her *shalom bayis*.*

---

* Whenever she is not available, siblings or grandchildren can/should be recruited.

Parents, says the *Sefer Chassidim*, "should be wary of asking something of their married daughter while she is busy with her husband and children, thus causing her to leave her primary responsibility. On the other hand, it is fitting that a husband, at times, allow his wife to put her parent's needs before his."[3]

A parent may not ask or demand that a son or daughter distress a spouse. This would be asking them to transgress the Torah, which, of course, they may not do.

BEING AN ONLY CHILD, born to my parents after many years of marriage, I guess you could call me spoiled and pampered. I will always be my father and mother's little girl.

I don't know how it goes in other families. In mine, my parents gave me everything. So, of course, I feel very indebted to them.

When I married, we moved to a beautiful home near my parents, which they bought for us. Everything was fine for many years.

As my parents got older, health issues arose. They went out less and less. I felt I should be there to fill some of their empty time, so I began going over in the afternoons with the kids to spend a few hours with Bubby and Zeidy.

The problem started when my parents urged me to remain for supper. Of course, it was nice for me and the kids. But it ran into the hour that my husband, Yossi, comes home.

My parents have even invited Yossi to come for supper. But Yossi likes the comfort of his own home, alone with me and the children after a long day.

Every time I leave my parents, they look so dejected and practically beg me to join them for supper. I've tried gently explaining that Yossi is coming home and I have to go home to serve him supper. On some level, I'm sure my parents understand that my place is at home, but in their eagerness for my company, they sort of lose it.

"Oh, Rivky," my mother said just the other day, "can't he use the microwave?"

She always offers to pack up a generous portion for Yossi so that he'll get a great meal when I — eventually — get home.

But Yossi insists that I and the children be there when he walks in.

Mostly, I'm good.

I'm embarrassed to admit this, but there are many times when I cave in. My parents' pleas and gloomy faces are too much for me. I think, "Look at all they've done for me, for us. How can I just walk out?"

When I finally do show up at home — usually at the eleventh hour, and often after — it's always with a beautifully wrapped dinner fit for a king, my parents' peace offering.

But it's nothing of the sort.

I know my husband is supposed to be my focus, and yet, I'm so torn. I know what I have to do, what I should do…but I don't always have the strength to do it.

Rather than navigate choppy waters with no compass, wouldn't it be better if Yossi and Rivky met with their Rav to get halachic guidance?

Yossi: I thought I was marrying my wife, not my in-laws!

Rivky: Doesn't hakaras hatov play a part in this? What about the fact that I'm an only child?

Yossi: Doesn't my wish as a husband to have my wife home when I arrive after a long day carry any weight?

Rivky: Well, isn't there any room for compromise? Can we say that the kids and I will join my parents for dinner twice a week? Shouldn't Yossi join us at least sometimes?

Yossi: Is it appropriate for a third party to speak to my in-laws if it turns out that they are wrong about this?

When conflicts arise involving parents and in-laws, both husband and wife should daven to Hashem to give them the wisdom and the desire to resolve the difficulties and achieve a peaceful solution.

When the point of contention can't be resolved, they should jointly consult a Torah authority. The brief outline given in this chapter may seem relatively clear cut, but applying it requires a breadth of understanding of halachic principles that only a Torah authority possesses.

Chapter 9
A Winning Presentation

A sprig of parsley. A drizzle of chocolate. A uniquely designed platter — a beautiful presentation.

The importance of an appealing and creative presentation is true in the spiritual realm as well.

Every mitzvah is like a presentation, an offering to the Almighty. When done properly, a mitzvah will ascend with a "pleasing fragrance like that of apples and roses and a variety of aromatic spices."[1]

Mitzvos, we are taught, have ingredients. Some are essential for the outcome. Others are great enhancers. All contribute to a beautiful finished product. Here are some of those ingredients, double and triple tested in countless Jewish homes throughout the generations for amazing results.

בְּדִקְדּוּק הַדִּין וְכָל פְּרָטֶיהָ	With attention to halachic details
בְּאַהֲבָה	With love
בְּיִרְאָה	With reverence
בְּשִׂמְחָה	With joy

מִצְוָה בּוֹ יוֹתֵר מִבִּשְׁלוּחוֹ	Personally
לֹא יַחֲמִיץ הַמִּצְוָה	By grabbing the opportunity
בְּהִידּוּר	By enhancing and beautifying it
דֶּרֶךְ כָּבוֹד	With respect and dignity
בְּכַוָּנָה	With intent
כְּשַׁמָּשׁ לְרַבּוֹ	With loyalty and devotion

These conditions[2] for fulfilling a mitzvah in its finest form apply to all mitzvos, while two pertain particularly to *kibbud av va'eim*.[3]

In the following stories, you will meet sons and daughters who delivered a winning presentation, pleasing those below and delighting the One above.

בְּדִקְדּוּק הַדִּין וְכָל פְּרָטֶיהָ
With attention to halachic details

WHENEVER MY PARENTS VISITED, it was always very stressful for me. I have a busy household with several high-need children.

When my parents came for Shabbos, they liked to arrive early Friday morning. Not only was I still frantically trying to "make Shabbos" when they walked in the door, but Grandma and Grandpa's arrival excited the children, disrupted our routine, and made my children especially hard to handle.

In addition, my parents expected to have lunch served to them. To make it even more difficult, my mother was dieting and could eat only certain foods. Convenience foods were out!

I always felt resentful and thought, "Can't they see how hard it is for me to make Shabbos and deal with the children? Instead of making things harder, why can't they make it easier for me by eating before they come or bringing food with them? Or why can't they just eat whatever I'm serving even if it isn't their ultimate diet plan — or just come later?"

On Shabbos itself, there were issues. My parents like to

eat soup at the Friday night meal. In my family, we don't serve soup, because we need to keep the meals shorter. I always thought, "Why can't my parents understand that there is a reason why we do it this way, and give up on that course!"

Then, there was the air conditioning. My father always feels hot, even when everyone else is comfortable. If I needed to run the a/c for him all Shabbos, I'd keep thinking, "Doesn't he realize how expensive this is and how we are struggling financially? The least he could do would be to offer to pay, since it's only for him!"

It wasn't until I was well into my married years that I learned about the obligations of honoring parents.

What a shocker!

Feeding, clothing, hosting parents and ensuring their comfort are minimal Torah obligations! How come I never knew about this before?

Here I was thinking all these years that I had difficult parents. Now I cried my eyes out over all the years I had wasted being angry, resentful, and unaccommodating. I had been so sure I was right. And I wasn't. This was so humbling.

It was amazing how learning the halachos properly helped me to totally reframe my thinking. It was a new approach that enabled me to replace "annoyances" with the word "opportunities."

Now, when I know my parents are coming, I work their Friday lunch into my schedule and plan ahead what to serve them. I make the foods for my mother's special diet the same way I would prepare a meal for the most important visitor.

I view the extra soup course in the same way that I view the extra course of simanim on Rosh Hashanah. I view the cost of the air conditioning as a special Shabbos expense, in the same way that on Succos we spend extra for a lulav and esrog, and on Pesach for matzos and wine.

I'm not saying that it isn't still difficult, but it's also difficult for a mountain climber to reach the summit. He must train, pace himself, plan carefully, and have a positive attitude. And that's what I did.

*My parents noticed the difference in my attitude imme-
diately, and commented on how pleasant Shabbos was.*

*And me? When they leave, instead of feeling relief that they
are "finally gone!" I am left with a feeling of thankfulness to
Hashem for the opportunity to care for them and make them
happy — and for the halachos that clued me in on how to do
it right.*

בְּאַהֲבָה
With love

*EVERYONE IN OUR FAMILY, even the little kids, knows
that Mommy's birthday is right after Purim. We start planning
as soon as we put away the Chanukah menorah. If you
would be in our house, you might overhear our whispered
conversations: "What can we get Mommy this year?" "What
will make her happy?" "What does she need?"*

*I, the oldest, have money from music lessons that I give.
My sisters have their babysitting money. My brothers have
prize money for extra learning in yeshivah. The little ones
save up Chanukah and Purim gelt.*

*Weeks before the special day, we older kids start scouting
out the stores. The younger ones find things in a variety store
not far from our house.*

*Finally, the big day arrives. We all gather around Mommy
— who is not exactly surprised, since we do this every year,
but seems to enjoy every minute.*

*This year, 7-year-old Avigail collected all the Purim sweets
given to her, and chose from them the ones she knows
Mommy likes. She put them all on a pretty tray, wrapped it
with cellophane, and presented it to Mommy, along with a
note (that a sister helped her write) addressed to, "To the
best Mommy."*

*Two children pooled their money and bought a garlic
press. Why did they think of that? Because once when they
were shopping together with Mommy, she mentioned that
it's useful to have a garlic press in the kitchen.*

Our 3-year-old, Avreimi, the baby of the family, wasn't going to be left out. One of the children in his kindergarten class had a birthday celebration and distributed party bags. Don't you think our cutie pie saved his bag to give to Mommy?

My sister, who learns computers in school, printed a picture of all of us children on special paper. Then she wrapped it around a chocolate bar.

I, who have the most savings, was able to get something special that I knew Mommy (and my father) would enjoy. Even though we spend most of Pesach with our grandparents, I bought them a matzah cover.

Every one, in his or her way, wants to express love and appreciation to our mother. We all feel that a birthday is the chance to show Mommy how much we appreciate all that she does for us.

We know it doesn't matter to Mommy how big or small the present is. What's important is the love that went into it.

בְּיִרְאָה
With reverence

What is the extent of reverence that the Almighty requires toward parents? Is it as much as we would show a head of state or another high-ranking political figure?[4]

MY HUSBAND IS ALWAYS TELLING the children what a wonderful mother they have.

"Go tell Mommy thank you."

"Go give Mommy a kiss."

Or, let's say, at the supper table, he'll compliment me on a delicious meal, and then tell the children to give me a round of applause.

Last week, he told the children that the mother of the house is "like a queen." He then told our sons, ages 8 and 10, to go to the store (about a five-minute walk) and buy me a plastic crown.

The boys liked the idea, and they went happily. When they

came back, both my husband and I were in for a surprise.

Apparently, they had dipped into their allowances, because they walked in with not only a crown, but a scepter and two toy trumpets.

They put the crown on my head, the scepter in my hand, and marched me around the house — the whole gang, plus these two trumpeteers, stomping, flapping, and blowing with all their might, in honor of me, the queen of our house!

And there was the queen, with a lopsided crown, a sparkling scepter, and tears of joy streaming down my face.

Truth is, this is not overstated. We are told that the honor due parents matches that due Hashem — much more than we would give a head of state! And three cheers for this father, who is pointing his children in the right direction, with a serious message presented in a most delightful way. [5]

בְּשִׂמְחָה
With joy

IT WAS SO HARD to focus. My thoughts kept running back to the conversation we'd had at the nursing home earlier that day, and the wrenching feeling it left me with.

I was listening to my sister, Malky, tell Mommy how her son Zalmy was preparing to say the Mah Nishtana, when Melissa, the nurse, came in. "He sings it nonstop, Mommy. It's so adorable. He was even trying to teach it to the baby. You're going to love hearing him at the Seder."

Mommy smiled, her eyes shining with anticipation. Even though she still couldn't speak clearly, it was so good to finally have her back with us and to see the Mommy we love, the Mommy we had longed for as we sat beside her bed, just weeks before, davening for her to come out of the coma.

Melissa, though, raised her eyebrows. "What do you mean, Mrs. Berkowitz, 'at the Seder'? Surely you don't expect your mother to be coming to you for the holiday!"

"I did, actually." Malky's voice was strained. *"Is there a problem with that?"*

"I would think so!" Melissa shook her head, as if unable to understand what on earth we had been thinking. *"Your mother is in no condition to leave the nursing home."*

"It would be only for a few hours," I rushed in. *"Malky and I both live nearby. And we could arrange to have a private nurse there, too."*

"Even for a few hours, I think it's out of the question." Melissa paused, looking at our faces. *"But if you want, I'll ask Dr. Perkovsky."*

When the doctor arrived, he refused to even consider it. *"Absolutely not,"* he said with a firm shake of his head. *"It would be far too risky for your mother."*

I nodded, as did my sister. Looking at Malky, I could see that we shared the same thoughts. Despite the smiles we kept stretched across our faces, there was a cloud of despondency and disappointment that was impossible to miss.

I quickly looked over at Mommy, and could see she felt it, too. So much more than we did, I was certain. Her eyes had dimmed, and the corners of her lips drooped slightly.

After everything she'd been through — the coronary, the open heart surgery, a massive stroke, four weeks in a coma, and then being transferred to a nursing home, barely able to move or communicate, speech-impaired and wheelchair-bound — after all that, the loss of this precious Yom Tov experience was a bitter letdown.

I wanted all of us to be together with Mommy for Pesach. How could any of us possibly enjoy the Seder knowing that Mommy was in the nursing home all alone?

What was that I had just thought? In the nursing home... Could I do it?

Maybe...just maybe all three of us could.

I reached for the phone.

"Leah, what happened?" With Mommy in such a precarious state for so long, late-night phone calls brought on a rush of anxiety for all of us. In my excitement, I hadn't thought about that.

I rushed to reassure my sister. "Everything's fine. But, listen, I figured it out! The Seder — we can make it in the nursing home!"

"What?" Malky sounded as if she hadn't heard right.

"We can make the Seder — a family Seder — at the nursing home. Mommy can't come to us, but we can go there. We'll make the food, bring all the dishes and everything, and it will be perfect!"

She was silent for a while.

When she finally spoke, I could hear the smile in her words. "You know, Leah, you might have an idea there."

Convincing the staff wasn't nearly as hard as I'd expected. Perhaps Melissa realized just how devastated we all were, especially my mother, because when I explained my idea to her, she jumped right into the planning.

"You can have the shul for the Seder. No one will be using it then. I'm sure of it." After a quick phone call to the administration, she gave us the go-ahead.

We sprang into action. I was cooking for the first Seder, Malky for the second, and our third sister, Frummie, was going to buy and deliver the paper goods and anything else that could be brought over beforehand. She was also in charge of technical details, of which there were plenty.

My daughters and I cooked up a storm. We chopped, peeled and cracked, cooked, baked, and fried, preparing our family's Pesach favorites.

When we were finally done, with all the dishes carefully packaged and stacked neatly in the fridge, we collapsed on the kitchen chairs, laughing at ourselves, our exhaustion, and the near-outrageousness of this plan we were putting into action.

We set off shortly after lighting. I had to chuckle at myself as I walked the mile to the nursing home, flanked by my daughters. From a distance, I'm sure I looked the same as any other woman pushing an old-fashioned baby carriage along the street.

But if anyone had stopped me, asked to take a peep at the adorable little baby bundled under the blanket — well, they would have been in for quite a surprise! Because nestled between the quilted walls of the carriage was the entire Pesach Seder, every container perfectly arranged in a culinary puzzle that maximized every inch the carriage had to offer. And though it wasn't a "real" baby in there, I pushed that carriage with just as much care as a doting mother would.

When we arrived, I went straight to my mother, letting the girls set up Seder in the shul. She was waiting for me, wearing the Yom Tov finery I'd asked her aides to dress her in. Tears in her eyes, and a smile that matched mine. A smile I was so grateful we'd been able to bring to her face.

As I wheeled my mother through the shul door, I stopped short, taking in the scene before me. The room had been transformed. Our Yom Tov tablecloth was laid with wine and matzos. Everything was in place just as it should be — the ke'arah, the charoses, the marror, a majestic cup for Eliyahu, even the pillows rested sublimely on chairs for our royal comfort.

We were ready to begin.

I sat right next to Mommy. She was so happy. There was a special glow on her face. It stayed there as we sang all the songs my father, alav hashalom, used to sing. We sang his beautiful "B'tzeis Yisrael," that he had brought from the Mir.

The songs, the minhagim that Mommy was used to, the Seder the way she knew it, surrounded by the people she loved and who she knew loved her — transported her to Pesach Sedarim of years gone by.

The nursing staff was very accommodating and let us continue until two in the morning. Mommy stayed at the table the whole time.

I thought about what might have been had we not made this effort.

That night remains vivid in my memory. As we left the home in the wee hours of the morning, I felt a joy well up in my heart. I think it can only be described as simchah shel mitzvah, the joy of doing a mitzvah in a truly complete way.

In fact, our Sages tell us, the reward promised for this mitzvah will be in proportion to the happiness with which it is done.[6]

מִצְוָה בּוֹ יוֹתֵר מִבִּשְׁלוּחוֹ
Personally

It is always preferable that a child assist personally. When this is not possible, he can find a substitute. For example, when a parent needs a letter mailed, bills paid, groceries purchased, and even assistance with dressing and food, the main thing is that it gets done.

There are, however, certain aspects of *kibbud av va'eim* that can only be done by a child. When the purpose is to show honor to his parents and to bring them *nachas*, this cannot be accomplished through a substitute.

"Yosef harnessed his chariot and went to greet his father, Yisrael."[7] Rashi comments: He himself harnessed the horses to the chariot, being eager to show honor to his father.[8]

Yosef HaTzaddik surely had servants who could harness horses. Nonetheless, he chose to do even this aspect of the mitzvah himself. Greeting his father was another matter.

Would it have served the same purpose had he sent strangers to meet his father?

SEVERAL YEARS AGO, I learned b'chavrusa with a very prominent and charitable New York businessman. He was running a multi-million-dollar business at a grueling pace. Nevertheless, he carved out time to learn with me every day.

One day as we finished our learning session, he mentioned to me that his mother was returning from Florida. Of course, he was sending his driver to pick her up.

Very nice, I thought. Still, I felt that this very special human being could do even better. So I ventured, "Your mother is arriving, and you're sending your driver?"

At first, he looked puzzled. A second later, his expression changed. He had heard me. (I told you he's a special guy.)

"You are 100 percent right!" he bellowed, banging the desk with his fist. After a quick glance at his watch, he reached for the phone and buzzed his secretary.

"Cancel the driver, and cancel all my appointments for the day," he told her. "Tell them to bring my car up to the front."

The next day, he thanked me.

"My mother's eyes lit up when she saw me walking toward her, knowing how hard it is for me to pull myself away from work in the middle of the day," he told me. Then, with a wink, he added, "That's it. From now on, this is my baby."

When hearing his father, R' Abahu, approach, Avimi always ran to open the door himself, saying as he ran, "I'm coming, I'm coming," so that his father would know that he was on his way.

Avimi had five grown sons who would have been more than happy to go in his stead and save their father the effort. They were responsible men, so Avimi knew it would get done. Still, he was particular to welcome his father himself.[9]

The Gemara relates: R' Tarfon's mother was walking in the courtyard on Shabbos. While she was walking, the strap of her shoe ripped, and the shoe fell off her foot. R' Tarfon witnessed this scene and ran to his mother's aid. He quickly placed his hands under her feet, allowing his mother to walk on his hands until she reached her couch.

Change the century and the weather, and listen to the following story.

THE GOLD-EMBOSSED INVITATION *read, "The kallah, Batsheva..."*

Our cousin, Batsheva, was getting married in a month. No question that we would offer to make sheva berachos. We ordered some of the food, but no one can order the weather.

As it turned out, the day of the sheva berachos dawned with heavy snow falling in Monsey. The weather report predicted that the snow would taper off by midday, which is what happened. Immediately, we hired some boys who shoveled and salted, so that by the time the guests arrived, the path from the street to our house was clear.

The mood was festive. Color-coordinated tables and ac-cessories offered an array of tempting courses, accompanied by leibidige *singing and speeches lavishing praise on the beaming* chassan *and* kallah. *All's well that ends well. Or so we thought.*

Many hours later, as the last strains of "Od Yishama" were heard, our bubby was the first of our guests to leave, my mother escorting her arm-in-arm. As they reached the front door and pulled it open, they were faced with an unexpected sight. Outside was a fresh layer of sparkling white snow. Surveying the scene, my mother assessed the walkway. Assigning someone to wait with her mother, she ran back into the house.

The rest of the story was told to me by our next-door neighbor, who saw the scene that I missed.

"That night," she said, "I saw a picture of kibbud eim *that is indescribable. You had to see it to understand the power it packed.*

"Your mother came back with a snow shovel in hand. There she was dressed to the nines, in her high heels, fur coat, jewelry, and Shabbos sheitel, *clearing the snow off the steps. She shoveled and threw the snow to the side, then your bubby took a step. Another shovel. Another throw. Another step.*

"Balancing on her heels, walking backward, shoveling, shoveling, throwing. Shoveling, shoveling, throwing, as your bubby proceeded forward in the path that your mother — at top speed — was clearing for her."

If you feel like asking, "Weren't there some stronger arms at this sheva berachos, *maybe some teenage boys who could shovel?" then you don't know my mother. "This is my* mitzvah," *she would tell them. "No one else is getting it."*

It's not that this story so surprised us. We children are familiar with our mother's extraordinary kibbud eim. *But for my neighbor, this was a glimpse into my mother's exceptional devotion to her mother, whom she cared for in our home for many years.*

My mother would always say, "A berachah *came to our home when Bubby came to live with us."*

Substitute a present-day woman for a Talmudic scholar of old. Both used their hands, walking slowly, step by step, backward, to protect the safety and ensure the comfort of their mother.

Yosef HaTzaddik could have recruited one of his assistants… The businessman could have sent a car service… You can hire an aide, or a maid…but nothing beats a child.

לֹא יַחֲמִיץ הַמִּצְוָה
By grabbing the opportunity

When an opportunity to do a mitzvah presents itself, don't delay. Grab it fast!

I WAS HOME FOR PESACH vacation. It was an hour before Yom Tov, and I was blow-drying my hair when my mother asked me to run out and pick up something at the store for my younger sister.

Well, the store isn't so close to my house. But I remembered what I learned about kibbud av va'eim. I immediately stopped what I was doing, and quickly drove to the store.

My mother was so impressed, especially since I did it with a smile and didn't say, "Why can't someone else do it?"

IN THE MIDST OF THE MORNING RUSH, the phone rang. At seeing my mother's number on the caller ID, I hurried to pick up.

"Faigy?"

"Hi, Mummy. I can hardly hear you."

"I know," came the unclear response.

As I heard these words, it suddenly dawned on me. There was no problem with the phone connection; it was my mother's voice itself. She was choked up with tears.

"What's wrong?" I asked anxiously.

"Bubby is sick," she managed to say. "Really sick."

"Do you want to tell me what happened?" I asked as I walked into a quieter room, where I could give the

conversation my undivided attention.

"She's in the ICU — on life support. It took a long time to put the tube in — a long time that she was without oxygen. No one really knows what will happen now. Usually within the first day, you can get a feeling of how things will go, one way or the other. It's just been a few hours. It was all very sudden..."

As my mother proceeded to tell me the story from beginning to end, she got caught up in the medical details, allowing her to control her emotions for the time being.

"Mummy," I asked, "should I come?"

"I don't know," she replied. "I don't know if it's worth it for you. It's an international trip. You have a family and work to consider. And Bubby won't even know that you're here."

"But Mummy, I would come just to be there for you."

"Oh...uh...I hadn't thought of that..." my mother said. 'Let's be in touch later today and see how things go."

On numerous occasions, my mother had dropped everything and sacrificed much to be a supportive presence at my side. Could I not do the same for her, and be there for her in her time of need?

I dialed my husband's cellphone.

"Of course you should go, Faigy," were his first words.

My heart said, "Go!" My husband said, "Go!" But a part of me hesitated. Leaving my family and making a big trip like this on a moment's notice was no small decision.

I heard my husband saying, "Call the travel agent and book a flight for this morning."

"This morning?!" I echoed, dumbfounded. That left me just a few hours to be packed, out of the house, and at the airport. Even I hadn't been imagining anything quite that soon.

"Yes, this morning," he repeated firmly. "Get on the first flight you possibly can. Your mother has traveled to be with us so many times. This is an opportunity — take advantage."

The travel agent booked the next flight out. I packed a few basics, spoke with my (kind and understanding) employers, called the school and gave a hurried explanation to my children, and was out of my house in record time.

As I was packing, my mother called. She wanted to discuss the options with me, and keep me posted on the situation, which was, for the moment, unchanged.

"Mummy," I said, "I'll see you soon. I booked a flight that's leaving in a few hours."

From my mother's reaction, I saw how much this meant to her.

On my way to the airport, and even in the airport itself, I worked out one last-minute detail after another, making the final arrangements for my ticket, for work, and for my family only a short time before the flight was to board. What was left, I knew that my husband would take care of.

Seated on the plane, my heart surged with emotion... thinking of my grandmother, anxious to be at my mother's side...and so grateful that I was on the way.

As the engines roared and the plane began its ascent, my husband's words buzzed in my ear: "This is an opportunity — take advantage."

בְּהִידוּר
By enhancing and beautifying it

We can't do better than to listen to what the *Mesillas Yesharim* tells about enhancement:

What is meant by giving *nachas ruach* to Hashem?

The mitzvos, which are incumbent upon all Jewish people, are common knowledge. However, one who truly loves *HaKadosh Baruch Hu* will not try to absolve himself by merely fulfilling these general obligations.

Rather, he will act as a son who loves his father. This son jumps at his father's slightest request, doing whatever he can to fulfill it. Though the father only made the request once — and very briefly — it is enough for the son to understand the direction of his father's thoughts, and he will do for his father even that which was not explicitly mentioned.

We see this behavior at all times between close friends, between husband and wife, between father and son. When two people truly love each other, they do not say, "I was not specifically asked to do more. I will do only that which I was asked." Rather, from that which was asked, they will discern the intent behind the request, and try to do for their loved one anything they understand will bring him *nachas*.[10]

MY MOTHER HAS LAVISH TASTE. If you would see the house she lives in, you would get a feeling for what I mean.

Every item in each ornate room has been carefully chosen and positioned. There are chatchkes *on every flat surface and then some — much like a museum, I always thought.*

My lifestyle is quite different, to say the least. My husband makes a modest living and our daily lives reflect this. So does our home.

When my mother visits, she never mentions the disparity between the home she just locked up and the one she is walking into. But, knowing her penchant for the luxurious, I'm just guessing her thoughts.

I can't duplicate my mother's home. I wouldn't dare try — both because of financial limitations and because her flair for aesthetics is just not me. Still, I wanted to do something for my mother to duplicate, in some little way, the elegance and chic that is so much a part of her.

When I finally came up with an idea, I giggled with delight, and was off to one of the swellest stores in town. There, I purchased (with my husband's generous approval) a plush down comforter, deluxe-quality pillows, and an expensive set of designer linen with pillows and accessories.

No one uses these except my mother. We take it out when she comes and store it away until her next visit.

All the kids know about Bubby's linen and the closet where it is carefully placed. Some of the older ones admire it and feel the softness as we set up her room.

Every time my mother comes, she again comments on our choice. "I just love this linen that you bought, Dina," or "I had such a cozy night's sleep." And we exchange smiles.

I surely wouldn't fargin this for myself, but I can truly say that I enjoy this purchase even more than if I had bought it for myself. It's the lush feeling of doing a mitzvah b'hiddur.

דֶּרֶךְ כָּבוֹד
With respect and dignity

"I'M TAKING MY MOTHER to a wedding tonight, so I won't be able to go. But thanks so much for thinking of me."

My mother and I were having lunch together. I had answered the call when I saw my sister-in-law's number. She had called to ask if I wanted a ride to the N'shei event scheduled that evening.

I pressed Off, and stood up to make myself a cup of coffee. As I turned to the counter, I heard my mother's gentle voice.

"Rivka'leh, sheifa'leh, sit a minute."

Obligingly, I sat down next to my mother.

Now that my mother is confined to a wheelchair after a stroke, limited in so many ways, we spend a lot of time together.

Notice what I just said: "We spend time together." I wouldn't have understood to phrase it that way if not for my mother's lesson to me that afternoon.

"Rivka'leh," she said, giving my hand a loving touch, "it's so much nicer to say, 'I'm going with my mother to a wedding,' rather than saying, 'I'm *taking* my mother.'"

With this one sentence, I experienced a major paradigm shift. I understood immediately what my mother meant. I was only ashamed that after the example she has shown us, it still took this reminder for me to get it.

Over the years, my mother has taught me many lessons just from watching her tuning in to the subtleties of feelings. Now, she is teaching me how to care for her in the sensitive way she demands of herself, in the path she hopes her daughter will follow.

That's why I now say, "I'm spending time with my mother," or "I'm going to visit my mother," rather than, "My mother needs my help."

Developing sensitivity to a parent's dignity is a lifelong challenge. We should daven for the wisdom to make the right choices, and the will to persevere.

בְּכַוָּונָה'
With intent

When we do mitzvos that are unique to *Klal Yisrael*, such as sitting in the succah, eating matzah, and lighting Chanukah candles, it is obvious that we do them only because Hashem commanded us. But what about those actions that humanity universally agrees are logical and proper, like honoring parents?

When we are engaged in virtuous behavior that is not unique to *Klal Yisrael*, it is essential to have the intention (*kavannah*) that we are doing so because it is commanded by the Creator. [11]

MY GRANDSON, who learns in a Chassidishe yeshivah, received a very good mark on his test. His rebbi told him to show it to his parents to give them nachas.

"Remember," he warned with a big smile, "first put on your hat and gartel. Then say, הִנְנִי מוּכָן וּמְזוּמָּן לְקַיֵּים מִצְוַת עֲשֵׂה שֶׁל כִּבּוּד אָב וָאֵם, *and then hand them the test."*

A NAME WAS SUGGESTED to us as a suitable match for our son.

The more we heard about Leah, the more enthusiastic we were about the shidduch. She sounded like an extraordinary girl.

We continued our inquiries, spoke to people who knew her well, and asked for more details.

One telephone call really clinched the deal. It was a close neighbor of Leah's family.

"You've come to the right address," the neighbor said, "because we know them quite well. I've watched Leah grow up and have seen her turn into the fine person she is. There are so many stories I could tell you — I've been in that house a lot — but this scene stands out in my mind.

"I passed by the kitchen when Leah was busy washing dishes. She didn't see me and didn't know anyone was listening. As her hands moved quickly, I caught her quiet words, 'I am doing this to be mekayem *the mitzvah of* kibbud horim *and the mitzvah of* gemilus chessed.'"*

כְּשַׁמָּשׁ לְרַבּוֹ
With loyalty and devotion

The last essential ingredient on our list is provided by the Rambam:[12]

A son should serve his parents in all matters like a *shamash* (personal assistant) serves the Rav (*Rambam, Hilchos Mamrim*).

When the *Chayei Adam* comments on this relationship, he uses the expression, "like a servant serving his master" (כְּעֶבֶד הַמְשַׁמֵּשׁ אֶת רַבּוֹ).

A personal assistant? A servant? A jarring image. Whatever could that mean? The relationship between parent and child should be one of warmth and love.

What lessons are meant to be conveyed from our Sages' description?

A personal assistant is "at your service," on call. He is there to make life more pleasant. The comparison of a *shamash*/personal assistant conjures up images of loyalty and devotion. The assistance we offer our parents should be seasoned generously with a big measure of both.

Honor

In Gratitude

Chapter 10

Opening a "Thank Account"

Sefer HaChinuch explains that gratitude is at the root of the mitzvah of honoring parents:

1. It is proper for a person to acknowledge the benefits done for him and to repay the source of that goodness with kindness.

2. He should not be an ingrate, who denies the good done him, as this is a lowly character trait, despicable both to Hashem and to mankind.

3. One should recognize that his parents are the reason he exists in this world. For this reason alone, it is truly proper for a son and daughter to give his parents any honor and benefit he can, because they brought him into this world.

4. In addition, his parents toiled and sacrificed for him when he was growing up.

5. When a person accustoms himself to appreciating the good done to him by his parents, it will be a steppingstone toward an appreciation of the Prime Cause of his existence and His kindness.[1]

EXACTLY ONE YEAR AGO I had the zechus to listen to a series of shiurim on the topic of honoring parents. While I have a close relationship with my parents, these shiurim opened my eyes as to how to approach this special mitzvah on an entirely new plane. I was introduced to a level of kavod that is not the norm in today's society, along with practical ways to achieve success.

One of the exercises recommended was to write a letter to our mother and father thanking them for the multitude of kindnesses they have done for us since our birth. I decided to do this, and I began with a letter to my father. While our relationship was a good one, he was a very intellectual man and he didn't always relate well to emotional outpourings. I thought this letter would be a perfect way to express my gratitude in words that were hard to say to him in person.

As I thought back upon my almost thirty-nine years with a father who was always giving, I found writing the letter easy.

I sent the letter and, as I expected, my father was very appreciative, though he didn't gush over it. Privately, my mother told me that he loved it and reread it many times.

Some months later, my father was diagnosed with a life-threatening illness. Though the doctors gave him a good five to eight years, he lived only three months. We are stunned and struggling to navigate through life without him.

My father had a folder where he kept his important papers. When my mother opened it to get the deed for his burial plot, lying there on top of all the papers was the letter I had written to him.

Why is it hard to be grateful?

Honoring parents should be an easy mitzvah, because there's so much we should want to repay and give back. Yet our Sages say that this is one of the most difficult mitzvos to fulfill properly.

What makes it so difficult?

Harav Shlomo Wolbe explains that Hashem created a baby helpless and dependent on others for survival, needing years of care and service before he is ready to assume adulthood. Indeed, often he is surrounded by many people catering to his every whim, jumping at his beck and call. Because of this, a child grows up accustomed to feeling that everything in his environment is put there to serve him. This is the way it is, always was, always will be, and is supposed to be. "The world was created for me." Gratitude has no foothold here.[2]

What purpose can this serve?

Hashem wants us to feel important, because we are important. Each of us has a unique assignment in this world that no one else can accomplish. This sense of importance is implanted in our hearts so that we will be drawn to achieve distinction by discovering the special talents and strengths that lie within us, and will utilize them maximally.

The danger comes when we misunderstand this lesson. If we do not wean ourselves from our childish version of "the world was created for me," it leads to a debilitating feeling of entitlement.

> *A WOMAN WAS COMPLAINING to a friend, "My parents have done nothing for me for the past thirty years."*
> *"But, Chani, didn't they buy you a home twenty years ago?"*
> *"Yes, but besides that..."*

How is it possible for this woman to overlook that purchase and make a statement that her parents never did anything?

The burden of a debt

When someone does us a favor — especially if it was big — we become indebted. I owe you. I owe you at least a thank you — and I might even have to return the favor! It's human nature to be uncomfortable with this feeling of being beholden to another person. So, what do we do? We'd rather forget about the favor that was done for us. We'd rather pretend that nothing happened. We deny or ignore what was given to us so that we can evade the burden of debt.

One who shows a lack of gratitude is called כְּפוּי טוֹבָה, from the root כפה, to cover — we cover the goodness with a covering, so that it won't be seen and we can avoid the burden of a debt.[3]

There is a natural inclination to feel this way. It's a lifetime of work to fight it.

The big I.O.U.

It is burdensome to be indebted to anyone, but parents present a greater challenge because we are placed in a position to constantly feel that we owe them. It is difficult to be constantly *anything*, and it is not pleasant to feel continually indebted. Which explains comments like, "What's the big deal anyway? That's what parents are for." "All my friends get the same things, and some get even more." "I didn't ask to be born. My parents wanted children for their own *nachas*."[4]

The premise that an act of kindness done for personal benefit is not a kindness and therefore not deserving of appreciation is a mistake.[5] When a person gives *tzedakah*, it is a kindness. The fact that the donor may be motivated by a desire for honor doesn't diminish the direct benefit to the recipient.*

Or take, for instance, a storekeeper. He gets up early in the morning to open his store so we can buy what we need. The fact that he earns a living doesn't change the fact that we are beneficiaries of his efforts.[6]

Becoming a grateful person means realizing how much we benefit all day long from the people in our lives. The mailman, a teacher, a dentist, a babysitter — they are all doing favors. Realizing that we are all constant beneficiaries of kindness is the first step to becoming grateful, with all the benefits that gratitude brings.

Gratitude begins at home

Our training in appreciation begins at home with an appreciation of parents. A father should be looking for opportunities to say to the children:

---

* The donor's intent will be a separate Heavenly accounting, not affecting the recipient.

"Who thanked Mommy for a yummy supper?"
"A big round of applause for our special, hard-working Ima."
*"Look at all the things Mom does for you. Even though she was
up at night with the baby, she still got up to send you off to school."*

A mother, likewise, should be looking for opportunities to
show the children how much they should appreciate their father:

"I'm sure all the good that we have in the house is due to Abba's
tefillos."
"Look what a fun vacation Daddy arranged for us."
*"You know, we have delicious food and pretty clothing to wear
because Tatty works so hard."*
*"Do you realize how lucky you are to have a father with a sense
of humor?"*

If a child did not thank his mother for the meal she just served,
says Harav Avigdor Miller,[7] you can be sure he had no *kavannah* in
Bircas HaMazon. Here he has in front of him an actual live human
being, his mother, whom he sees cutting, stirring, standing over
pots, serving him and cleaning up after him, yet he feels no need
to express any appreciation. Surely, he will not reach the next
level of sincerely thanking a Being he cannot see.[8]

From the tangible to the intangible

Of the many benefits parents offer us, an important one is the
opportunity to recognize the good being done for us, developing
our *middah* of *hakaras hatov.* A child spends his early years at home,
a boot camp for developing gratitude. In our childhood years, we
serve a long apprenticeship in becoming expert thankers. Once
we've finished our training period, we can learn to extend gratitude
to other benefactors. The ultimate purpose of all this training is to
move from the tangible to the intangible — from people to G-d.
Once our hearts and eyes are open to the constant good bestowed
by parents, it's easier for us to grasp the goodness of a Higher
Being — to recognize and thank the Ultimate Source of all good.

Modeh ani means "I thank" and also "I acknowledge." When
I thank, I admit that on my own I could not have attained that

which I needed. I needed someone's help to put me on my feet. And I acknowledge that debt.

Most of us keep a watchful eye on our bank account, but are we as careful to monitor our "thank account"?

One of the best ways to cultivate a grateful heart is to record our feelings of gratitude. Take the time to write down your blessings and to acknowledge those who helped you along the way.

> *Do I think...*
>
> *who burped me, rocked me, sang to me, talked to me, hugged me, and so much more that I don't even know about?*
>
> *who dragged him/herself out of bed to feed me?*
>
> *who carried me before I could walk?*
>
> *who encouraged me to take my first step?*
>
> *who strapped and unstrapped me into my car seat, booster seat, and high chair?*
>
> *who paced the floors with me when I was teething?*
>
> *who taught me to eat solid food and patiently fed it to me?*
>
> *who taught me to drink from a cup?*
>
> *who taught me to say Modeh Ani and Torah tzivah lanu Moshe?*
>
> *who dressed me in the morning when I was too little to do it on my own?*
>
> *who gave me thousands of baths?*
>
> *who cut my nails thousands of times?*
>
> *who taught me colors and numbers?*
>
> *who pushed me on the swing?*
>
> *who wiped away my tears and hugged away bumps and scratches?*
>
> *who made all that effort to make me eat, imitating planes, boats, helicopters, while cajoling, "Just three bites."*

Dear reader, dear child, don't rush through this list. Consider each act of kindness and the effort that went into it. You may be skimming over a sentence without realizing that it represents thousands of days of sacrifice for YOU.

> *Thank you for...*
>
> *all the Shabbos parties, birthday parties, and the presents every year.*

letting me help even when it wasn't much of a help.

taking out my splinters.

all the treats that I got.

teaching me to cross the street.

walking me to the bus stop and waiting.

standing hours in line at PTA meetings.

coming to my Siddur parties, Chumash parties and Chanukah skits, high school productions, and graduation.

buying me my first siddur.

helping me with homework, reports, and all my projects.

paying years of tuition.

sending me to sleep away camp, shopping, sewing on labels and packing my luggage, being there to listen when I was homesick, and paying for the luxury of going to camp.

taking me to the doctor when I was sick, or even just for a routine checkup.

staying home from work to be with me when I was sick.

paying for my braces and retainers and taking me to and from the orthodontist.

taking me to eye exams and buying me glasses.

holding my hand as they wheeled me into the operating room, reciting Tehillim and being there when I came out.

cooking, peeling, slicing, sautéing, baking, grilling, roasting, serving, cleaning up, and then doing it all over again and again and again.

buying me a summer wardrobe, a winter wardrobe, and then again a new summer wardrobe in a never-ending cycle.

sewing on my buttons.

buying me sneakers, shoes, slippers, sandals, boots, and swim shoes.

being my human alarm clock.

laughing at my jokes even though they weren't funny.

teaching me so many skills, like riding a bike, tying shoelaces, making my bed, braiding challah, reading a map, parking a car, putting in contact lenses, and setting a table.

insisting I write an apology letter to my teacher when I misbehaved.

listening to what I had to say and showing that it mattered.

driving me to and from friends, school, weddings, parties, and sleepovers.

staying up late and waiting for me to come home.

Thank you for letting me sleep at night — because you were up doing the worrying.

Were you a recipient of many of the above? Did you — and do you — feel grateful?

This is just a puny attempt to recreate the abundance of kindness bestowed on many children.

Do I think who taught me to shake a lulav and esrog, who taught me to make berachos, who showed me to live with less and still be happy?

Do I think who taught me not to join in neighborhood gossip?

Do I think who said Shema with me every night?

Do I think who davened for me before I was born and still does every day?

Do I think who cries out his heart to Hashem for my well-being?

Do I think who bentched me on erev Yom Kippur and took me to Zeidy for berachos?

Do I think who taught me to give?

Do I think who taught me to love?

Do I think who taught me right from wrong?

Do I think?

Do I think enough on a regular day to realize how much you do for me and how grateful I should be?

Do I think that you don't have to do all this?

Is it time for me to start thinking?

OUR TEACHER TOLD US to write a thank you to our parents for everything they do for us. So my friends sat down and wrote long, detailed lists of thank yous for everything their parents had done for them since they were born.

Mommy, I have something different to thank you for. I want to thank you not for what you gave me, but for what you haven't given me. I want to express my hakaras hatov for all those times you looked beyond my pleading eyes to see what was really good for me — and said no.

My friends are saying thank you for their cellphones. I want to thank you for the fact that I did not receive my own cellphone until I was 18.

My friends are saying thank you for their full wardrobe of clothing, and I am saying thank you for the chinuch *you instilled in me that clothes are not the* ikar, *even when money is not an issue.*

My friends are saying thank you for all the times their clothes were washed, their dishes were cleaned, their beds were made. And I am saying thank you for insisting that I help around the house with the laundry, dishes, and yes, even cleaning my own room.

My friends are saying thank you for letting them have an easy life and for giving them their way. I am saying thank you for all the times you did not let me have my way.

Mommy, I wasn't always able to thank you for these things. There were definitely times in my childhood when I felt resentful that I couldn't always have my way. There were times when I felt you demanded too much of me. But now that I'm at this point in my life, and I see the person I have been able to become as a result of your restrictions and demands, I want to thank you so much for the amazing chinuch *you have given to me.*

Just how important is this thank account? How much do we have to be concerned to make deposits, to fill it up, and to constantly check our assets?

The answer is implanted in our heart on the Seder night with the exuberant singing of *Dayeinu. Dayeinu's* lesson is that each and every favor bestowed upon us was so great and valuable that it *alone* requires our thanks.

To My Dear Parents,
Had you only given birth to me
And not raised me
Dayeinu! For this alone, I would have reason to thank you.

If you had only raised me
And not straightened my teeth

Dayeinu! I would also have much to be thankful for.

Had you only straightened my teeth
And not prayed for me continually
Dayeinu! Yes, I would still have so much for which to be thankful.

(And here's the space to fill in your own Dayeinus.)

Had I considered how much you gave
And not brooded on what I was missing,
Dayeinu! Dayeinu!
...It would have been enough, I would have had enough.

A **STUDENT APPROACHED ME** after class to speak with me privately about the assignment to write a "thank you" letter to parents.

"I wrote one page, two pages, three pages," she told me, "and I couldn't stop. For each point I made, six more popped into my mind. I continued filling up page after page. I wrote for several hours and saw it still wasn't ending. Meanwhile, I sent those six pages to my parents."

Her voice caught. "I'm just imagining the feelings my father and mother will have when they read it."

By now, the tears that had been close to the surface were visible as she added, "Too bad my parents had to wait eighteen years to hear me say this."

Chapter 11

The Gift of Life

> ...One should recognize that his parents are
> the reason he exists in this world. For this
> reason alone, it is truly proper for a son and
> daughter to give his parents any honor and
> benefit he can, because they brought him
> into this world... (*Sefer HaChinuch* 33).[1]

A person who is drowning and is pulled out of the water will always be thankful to his savior for rescuing him.

The accused is forever grateful to the judge who found him innocent and set him free.

A patient who was hovering between life and death is overwhelmed with gratitude to the doctor who cured him.

Our parents have given us the gift of life. Yet do we feel overwhelmed with gratitude to them?

As Hashem has commanded

As we saw in the previous chapter, *Sefer HaChinuch* explains that it is proper for a child to acknowledge the benefits done for him, the toil and sacrifice day-in and day-out. But what if that was not so? What if his parents did not meet his needs? What, then, is his obligation to his parents?

The answer is found in the wording of the mitzvah itself:

The fifth commandment instructs: כַּבֵּד אֶת אָבִיךָ וְאֶת אִמֶּךָ, כַּאֲשֶׁר צִוְּךָ ה' אֱלֹקֶיךָ, "Honor your father and mother as Hashem, your G-d, commanded you."[2]

What do we learn from the addition of these four words כַּאֲשֶׁר צִוְּךָ ה' אֱלֹקֶיךָ, *as Hashem, your G-d, commanded you?* Isn't every mitzvah done because we are commanded?

Its placement here is stressing that the primary, compelling reason for our fulfillment of this mitzvah is because it is Hashem's command.

Kibbud av va'eim is not based on how much my parents gave me, or how much time they spent with me. It's not dependent on how supportive they were — physically, monetarily, or emotionally. We honor them "as Hashem commanded."

How do we know this is so? When we consider the following:

The commandment to honor parents was given to the generation that lived in the Wilderness,[3] where parents were not responsible to provide for their children's needs. In the Wilderness, food, the manna, was provided straight from Heaven. No cooking, serving, or stacks of dishes! Water came from the *be'er* — no lugging heavy bottles! Clothing never wore out (no shopping!) and never needed laundering; they were cleaned by the *Ananei HaKavod*, the Clouds of Glory — no piles of laundry, folding, ironing, or running to the cleaners. Not even any carpooling. Against this backdrop, where parents were *not* caring for their children's basic needs, Hashem introduced this mitzvah.[4]

A child might think, "I'll evaluate my parents on a scale of one to ten and decide my obligations to them." But this mitzvah is not contingent on a child's judgment of his parents' worth or upon their having given him anything other than life. We are here in the world because of our parents and that alone obligates us.

Yes, it's true, most parents give their children many reasons to be devoted, but the basic reason we keep this mitzvah is because it is Hashem's Will.

Parents who don't meet our material/physical needs

WHEN MY GRANDPARENTS MARRIED, there were no signs that trouble lay ahead. But three short years later, they divorced.

The two children of this broken home, my mother, age 1, and her brother, age 2, returned with their mother to her parents' home. Likewise, their father returned to his family. The year was 1946. The city, Tel Aviv.

Divorce was rare in those times. For this unusual situation, there were no precedents, no rules, and no guidance. I imagine that my grandfather felt like persona non grata when he went to visit his children in the home of his former wife and her mother. With no one to intercede for him, those visits were not viable, and eventually petered out.

I'm not sure what prompted this, but when the children were 6 and 7, he started visiting them again. Not often — once or twice a year. They were not pleasant visits. All three sat very stiffly, not sure what to say. It seems that everyone was very happy when these meetings were over.

When I think about those visits, I feel so sorry for my grandfather. He didn't know how to relate to his own children, having never raised a child and having had no contact with them.

The situation continued like that. Eventually my mother married and moved across the ocean, to the States, which spelled the end to even those annual or semi-annual encounters.

Years passed. Actually, decades. Then, one day, my mother picked up the phone with no warning of the upheaval that was about to take place in her life.

An unfamiliar voice identified himself. "This is Abba." Her heart pounding, her feet barely holding her, she listened as the voice announced, "I'd like to visit you."

What thoughts do you think were running through my mother's mind when she heard that request? She never spoke about it in detail but she did tell us that her very first thought was, Abba? — 'This is Abba?' What kind of a father had he been to her? During those few stilted, awkward meetings over the years, she had never related to him, certainly never called him Abba. My mother told us that she simply could not get the word "Abba" out of her mouth. And now here he was, asking to come over for a little visit.

What would you have said? What would you have done?

My mother invited "Abba" to her home.

Zeidy became a presence in our lives. It was awkward at first, as you can well imagine. After that first visit, my grandfather came once a year, arriving around Purim time and staying with us until after Pesach. We slowly warmed up to this surprise grandfather, taking our cues from our mother.

We also saw Zeidy at happy occasions. He was invited to all family simchas *and would occasionally come in for* bar mitzvahs *or weddings.*

As the years went by, Zeidy's health deteriorated. During one of his visits, he collapsed. Hatzolah took him to the hospital where blood tests revealed he was suffering from a fatal illness. He wasn't able to be on his own anymore. Without hesitation, my mother insisted that he move into our home. He lived with us for the last four years of his life.

During those years, we got to know Zeidy well and learned new things about my mother too. More than ever, her greatness shone forth. Considering her upbringing, or, to be more accurate, lack of paternal care, my mother's care for her father was awe-inspiring. I will describe to you things that I saw with my own eyes and heard with my own ears, and tell me what you think!

When I went shopping with my mother during the years that Zeidy was living with us, we would go up and down the aisle. At each aisle, the major concern was, "What can I get for Zeidy?" The steady refrain was, "What would Zeidy like?" "Come, let's get this for Zeidy." "He'll really like this." "Zeidy likes_____, so we can't forget it." "Remember, we must get that special drink."

Let me add that Zeidy's food and meals were no simple matter. He didn't want to eat food that had been

*refrigerated(!!). So everything was warmed to room temper-
ature. I remember distinctly — it was Erev Pesach — and
while we were all making do with whatever, Zeidy was seated
at the table and served a complete* chametzdik *breakfast.
Who would consider causing Zeidy any discomfort?*

*That was when he was well. When he became ill, there were
new food issues. His taste buds were apparently affected
and all the food my mother lovingly prepared tasted awful
to him. He had no idea how sick he was, and my mother
wouldn't tell him. She shouldered his insults and ravings
(which I remember clearly) with no self-defense — only an
apology and a promise to do better next time.*

*My mother washed, ironed, and mended Zeidy's clothing
and made sure to buy him new clothing, especially for Yom
Tov — just as if he had been a father who had raised her,
clothed her, fed her and now she could repay him.*

*During those four years, my mother accompanied Zeidy
to shul daily. She remained there until he was ready to leave,
and then walked him home carrying his tallis and tefillin in
her hand.*

*My mother was a soft-spoken person by nature. But Zeidy
suffered a hearing loss and in order for him to hear, she had
to shout. How unnatural for her and how difficult this must
have been for this genteel woman.*

*She would rise for her father when he came into the room
— but just a little. Although she was aware of the halachah
that a child should stand fully erect, she understood that her
father would be uncomfortable. She felt that he "wouldn't
go for it," so she stood just a bit.*

*To my mother's everlasting credit, he was a regular grand-
father to us. We were raised without any feelings of animosity,
and, in fact, with feelings of sincere warmth toward my
mother's "father." It was surely my dear mother who created
and nurtured these feelings. She took those quotation marks
away from "father" and we followed her example.*

*Extended family members who saw how hard my mother
worked would say, "We're not telling you to neglect your father.
But what's so wrong with a top notch nursing home?" Even*

in the early years when Zeidy first started coming, my mother davened, "Please, Ribbono shel Olam, let me do this mitzvah."

Was she oblivious to the fact that he hadn't been there for her when she was a child? Not at all. My mother once hinted that she never felt totally comfortable with her father, and it took her a very long time before she was able to call him "Abba."

Where did my mother get the strength to weather this challenge? I think, knowing my mother, that it was her deep-rooted connection to Hashem. She never questioned why this happened to her, why she was given this type of family situation.

Most remarkable, I would say, is that she didn't use her less than perfect childhood as an excuse to bow out of her obligation of kibbud av. She used to say, "My father gave me life. Hashem decided what kind of a life it would be. He decided in His wisdom that this is the father He wanted me to have."

Her spoken and unspoken message to us was: Honoring parents is the training ground for all of life's challenges. Acceptance of our family's circumstances — how we accept Hashem's decree for us at this primary and basic level — will prepare us and affect our attitude and behavior for everything that comes later in our lives.

We watched her live her ideals.

Every day my mother puts money in a pushka l'ilui nishmas her father.

He told her on several occasions that she turned out exactly as he would have wished.

Don't you agree?

Parents who don't meet our spiritual needs

Our *mesorah*, our Jewish tradition, is based on a parent-child, teacher-student chain of transmission. Hashem created man, of all His creations, with the longest nurturing period, with enough time for values to be transmitted and deeply absorbed.

But what if these values weren't transmitted by our parents? Even if we did not get spiritual guidance from our parents, even if we did not receive our *mesorah* from them, we are still commanded to honor them — "as Hashem commanded."

Where do we learn this? In the Wilderness, where we were first commanded to honor parents, it was Moshe Rabbeinu who instructed the nation. Spiritual guidance was not the realm of parents. Later, when we stood at Har Sinai, every individual received the Torah firsthand from Moshe Rabbeinu. In neither instance did parents pass on the tradition to their children. Yet, it was then — under those very circumstances — that we were commanded to honor and revere parents.[5]

I CAN'T SAY MY RELATIONSHIP WITH ESTELLE has always been an easy one. When your child turns her back on everything you raised her to value — on everything you yourself stand for — well, it's a slap in the face, that's the only way to put it.

Not that Esther — that's what she goes by now, not the name I gave my baby girl — is ever disrespectful. No, she's always polite, and the truth is she really does make an effort to steer clear of controversial topics. But it's there, it always is. In the words she doesn't say, in the pictures she sends, everyone buttoned up in black and white, in the packages of food she brings when they come to visit — because Heaven forbid she should actually eat in her own mother's house!

No, it's always there. And though she calls me nearly every day, chatting about anything and everything, that elephant in the room — this new lifestyle — drives a wedge between us. There's only so much we can share, after all. Our lives are so very different.

It's always made me wonder — though of course I'd never tell this to her — just how much she really loves me. You know what I mean? If all those endless laws are so important that they push away everything I value, everything I raised her with, everything I am, then is there any love left? Is there any left for me?

But I've stepped back. I try not to be imposing, try not to make demands, let her live her life the way she wants to, swallowing the sting of knowing that I do — and always will — come in second.

At least, that's what I thought. For a long time, too.

But last week… Well, last week something happened that left me speechless. Left me wondering. And left me feeling very loved.

We were on the phone, in the middle of our daily call. I was in the middle of telling her about the trouble my gardener was giving me over that rosebush out back. But I heard the other line ringing in the background, so I told her to take it.

"It's okay, Mom," Esther said. "Danny" — that's her husband — "will get it."

So I went on, telling her about how he'd insisted it was dead even after I told him it wasn't, and he went and dug it up, when I heard Danny saying something to her.

"Just a second, Mom," she told me. Then, to Danny, "Tell Avi I'll call him after I finish speaking to Mom."

Now, Avi is her son, and he lives in South Africa. I know Esther doesn't get to talk to him that often, what with the time difference being so big. On top of that, his wife Chani is expecting their first baby any day now, and if he was calling in the middle of the week like that, there was a good chance it had something to do with the baby. Esther must have been dying to speak with him and see what was going on.

"No, no," I told her. "You take Avi's call; that's more important."

"It's okay, Mom," she said. "I'll call Avi when we're finished."

But I didn't want her to stay on the phone with me just to be polite. I knew she must really want to talk with Avi, so I told her again that I didn't mind, that she should take his call. "I'm sure you have important things you want to discuss," I said.

But again, she said no. "It's really fine, Mom," she told me. "It can wait. I'm talking with you right now."

And then I couldn't say a word. I was too choked up to speak.

Because she meant it. I could tell that she meant it. Here her son — who she rarely gets to speak to, let alone see

— is on the verge of becoming a father, of making her a grandmother for the very first time, and he's asking to speak to her... and she'd rather stay on the phone with me.

I was totally, utterly speechless.

"Mom? Are you still there?"

Esther thought we'd been disconnected!

"I can't believe you did that for me," I whispered.

I was so choked up I wasn't sure if she could hear me. But she did. And when she answered me, there was such tenderness in her voice that I had to reach for the tissues.

"Of course, Mom." I was pretty certain she was crying, too, on the other end of the line. "You are so important to me."

Don't ask me what we spoke about for the rest of that call, because I can't remember a single word of it. But I will remember those six words as long as I live. And I know, now, that it's true what she said. I am *important to her. So very, very important to her.*

And it means more to me than she could ever imagine.

———◆•◆———

Honoring parents is something that can be arrived at intellectually, something that logic can process and grasp. Therefore, we see outstanding examples of devotion toward parents in many cultures, men and women reciprocating with devotion to those who were devoted, caring for those who cared, responding with good for good received — all stemming from a sense of human decency.

But if the devotion to our parents would be because logic dictates it, what happens when, one day, our logic tells us the opposite?

While the nations of the world may act out of ethical considerations, *Klal Yisrael* honors their parents not primarily because decency demands, but because the Almighty commands.[6]

Honor
In Speech

Chapter 12

It's What You Say *and* How You Say It

When the Torah teaches us "honor your father and your mother," our Sages tell us it is especially referring to respectful speech.[1]

No matter how much we do for parents materially or physically, no matter how many gifts we buy them or how many invitations we extend, no matter how many visits we make, if we speak disrespectfully, hurtfully, when we compromise their dignity, the gain is offset by the loss.

A son may feed his parents the finest delicacies or spend loads of time and money on their care, yet still be faulted. Another son might seem to be making demands on a parent, yet earn eternal reward.

Our Sages tell us two stories to illustrate this principle.

> A son gave his father the finest costly foods. Once, as they were dining, the father asked his son, "Tell me, my son, from where do you have all this [money for such a meal]?"
>
> The son responded, "Why is it your business? Just eat."[2]

The son is thinking, *Yes, it's costing me a fortune, and it's my hard-earned money paying for this meal.*

It doesn't matter if it's rib steak served at the best restaurant in town. Can a parent possibly enjoy the meal after such a response? No matter how impressive the gift, this son lost credit for the mitzvah and earned for himself Divine displeasure.

The second story is about a son who worked at grinding wheat.

> One day, this son's elderly father received a notice to appear for army duty. The son told his father, "Take my place at the grinding mill [the son needed to bring in income for his family, so he couldn't just relinquish his job], and I'll take your place in the army. It's better that I suffer the grueling demands of army service, and you, Father, take the easier job of grinding wheat."[3]

Here is a son who is suggesting to his elderly father that he take his place at the grindstone! Is this an example of a respectful son? In fact, it was the best option possible, and a favor to the father.

The son spoke to his father kindly, made his request gently. He explained patiently that this was the best plan and a different option would have more drawbacks. As a result, the father was appeased.[4]

Even if we can't serve parents as much as we or they would want, or can't provide the time and effort desired — or even if we ask a parent, for his benefit, to do a tedious task — because we did the most we could pleasantly, explaining patiently, and apologizing humbly for what we couldn't do, our reward is great.[5]

Putting honor into words...

While the *Shulchan Aruch* brings six examples of honoring parents in deed, only one example is brought of honoring in speech.

> If a child finds himself among people who admire his parent, and the child needs a favor, he should ask for the sake of his parent rather than his own sake, even though the people would do it for him without

mention of his parent. [6]

"I know my father would appreciate it if you could…"
"Would you be able to do this for me? It would be important to my mother."

On the other hand, if mentioning a parent's name would detract from the parent's honor, then we don't do so.

Why is this example singled out to exemplify honoring through speech, a subject that has so many facets?

The Rambam explains: "This example, which would include anything similar, [is establishing a general principle]: Our words should always reflect both our respect and deference for our parents." [7]

By saying, "Do it for my parent," i.e. a person whom you admire/respect, a child is honoring his parent in two ways. First, he shows desire to afford honor to his parents, by bringing them into the picture. Second, he gives his parents the additional distinction of having people do a favor out of respect for them.

The lesson: Even when our parents are not present, we should keep their honor uppermost in our mind and think about what we can say to increase their prestige and enhance their image so that others will think well of them. What can we say *about* them, and how much more so *to* them, to express our respect?

The *Shulchan Aruch* brings only one example because this says it all. **If it gives honor to your parents, say it. If your words detract from their honor, leave them out.**

…by speaking to parents with all due respect

Here are some directives offered by our Sages concerning the manner and style of speaking to parents:

We should strive to speak

❖ calmly, softly, and deferentially[8]

❖ unpretentiously, patiently, asking rather than demanding[9]

❖ not raising our voice or using unrefined words, and with *derech eretz*[10]

❖ To speak in an unrefined way to others, in front of our parents, is also disrespectful.[11]

...by answering promptly

When a parent calls, it is a mitzvah to answer promptly. Ignoring a parent diminishes his honor.

> At hearing his father knock, Avimi always ran to open the door promptly, calling out as he ran, "Yes, yes! I'm coming," so that his father would have the least distress while waiting, knowing that his son was on his way (*Kiddushin* 31a).

We learn from this that when a child is called he should respond without delay.

> *"I'm upstairs. I'm coming."*
> *"Yes, Dad, I hear you. I'll be right there."*
> *"Mom, I'm saying good-bye to my friend. Can I come in a minute?"*

Children can be encouraged to respond this way while they are still young, each parent doing his bit.

> *Little Sari and her dad are sitting in the den. Sari is coloring. From the kitchen, Mommy's voice rings out, "Sari, I need you."*
> *Sari is engrossed in her crayons.*
> *Dad, who has heard his wife's call, says, "Sari, I hear Mommy calling you. Please put down your crayons and see what Mommy wants."*

An extension of answering promptly in person is responding to phone calls. When we know a parent is calling, it is proper to pick up.

Q I'm studying away from home this year. Lots of times, I'm in the middle of a casual phone conversation with a friend when I see my mother trying to call. Do I have to pick up?

A Answering your mother's call demonstrates your respect for her with words and is an aspect of *kavod b'dibbur*.

Q What if I'm on the phone with my grandmother? My principal? A doctor? A *shadchan*?

A What would your parent want you to do? "Their will is their honor."

MY FRIEND SHULA *buys interesting toys and books that she knows her children will enjoy, and then stores them away. She takes them out only for that special time when her mother calls. That way, the children are happy and entertained, and Shula gets a few quiet minutes with her mother.*

...by bringing joy[12]

When parents are dispirited — or really, any time — it is a mitzvah for children to cheer them up with good news, encouraging words, and other upbeat subjects.[13]

Just as a person needs food and sleep, he also needs joy.

When a child gladdens his parents, he is meeting a basic need, in the same vein as food and drink.[14] Therefore, when we tell our parents good news, happy news, our intention should be to fulfill the mitzvah of *kavod b'dibbur*.

"Hi, Dad. I know you'll be happy to hear the good news. That's why I'm rushing to tell you. They gave me that raise I was hoping for."

"Hi, Ma. I'm calling because Hindy just showed me her report card. I know you're going to be so proud of her."

WHEN I GOT MARRIED, *I envisioned that my life would be more or less a copy of the model my parents had provided.*

This model is what I dreamed of giving my own children.

The only thing is, Hashem had something else in store for us.

One year turned into five. Our arms were still longing to hold a child. We sought medical help, from which ensued a decade of unsuccessful treatments.

During this time, my mother (mostly at a distance of three thousand miles) lent me restrained and unobtrusive empathy. The situation was delicate. She didn't want to pry into our private affairs, yet at the same time, she didn't want to appear indifferent to our pain and anguish. The balance she maintained was perfect.

Then, without warning, a phone call brought distressing news. After being in remission for over twenty years from a life-threatening illness, my mother was re-diagnosed with a aggressive form of her disease. She immediately embarked on a new set of treatments and surgeries. Suddenly the distance between us was enormous.

Not long after this, a 3-week-old baby came up for adoption, and my husband and I became the fortunate ones offered to raise her as our own child. We accepted without hesitation. This meant, though, that I was not able to fly to be at my mother's side to give her the succor she richly deserved.

My mother fought valiantly against her illness for more years than her doctors predicted. Following five years of unpleasant, invasive procedures, my parents made a momentous decision.

They surprised us by buying a house right near ours.

Now my mother, though riddled with pain and discomfort, could see her (by-now) two adopted grandchildren up close, kiss and cuddle them, and even play with them for short periods.

Sadly, as time went on, these occasions became fewer and further between. The pain my mother often suffered was awful to bear, and the side effects of some of her medications caused her distress and indignity.

In the midst of the turmoil, after seventeen years of marriage, tests showed that we were awaiting a simchah! I knew immediately that this was an answer to my prayers in more ways than one. For in fact, Hashem blessed me doubly. I was given a long-awaited gift just at the time I could present it to my mother.

I could hardly contain myself as I rushed to my mother's side.

"Mommy, I want to give you a wonderful piece of news. Something you've been waiting to hear for a very long time — I want you to be the first to know."

Because this was so unexpected, my mother had no idea
what I was about to say.
My heart was racing as I told her the awesome tidings.
With tears in her eyes, my mother pulled me close to her in
a tight embrace. I heard her unspoken words: "You've given
me a reason to live."

"I want you to be the first to know" — what a powerful
sentence to say to anyone. But saying it to a parent becomes the
mitzvah of bringing them joy.

...by greetings and farewells

A greeting is a form of recognition, a way to express *kavod*
b'dibbur. Not greeting someone, ignoring a person's presence,
diminishes his status. Imagine walking into your boss' office
and then ignoring him!

When a child lives at home, it is a gesture of respect for him
to say hello to his parents when he returns home. It is likewise
proper for him to say good-bye when he leaves. A son or daughter
should not leave home without telling his parents he's leaving.

He [Elisha] left the oxen and ran after Eliyahu, and
said, "Please let me kiss my father and mother, and
then I shall go after you."[15]

The Ralbag comments:[16] One should not leave his parents'
home without letting them know. To be uninformed of a child's
departure and whereabouts is worrisome. We learn this from
Elisha. Despite Elisha's strong desire to follow Eliyahu, he was
moved to return to his father and mother to kiss them, to tell
them of his plans, and to bid them farewell.

...by asking for a blessing

When Eisav heard that his father had blessed Yaakov in his
stead, he cried bitterly. The *Midrash* says that all the dominion
that is enjoyed by Eisav's descendants is the result of the fact

that Eisav valued his father's blessing to the extent that he cried out a great and bitter cry when saying, "Father, please bless me as well!"[17]

From here, we learn how much a son or daughter should desire a parent's blessing.

What is so important about a parent's blessing?

The strength of a blessing depends on the intent. A blessing from parents is given with wholehearted intent. Who wants our success more than our parents?[18]

Additionally, we ask for a blessing only from someone we respect, someone we feel is worthy of giving a blessing. By asking our parents to bless us, this is the message we are sending.

"I'm starting a new job this week. Your blessing would mean a lot to me."

"Mom, tomorrow is my interview/driving test/big presentation. I sure could use your berachah."

The traditional time for blessing children is Leil Shabbos and Erev Yom Kippur.[19] There is a special prayer text for each.*

WHEN MY GRANDPARENTS were no longer able to look after themselves, they came to live with us. We learned many things from Opa and Oma. They were from Germany, and brought their minhagim with them.

On the first Shabbos, our father and we, the grandchildren, watched as Mommy went over to Opa and lowered her head. Opa lifted his hands and proceeded to bless her.

My father was from Russia, and his family didn't have this custom. After watching this moving scene, my father decided that he would make this his custom also. Not only he, but my mother as well, offered my sisters and me the traditional blessing that Hashem make us like the Matriarchs.

It's now many decades later. My father is gone. My mother is living in a wonderful facility in London.

Once, on a quiet evening, I was thinking of the blessings my mother always gave me Leil Shabbos, and how much I miss them.

---

* These blessings can be found in the *siddur* and *machzor*.

Why not ask her for a blessing when I call to wish her a good Shabbos? *I thought.* Couldn't she do that on the phone?

When I called the next time, I told my mother my idea. She listened and then said quietly, "Thank you so much for asking." I realized that I wasn't the only one who missed that weekly ritual.

Recently, I visited *my mother in England and spent a Shabbos with her.*

When my visit was over, and my bags all packed for my trip back home, I asked my mother if she would bentch *me. I bent my head, and my mother raised her hands and recited lovingly, "May Hashem make you like Sarah, Rivkah, Rochel, and Leah."*

Every word was so precious. One never knows how many more times I will feel my mother's hands and merit to receive her blessing.

...by giving parents a blessing

It is an accepted custom to say a blessing for the welfare of one's parents in *Bircas HaMazon.* Every time we sit down to a meal with bread, we have a chance to ask Hashem to shower our parents with blessing.

If we are at home, we say: הָרַחֲמָן הוּא יְבָרֵךְ אֶת אָבִי מוֹרִי בַּעַל הַבַּיִת הַזֶּה וְאֶת אִמִּי מוֹרָתִי בַּעֲלַת הַבַּיִת הַזֶּה... — "May Hashem, in His compassion, bless my father, my teacher, the master of this house, and my mother, my teacher, the woman of the house..."

After any meal, no matter where we are, we can beseech Hashem for our parents' welfare. In that case, "master of the house, woman of the house" is deleted.

The *MiSheberach* prayer offers another opportunity to bless one's parents in a special way.

The custom of blessing those who are given the honor to read from the Torah, called a *MiSheberach,* is centuries old. The blessing includes a prayer for the one who is called up to the

Torah, the congregation, and certain individuals, such as people who are ill, new mothers and their newborn infants, parents and other relatives. The concept behind the *MiSheberach* prayer is that the merit of the Torah reading is a source of blessing.

> **IN MY FRIEND** *R' Yehuda Aryeh's minyan, where I also daven, they sell the* aliyos *on Yom Tov to help cover the expenses of maintaining the minyan.*
>
> *Every Yom Tov without fail, R' Yehuda Aryeh buys an* aliyah, *even if the bidding is very steep. I know that he is not a man of means, so once when we were walking home together, I asked him about this rather costly custom of his.*
>
> *"I buy an* aliyah *on Yom Tov to say a* MiSheberach *for my parents,"* he answered. *"You know, on Yom Tov, there is an addition to the usual text of the* MiSheberach. *We add* וְיִזְכֶּה לַעֲלוֹת לָרֶגֶל, *'May he be privileged to ascend to Jerusalem for the pilgrimage [together with all Israel].' I'm not going to miss a chance to* bentch *my parents that they greet Mashiach."*

...by requesting and not demanding

When children are young and dependent, it is a parent's responsibility and (mostly) pleasure to provide for them, while encouraging "please's" and "thank you's." Even at a young age, children can learn that "Make me pizza," and "You have to sew on this button for me by tomorrow," are not the way to ask.

As children grow and become more independent, they still have needs. And the requests continue to tumble in. However, a request should remain just that, **a request and not a demand.** * Though a parent willingly performs services similar to those of paid help (maid, butler, laundress, tutor, chauffeur), sons and daughters shouldn't give the impression that they view parents as being *obligated* to serve them.

---

* *Sefer Chassidim, Se'if* 562, and *Otzar Kibbud Av Va'eim* 693 quoting Rav Chaim Kanievsky in *Sefer Ben Chacham*: שהרי האמא רוצה שהבן יבקש ממנה מה שחסר לו, If a son or daughter knows that for his parent, it will be a pleasure to help and a *tza'ar* if they knew you were refraining from asking, it is certainly permitted to ask, as long as it is a request, not a demand.

Minimal courtesy requires a please and a thank you, could you, would you. As opposed to: "I have to be at practice at four o'clock." It is as if the child is saying, "Now it's your problem, Ma."

No demanding and certainly no threatening: "I'm not going to school until I have a new briefcase."

Even better is to phrase the request in a way that acknowledges that we only want our parent to do this favor **if it is okay with them**.[20]

> *"Would it be too hard for you to...?"*
> *"Is it a good time for you to...?"*
> *"Would it fit into your schedule...?"*

"Can I do this myself?"

When children are young, they must be served and serviced. As soon as this is no longer necessary and children become more self-sufficient, a son or daughter should ask himself, **"Can I do this myself?"**

Take mealtime, for example:

> *"Ma, there's no ketchup. And while you're there, there's no mustard."*
> *"There are no knives on the table."*
> *"Any salt around?"*
> *"I didn't get a glass."*

Some parents prefer to serve while everyone else remains seated. Respect their preference. But if your mother would appreciate your help — then get up and get it yourself.

Sometimes it's a pleasure, and sometimes it's not

Generally, parents want to do favors for children if they can, even after their children are married. Empty nesters especially may be more than happy to be helpful. When we know that it is their pleasure, then asking a favor of parents is actually fulfilling the mitzvah of *kibbud av va'eim*.

But what if a parent can't or doesn't want to do that favor? When we make a request, are we listening for hesitation? Does it matter to us that our parents are hemming and hawing? Are we considering if this is in our parents' best interests? Do we persist despite their hesitation?

> *"I'll be over in a half hour. I have a few errands to run, so I'm dropping off the kids."*
>
> *"We're going on vacation, so I need you to water the plants and bring in the mail."*

Once again, *Chazal* reveal to us another principle that helps crystallize the proper approach to the parent-child relationship. Once a son or daughter is able to care for his/her own needs, "it is considered a *'chutzpah'* to request an errand or other service of a parent"[21] **unless the child knows that the parent wants to be asked**.

> **MY SON, HILLEL,** and daughter-in-law, Zahava, wanted to travel cross-country for Zahava's sister's wedding. They asked me if I would watch Shimmy, their 2-year-old. Though I am usually an available bubby and enjoy this job, this time I felt I wasn't up to it. I explained to them that I was having strong back pains, so caring for a lively 2-year-old wasn't going to be possible.
>
> "Ma, I'm sure it will be fine," Hillel answered. "We really don't have a choice. You know we have to be at this wedding."
>
> "I understand," I said. "But can't you just fly up and back? Why does this have to be for a week?"
>
> "Well, we get a better price on the ticket, and this gives Zahava a chance to be with her family for the whole celebration."
>
> I tried to explain my difficulty, but Hillel wasn't hearing.
>
> "I know this is a big favor, Ma, and I really wouldn't ask, but now I'm stuck. And besides, only a bubby can care for our Shimmy the way we like."

How fortunate we are to have this built-in alarm clock. Halachah rings! "Wake up, sons and daughters! Look around! **It's not *only* about you and your needs**. There's someone else involved here: your parents. Do they *want* to do this favor? Can they do it physically? Can they do it financially?" This is one of the many halachos that move us toward greater sensitivity to the needs of others.

It's nice to be nice to everyone — "please's," "thank you's," "could you's," and the like — but a request to a parent has a trademark that's patented, legally registered and owed to a father and mother. A trademark is defined as: "A word pointing distinctly to the origin or ownership of merchandise...legally reserved for the exclusive use of the owner as maker."

It's something more than the generic "please" we offer to anyone and everyone. It's against the law (read: halachah) to demand, command, or boss a parent around. How much more so in front of others.*

...by asking for advice

The Torah tells us that Shimon and Levi undertook a rash act without consulting their father, Yaakov Avinu. They acted, says Rashi, "like strangers" rather than sons, who, out of respect, should and would confer with their father, especially since their actions directly affected their father.[22]

Even in matters not relevant to a parent, when we ask their advice, it is a statement that their opinion is valuable to us.

Parents have more life experience than their offspring. When you avail yourself of it, you may get a benefit for yourself, but one thing is for sure: you are fulfilling the mitzvah of honoring with words.

...and reporting back

A continuation of this theme is letting parents know how helpful and appreciated their input — recommendations and advice — has been for us.

"Dad, I had to make a hiring decision at work. I thought about the advice you gave me when this type of issue came up a few

---

* See endnote 6 in Chapter 7: "Rise to the Occasion" for a discussion of certain halachos whose purpose is that onlookers should not think that we are compromising the respect due a parent.

months ago. I ran with it. You'll be happy to know that my boss gave his full approval."

This is *kavod b'dibbur*.

...by giving credit where credit is due

MY FATHER GOES to physical therapy every day, and I go with him. He likes the therapist very much. Once, my father said to him, "You know, Roger, you are such a nice person." Without blinking, Roger responded, "That's because I have nice parents."

Plenty of people are where they are largely because of their parents, though few *instinctively* credit their father and mother for this.

WHEN PEOPLE COMPLIMENT my Shabbos food, I always say the truth: "I come from a long line of good cooks."

YESTERDAY, MY SISTER Tzivia called me.
"You know, Dassi, I recently went to a class on nutrition, and I didn't learn one thing. You know why?"
"I think I can guess."
"Everything they said, Mommy has been telling us for years. She was so ahead of her time. All the great food we give our kids is really to her credit."
"You know what I'm thinking?"
"What?"
"Why don't we call to tell her?"

Yes, why *don't* we call to tell?

Quote, unquote

When we quote our parents or speak about them in a way that makes people feel they are wise or insightful, causing them to be respected, that is *kavod b'dibbur*.

My mother/father always says...

"THE AX FORGETS, but the tree remembers."
How many times did I hear that growing up! Our mother

instilled in us an unusual concern for the feelings of others, which, by the way, she learned from her *mother. Now my children hear this from me. If I ever see them tease each other, they know that they are going to be reminded about Bubby's tree. This is a family tradition.*

WHEN WE KIDS *complained that we weren't getting "enough of...whatever," our father would invariably remind us that his father always used to say, "I complained because I had no shoes until I saw a man who had no feet." That was enough to cool us down.*

That was only one of the many words of wisdom my father told us from Zeidy. Zeidy lived far away, but was a constant presence in our lives.

At what point do we make the shift from being a "taker" to a "giver"? When do we flip from being almost exclusively on the receiving end of a relationship, showered with the largesse of parents, to becoming a giver, a bestower of benefit, a provider of kindnesses?

The change doesn't happen suddenly. It starts when we're young, when we learn that we are obliged to answer when we're called, to greet our parents when we come home and to say good-bye when we leave, to approach with requests and not demands, and to give credit where credit is due.

This mitzvah takes us by the hand and leads us out of our cocoons of childish egocentricity, shows us how to shed our toddler mentality — the "me, me, me" — to adjust our focus from inward to outward.

It's a slow shift in gears, smoothed by the mitzvah of *kibbud av va'eim.*

Chapter 13

"And His Name Shall Be Called..."

I WAS SITTING AT A TABLE WITH TWO OTHER WOMEN in the mother-child convalescent home, enjoying the relaxed atmosphere, caring service, and the generous portions of nutritious food.

Shifra, Devorah, and I were chatting when in walked Chaya, another kimpeturin. She stood at the doorway looking for an empty seat, and then chose our table.

"Do you want to hear a chutzpah?" she said as an opener.

Before we could answer, she forged on. "My mother-in-law just called to ask if I would name my baby after her father. Since he died, only girls were born in the family, so no one has been given his name. Isn't that a chutzpah?"

Shifra looked like she wasn't following. "Why is that a chutzpah?"

Chaya didn't bother to answer. "Want to hear another chutzpah?"

"Not really," Devorah said. "Can you please pass me the juice?"

> *Too worked up even to hear, Chaya went on. "Ten minutes later, my husband's grandmother called to ask if I would give the name for her husband, that same grandfather. She says she wants to give a Kiddush cup to whoever gives the name, and wants to know if we'll consider. What nerve!"*
>
> *"What's the matter?" I asked. "Don't you like the name?"*
>
> *"No, the name's okay. It's Chaim. It's a nice name."*
>
> *"Don't you want to do this for your husband?" Shifra asked. "After all, it's his grandfather, and it would make his mother happy. Wouldn't it be* kibbud eim*?"*
>
> *"The name is none of their business, and it's a* chutzpah *to even suggest it —"*
>
> *"But they only asked," interrupted Shifra.*
>
> *Disregarding the comment, Chaya continued, "I told my husband to tell his family that this is our baby. Why should they feel they have any say in his name?"*
>
> *"Is it the controlling issue that's getting you?" I asked.*
>
> *"A better word is 'butting in where they do not belong.' This is our baby. Period."*
>
> *Just then, Devorah knocked over her glass of juice, and the topic changed from names to stains.*
>
> *The next day found the four of us sharing the same table.*
>
> *"Mazel tov!" we called out to Chaya as she walked in. The bris had been that morning.*
>
> *"Nu, what's the name?" we wanted to know.*
>
> *"Chaim."*
>
> *Our jaws dropped. But she said...*
>
> *"I told you I liked the name. I just wanted to make it clear that no one is going to decide for me."*

What do you think? Was Shifra right? Or is it out of bounds for parents to even suggest a name, as Chaya felt?

Naming a child is no small matter, for a person's name has a deep and powerful connection to his very essence,[1] his soul — and his destiny.[2] For this reason, our Sages encourage us to choose the name of a righteous individual,[3] linking our child to the sanctity and noble deeds of that elevated person. In fact, this is one of the first acts of kindness a parent can do for his child.

Many considerations can go into choosing a name. One significant and time-honored choice is to name a child after a family member.

The *Midrash* tells us that our ancestors didn't name for grandparents, since people lived longer lives, several generations alive at the same time. But we, who don't want to forget from whom we descend, choose names from our forefathers."[4]

❖ In naming our children for ancestors, we remember former generations and declare their value and importance to us, confirming our desire to add links to this lineage.

❖ We are told that giving a name for a departed relative is a benefit for the departed and a remembrance from generation to generation.[5]

❖ We name for grandparents because of the gratitude we owe them for their share in our lives. After all, we are in the world because of them. If we, their descendants, don't choose to name for them, who else will give this benefit to their *neshamos*?

❖ One of the most important reasons to name for an ancestor is to fulfill the mitzvah of honoring parents.

In Sephardic communities, it is an honor for living parents to have grandchildren named for them. In doing so, the child gives his parent pleasure, honor, and glory.[6]

> **BOTH SETS OF PARENTS** *were delighted about our first baby's imminent arrival and flew in from the States to be with us.*
>
> *When our baby was born and it was a boy, it added to the* simchah *that both grandfathers and grandmothers would be at the* brit. *The baby was being named for my father-in-law, who would be the* sandak.
>
> *As it turned out, because of health issues, the* brit *was delayed. What a disappointment to those who had flown in, especially my father-in-law, who wasn't able to stay longer, due to business obligations.*
>
> *At the* brit, *when everyone strained to hear the name,*

many of the women approached me with mazel tov *wishes and the usual question, "Who is he named after?"*

"My husband's father," I answered. "He so much wanted to be here, but it just didn't work out."

I received strange glances from some of my guests. To make it clearer, or so I thought, I added, "He had to get back because of his business."

As a girl born into the Syrian Jewish community in New York, I grew up knowing that a couple's first two boys and first two girls would be named after their two sets of grandparents. It was, as we say, "a given." No questions asked.

The brit *of my first two sons brought no surprises. The first boy is named after the baby's grandfather on the father's side, and the next son is given the name of his mother's father. Ditto for the girls. No, it doesn't matter if the grandparents are alive or not. In fact, this is considered Grandma and Grandpa's real* nachat, *hearing one's children calling their sons and daughters by their own names.*

When we moved to Israel, soon after our sheva brachot, *I began to meet more Ashkenazi families. It took time, however, for me to learn their customs and traditions, many of which I was unaware. I didn't know that a baby was named only after someone who had passed away. I was so surprised! And… so were they.*

When I explain to them that naming after the living is a strong expression of kibbud av va'eim, *I understand that for some this is a new idea.*

Now that I am blessed to have grandchildren, I appreciate our custom even more. I consider it a zechut *that my children continue this* minhag *by naming their children after my husband and myself.*

In Ashkenazi communities, to name a baby after one's deceased parents is fulfilling the mitzvah of *kibbud av va'eim* posthumously (מְכַבְּדָם בְּמוֹתוֹ). To name after a parent's parent or other relative is an honor for one's living parents (מְכַבְּדָם בְּחַיָּיו).

If we name a child for an ancestor, we give pleasure to our parents, and perform a kindness for the *neshamah* of the namesake.[7]

Rav Binyamin Zilber in *Oz Nidbaru* writes:[8]

Though we have many sources that say it is correct to name for a tzaddik or for the parent's rebbe who taught him Torah, nonetheless one should not push away the *zechus* of being able to name for deceased parents who were upright in their ways, even though there are people more virtuous, since this is considered an honor to parents (מְכַבְּדוֹ בְּמוֹתוֹ).

How much more so if our living parents themselves are asking us to name for their parents! Don't be a pious fool (חָסִיד שׁוֹטֶה) to refuse this request, because you are missing out on the fulfillment of a mitzvah of the Torah of honoring one's father and mother (מְכַבְּדוֹ בְּחַיָּיו).

For this mitzvah we are promised an extra measure of success, which includes the spiritual success of children.

REB YOSEF HEARD the first wails of his newborn daughter. Coming after three boys, he knew his wife would be ecstatic, and he no less.

This time, the name wasn't up for discussion. They were all waiting to honor their beloved grandmother who had recently passed away.

When he called his mother to give her the good news, Reb Yosef was in for a big surprise.

The grandmother's name was Sarah, and Sarah would surely be the name given. But Reb Yosef's mother strongly suggested that they add a second name.

"One day, Yosef," she said, "you will be looking for a shidduch for this daughter. Sarah is such a common name that you might easily have to refuse a wonderful shidduch because the future mother-in-law's name is the same. If you give the baby two names, there will be much less chance of this happening."

Reb Yosef said nothing to his mother, but he was very unhappy with this suggestion. As far as he was concerned, such a far-fetched problem was not a valid reason for adding a second name.

However, he did not want to upset his mother. He decided to ask his Rosh Yeshivah, Rav Yitzchak Hutner zt"l, and this was the answer he received: "You are 100 percent right. That's not a reason to add a name. But if you can stick a kibbud eim into your daughter's name, that will surely be a big zechus for her."

In addition to the above guidelines, we have community traditions that help keep the naming of a baby a peaceful event. In some communities, the custom is for the father to name the first child, the mother the second, and to alternate for subsequent children. In other communities, the mother picks the first child's name, in recognition of her efforts in bringing children into the world, and then they alternate. Of course, either spouse may give up "his turn" for appropriate reasons and for the sake of peace.

That said, the preferable way to choose a name, no matter whose turn it is, is *together*. Even if we are not prophets, and even if we don't have *ruach hakodesh*, every parent has unique *siyata d'Shmaya*[9] when naming a baby. Knowing the mission given to this *neshamah*, the Creator puts into a parent's heart the desire for a particular name, one that seems "just right," an appropriate name, one that expresses the *neshamah's* essence.

This being so, couples may still turn to their Rav or Rebbe to help them make a decision on a baby's name. For example, they may bring these considerations to his attention: "We have a good feeling about the name _____." "Grandma is insistent on the name _____." "It's the *yahrtzeit* of the *tzaddik* _____." "The baby was born on Purim, so we thought he should be named Mordechai." The Rav, who understands priorities in the Torah, can help the parents understand which issues take precedence. With that in mind, the parents can then make the best possible decision.

Questions are bound to arise in the process of naming a child. We do not have to decide them for ourselves. All questions such as those that follow should be discussed with *daas Torah*.

❖ My parents asked us to name the baby after my uncle, who passed away at a young age. My wife and I are worried about doing this.

❖ My father wanted us to name the baby Baruch, after his father. Surprise! It's a girl. Can the name be Bracha? Is that considered naming for the grandfather?

❖ My father-in-law wants us to name our son after his brother, who had two names. It's not our style. Can we just use one? Is that considered naming for that person?

❖ My mother wants us to name for a relative who had a difficult life. We'd rather not. What should we do?

❖ A close relative on my husband's side passed away recently, and my father passed away several years ago. I know my mother would be devastated if we don't give my father's name. What's the right thing to do?

The Chazon Ish writes that one should not give a child an unusual name that would be difficult for him to live with. To consider: Can the name be changed slightly? Will the parents be satisfied giving it as a middle name?

> *MY DEAR BUBBY* *had a name that most people in our circles would not choose. My father sort of took it for granted that all his children would give the name of his beloved mother and use it as a first name. We children didn't have the heart to disappoint him.*
>
> *We all managed to get around this name in different ways. My wife and I worked out a shortened version of Bubby's name that is acceptable to everyone. It sounds similar, and it's the name our daughter will use except on official documents.*

------◆------

The grandparents of a newborn often want to honor their own parents by having that name given to descendants, both as a remembrance and because it is a merit to the *neshamah* of the deceased. It would actually be unnatural and uncaring for them not to have a preference.

However, at the moment of a baby's naming, when we want to thank Hashem for His great goodness, we don't want to cause our children pain and create dissension. We certainly are not giving a benefit to the *neshamah* of the *deceased* if there is *machlokes* (dissension) involved.

> *TO MY DEAR BROTHER,*
> *I'd like to put in writing some of the thoughts that have been going through my mind this past year.*
> *Don't think that the whole family takes for granted the*

way you took care of Mommy and Daddy the last years of their lives. We all witnessed the efforts you and Malki put into having them move in with you, and the daily, loving attention you gave them for years. We know it was no easy thing, especially with children still at home.

At your grandson's bris, I saw your stricken look when Benny didn't give the baby Daddy's name. Believe me, I fully understand how devastated and hurt you were. It was surprising to me too.

We spoke to Benny about this at length. He had no intention to hurt you.

Unfortunately, what was already done can't be undone. But life must go on.

You've got a beautiful family, a family to be proud of. I'm begging you not to let this ruin what you have (and what you worked hard to achieve).

Think a minute, Dave. Didn't we all do things to Daddy and Mommy that hurt them?

Benny is still your son. Maybe he made a mistake, but you are making one too.

For the sake of Daddy's neshamah, *for the sake of those still living — Mommy and the rest of our family — try to find a way past this. Let's count our blessings, and look at how much Hashem has done for us. You know Daddy would want us to make peace, as he always did.*

Shimmy

If this father only realized the disservice he is doing to his deceased father, the harm that is brought through *machlokes* he insists on fueling, if he could picture the *yetzer hara's* glee.

If someone would just tell him…

Arguing about the name is not a good omen for the baby.[10] In fact, a *machlokes* is not a good omen for anyone. The Torah places a high premium on peace and warns about the evils of *machlokes*. The Rambam tells us that though our Sages have spoken at length concerning the evil of dissension, its destructive force can never be adequately described.[11]

We are fortunate that when opinions differ, halachah and *minhag* guide us to peaceful solutions.

This telegram was sent by Rabbi and Rebbetzin Eliyahu Dessler (the *Michtav MeEliyahu*) upon the occasion of the birth of a grandson born to their son, Rav Nochum Zev Dessler (Dean of the Hebrew Academy of Cleveland). Note the sensitivity: "with dearest Miriam's permission" (Miriam is their daughter-in-law), and "would propose" — though Rav Reuven Dov Dessler, his father, was as yet "unnamed for thirteen years"!

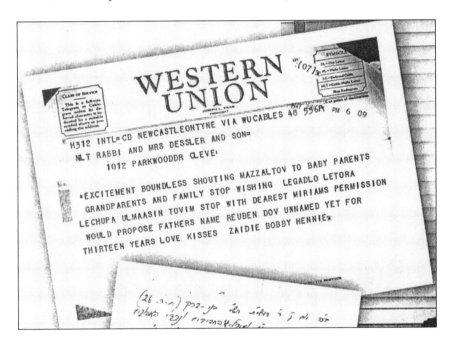

Just as our livelihood is decided on Rosh Hashanah yet we must still make an effort for our sustenance, so too it is with baby naming. It is Hashem's will that we make an effort to find the proper name for our child. Therefore, it is fitting to daven to Hashem for success in this undertaking.

A name has the potential to influence a person's ability to serve Hashem in holiness. Therefore, we ask of *HaKadosh Baruch Hu*: May it be Your will that the name I choose be pleasing to You, *Ribbono shel Olam*, and beneficial to the newborn child.[12]

Honor
In Thought

Chapter 14

Getting to the Heart of the Matter

In addition to honoring parents in deed (*ma'aseh*) and with speech (*dibbur*), there is a third aspect to honor: honoring parents with our thoughts (*machshavah*). A proper attitude not only completes the mitzvah, but is, in fact, the crux of *kibbud av va'eim*.

The way we speak to parents and the way we behave is an expression of our heart — how we feel inwardly. One cannot expect his words and actions to be proper if his attitude to his parents is one of disrespect and belittling (*zilzul*). Our attitude directs our behavior. Our attitude forms our words.[1]

Improve your vision

The *Zohar HaKadosh* tells us that each of the 248 positive mitzvos correspond to a limb of the human body. *Kibbud av va'eim* corresponds to the eyes. At the heart of *kibbud av va'eim* is how we "see" our parents.[2]

Kibbud, honor, is from the root *kaf-beis-dalet* (כבד), which means "weighty." We are to consider the weightiness, that is, the strengths, of the ones being honored, our parents.

Honoring in thought means making the effort to see our parents as people of stature (בַּעֲלֵי מַעֲלָה), because a person of stature is treated differently. Even if a parent holds no communal position, receives no public recognition, it is a child's job to discover and then concentrate on his virtues and even his uniqueness.

WHEN MY PARENTS came to live with us, I was delighted with the added bonuses that came along with the territory.

For starters, my parents have wonderful Torah values. In my youth, I learned many of these values and was able to internalize them. But there were still plenty that had fallen by the wayside. With my parents living in close proximity, I was able to have "a second chance."

In all honesty, this second chance worked easily for only some of my parents' values. Though we are taught to put our parents on a pedestal, it's not easy. It's natural to look at the clay feet and fail to focus on the good.

But Hashem was kind to me, and the second chance was not lost. He sent me people who did not carry with them the same baggage I did, and so were free to see my parents with fresh eyes.

I'm talking about the aides and volunteers who helped me with my parents' needs, and after my father's passing, with my mother's needs.

I searched carefully for the right people. The two most important qualifications were that they be responsible and capable. The third most important trait for me was that the person would like my mother, appreciate her, and enjoy talking with her. I managed to find caregivers who met these criteria.

Over the months, they got to know my mother. From time to time, they would share with me some of their observations.

Here they were, people who had only recently become acquainted with my mother, yet they opened my eyes to things I had missed or dismissed.

Here is what one of the caregivers wrote in her goodbye letter. Emphasis mine:

"It has been such a privilege to spend time with your

*mother. She is **smart** and **funny** and **kind**. She is **grateful** and* **positive**. *She is so much* **fun to be with**, *and she really has become a* **role model** *for me. She has an amazing* **relationship with Hashem**, *an outstanding* **devotion to her family**, *and an* **expectation for herself** *that is beyond compare."*

Of these ten attributes I highlighted, three were new to me. What an eye-opener — and this is only from one person!

Shlomo HaMelech tells us that "foolish people look to condemn, while upright people are satisfied" (*Mishlei* 14:9). Why are the upright satisfied? Rabbeinu Yonah explains that they are satisfied because they downplay the negative and concentrate on the assets in any person and the good in any situation.[3]

If we notice a negative trait in a person, our tendency is to invalidate that person and overlook any good. This works to our disadvantage, because when we get bogged down on a shortcoming, we lose the benefit of all the strengths.

In one of his famous Thursday-night talks, Harav Avigdor Miller, *ztz"l*, gives us this suggestion to develop a good eye:

> Choose someone with whom you feel you would like to improve your attitude. Now, when you are on a break from your working or learning…work on discovering the strengths of that person. For example: "Moshe is always the first to say hello." "Berel is always on time." "Chaim never makes personal calls."
>
> This is especially effective if the person has strengths that we are lacking. Give Moshe a week of *ayin tovah*, and soon, we will begin associating Moshe with his strengths, rather than dwelling on the negative, which we did until now.
>
> This is called developing *ayin tovah*, a good eye.

When do we start? When we are young, by developing a good eye for our parents, looking for reasons to be satisfied.

I HAD THE MOST AMAZING experience.

I am having a difficult time getting along with my father. I know it's partly my fault. I spoke with my guidance counselor, Mrs. Schiff. After listening patiently to my tirade, she suggested that I tell her some of the things I admire about my father. I answered that I don't admire anything.

Her eyebrows shot up. "Nothing?"

"No," I answered bluntly. "I can't think of one nice thing to say."

We sat in brooding silence for a few minutes.

Mrs. Schiff then asked me if I was willing to do a short exercise.

I couldn't imagine where she was going, but I accepted the pencil and paper she offered.

She explained that she would read to me a list of adjectives. If I thought that one of them described my dad, I should jot it down. She said she would read slowly, giving me time to think about each word.

Honestly, I was anticipating an empty page.

There were about two hundred words altogether. She started to read at a snail's pace.

It was harder than I thought. Sometimes a word caught me unaware — like when I heard courageous, ethical, reliable. It was as if I were shaken awake out of a deep sleep. Sometimes the pencil hit the paper — like when she said forgiving — and I was jolted by the surprising realization that it fit.

When she finished, I had thirty words I was sure about, and another ten maybes.

Mrs. Schiff told me that they were all virtues.

What could I say?

She said that this was a good beginning. She told me to go home and think about the things I had written. Next time we would have a lot to talk about.

Honoring in thought means looking for reasons to admire our parents despite their shortcomings — which they share with all humanity, us included. We should do this for all people, but for parents there is an extra obligation.

We tend to recognize as a virtue only something from which we benefit directly. In truth, though, parents may have many strengths that do not directly benefit their children. They are nonetheless positive attributes.

Developing the *middah* of *ayin tovah* toward parents, focusing on their unique strengths, was the goal of essays written by a group of seminary students. Here is a selection of their thoughts:

"I admire the way my father gives *tzedakah*. When someone knocks on the door for *tzedakah*, my father welcomes him in and sits him down in his office. My father then patiently listens to what he has to say, and then gives the *tzedakah*. Although he is a busy person, this interest he shows in their difficulties is what makes his mitzvah so special."

"When I have to bring my new clothing to a seamstress, my mother is very careful to remove all the tags. She says, 'The poor lady is working so hard to earn a few dollars. Why does she have to see how much you spend on your clothing?'

"My mother really looks out for other people and truly cares for their feelings. She will do anything not to cause someone pain."

"In my father's business, he goes out of his way to employ people with mental and physical challenges, giving them a sense of worth and purpose. Even if it would mean a loss or delay in output, my father feels the gain overrides."

"My parents act the way they know is right, even if it is something that not everyone does. They are very open to growth and improvement. If one of my siblings comes home from school having learned a halachah that we may not have kept so carefully at home, my parents will gladly implement it."

And comments:
"Thank you so much for giving me this assignment. As I started writing, I realized more and more *maalos*. It really made me realize how special my parents are."

"This was an incredible journey."

Judging favorably

Pirkei Avos teaches us, "Provide yourself with a teacher, acquire a friend, and judge everyone favorably."[4]

Whether it's an authority figure in your life such as a Rav, or a friend, colleague, neighbor, or business acquaintance, to keep that connection positive and lasting, it is vital to tap into the power of judging favorably. Parents, our first and foremost authority figures, should be recipients of our *limud zechus* (finding merit).

In addition, judging favorably is crucial to our success in fulfilling the mitzvah of honoring parents. In his *Sefer Vayevarech Dovid*, Rabbi Yisroel Dovid Harfenes writes:

> When a son or daughter has complaints about his parents' actions, he should invest serious effort to understand their point of view so that their worthiness is not diminished in his eyes. And while it is true that we must judge every person to the side of merit, our obligation to our parents is even greater.[5]

MY FATHER WAS A HARDWORKING, honest, and caring chartered accountant. He built up a successful business practice, which earned him a good reputation and a decent living. He ran his affairs with great efficiency and competence.

As a teenager who wanted to earn a bit of money during the summer vacation, I would go to my father's office, do the filing or man the phones, or sit in for a receptionist on sick leave and see how well my father managed his office and staff. Here was a man who knew how to get things done, and his competency was formidable.

After my mother passed on, it was now his turn to start visiting the health clinic and doctors and therapists, because his own health started to decline quite seriously.

One day, while I was visiting him at his apartment, he announced that he wanted me to reorganize his study. He also wanted me to help him do his tax returns.

After explaining which files he wanted me to extricate from his cabinet, he described a new type of folder — without rings or metal prongs. He wanted me to go out and buy them and then transfer all his papers to these new folders. My father's skin had become so thin and delicate that sometimes the slightest knock would cause bleeding. His present files were "lethal" in this regard.

Then he told me which books he wanted put on different shelves or taken to another room, and which papers needed copying ten times and placement in ten different folders, and who I should phone or e-mail or fax and get information from...

Okay. It was a tall order. But I dived in with the best intentions. I mean, I intended to do my best, but my father immediately got annoyed at my inefficiency. Why was I just standing there doing nothing? Why hadn't I started doing anything yet? Ten minutes later, why was I taking so long to get things done?

I didn't answer. I didn't try to defend myself. But I was bursting with feelings of outrage: Wait a minute! Haven't I just driven almost an hour to get here, like I did two days ago, and a week ago? What about all the other hours and days I have given you over the past year? What about how I sacrificed the pile of administration, laundry, shopping, and family-related chores I have to do at home, in order to help you?

Feelings of entitlement swept through me: I deserve to get a please and thank you for this, not discontent and lack of appreciation...and anger.

Feelings of humiliation followed: Why are you making me feel like I'm still your little girl, not a grown woman who's also competent? You know that I know how to run an office. Can't you give me some breathing space to work out what to do first without overwhelming me with continual instructions?

So far, these feelings of resentment were contained. A little more, and I was sure they would spill out.

I excused myself, claiming I had a quick errand and would be back in a few minutes. I drove my car around the block and parked it.

What's going on? I came here to help, and all I'm doing is getting aggravated. I took off the day from a hectic schedule to bring my father some happiness and to try to alleviate his pain, certainly not to cause him distress. I can't ruin this.

I continued sitting there in the car in brooding silence, with one sentence revolving in my mind: What is going on with my father?

Why was he so upset with me?

I was staring out the window, feeling I was at a dead end, when a thought leaped out at me. The way I'm going to make some headway is to stand where my father's standing and see how this looks.

With this new direction, a switch turned on in my mind, and a flood of thoughts surged into my brain.

How hurt must my father feel that he has to ask his daughter to do things he wished he could do himself! How humiliating must it be to have your daughter (not even trained in bookkeeping) enter your accounts when, once upon a time, all this was second nature to you?

Wouldn't my father love to reach up to the top shelf or crouch down to the bottom and remove a file? Wouldn't he prefer to type out letters, print them, fold the paper, insert them in envelopes, address them in his own handwriting, and take the stamped envelopes to the postbox himself?

At once, I appreciated my father's vulnerability, and a wave of empathy welled up inside me. My initial resentment and indignation dissipated, and I was ready to go back.

I found my father in the kitchen. I made myself a cup of coffee and joined him. I turned to my father and asked him patiently, "Daddy, it must be very frustrating watching me do something that you could have done so much more easily yourself a year ago. What would you like me to do first? Tell me exactly the order you would have done things, and I'll try and do it the same way."

Patiently and carefully we worked our way through the "To Do" list and the "How" list. I dedicated many hours, days, and visits to achieve this. It became an absolute privilege for me to do everything my father asked, and each time I had to take my leave, my father would look at me with a loving, grateful glance and proclaim, "You are an angel for being so kind and patient and understanding. I always look forward to your visits, and I love you so much."

One aspect of honor in speech (*kavod b'dibbur*) is making our parents look good in other people's eyes. Honoring in thought (*kavod b'machshavah*) is making them look good in *our own* eyes.

> MY FATHER IS THE TYPE *who goes around the block ten times to find a parking meter that still has time left in it. He and my mom mostly buy in thrift shops. My father can't understand why we would want to buy new appliances, new beds, or a new couch rather than looking for second-hand items.*
>
> *This approach is hard for some of my siblings and their spouses. As for me, well, the truth is I'm not at all like my father, but I understand him and where he is coming from, and because of this, I can avoid annoying him.*
>
> *Recently he offered to buy me a new suit and asked me how much it would cost. If I had told him even a low-end price, I know he'd have hit the roof. No store can compete with a thrift shop! So I just made up a price that I figured he could handle, and then I'd do the rest.*
>
> *I understand that my father isn't like most people. The best thing for all of us children is to accept his nature and appreciate the fact that despite his low income, he was able to lead a stable, responsible life, stay out of debt, and never ask anyone for help, only because he lived like this.*

Judging favorably: What is it, and what is it not?

Rav Alexander Ziskind, the *Yesod VeShoresh HaAvodah*, tells us that the mitzvah of judging favorably and the mitzvah of *v'ahavta l'reiacha kamocha*, love your fellow as yourself, are interdependent and intertwined.[6] When we truly love someone, we automatically, without any prompting, find ways to interpret his actions to "the side of merit."

This works in reverse as well: When we judge favorably, love is created or restored.

Seeing people in a favorable light is an act of humility, an admission that our perspective is just that — ours. It is a conscious decision not to allow one perspective to draw us into hasty conclusions.

Judging favorably means searching for acceptable reasons for behavior that is difficult for us to understand or accept — reasons that make sense to us and leave us with a more positive attitude.

❖ Maybe what he did wasn't really wrong.

❖ Maybe he knows something I don't and is acting for my benefit.

❖ Maybe I misunderstood what he meant.

❖ Because he wasn't successful, that doesn't mean he didn't try.

Finding merit (*limud zechus*) is like finding the missing pieces of a puzzle. Place them where they belong and the picture is complete, clear. And often beautiful.

Judging favorably is based on a willingness to see the best in others; to recognize their good qualities despite what we may perceive as shortcomings. Although we owe this to all people, we have an extra obligation to parents.

Judging favorably is *not* whitewashing wrong actions. Judging favorably does *not* mean living with apathy or resignation, nor should it hamper our efforts to help ourselves or others.

Judging favorably quells our anger and resentment. It is the antidote to *lashon hara*, and is the road toward a peaceful home. The tools of *limud zechus* may not always leave us completely at peace, but we can often ease our pain if we slip into our parents' shoes and consider their point of view.

The more we judge favorably, the less likely we are to speak against people — including, of course, our parents — or even to think ill of them, because the desire to understand a person and the choice to condemn him are mutually exclusive.

A journey back in time

Judging favorably might mean putting parents back into the perspective of the time in which they grew up, with the values that they and their peers shared. If we could read the story of their lives, see them growing up, puzzling pictures might become clear.

> **WHEN I TOLD MY MOTHER** that I was going to the graduation party of my daughter's kindergarten class, she started to carry on. "Dvora, you're a week after birth. In my day..." Then I got a big speech about women after birth. In her day, a woman after birth didn't go out of the house before...
>
> When I attempted to add "But Mom, all my friends go out after a week," it only elicited a second speech.
>
> I told myself, "Dvora, this is the way it was when Mommy was young. If you try to understand where she's coming from, you'll be able to deal with this much better."

Keep in mind — it is likely that one day our children might question things that *to us* are self-understood.

In their shoes

Pirkei Avos (2:5) gives us another strategy for judging favorably: "Don't judge your fellow until you reach his place."[7]

We grow up in our parents' homes, with their "policies," some of which generate no small amount of discontent. It may take years for a son or daughter to acknowledge their value, which often happens only when we reach "their place."

> **GROWING UP,** I was just like any other child, though my siblings will disagree and say that I'm "spoiled," being the baby of my family.
>
> My parents were always very supportive and loving. That's how I see it now, in the eyes of an adult and as a parent myself.
>
> But when I was growing up, I can't say that I always felt that way. My father has this "thing" that I thought was very annoying and unnecessary. He used to come to my school once a week to speak to my teachers, to see how I was doing. None of my friends' fathers ever did that. Some just about made it to the PTA — almost by force.

I remember when I was a kid it really bothered me. I was embarrassed and annoyed, as if I were always doing something wrong and always needed to be watched. Even though my teachers always told me how impressed they were and what an amazing thing it was, and how special of my father — my childish mind just wouldn't accept it.

It was only when I was older that I started appreciating and respecting the devotion and love that my father really has for me and the time he set aside to show it.

This devotion only grew when I was 14 and went to an out-of-town yeshivah. Then, about once a month my father had to schlep to come see how I was doing, always bringing with him a bag of goodies from home. That was on top of a weekly call to my rebbis and teachers. By the way, no matter what really happened, when my father called, he always told me that he got an amazing report.

It's only now that my kids are enrolled in school that I really appreciate what my father did. Especially seeing how time consuming it is and the reaction I get from the teachers when I come. "Is this your only child?" Or like, "Wow, this is real caring." Or even a few weeks into the school year, I was told, "You are the first parent in this class to ask about your child this year."

It's only when I got older that I realized there's a lot more behind our parents' behavior. It's called love.

Judging favorably is a broad subject. We've touched on only a few of the many successful strategies our Sages have given us. Additional ideas can be found in *The Other Side of the Story: Giving People the Benefit of the Doubt — Stories and Strategies* (ArtScroll/Mesorah).

Judging favorably is the foundation that will enable us to fulfill the mitzvah of *kibbud av va'eim* in its fullest form.

Chapter 15

Must We Love Our Parents?

"**Honor** your father and your mother" is universally quoted and colloquially used as an umbrella term under which a multitude of filial responsibilities are clustered.

Less quoted is the other major Torah obligation: "**Revere** your mother and father."

Honor and reverence. But does it say anywhere in our tradition that a child is required to **love** his parents?

The first question is, what *is* love?

In the *Midrash* (*Sifra, Kedoshim*) we are told that Rabbi Akiva said: "Love your fellow as you love yourself" — this is a fundamental principle of our Torah.[1]

How do our Sages explain this love, this *ahavah*?

> The Rambam writes: It is a mitzvah incumbent upon every person to love each and every one of his fellow Jews as he loves himself. Therefore, he must speak well of others and be concerned about their material well-being, just as we care about our own material well-being and want people to respect us.[2]

Here, the Rambam is saying that "to love" someone entails being concerned about his concerns: (1) Speaking well of him — guarding his reputation; (2) looking out for/showing respect for his property and possessions.

The Gemara tells us succinctly: ...what is hateful to you, do not do to others.[3]

The *Sefer Chareidim* tells us: He should want another person to be honored just as he wants to be honored. His love and compassion for another should be like his love and compassion for himself. He should seek [the other person's] benefit, rejoice in his good fortune, and share the pain when he is in pain.[4]

These classic sources teach us that "love" is principally used as a verb, meaning to care about the well-being and success of others, and to take action to ensure this outcome. Our Torah gives us a way to measure the extent of the love/caring we are obligated to give others. The key word is כָּמוֹךָ, the kind of caring and concern we want for ourselves.

All of these sentiments and benevolent behavior — love! — should be applied to parents.

The Chayei Adam gives three reasons why sons and daughters are obligated not only in honor and in reverence, but also obligated in *ahavah*.[5]

REASON #1

פְּשִׁיטָא שֶׁצָּרִיךְ לְאַהֲבָה אוֹתָם כְּגוּפוֹ שֶׁהֲרֵי הוּא בִּכְלַל וְאָהַבְתָּ לְרֵעֲךָ כָּמוֹךָ

We are commanded *v'ahavta lereiacha kamocha*, to love others as we love ourselves. Parents are included in this mitzvah.

REASON #2

אֶלָּא שֶׁבְּאָבִיו וְאִמּוֹ הוּקְשָׁה אַהֲבָתָם לְאַהֲבַת הַמָּקוֹם

Our obligation to love our parents is
likened to our obligation to love Hashem.[6]

Parents are singled out and elevated to an awesome pinnacle;
we see that *HaKadosh Baruch Hu* has equated their honor and
reverence with His own.

While we must express love and concern for everyone, love
and concern for parents should be even greater.

REASON #3

דְּכָל מִצְוֹת הַבֵּן עַל הָאָב וָאֵם, הוּא פֵּרְעוֹן חוֹב שֶׁהַבֵּן
חַיָּיב לִפְרוֹע לְאָבִיו וּלְאִמּוֹ הַטּוֹבוֹת שֶׁגְּמָלוּהוּ ...
בִּכְלַל הַפֵּרְעוֹן שֶׁיֹּאהַב אוֹתָם אַהֲבָה עַזָּה כְּדֶרֶךְ
שֶׁהָיוּ אוֹהֲבִים אוֹתוֹ וְלֹא יִהְיוּ עָלָיו לְטוֹרַח וּלְמַשָּׂא

The mitzvah of *kibbud av va'eim* of a child
to his parents is considered repayment of
a debt for all the good our parents did for
us ... included in this repayment is to love
them deeply, as they loved us, and not to
consider them an unwelcome burden...

Here is what some "children" had to say, when asked to
imagine a letter they would write to their parents, outlining the
"debt" they had to them:

"If I were to combine all the devotion, dedication, and caring
that I got from all the other people in my life, it would pale in the
light of what I received from you..."

"When I couldn't get into school... I think now of the scores
of phone calls you made... the embarrassment it caused you...
pulling every string...and crying together with me.

"...for always forgiving and forgetting. And even if you didn't
forget, at least you pretended that you did..."

"...how you always wanted the best for me and would have
done — and did — anything to make it happen."

"You always provided for my needs with a 'no big deal' attitude."

"...from amenities to accessories, from necessities to luxuries..."

If you identify with the statements above — *repay that debt.* Both with what was given, and the strong love with which it was delivered.

If you were front and center in your parents' lives, day and night, in all seasons and throughout all the years, in-between their many struggles; if they took care of all your needs — much of the time, even before you asked — with attention, interest, sacrifice and love — this is what you should return.*

Every age and stage is the time to repay. But especially as the years pass and parents become needy, remember the debt of intense love they lavished on you.

❖ "You listened to my stories with enthusiasm and showed it mattered to you. You paid attention to me as if I were the only one in the world.

"Now that you are retired, with long stretches of hours before you, when you doze from boredom and are anxious for a listening ear, I offer you my ear — but more important, I offer you the heart you so willingly gave me."

❖ "When I was little, we lived out of town, where my father got his first job as a social worker. Every few months, we made a five-hour car trip to visit our grandparents.

"I remember those trips, and I remember driving you crazy, Dad, with my endless questions: 'But how much longer?' 'When will we get there already?' Again, and again, and again, you patiently answered.

"My dear father, now, in your declining years, would I dare be impatient with you?"

❖ "You made every effort to make me eat — just three more mouthfuls. I would complain about the supper after you

---

* Should one feel that care and concern were missing, this would not exempt him from his Torah obligations of honor and reverence to parents, with all their details.

worked so hard on it. And the next night, you still made supper again.

"And now that you have problems swallowing and I prepare special food, do you taste my tears which fall as I mash, and think of all the love that went into the food you made for me? I tasted your love. Do you taste mine?"

❖ "You stayed home because you said a babysitter is not a mommy.

"Should I not realize that an aide is not a daughter?"

❖ "I remember how you'd run out at seven in the morning or eleven at night because I needed something desperately.

"So when you call me a few hours before Shabbos, desperate… well, of course, I should go quickly and eagerly."

❖ "You always took care of me when I was sick, whether it was taking me to the doctor or being my doctor.

"And now that your health is failing…

"You didn't just do things to tick them off a list — and I won't either."

———————◆———————

Are you head over heels in debt?
Are you in the red — overdraft?
Are you making payments on your IOU?

Chapter 16

Imperfect Parents Who Are Perfect for Us

The Gemara speaks of R' Tarfon's dedication to his mother:

R' Tarfon had an elderly mother who found it difficult to climb into her bed. R' Tarfon would get on his hands and knees beside her bed to let her use him as a stepstool every morning and evening.

One day, while discussing the mitzvah of honoring parents with the other Sages, R' Tarfon told them about the manner in which he helped his mother.

They responded: You still have not fulfilled even half of the mitzvah of honoring parents. If your parent took your wallet filled with gold coins and threw it into the sea before your eyes, would you become upset, berate, and embarrass her?[1]

A second story is told of Rabbi Tarfon's devotion:

R' Tarfon's mother was walking in the courtyard one

Shabbos when her shoe tore and came off. R' Tarfon placed his hands under her feet, and she walked in this manner until they reached her couch.

Once, when R' Tarfon became ill, the Sages came to visit him, and his mother said to them: "Pray for my son, R' Tarfon, because he honors me exceedingly."

They asked her: "What did he do for you?" And she told them what happened with her shoe.

They responded: "Were he to do that a thousand times, he has not yet bestowed even half the honor demanded by the Torah."[2]

Each story leaves us astonished.

To make our back a stepstool or offer our hands in lieu of a shoe — what could express greater devotion? Yet our Sages seem to minimize R' Tarfon's unique dedication. There is apparently another dimension to honoring a parent.

The Gemara continues:

The Sages once asked R' Elazar, "How much must we honor our parents?" He answered, "If you really want to see what it means to honor a parent, go and ask Damah ben Nesinah."

Damah ben Nesinah was a [Roman] mayor and army commander. Once, he was standing in front of his soldiers when his mother [who was mentally unbalanced][3] came up to him and hit him with her shoe, which then fell from her hand.[4]

Damah bent down, picked up the shoe, and handed it back to his mother, attempting to calm her with gentle words.[5]

What do we see in the story of Damah ben Nesinah that we don't find with R' Tarfon?

R' Tarfon had a fine mother. Damah didn't.

If a child is devoted and respectful to his parents who gave him not only life itself, but years of devotion and sacrifice of every kind, that's the *middah* of *hakaras hatov* — paying back good with good. This is universally understood. We would be grateful to anyone who gave us even a fraction of what parents give.

We give our back — to a parent who carried us on his back. We use our hands as shoes — for a parent who has shod us.

That was R' Tarfon's world.

Damah ben Nesinah had a different reality. He had a mentally unbalanced mother who accosted and humiliated him in public. If you want to know what honoring parents means, go to Damah, say our Sages. Look at sons and daughters who are challenged by the parents they were given, and watch how they overcome.

MY SISTERS AND I always knew that it wasn't an ideal life setting.

We grew up the children of divorced parents, uprooted from city to city every other year, our primary caretaker the woman who replaced our mother.

Our story goes like this:

My name is Jason (Yaakov) Stone. I am the middle child, sandwiched between two sisters.

It was 1981. Everything looked like it was going well. The family had just moved to Boulder, Colorado after my parents, on a vacation five years earlier, became enamored with the Rocky Mountains.

The joy was not to last. Though on paper my parents seemed to be a perfect couple, they divorced. The childhood of Joyce Stone, 8, Jason Stone, 4, and Amanda Stone, a baby, came to a sudden and unfortunate end.

My mother would remain incapacitated by the divorce and the collapse of her life, depressed and unable to care for her brood. The responsibility fell to my father.

To save himself and his children, he remarried a year later. Her name was Stella.

Here began our new life. For the next twenty years, they would be married, and when I referred to them in conversation, they were "my parents."

What was our home like? Well, we were never hit or made to suffer some kind of gross punishment for a relatively minor misdemeanor. We were never sentenced to our room with no dinner. Our clothes were replaced when worn, our bellies filled when empty, and our teeth braced when crooked. We were physically cared for.

But there was nothing more than that.

I was never asked if I had homework, what I learned in school, or if there was some kind of activity I'd like to participate in. We were left to fend for ourselves, to figure out a new school each year we moved — eleven times in total — to learn how to survive "out there."

My mother was out of the picture, my father was swallowed up by work, and then there was Stella and her "quirks."

If ever I wanted to eat something, she would have to have the first bite, before our hands could touch it, because she didn't want our "cooties." There was always "hers" and "ours." Her salad dressing, her markers, her stereo, her treats.

They came in the front door, with shoes on; we came in the back door with the dog, shoes off. We were never physically whipped with a belt, but we were whipped with the steady, repeated, repeating message: "You children are not welcome here. You are ruining our life. Don't touch anything, and don't bother us."

Eventually, I moved on, first to college, then to Israel, to Torah, and a world I had never known about. I picked up my sister Amanda along the road back home. Now we're both married and are busy building families, working, learning, and growing more and more.

This story of our return is in itself a marvelous one and I could end here if not for a surprising twist of hashgachah.

When you're from Colorado, it's called an "upslope" — one of those blizzards that catch everyone off guard and decimates the ill prepared. That my father's twenty-year marriage to Stella finally ended was not a surprise. But that he would return home to my mother, apologize for twenty years' worth of damage — the carnage left behind the day he walked out and the whole train derailed — and ask for another chance, and that she would accept... I was sure that when Chazal *say that it's more difficult for Hashem to bring a couple together than to split the sea, this was surely the couple they were speaking of.*

And just like that, they started anew. They realized their joint mistakes, and vowed to move on into greener pastures.

Because I was only 4 at the time of the divorce, Mom and Dad had always had their own place in my mind, never together. The expectations, behaviors, and roles in these two worlds were exactly that — two separate worlds. And once they collided, an emotional supernova exploded inside me. I had managed to keep all this in and maintain a "normal" relationship with them when they were "Mom's world" and "Dad's world." But the shock and turmoil of the "collision," and the way it was handled toppled me.

Dad went around to Gramma, Uncle Paul, and everyone else to ask forgiveness. As a kid, I had been ignored, and now, in the most significant moment in this family since the divorce twenty-five years earlier, I was being ignored again. No one asked me how I felt about my parents' divorce, the years in between, and now, no one was asking me how I felt about everyone pretending that nothing ever happened, the myth of "let's just be a whole family once again." The only thing I was being asked was to not make anyone feel guilty by bringing up the past.

In other words, "Don't rain on our parade" — the same message at 5, 15, and now, at 30.

I felt I had every reason to end this painful relationship. I could have and would have played the "if only" game until the anger totally consumed me. If not for the Rabbi in Boulder, it might have been impossible to have a happy ending. It would have been just an ending of me and them.

The Rabbi and I spoke at great length. He explained that my approach to my parents was wrong. My feeling that I "owe them nothing" was off base. We spoke about the many things I did get, benefits that I hold in my hand today that can be traced back to my parents. As far as my "account" with them, items missing from my list of life's necessities, that does not allow me to subtract from my obligations.

The message of those conversations, if it needed to

be summed up, was: Your father and mother are not bad people. They have made mistakes in life and want another chance.

What has happened is that I have slowly come to realize that my parents are also just people — imperfect, like the rest of us. They also live in a confusing world and are trying to find their way. To the extent that they are capable of having a relationship with me, I'll match it and give it to them. They want another chance, and I must oblige, because we are Jews, and life is about teshuvah.

Every person has his mitzvos that challenge him, and this is mine: to give honor to my parents. Whether I feel they deserve it or not, Someone Above has already answered that question for me.

It's still a challenge, especially when they ignore my kids — their grandkids — like they ignored me. The pain is there. But I have the Rabbi's words in my head, and I have a support system of people to talk to. And Hashem has blessed me with a great wife, who is always by my side, and who gets me back on track in the darker moments.

I know I made the right decision to stick with them. I'm still fighting with the "if only," but it's not consuming me.

Now, a few years later, that supernova has cooled, and other things in life have become more important. My kids have a Gramma and Grampa in their lives — maybe not ones as warm and loving as I might have chosen, but, as the Rabbi explained, Someone chose them for me.

My kids know nothing about any of this. They're happy, my parents are happy, and so am I.

"How far do we have to go in honoring parents?" the *Shulchan Aruch* asks. "Even if a parent took your money and threw it into the sea…"

When the Torah commands us to honor parents, it is mainly referring to parents who caused us a "loss" — whether financial (like throwing the wallet in the sea), or any other loss we feel we faced: parents who disappointed us, parents who haven't lived up to our expectations (what we think we should have gotten when we look around and see what others have), parents who have dashed our dreams of what could have been.

R' Chaim Palagi explains this point:

> The obligation to honor and revere our parents refers even to parents who are tough and unaccommodating, parents who are bothersome and make life difficult for children with their numerous complaints and demands, and parents who are prying and meddlesome. Especially as they age, parents might become quarrelsome, curse their children, become stubborn in their ways and ideas, are ill mannered, or even act strangely.
>
> Even if the whole world maintains that a child has no obligation to such parents, this is not true. A child is obligated in the mitzvos of honor and reverence. And it is certainly forbidden for a child to hit, curse, or embarrass such [or any] parents.
>
> **In fact, the Torah's commandment to honor parents refers primarily to parents of the abovementioned type.**
>
> Logic alone would indicate that a person honor parents if only because they are older and because they brought him into the world. If they are, in addition, loving and nurturing, even a stranger would honor and revere someone who raised, fed, and dressed him, so as not to be an ingrate. Is the Torah, then, coming to teach what is just common sense? If logic demands honor, what does this mitzvah add to our understanding of filial obligations?
>
> The fifth commandment comes to teach us: When our logic would exempt us from honoring parents of the type mentioned above, even if a son or daughter would insist, "I'll treat my parents the way they treat me," the Torah warns: Honor your father and mother as Hashem told you; honor parents even when they present challenges. This mitzvah is between you and the Almighty, and this is His will.[6]

Retrievable and irretrievable loss

A child may make an effort to prevent a loss caused by a parent — whether physical, financial, or emotional in nature.

If a loss has already occurred, he may take measures to reverse it or retrieve it.[7] But, in doing so, continues the *Shulchan Aruch*, he may not shame his parents or respond in anger.[8]

WHEN MOTTIE AND I GOT MARRIED, we lent my father our wedding gift money for a purchase he was making at the time. About three years later, when our son Yaakov was born, we thought about investing the sum, $18,000, for our future, and asked for the money back.

My father refused to return the money, saying that because he paid for the wedding (which cost $40,000), the $18,000 we had received in gifts belonged to him. He added that he wanted to invest all the money in his new grandson's name.

Though that was a kind gesture, we felt that the money was ours to use as we wished. We never made such an agreement with him before the wedding, and I was unsure if he had a legitimate claim to the money.

We asked our Rav, who said that the money belongs to us. If it was a small amount, he would advise us to look away for the sake of peace. But because it was a significant sum, we are justified in pursuing our claim.[9]

We were advised to be careful with how we attempted to retrieve the money because we were dealing with a parent.*

P.S.: The Rav made one final observation: A parent's natural love for his child would come to the fore. This proved to be true. My father did indeed return the money shortly after.

---

* If financial matters cannot be worked out between child and parent, a son may bring the matter to a *beis din* to recover a loss, reviewing this matter carefully with a Rav before taking action.

There are opinions that a child should act beyond that which halachah allows (לִפְנִים מִשּׁוּרַת הַדִּין) and refrain from summoning a parent to *beis din*, even when he is sure he has a valid claim. Rather, he should go to an authoritative third party who will hear the arguments of both sides and broker a compromise.

But there's another kind of a loss. An irretrievable, irreversible loss.

"I wanted to be a lawyer. My father gave a lot of money to charity, but wouldn't finance my education. This has been a low simmer for me."

"My mother was chronically ill. My father worked long hours. No one was there to take an interest in my life. I suffered, and it didn't have to be like that."

"If only..."

"If only I would have had _____ for a father..."
"If only I had a mother who...didn't/wasn't/would have...like my friends' moms."

When we feel we have lost out and are obsessed with an "if only" scenario, we can move forward by reversing the order of those two destructive words, the "if only" becoming "only if." *Only if* we include Hashem in the picture will we accept our parents as a match made for us in Heaven.

This can be explained with a parable:

The Almighty sends us on a journey. There will be stops along the way. We are given a suitcase packed with whatever we will need at each junction. Included is our parents, maybe stepparents, and on occasion absentee parents.

Did we need a lighter suitcase? Did we need all those things we're carrying?

That suitcase was packed especially for us. Every item it contains is placed there to ensure us a successful journey.

Hashem has a special purpose in creating us. Each of us is a unique individual with a unique mission, put into this world to accomplish something that no one else can. We are given our own unique circumstances, tailor made for us, the "props" of our life, to bring out our potential and help us fulfill this mission.

"But he has a suitcase with wheels. Look how easy it is for him!"

If we lack what others have, it's because we don't need it for what we must accomplish.

In the *Aseres HaDibros* we can learn important messages from the parallel placement of the commandments. The first is parallel to and connected to the sixth; the second to the seventh; the third to the eighth; the fourth to the ninth; and the fifth to the tenth.

The fifth commandment tells us to honor our father and our mother. We move our eyes to the other side and see, "Do not covet, do not be jealous."

What's the connection?

From the millions of *neshamos*, from the tremendous pool of possible parents who could have been chosen for us, Hashem chose the ones that are best matched to our *neshamah*. If we needed parents who were smarter, healthier, wealthier, more successful, more prestigious, warmer, more available — then that is what would have been given us.

We might ask: Why does Hashem allow a child to be a victim of his parents' failures? "My parents were…critical, controlling, stingy, constantly exploding, icy…and I feel I'm under the crippling influence of their shortcomings."

In fact, Hashem wants us to function in what seems to be an imperfect system. He wants us to function with "imperfect" parents, developing ourselves in an "imperfect" environment.[10]

The challenge our parents provide us, by being who they are, serves to train us in areas in which we need training, like a personalized *middos* development program. Different parents are just not going to help make us what we're supposed to become.

"Do not covet" is an integral part of our belief in a Creator Who is running a purposeful world, which is the basis for acceptance of our parents, who are custom made for us.

Making it work

Back to Damah ben Nesinah, whom we met at the beginning of the chapter. We're meant to take away a lesson from the exemplary behavior of Damah and not from the disturbing behavior of his mother. Of course, parents may not "beat" their children physically (*Shulchan Aruch* 240:20).

Or verbally.

Put-downs are an old story, the severity of which was taught to us at Har Sinai over 3,300 years ago, when the mitzvah "Do not aggrieve your fellowman" (לֹא תוֹנוּ אִישׁ אֶת עֲמִיתוֹ) was given to us as one of the 613 mitzvos.

"The warning against paining with words applies **even with a person's own children**," says the *Sefer HaChinuch* (338). "One who is careful about not causing them pain will be rewarded with life, blessing, and honor."

The difference between insulting all other people and one's own children is a significant one. While we can be devastated, sometimes nonfunctional, from any put-down or hurtful comment, those punches coming from a parent carry much more weight. To a child, all the weight in the world.

So, you're in the ring, and you've knocked down your child. If there would be a referee (Oh, how good that would be!), he would announce, "And the loser is…" and point to you.

Tanach and Gemara are full of severe warnings about causing pain with hurtful words, yet who can claim that he has not pained others with his inconsiderate comments? Harried parents, who do love and care for their children, will almost certainly make mistakes. That's not our discussion here.

What we are discussing is a situation of debilitating, crushing insults. There can never be justification for a pattern of humiliation, mockery, or toxic criticism.

That said, there are, unfortunately, homes where parents do lash their children with their words. Many sons and daughters have succeeded with difficult home situations, but this will not always be the case. When a parent — for whatever reason — doesn't see the pain he is causing; when it doesn't help for the child to explain to his parent how he is hurting, or he doesn't know how to verbalize his pain; when he is too intimidated by harsh words or harsh hands to respond, and the second parent either emulates this harmful behavior or lacks the ability to prevent the mistreatment, ideally an influential person should be asked to intercede.

Additionally, a child can be encouraged to turn to a teacher, a Rav, a counselor, or other adults for guidance and assistance.

When children share their pain many benefits can result: they can hear advice on how to deal with the existing situation and find ways to prevent future pain. And sometimes just having a sympathetic ear can go a long way to relieve a child's distress.

The direction should always be "to reconcile parents with children and children with parents" (לְהָשִׁיב לֵב אָבוֹת עַל בָּנִים וְלֵב בָּנִים עַל אֲבוֹתָם). Sons or daughters of all ages want and need a relationship with their parents. They may need help figuring out how to make it work.

I WAS CALLING MOMMA when my heart froze in my chest. I started to cough and tried to hang up. Too late.

"Who is this? — What is this? — Shea is it YOU? Are you okay?"

My father was nervous at the best of times. This wasn't the way to begin a conversation I definitely didn't want to have anyway.

"Yes, Tatte," I choked. "One second..." I put down the phone, got a glass of water, and tried to just breathe easily even though my heart was pounding. I had called for Momma, but it was poor timing — my father was home!

Back on the phone...

"Hi, Tatte, sorry about that... Just somehow started coughing... How are you?"

"Trying to kill me or something?" my father snapped at me. "You know I have to take care of my heart and not get upset about anything, and you call and begin to cough?! What are you hiding from me? What's the matter with you, and when are you going to see a doctor about it?"

The sentences ran into one another almost unintelligibly.

I tried to maintain my equilibrium. My father was already upset and we hadn't gotten to hello yet!

"Tatte," I said, "please, Tatte, let's start this conversation from the beginning. Hi, Tatte, it's Shea — "

"ALRIGHT!" My father took a deep breath. "How are you, Shea? How was your week? So I hear from Momma you made a delivery of that pizza of yours."

I stiffened — was that sarcasm in his voice?

"No one else in your town makes pizza? They have to get it from you?"

I tried to be mechubadig, *even as I began to boil. "Tatte?"*

"You delivered that pizza yourself, Shea, didn't you? Weren't you covered in flour and looking like a schlemiel?*"*

My father knew me well. My pants were covered in flour. I had thrown a coat over them and the coat had floured fingerprints on it where I had buttoned it up. But the pizza was delivered on time. Ruchel'eh's recipe was delicious and many people enjoyed it. Bais Bnos was happy with the order and would order again.

I gave my best shot at saving this conversation. "Tatte, they like my pizza. I am supporting my family honestly."

"You could have been a pride to this family," my Tatte hissed. "Instead, you are selling pizza. You had a good Gemara kop, you could have been a chushuveh balabus, poisek, *a* shoichet. *At least, someone involved in Torah, in halachah."*

I lost it after that.

"What's wrong with supporting my family? Are you offering to support? Why do you constantly criticize me? What do you want me to be a SHOICHET for! I will NEVER be a SHOICHET, do you hear me? NEVER! This is as close to a cow as I will ever get — CHEESE!"

I was shouting by this time, screaming the words into the phone.

"You think there's no halachah in the pizza business?" I kept screaming. "You think I'm an apikoirus? *You think I never call a Rav? You think I don't learn Gemara every single day no matter how tired I am?"*

Through the phone, my mother's voice pierced my tirade.

"Avruhum!" she called to Tatte, "what's the yelling about? You have to hang up right now — your blood pressure!" She took the phone from my father. I heard her as she began to settle him into a chair.

"Who is this?" Momma demanded.

I was too embarrassed to answer and was just breathing to calm down.

"*Shea! Is it you?*"

Momma recognizes my breathing!?

"*Shea! How could...*" *Momma doesn't finish. Controlling herself, voice very cold, she says, "I have to attend to your father now. Shea, we will speak at a later time.*"

I put down the phone, my hand shaking uncontrollably. I turned to my wife, who had witnessed the scene.

"*Ruchel'eh,*" *I announced, "that's it! Enough! I'm simply going to cut ties with him.*"

"*What will that mean, Shea? You can't just cut your father out. Where is* kibbud av? *And what about hurting your mother?*"

"*Ruchel'eh, I am not speaking with him again. I won't be able to stand it, and it bothers you too. The best* kibbud av *will be silence.*"

And that's the way it went. When I knew my father wasn't home, I'd call to speak to my mother. On rare occasions, if he did pick up, I kept it short. "Hi, Tatte. Is Momma home? Please tell her I called. I have to go now. Have a nice day." I paid no attention to the times my father actually tried to converse with me. Just kept on my pain-free, predictable track.

This remained my plan. In my mind, I saw the years go by without my father in my life. He would never be the father I needed, and I didn't need or want the father he was.

Several years passed. Like a worm wriggling around inside me, it played on my conscience. What seemed a simple, workable solution was now questionable.

Ruchel'eh wanted me to go to the Ruv, our Dayan.

"*Shea, going to the Ruv needed to be done years ago when this situation began. You just weren't open to the idea.*"

I wasn't buying it, but this time Ruchel'eh wouldn't back down.

"*We ask the Ruv all the* shailos, *bar none. How did we miss going to him for this one?*" *she said, shaking her head.*

It took more coaxing on her part, but this time she was insistent.

"*Shea, right is right.*"

That's how I ended up in the Ruv's book-lined study, where everyone came. The Ruv is closer to 80, though his bright kind eyes twinkle like those of a much younger man. He is a stalwart pillar of Torah. The Ruv, the Dayan, has led our community for years. He is revered even as he is profoundly loved.

The Ruv's kind eyes and gentle demeanor comforted me as I spilled out my story and my decision. I was wracked by heaving sobs, my head on the Dayan's desk, tears soaking the highly polished wood. I was definitely not the first or the last man to cry here.

"Shea, kibbud av va'eim is a hard mitzvah," I heard the Ruv saying.

I tried to raise my head, but my shoulders still sagged in defeat.

"Sometimes, there is a heter in extreme cases, when fixing is not possible. Your situation doesn't fall into that category. A person is capable of changing his attitude toward his parents in adulthood." The Ruv hesitated but a moment. "Your approach until now with your father has some merit."

I looked up surprised — I did something right?!

The Ruv continued, "Let's add one feature. Nachas. You are now appointed your father's 'nachas-giver.'"

It was an utterly unthinkable statement, and I was hard pressed to prevent more tears from dripping from my eyes. What did the Ruv mean?

"Conversations between you and your father are to be short and, from your end only, contain nachas messages. For example, Fraidy got an 80 percent on her Chumash test. Chayale told a story about Rebbi Akiva at the Shabbos table. Shmeili kept his bib clean. Then wish the Tatte well and hang up the phone, or speak to your mother as you do now."

Is the Ruv saying there is hope?

"This has to be done with commitment every week. What day will you do this? Friday isn't a good day for this because ken ayin hara your father has many children, and Fridays are short. How about a Wednesday or Thursday night? Let's choose the time now, and you will speak to your father for five to ten minutes only, listing the nachas moments of the eineklach."

We chose Monday afternoon. In the pizza business, it's a touch slower — after lunch, before school ends, in advance *of the dinner hour. Since the business had moved from the house to the store, privacy was less of an issue, and I could talk undisturbed by the* nachas *makers — our* baruch Hashem *numerous children.*

The advantages of this method were profound. I became way more aware of my children's antics and milestones. I had to ask Ruchel'eh daily, and keep a list for my father's Monday call. A few minutes stretched to a few more minutes.

Momma told me that Mondays had become a good day in my father's book. Taciturn at other times, for my father Mondays had become a lighter day.

The years flew by and Shmeili's bar mitzvah *was coming up. The first time our boys put on* tefillin *is with the Dayan. It's a big* simchah *and* chashuveh *event.*

My father and mother came in for it. My in-laws live in town. Tatte accompanied us to the Ruv. The Ruv awaited us, his eyes lighting up like a zeidy when he saw Shmeili. The Ruv greeted my father, my father-in-law and me by name and wished us mazel tov *on this occasion.*

"Reb Avrumele, Reb Reuven," the Ruv addressed my father and father-in-law when the tefillin *were stored away. "My ir* eineklach *tell me how much they enjoy your son's pizza."*

I didn't dare turn to Tatte, afraid of his reaction.

"And by the way, Reb Avrumele," continued the Ruv, "while in our community we don't keep yoshon, *others in the wider community do, and Reb Shea, your son, is very particular with these halachos.* Yiras Shamayim *and delicious, nutritious food rolled into pizza pies. Nachas, Rav Avrumele, Reb Reuven, nachas."*

I was rooted to the floor, my vision clouded over. I felt my father grab my arm tightly. Startled, my vision clearing in seconds, I saw tears in his eyes. We could not speak.

The Ruv cradled Shmeili's chin in his gentle hand. "Shmeili, mazel tov. *May you grow to be a* yirei shamayim *like your Tatte and your zeides."*

Smiling, Shmeili kissed the Dayan's hand. We all followed suit and slowly backed out of the Dayan's study.

Exceptional situations

It is sad to say that in exceptional cases, after having attempted alternative solutions, a child may be compelled to distance himself from a parent(s).[11] He may be advised to avoid contact as much as necessary,* particularly when it affects his physical or emotional well-being,[12] and with married children, if it disturbs their *shalom bayis*.[13]

Because it is a serious and consequential decision to close a door on a parent, even partially, it is most essential that such a determination be made only with Rabbinic approval and guidance.

Even when distance is required, hopefully it need not be completely or forever.

——————•·•·•——————

As we read the *Haftarah* of Minchah on Yom Kippur, the holiest day of the year, we are reminded that we cannot run away from Hashem and the task He wants us to accomplish. The prophet Yonah was given a mission by Hashem. He was asked to go to Nineveh, but he ran away instead. After a Divinely directed turn of events, Yonah fulfilled his mission.

A person can sometimes be tricked into thinking that his lot has been decided by his own choices. We can't make that mistake with parents. Clearly they were Hashem's choice for us. Whatever challenge a parent presents is part of our *tikkun*, our personal mission in this world and our unique and special part of His plan for Creation.[14]

You have given me imperfect parent(s) that You know are perfect for me. May I earn a long life to figure out why.

---

* Avoiding contact is not a license to shame, pain, or respond in anger. Because the time we spend with them is limited, we should bend over backward to make sure to be especially respectful. Avoiding contact is likewise not a license to speak *lashon hara* and badmouth one's parents.

HONOR:
A Final Thought

The *Aseres HaDibros* were given on two *luchos*, with our responsibilities to Hashem *(bein adam laMakom)* on one side, and our responsibilities to our fellowman *(bein adam lachaveiro)*, our societal obligations, on the other.

Yet the Fifth Commandment, honoring parents, relates to human obligations. Why, then, is it among the first five, on the side of Divine obligations?

To teach us that Hashem elevates and equates the honor of parents with His own!

In an amazing statement made by the Sage Rav Yosef, we find a validation for this awesome equation. Rav Yosef heard the footsteps of his mother and he stood up, saying, "I am standing up in honor of the *Shechinah*" (*Kiddushin* 31b).

How could Rav Yosef say he was standing in honor of the *Shechinah*, when in fact it was his mother who was entering?

Only because Hashem Himself has drawn this parallel:[15] "Three partners join in creating man: the Almighty, a father, and a mother" (*Kiddushin* 30b).[16]

If we reflect on this truth, it is almost too huge to absorb — the Almighty has allowed the finite to partner with the Infinite.

Parents are given the privilege of partnering with Hashem to create a human being, parents contributing the physical, temporal body, and Hashem, the eternal soul, the breath of life. Says the Almighty: The first four commandments concern My honor. The fifth concerns the honor of My partners.

To quote the Almighty Himself:

> When a child honors his father and mother, Hashem says, "I consider it as though I am dwelling in their midst and **they are honoring Me**."[17]

Respecting parents — in attitude, word, and behavior — brings the *Shechinah* and the accompanying blessing into our lives.

Parents' Accountability

Chazal refer to *kibbud av va'eim* as being one of the most difficult of all the mitzvos of the Torah — חֲמוּרָה שֶׁבַּחֲמוּרוֹת. Because of the challenges surrounding this mitzvah, children need a helping hand.

There are 34 *se'ifim*/paragraphs in the *Shulchan Aruch* devoted to children's obligations to parents (240:1-25, 241:1-9). Right in the middle we find two seemingly incongruous paragraphs. Paragraphs 240:19-20 present the obligations of parents!

Chazal are stressing that parents must help children succeed by not creating situations that make it difficult and sometimes nearly impossible for their children to be respectful.

This lesson for parents is built right into the mitzvah.

The Torah verse that teaches us *yiras av va'eim* — אִישׁ אִמּוֹ וְאָבִיו תִּירָאוּ — begins with the singular noun, אִישׁ, and ends with the plural verb תִּירָאוּ.

Says the Shelah HaKadosh: The plural usage of the word תִּירָאוּ incorporates parents into this mitzvah. They have the responsibility to make sure that they are not the cause of their children's stumbling.

Chapter 17

Are We "Tripping" Our Children?

One of the two paragraphs in the *Shulchan Aruch* that discuss parents' obligations to children is:

אָסוּר לְאָדָם לְהַכְבִּיד עוּלוֹ עַל בָּנָיו וּלְדַקְדֵּק בִּכְבוֹדוֹ עִמָּהֶם, שֶׁלֹּא יְבִיאֵם לִידֵי מִכְשׁוֹל. אֶלָּא יִמְחוֹל וְיַעֲלִים עֵינָיו מֵהֶם שֶׁהָאָב שֶׁמָּחַל עַל כְּבוֹדוֹ, כְּבוֹדוֹ מָחוּל.

A parent is forbidden to place a heavy yoke on his child, to be exacting, overly demanding with his own honor, so as not to cause him to stumble. Rather, he should waive his honor and look away [from certain infractions], since a father has the right to forgo the honor due him *(Shulchan Aruch* 240:19).

What is meant by a *heavy yoke* and *overly demanding*?
To ask for more than the child is capable of.
A parent is prohibited from weighing too heavily on his

children, being too "weighty" in his demands. When parents set the bar too high, they set up their children for failure. When they are exacting in the honor due them, in the service given to them, or the deference shown them, to the point where a son or daughter can't measure up to their standards and falls short of their expectations, they have created a stumbling block, a *michshol*. This is a transgression of the commandment (*Vayikra* 19:14), "Do not put a stumbling block in front of an unseeing person" — a person who clearly cannot navigate that hurdle.

When a child trips on the mitzvah of *kibbud av va'eim*, both parties are faulted: the child who tripped *and* the parent who caused the trip.[1]

To forestall this, it is the parent's responsibility to make a realistic evaluation of his child's abilities. Requests made and standards set should be relative to a child's ability to fulfill them.[2]

The waiver, *mechilah*, is a response to that assessment.

The waiver (mechilah)

The mitzvah of honoring parents is difficult to fulfill properly. It demands from children physical, emotional, intellectual — and sometimes, financial — investment. To help their children succeed with this mitzvah, parents were given a powerful tool: the waiver, *mechilah*, the option to look away from less-than-perfect behavior.

Mechilah here means being flexible in matters of a child's multiple responsibilities to parents. Once a specific responsibility to parents is waived, a child is not guilty of neglecting his obligation, because his parents have excused him from it.[3] The validity of a child's obligation doesn't change. The standards of *kavod* and *yirah* are not discarded, but at that moment, they are not demanded. As the *Pele Yo'etz* says:

At times...look away

The principle is that [we go according to] the comprehension (דַּעַת) and the personality of the child...

We should not be overly exacting with children. At times, a parent should act as though he is deaf and "not hear" or pretend as if he does not see. Now and again, a parent should give in to what his child wants [although the parent would prefer otherwise]. This is an important guideline for one who wishes to accrue merit for himself and for his children (*Pele Yo'etz, Ahavas HaBanim VeHabanos*).[4]

Torah wisdom cautions us: *chanoch lana'ar al pi darko*, each child is a study unto himself. A parent should ask himself, "For *this* child, will this be *a heavy yoke, overly demanding*, or *cause him to stumble?*"

The waiver is a parent's prerogative. It may be willingly given by the wise and discerning parent. A child cannot expect it or demand it, but may request it.

Even with a waiver...

Even when a parent makes allowances and excuses for his child — "It's okay. I see it's going to be a hassle for you to get to the airport to pick me up" — the child still gets a mitzvah if he performs the service.[5]

The waiver and neglect

But if a child knows his parent can't manage with the baggage...

It is important for a child to sense how the waiver was given. Was the parent's heart in it? Or was it given because he didn't want to bother the child, or he sensed the child didn't really want to be bothered?

If accepting the waiver, and not doing the service for the parent, will result in neglect or harm, a son or daughter should disregard it:

> *"You don't have to bring me supper tonight."*
> *"Esty, you don't have to take me to the doctor tomorrow."*

Will your father have food to eat if you don't bring it?

Will your mother keep her appointment even if you don't take her?

Overusing mechilah

One of the purposes of the mitzvah of *kibbud av va'eim* is to develop the trait of gratitude in children. First, to realize that we have been recipients of benefits, then to acknowledge the source of these kindnesses, and then to reciprocate in kind. If a parent waives all services, releasing his son and daughter from any assistance (or a child requests this), he is withholding from his child *tachlis hamitzvah* — this goal of flexing the gratitude muscle, resulting in an atrophied gratitude, arresting the development of this essential trait.[6]

Being flexible is good for all relationships, but even more essential when raising children. Because of the constant interplay, the possibilities for clashes are abundant, and the need to look away, at times, is imperative.

Some things, however, should *not* be overlooked.

When looking the other way is looking in the wrong direction

While a parent may look away from some slights, he may **not give permission** for the following:

1. Striking parents, וּמַכֵּה אָבִיו וְאִמּוֹ (*Shemos* 21:15)
2. Cursing parents, וּמְקַלֵּל אָבִיו וְאִמּוֹ (ibid. v. 17)[7]
3. Belittling parents in speech or action, אָרוּר מַקְלֶה אָבִיו וְאִמּוֹ (*Devarim* 27:16)[8]

Striking

Even though a parent might see the following as a solution, the Torah does not allow a parent to say:

Father: Let's make a deal. No hitting in school, but when you come home, I'll be your punching bag.[9]

Even with express permission, striking a parent is not permitted.

Cursing

If a child loses himself, and out of anger, wishes a parent ill… An improper response would be:

Father: You can say whatever you want about me, wish me what you want. The important thing is just to get it off your chest so that you'll feel better.[10]

Even with this express permission, cursing a parent is not permitted.

Belittling

And a parent may not condone blatant belittling (בִּזָּיוֹן מַמָּשׁ).[11]

Child to mother: This meat is inedible. You are a terrible cook.

Improper parental response:

"In this house we let everyone express their opinion."

Maybe — but not when that opinion is one that belittles parents.

Even with parental permission, blatant belittling of a parent is not permitted.

Better parental responses:

"Maybe you'd like to rephrase that."
"You probably weren't thinking when you said that."

To our sorrow, for some, blatant belittling is the order of the day. Far from condoning this *chutzpah*, parents ache that such disrespect can burst forth from the mouths of their sons and daughters. This should not, however, deter us from aspiring to the home that the Almighty wants us to build.

After the fact

Though a waiver can never help to permit demeaning behavior toward parents, it does help after the fact.

It is proper for a parent to forgive his children in order to lessen the Heavenly judgment on the son or daughter (*Pele Yo'etz*).[12]

It is proper for those who have fear of Hashem to forgive their children (in their hearts) even when the child is not aware of the *mechilah* (*Sefer Chassidim* 152).[13]

OUR FAMILY CONSISTED of my husband, our daughter, Debbie, and me. I am thankful that we were blessed with many good years, but there were many hard ones, too.

My husband and our daughter were two strong-willed individuals, with opposite temperaments — he, punctual and disciplined; she, artistic and sensitive.

They loved each other, and wanted to love each other, but their extreme differences were blatant, especially when she reached her adolescent years. I tried to be the peacemaker, but I couldn't always save the day. The hurtful words rang in my ears.

Debbie finished school and found a job an ocean away from us.

We move ahead to my husband's final illness. I'd been in the hospital with him for about forty-eight hours. He took a turn for the worse and it seemed that the end was near. My good friend Pearl was on the phone with me. She asked if Debbie knew what was going on.

Yes, she knew that her dad was very ill, but she didn't know about the recent developments. I had no way to call her (no international call plan on my cell phone) or e-mail her from the hospital. So Pearl sent her a message in my name to let her know. Debbie received the e-mail and answered immediately — a tender and supportive message.

I guess she realized that it was now or never. She ended her e-mail, by saying, "I forgive Dad for everything and ask him to forgive me."

I listened to Pearl read those words to me, trembling with emotion. The result that I had worked for, dreamed about, and davened for so much — that they would somehow make peace while both were still in this world — came about.

Pearl sent my dictated message back to Debbie. I thanked my daughter for her support, which I deeply appreciated. I told her that I would relay her message, and that her dad would rest better.

"And, Pearl, I have one more thing to add. Please tell Debbie" — I forbade my voice from breaking — "please tell her that her dad forgave her years ago."

This took place sometime late Wednesday night. Thursday morning my husband passed away.

———————

A child has an obligation to aim to please. A parent has an obligation not to make it too hard to please, giving his child a helping hand to succeed.

Reverence

Honor, *kavod*, as we saw in the previous section, encompasses the following:

- ❖ proactive, positive actions done for the benefit and convenience or pleasure of parents
- ❖ assistance given joyously and with alacrity; loyal and dedicated attentiveness, with an emphasis on that which your parent particularly enjoys
- ❖ reflecting honor in our speech
- ❖ raising parents' status by zeroing in on their strengths, focusing on reasons to admire them
- ❖ rising as a sign of respect

Reverence, *yirah*, in contrast, is **refraining from behavior** that diminishes a parent's esteem, and stems from an inner feeling of deference.

While honor is expressed through active gestures, reverence is **purposeful inaction**.

The Aruch HaShulchan gives us a general definition of reverence/*yirah*: "Anything that diminishes a parent's honor is also considered lack of *yirah*."

Both sons and daughters, whether single or married, are obligated in the mitzvah of reverence.

Chapter 18

Awe-some Examples

וַיְדַבֵּר ה׳ אֶל־מֹשֶׁה לֵּאמֹר. דַּבֵּר אֶל־כָּל־עֲדַת בְּנֵי־יִשְׂרָאֵל
וְאָמַרְתָּ אֲלֵהֶם קְדֹשִׁים תִּהְיוּ כִּי קָדוֹשׁ אֲנִי ה׳ אֱלֹקֵיכֶם.
אִישׁ אִמּוֹ וְאָבִיו תִּירָאוּ.

Hashem spoke to Moshe, saying: Speak to
the entire assembly of the Children of Israel
and say to them: You shall be holy, for holy
am I, Hashem, your G-d. Every man: Your
mother and father shall you revere

(*Vayikra* 19:1-3).

The parent-child relationship is meant to be a warm, loving, positive attachment. A "friendly" connection with parents, though, is not the same as the one we have with a friend. Certain behavior that might be appropriate and acceptable with a friend is inappropriate and unacceptable with parents.

Our actions — and in the case of reverence, primarily **nonactions** — acknowledge the qualitative gulf in status separating parent and child that is demanded by our Torah. We aspire to refrain from behavior that diminishes that status.

There was a time when *yirah* was easier to access. There were kings and queens who inspired awe in the populace. People trembled in anticipation of a personal encounter with royalty. *Yirah* was in the very air.

IT WAS A FAMILY GATHERING, three generations around the table, easy conversation about this and that. Somehow, we meandered to an interesting observation — children seem to be taller than their parents. We noted that Uncle Gershon's kids were, and Aunt Reva's were — at least most.

As we were debating the accuracy of our premise (and its possible causes: better nutrition? more sleep?), my brother, Yitzy, wondered aloud if something about the transfer from European shores to the American frontier contributed to this (supposed) new physical phenomenon. Turning to his right, where our dear zeidy was sitting, he asked for his input.

"Zeidy, what would you say? Did you also see this when you were growing up? Were children in Europe also taller than their parents?"

"In der heim, children wouldn't dare be taller than their parents."

So what happens today, when we can only smile or weep over lost times? Living in times of equality for all, how do we approach the mitzvah of *yirah*?

How should yirah "feel"?

What is yirah, *reverence? The specific definition of* yirah *that's given by the Sages*[1] *is: One may not **stand or sit in his parent's usual place**. He may not **contradict** a parent* or **validate** a parent's opinion in front of him [in case of disagreement with another person]. He may not **call or refer to a parent by his/her first name**...*[2]

Reverence is a positive commandment, yet the definition above contains all negatives: don't sit in their seat...don't stand in their place...don't contradict... Where is the positive action that delineates reverence as a positive commandment? Where is the

---

* Contradicting and validation are discussed in the two chapters that follow.

performance, the achieving, that defines a positive commandment? The answer takes us to the core of this mitzvah: the heart. The primary fulfillment of the mitzvah of reverence takes place in our mind and heart. It is a command to cultivate an attitude of deference — an internal, positive feeling of regard for our parents that gives us the understanding to refrain from less than respectful behavior.

How do we cultivate this attitude?

Our Sages give us this advice: Try to simulate the feeling you have when you meet someone you greatly respect. For one person that might be a Rosh Yeshivah or a Rebbe; for another, a school principal or a senior teacher. For yet another, a CEO, a professor, or a political figure.

Then, think about how you feel when this person makes a request of you. Or, even without a request, just knowing what he would prefer, how he likes to have things done. Or, consider how you would make a request of him or converse with him. [3]

Take that feeling and bring it to your home, to your parents. Feel that deference and hold onto it.

This is one way to cultivate *yirah*.

Another approach to help cultivate feelings of *yirah* is taught by *Mesillas Yesharim*[4] based on the principle that external actions influence inner feelings. In discussing the trait of *zerizus* (alacrity), the author says that alacrity is external enthusiasm born from internal enthusiasm.

What if one is naturally unenthusiastic? He can still acquire an internal flame by acting with alacrity until it becomes more natural. If we do what is within our grasp, we will be able to acquire what is beyond our reach.

So it is with *yirah*. If we act with deferential behavior as outlined by *Chazal*, our actions will impact on our heart — molding it, teaching it, habituating it to feelings of deference.

MY FATHER'S PARENTS were a very special part of our childhood. They came to visit often, and they would stay in our home for two to three weeks at a time.

These visits were special in so many ways, but one of the things I loved most of all was how Gramma came and sat with me on my bed before I fell asleep. I would rest my head on her lap, we said Shema together, and then… "Gramma," I would ask, "tell me a story of when you were a little girl." Gramma had so many good stories, but my favorite — and one of the few that stands out in my mind until today — was about "The Big Papa Chair."

"My father, whom we called 'Papa,' had a special chair at the head of the table," Gramma would relate. "We called it 'The Big Papa Chair." No one was allowed to sit in Papa's chair…and we didn't dare. That was his special place — and keeping it special for him was the way we showed respect for our father. Sometimes, as a treat, when we were good, Papa would let us sit in The Big Papa Chair."

Short and sweet — yet I asked Gramma to retell this story time and again over the years. There was a special thrill about this big, imposing chair that was completely off limits. I would try to imagine it, how big and grand it must have been, from the way Gramma spoke about it with such reverence.

Reminiscing, I wondered…how ornate a chair, or even comfortable a chair, could The Big Papa Chair really have been? Probably not very, judging by the standards of the time. Now, years later, it finally occurred to me to ask Gramma what The Big Papa Chair looked like.

Gramma thought a moment, before saying, "It was the chair from the dining room set that was a little different from all the others — the one that went at the head of the table."

I could hardly believe what I was hearing. The Big Papa Chair was just a regular dining room chair! And yet, it was huge in the children's' eyes — a big, imposing, special place — that was reserved only for Papa.

The feeling that went along with The Big Papa Chair was so strong that it is forever engraved in Gramma's mind.

Standing or sitting in a parent's usual place

אֵיזֶהוּ מוֹרָא?

לֹא יַעֲמוֹד בִּמְקוֹמוֹ הַמְיוּחָד לוֹ לַעֲמוֹד שָׁם...

וְלֹא יֵשֵׁב בַּמָּקוֹם הַמְיוּחָד לוֹ...

What is reverence? One may not stand in his parent's usual place...nor sit in his usual place... (*Shulchan Aruch* 240:2).

A son or daughter may not stand or sit in his/her father's or mother's usual place unless necessary, and permission was given. This is one way to show: "I don't feel myself equal in importance to my parent."[5]

Reverence in standing

The *Shulchan Aruch* gives this example: When a parent has a special place that he/she frequents to discuss important matters... a son or daughter should not stand there.[6] For example, if a parent is a teacher or lecturer and a child is substituting, he should either teach from a different place or move the lectern to a slightly different position. This is to avoid giving the impression that he views himself as equal in importance.

Reverence in sitting

Similarly, a son or daughter may not sit in a parent's designated place.[7]

The most common example would be at home, at the table. If a parent sits in a particular place at the table — for example, the father at one end and the mother at the other — and these are their designated, regular places, a son or daughter should not sit there without permission, even when not sitting down to a meal.

If all the chairs are similar, the chair that happens to be at the head can be moved to be used in a different place.

This mitzvah applies:

❖ During a parent's lifetime[8]

❖ In a parent's presence and/or in the presence of others

❖ When a son or daughter is alone, there is a difference of opinion. Some permit sitting in a parent's seat.[9] Others say since the feeling of *yirah* is an internal, private affair, it would be applicable even in total privacy, reflecting a heart that feels the significance of a parent's "place."[10]

We find the name Damah ben Nesinah in yet another incident, this time illustrating his sensitivity toward his father's "place." Nesinah had a particular stone that he used to sit on. That was his "seat." His son, Damah, never sat on that stone.[11]

A parent's special chair

If a father or mother has a chair that only they use, such as the "big Papa chair" in the story above, or a rocking chair, a recliner, or a chair at the table that is specifically set aside for the parent (for example, a chair with arms), a child should not sit in that chair even if it is moved.[12]

A parent's place: a direction

The Gemara and *Shulchan Aruch* give us this first expression of reverence: Do not stand in your parent's special place. While this is a commandment in its explicit meaning, it is also significant as suggestive of an attitude.

> *OUR SON AND DAUGHTER-IN-LAW traveled abroad for a family* simchah, *along with the youngest, a baby. Aunts were happy to pitch in with some of the other children, and I got three of the most adorable* eineklach *imaginable.*
>
> *On Friday, opening 7-year-old's Yochanan's briefcase, I discovered the once-familiar* parashah *sheet and had in mind that this needed to be filled out and signed.*
>
> *Motza'ei Shabbos, I asked Yochanan's 16-year-old brother Chaim if he would give us a hand filling in the necessary information and proper responses. Quite clearly, my husband and I have been out of this "*parashah*" for a long time. Chaim hesitated. Usually a very accommodating boy, we weren't sure what his reservation was.*
>
> *"Chaim, is there a problem filling this out?"*
>
> *He seemed reluctant to say.*
>
> *"Do you prefer not to?"*

Concern was written on his face. About what, I had no clue. So I just smiled encouragingly.

"Umm…" he stammered. "Umm…" And then it came out. "Usually my father fills these out," he answered softly.

I was stunned. To Chaim, filling out the parashah *sheet was taking his father's place.*

My husband jumped to the rescue. "I'll sign it," he said, with a look that beamed with pride. He walked over and put his arm around this precious child, who we now understood had been grappling with his grandparent's request and what he felt was his father's due.

"You're really doing us a favor by filling it out," he said to our grandson. "It's been years since we did one of those things. But, of course, I'm in charge. So I'll do the signing."

A parent's place is certainly spatial and literal, but it is also symbolic and not to be usurped. The equalization of family members that we see today comes with a price — the parent's "place" is compromised. So, while it is great to be helpful — in the kitchen or anywhere else — caution is in order. An attitude of "I'll help, but *my* way" — I'll cook and bake, but only what *I* am in the mood to do in the way I want to do it (as opposed to offering suggestions and making requests, which *are* in order) — smacks of overstepping a boundary.

Parents are entitled to a title

אֵיזֶהוּ מוֹרָא … לֹא יִקְרָאֶנּוּ בִּשְׁמוֹ לֹא בְּחַיָּיו וְלֹא
בְּמוֹתוֹ אֶלָּא אוֹמֵר אַבָּא מָארִי…

What is reverence? … One may not address or refer to a parent by his name during the parent's lifetime and even after a parent's death; rather, a parent must be titled…
(*Shulchan Aruch* 240:2).

Parents are entitled to a title.
This is so it be apparent to all that this is your parent. Others

should take note that to you, your father and your mother are VIPs in your life.

And foremost, it should be apparent to **you**.

Addressing parents by first names

We may not address a parent by his first name:

> *"Chaim, can you help me with my homework?"*
> *"Leah, do you have time to sew a button?"*
> *"Hi, Yosef. What's up?"*

Even with parental permission, this is not permitted because it is considered a *zilzul* (disrespect).

Instead, we should address our parents using customary titles such as Abba, Dad, Daddy, Tatty, Papa, Father, Ima, Mommy, Mom, Mama, and Mother.[13]

Referring to parents by their first name

When speaking of our parents, we should not refer to a father or mother by first name alone, even when not in their presence and even after their passing; i.e. "This is Miriam" or "Miriam was an avid reader." Rather, a parent should be titled,[14] for example, "Rabbi," "Dr.," "Reb," "Rebbetzin," "Mrs." and the like. "This is my mother, Mrs. Dina Gross."

According to some opinions, "father" or "mother" is a sufficent title. "My father is Dov Gross."

According to other opinions, one should refrain from referring to a parent using his or her first name, even with the addition of a title. "This is my mother, Mrs. Gross."

There are times when it cannot be avoided, such as in response to a question or when necessary for identification. For instance, you're in a bank and the teller asks you for your father's first name. Though his interest is only in the first name, a son or daughter should say, "My father is Mr. David Miller," or simply, "Mr. David Miller." Another example would be when a son is called for an *aliyah* to the Torah. When he is asked by the *gabbai* for his name, the son should respond by adding a title before his father's name. For example: Asher ben avi mori Yaakov or Asher ben Reb Yaakov.

WHEN I BEGAN *the school year and looked over the attendance sheet, one of the girls' last names was very familiar to me. It is an uncommon name, so I was quite sure it must be the family I know. I wondered which one of the four brothers is her father.*

When I asked her, she answered, "My father is Reb Shmuel."

I was impressed by her response, and also curious. "How did you know to preface your father's name with 'Reb'?"

She answered with a shy smile, "My mother taught me."

IN MY MOTHER'S OFFICE, *they only know her as "Bracha," and that's how I asked for her whenever I called.*

Then I learned this halachah in school. Now I say, "May I please speak to my mother, Mrs. Bracha Miller?"

IN RECENT YEARS, *Gramma has become forgetful. It's hard for her to identify which of her many grandchildren is calling. When I call, I have to identify myself. I say, "Bubby, it's Yitzchak. I am Reb Avrohom's son."*

Davening

When we daven for a parent's welfare, we say their given name without any additional title. When we are addressing Hashem, we don't give honor to anyone else.

On the other hand, when we submit a parent's name for davening, it is proper to title; e.g., "Please daven for my father, Reb so-and-so." Some preface the name with "Reb," "Maras," "avi mori" or "imi morasi."

A special refinement

In some homes, families are careful not to refer to parents as "he/she" or "him/her."

IN OUR FAMILY, *we are all careful not to say "he" or "she" when speaking about our parents. If one of our little siblings* *says something like, "She said she would take us," or, "I gave it to him," we older children all chorus, "Who is she? Who is him? You mean, 'Mommy said she would take you,' or, 'You gave it to Tatty'?*

It doesn't take them long to get the hang of it.

Writing a parent's name

There is a difference of opinion as to whether you are allowed to write a parent's name without a title. Whenever possible, one should title parents. This would include writing a check or addressing an envelope to parents.[15]

When making a dedication in honor of parents, rather than "In honor of our beloved parents, Saul and Esther Miller," it is proper to title: "Mr. and Mrs. Saul and Esther Miller."

When writing a story about parents, one should not write, "Shimon was born in Russia," but rather "My father, Reb Shimon, was born in Russia."

When filling out official documents or forms that do not allow for titles, it is permissible to write the name alone.

Parents-in-law

One should not call parents-in-law by their first name.[17] If they insist, one should discuss options with a Rav.

Grandparents

When a son is talking to his children about his mother, for instance, he may refer to her as "Bubby Leah," since she is titled. Some people prefer to avoid a personal name and instead say "Bubby Katz."

———◆———

Here we have the parent-child relationship from a Torah perspective: close, but respectful. It's a loving bond, with the accompanying qualities of devotion, affection, attentiveness, loyalty, trust, and sympathy that are part of all true relationships. But it differs from our other relationships because the Torah adds the obligatory attitude of deference.

The Torah teaches us that parents and children do not share the same status in the home. The mitzvah of *yirah* and all its halachic details establishes this inequality.

Chapter 19

Learning to Speak a New Language

אֵיזֶהוּ מוֹרָא... לֹא סוֹתֵר אֶת דְּבָרָיו...

What is reverence? … One may not
contradict a parent...

(*Shulchan Aruch* 240:2).

How many languages do you speak? Do you speak the
language of *yirah*? This language is our mother tongue, unique
to *Klal Yisrael*.

The word for contradict, סוֹתֵר, is the same word used in the 39
Melachos of Shabbos for the *melachah* of סוֹתֵר, *undoing*, *breaking*,
or *throwing down* in order to rebuild *our* way. This gives us an
understanding of what סוֹתֵר means in the context of this mitzvah:
stating that parents are wrong, throwing down their opinion.

When a parent makes a statement or has an opinion with
which a son and daughter does not agree, he or she should
not "throw down" that statement with an explicit statement of
opposition or disagreement.

Contradictions that serve no purpose

Mother: The baby looks just like Aunt Chava.
Daughter: Not in the least. She looks just like Sarah.

Father: That man has a South African accent.
Son: Definitely not. It's clearly Australian.

Mother: I love those pink flowers.
Son: They're not pink, they're fuchsia.

Mother: She made a delicious pudding.
Daughter: It's not called a pudding. It's called a quiche.

Notice that these responses have one thing in common: they are all of no consequence and do nothing but feed the poor habit of contradicting for no constructive purpose.

While we may not contradict a parent, we need not agree. A son/daughter may maintain his or her own ideas. What is prohibited is a blatant expression of opposition, a comment to the contrary.

It makes no difference if it's opinion or fact:

Opinion

Father: X is a beautiful city.
Son: There's nothing beautiful about it at all.

In the above example, the son is saying, "I have my opinion as a child, and you have yours as a parent, and mine is as valid as yours."

That may be so, but it can't take the form of a contradictory statement.

Fact

Parent: I went to the Cohen wedding last week.
Son: It wasn't last week, it was two weeks ago. And just for the record, it wasn't a wedding, it was a bar mitzvah.

It's as if the child is saying to the parent: "You have your facts wrong. I know better." This may be so, but a son or daughter still is not allowed to contradict a parent even when he is 100 percent sure he's correct.[1]

A son and daughter would do well to remember that not every comment needs a response. In these instances, reverence is expressed through silence.

When correcting is correct...

On the other hand, what if a parent might suffer a loss or an embarrassment if their statement is not corrected?

> *"Company is coming at seven," says mother — and you know they're coming at six and your mother won't be ready.*

> *Dad says, "It will take two hours to get there" — and you know it will take three and a half, as it did last time, and then your father will be late.*

...but with Torah tact...

If the purpose of the response is to protect our parents from loss or embarrassment, surely the form of response should reflect that purpose. How do we respond?

When it is beneficial to bring a point of information to a parent's attention, but this would necessitate contradicting the parent, Torah tact means using a nondecisive questioning form:[2]

> *"Do you think...?"*
> *"Should we check...?"*
> *"Maybe it was...?"*
> *"Could it be...?"*
> *"Is it possible...?"*
> *"Would you want me to make sure?"*
> *"Do you want me to call and find out?"*

A questioning form delivered in a nonauthoritarian and nondecisive tone allows us to present contradictory information while demonstrating deference for parents.

Parent: The phone is ringing. Please answer.

   ✗ Our phone is not ringing. It's the neighbor's phone (an oppositional statement).

✓ It could be that the ringing is from our neighbor's house. Do you want me to check?

Parent: I have time to go with you today to buy shoes. Let's try Best Buy first.

✗ Best Buy? Not in a million years! I would never walk into that store.

✓ Can we try R&S first? I like the shoes there better.

A response does not always have to be in a question form, as long as it's said respectfully, in a non-conclusive, non-emphatic manner, conveying in its tone and content the message of "perhaps..." "I think it may be..." "Maybe it is..."

Some are fortunate to live in a home where please, thank you, and excuse me have been taught and ingrained, where these expressions and similar ones are recognized as a mark of thoughtful, well-bred youth. Less familiar, but nonetheless indispensable in a Torah home, are the deferential introductory phrases listed above. They should be taught *bedarchei noam* — pleasantly, until they are second nature.

When we are accustomed from early on not to contradict our parents, we will instinctively react in ways that are both permissible and effective later on, if an elderly parent whose mind is not clear makes a statement that is obviously incorrect.

Parent: Today is Tuesday.

✗ It's not Tuesday, it's Friday. Don't you see the table is set for Shabbos?

✓ Should we check the date in the newspaper to be sure?

Mother: I already took my medicine.

✗ No you didn't. It's right here in the box.

✓ Maybe some pills were left in the box?

Father: No one gave me lunch yet.

✗ Of course you ate — look at the dirty dishes in the sink.

✓ Let me give you something delicious to eat right now.

A direct contradiction does little to solve these predicaments since imposing our reality on our confused parent is not possible. At this challenging junction, years of practicing nonconfrontational, noncontradictory patterns of response comes to our rescue — yet another benefit of becoming fluent in the language of *yirah*.

Responding to an accusation[3]

Father: Why do you always contradict me?
Son: I do not!

When a son or daughter feels **unjustly** blamed by a parent, he naturally wants to defend himself by saying, "I didn't do it." While replying is permissible, the defense should not take the form of a contradiction. Because halachah doesn't allow answering to the contrary, a child must find an alternate response.

Father: I told you to come home at ten.

✗ You never told me a time.

✓ I'm sorry for worrying you. I don't remember you saying it.

Father: Why did you take the car without permission?

✗ That's not true. You said I could.

✓ I thought I heard you say it's okay.

If, for instance, a parent says, "Why did you break my camera," an instinctive defense is, "I did not." Since this type of response is a definite contradiction, it is not permitted.

But how else can you answer?

Here comes the "questioning form" to the rescue: "Can I tell you what happened?" This is an alternate way of saying "I didn't do it," deflecting the blame and avoiding contradicting a parent.

"Is it possible…?" "Could it be…?" "Perhaps…"

We probably can't imagine hearing such responses, and certainly not saying them.

This chapter on *yirah* may be difficult to digest. Having been accustomed to speaking a different language all our lives, these expressions may sound stilted and seem almost impossible to incorporate into our vocabulary. For many, it is considered among the ancient languages no longer spoken, used only by a select few who stubbornly hold on.

Take heart! We have been fortunate to see in our times a major reawakening in many areas of speech. *Klal Yisrael* has been able to change its mindset and the resultant speech patterns. With more knowledge, the help of idealistic and dedicated educators, and *siyata d'Shmaya*, we *can* revive and rediscover the treasures of *yiras av va'eim* (reverence for parents).

IT WAS QUITE A NUMBER of years ago that we in Camp Morris bungalow colony were invited to hear a series of lectures on kibbud av va'eim.

One of the charms of Camp Morris for me is the diverse ages of my neighbors. As I was making my way to the spot on the lawn where the rebbetzin was to speak, I overheard a much older friend say, in jest, but with a strong undercurrent of sadness — "Well, I'll go listen, but she's a few years too late for a lot of us!"

She was so wrong. The rebbetzin covered so many facets of kibbud av va'eim, *including how to be* mechabed *one's parents even after they leave this world. She was able to talk about* kibbud av va'eim — *for most people, a subject murky with half-remembered lessons from childhood mixed with layers of guilt — with wisdom and humor. In fact, looking back, I believe that many of the practices that have become second nature for me and my family have their roots in those classes on the lawn.*

For example, she taught us that one should not contradict one's parents (or teachers). If a parent makes a mistake and he needs to know about it, one should preface the corrective statement with something like "is it possible that..." This has become part of our family lexicon. We actually use it in a humorous way, but the message gets across.

For instance, we had ordered a platter of wraps for a shalosh seudos simchah. A huge colorful platter was delivered on Friday.

Mom (catching sight of the platter): "Oh no! They sent

*sushi instead of wraps! Why did they do that?! We can't wash
on sushi!"*
    *Me (after carefully checking the platter): "Ma, is it possibly
possible that this platter is actually wraps and not sushi?"*
    Mom: "Possibly."

It's a new idea. A new language. More time is needed to learn
its syntax. But it's a pleasure to know the language of *yirah* is
being learned and spoken.

Questions that are out of the question

A son or daughter should not pepper a parent with questions
that expose the parent's error, exaggeration, oversight, or
misinterpretation. This is another version of "throwing down"
a parent's words.

> *Father: I am going to need a week to recover from that vacation.*
> *Child: Didn't you say you never slept so well at night?*
> *Father: Well, the day trips were exhausting.*
> *Son: What's exhausting about sitting on a bus?*

Discussions and debates

Torah learning is based on questions asked and a quest for
answers — probing, exploring possibilities, challenging — with
the intense desire to arrive at the truth. Our tradition has been
transmitted from one generation to the next — father to son,
teacher to student — in this way.

Difference of opinion, arguing a point to arrive at the truth, is
our strength; outright contradicting and demeaning statements
to parents is a failing and a prohibition.

Debating with a parent to clarify a halachah or a Torah passage,
even though it involves disagreement and challenge, is in place.[4]
What is not in place is arguing *derech hachlatah*, a definite statement
that leaves no room for other ideas, and *derech nitzachon*,[5] a
gloating attempt at one-upmanship with the goal being to prove
we are more intelligent or have more information than our parent:
"I'm going to win this one. I'm going to get him this time."

HARAV YECHEZKEL SHRAGA HALBERSTAM, the Shinover Rav (the Baal Divrei Yechezkel), was the son of the Divrei Chaim of Sanz.

A difficult question regarding an agunah *was brought to him. The Shinover Rav decided to travel to his saintly father to present his understanding of this complicated matter, to see if the Divrei Chaim agreed with his conclusion.*

The question was presented to the Divrei Chaim, who asked his son to return the next day for further discussion of the delicate issue.

Upon returning home, the Rav entered his study and promptly removed a Shulchan Aruch *from the shelf. Those present were not at all surprised. He was surely reviewing the sources for his position, which he would have to defend before his father the next day. What was surprising was that instead of taking the* Even HaEzer, *where the laws of* agunah *were found, he reached for a* Yoreh Deah. *Respectfully, his mistake was brought to his attention. To which he replied, "It is not the sources for my argument that I wish to review. I am reviewing the halachos of* kibbud av va'eim. *Tomorrow, when I have to prove my points and justify my claims, these halachos will be fresh in my mind."*

Not only Torah discussions, but also speaking about our daily lives, exchanging ideas, dissecting issues, discussing the pros and cons and bringing proofs, having heart-to-heart talks, disclosing and exposing our deepest feelings, are the cement that bonds the family unit.

Children and parents connecting meaningfully is important and desirable, provided that the interchange causes **no embarrassment** to parents, is **not demeaning,** and contains **no contradicting statements** that show disrespect: "You're wrong," "That's illogical," "What you're saying makes no sense," "I still don't agree," "I never heard anything so_____." Included as well is using a tone of voice or gestures that convey the same disrespect.

Father: Miri, Mommy and I decided that you're not going to seminary in Eretz Yisrael. We feel you should spend your seminary year locally.

✓ Miri: Is this open for discussion?*

If the answer is yes, Miri can let her parents know how she feels about it without:

Embarrassing them (particularly in front of others):
Father: We don't feel it's worth the expense.

✗ Miri: How come you have money for vacations, but not for seminary?

✓ Miri: Would it be possible if I earn part of the tuition?

Demeaning them (*zilzul*):
Father: You're not going to gain that much more from going.

✗ Miri: How can you say that? You were never in sem.

✓ Miri: Perhaps the gain is not only in learning more but also in maturing — learning to manage on my own.

Contradicting them:
Father: Not everyone in your class is going.

✗ Miri: Yes, they are.

✓ Miri: As far as I know, all my friends are going.

We all know the expression, "Think before you speak." The Torah demands that we all think before we speak: Is what I'm saying honest…truthful? Will it cause pain? Will someone lose his job or social standing because of what I said? Will it cause an argument?

Where do we first learn this essential *middah* of "think before you speak"? In our home, with our parents:

Learning that not everything needs a comment.

Considering, "Can I say this in a more respectful way?"

Controlling the knee-jerk reaction to accusations.

And realizing that not every question should be asked.

By following these and all halachos of *yirah*, we are placed in a "let me think a minute before I speak" mode, preparing us for the life of filtered speech required of every member of *Klal Yisrael*.

---

* Requesting permission to give your opinion is a way to avoid the problem of contra-dicting.

Chapter 20

In the Public Eye

In the previous chapter, we saw that contradicting a parent is prohibited. Contradicting "in the public eye," in front of others, is even worse.

Mother (describing a party to her friend): For the first course, she served a fruit cup —
Daughter: The roll with the salads was really the first course.
Mother: ...and then, I think she had a pumpkin soup with some pine nuts sprinkled —
Daughter: The proper name for those nuts is pignolia.
Mother: ...and then for the main dish, it looked like broil —
Daughter: I think it was roasted.
Mother: How can you correct me before I even say anything?

> If you are in the company of people you must honor, for example your father or mother, honor and revere them. Do not contradict them. If they say something and you know it is not so, do not say, "It's not like that" (Rabbeinu Yonah, *Sefer HaYirah*).[1]

"That's not the way it was!"

The contradiction serves no essential purpose

In general, if your parent is relating a story or making a statement in public ("public," meaning at least one other person is present), you should not contradict.

> *Mother (at a family gathering): You won't believe what happened at the zoo. We were standing in front of the lions, and Mutty stretched out his hand —*
> *Daughter: That's not the way it was. The story goes like this...*

> *Father to a neighbor: We were traveling 60 mph when the police stopped us.*
> *Son: It was more like 80.*

These are examples of unimportant corrections that should not have been made. If, as we learned earlier, an inconsequential statement should not be corrected in *private*, it certainly shouldn't be "fixed" in public.

What if your parent is telling a story about *you* in front of others, and you feel that what he is saying is inaccurate? If a parent exaggerates and gives people the impression that you are "more" than you really are, or different from the image you would like to project, may you set the record straight?

Father: This week, my son snagged a million-dollar contract for his company.

✖ Son: Actually, my partner did most of the work.

Not every statement of this type made by a parent requires a response. When the correction serves no essential purpose for the listener or for you — there is no loss involved, and your main purpose in commenting is merely to "set the record straight" — the best response is no response at all. Unless you say something like:

Mother: I never could have made this *simchah* myself without my daughter's help.

✓ Daughter: It was my pleasure.

I OWN A SMALL HARDWARE store that serves our local community. Business is steady, and profits are enough to support the family comfortably.

My father always worked in an office and was never self-employed. He sees my store as a shining example of what personal initiative can accomplish.

"My son, Chaim," he'll say proudly, "is the owner of Handy Hardware Store. You've heard of it, I'm sure. It's one of the biggest hardware suppliers in the whole Northeast."

Sometimes I'd like to say, "Come on, Dad. No way is my little store what you're making it out to be."

But then I think, leave it. No harm done. And it gives my father a lot of nachas.

Averting a loss (נֶזֶק)

While sons or daughters may protect themselves against loss,[2] correcting a parent in a public setting comes with rules and conditions, using the language of *yirah*.

Corrections that can wait should be done later, privately.

Corrections that can't wait may be done on the spot, using Torah tact.

Margalit Frankel gives music lessons. Mrs. Frankel is proud of her talented daughter. She is telling a friend, Mrs. Baum, how successful Margalit is as a teacher. Mrs. Baum, duly impressed, mentions that she would love her daughter Simmy to take lessons.

Mrs. Frankel promptly calls in Margalit, and announces, "At $20 an hour, she's giving you quite a bargain."

Margalit has just heard her mother quoting a price that is much lower than what she takes. Giving lessons for that price would leave her with an ongoing loss. If the mistake isn't corrected on the spot, it could prove sticky to correct later.

In this case, Margalit could say: "Mommy, I probably wasn't clear about…" Or, "It's true I used to take twenty, but now I charge thirty."

As long as Margalit makes her correction without annoyance or impatience, she may do so to prevent a loss — and most likely, her mother would want to be corrected.

Public embarrassment (בּוּשָׁה)

What if your parent tells a story about you that is not only inaccurate, but also humiliating? You want to say, "That's not true!"

Embarrassing any person is a serious transgression. To do so in public is worse.

This includes children.

If a parent has embarrassed a son or daughter in public the parent has transgressed a Torah prohibition and the child is allowed to defend himself, to deflect the humiliation — *as long as it is not done in a demeaning or contradictory manner.*[3]

> *I WAS SITTING WITH MY FATHER and a few friends discussing the purchase of my new home. Though I consulted with experts, I later discovered that the building rights that I had counted on were illegal.*
>
> *"How could you be so negligent?" my father said. "Who buys a house without consulting qualified lawyers? Where are your brains?"*
>
> *"Maybe this is an unusual case, Dad. I consulted with people who are known to be experts in the field."*

To save ourselves shame by causing shame is not an option. Parents, whose reverence is likened to that of the Almighty, are in a category of their own. No matter how tempting, embarrassing a parent is not an option.

Parents beware

Embarrassing children and then expecting them to be silent is a major "trip." Don't take your children there!

"My father's right!"

אֵיזֶהוּ מוֹרָא...לֹא מַכְרִיעַ אֶת דְּבָרָיו בְּפָנָיו...

What is reverence? … He may not...validate (i.e., feel a need to confirm) a parent's opinion in his presence...

(*Shulchan Aruch* 240:2).

When a parent is involved in a disagreement with someone, a son or daughter should not feel the need to "tip the scales" in his parent's favor by saying, "My father is right," or, "What my mother is saying makes more sense."[4]

You might think, what's wrong with that? Wouldn't most parents be thrilled to hear their child say, "I agree with my father?" Especially in front of other people!

Living in a time when reverence for parents is in such a sorry state, it would serve us well to hear the Torah's answer: It is considered arrogant to suppose that we need to lend support to our parent, implying that our parent needs our assistance and giving the impression that our opinion is weightier than theirs. When a son or daughter says something to the effect of "What my father is saying makes more sense," this translates to, "I'm the expert here."

A son and daughter might very well be more qualified. But this is the humility demanded of a child in the family setting.[5]

What if you're asked, "What's your opinion?"[6]

If a parent asks, "What's your opinion?" or, alternatively, if a child asks, "May I give my opinion?" and gets an okay, that's fine. No lack of reverence is involved, because your parent has given you permission to state your opinion, even if it's contradictory, as long as this is done in a non-demeaning manner.

Bringing in outside sources as proof[7]

If a son has proof to bolster his father's opinion, he should bring it. This is not considered "throwing around his weight." This is bringing tangible proof, as opposed to a son or daughter's personal opinion.

My father and his brother were arguing about a political issue. My uncle had his views, and it seemed like my father had little to back up his argument. I had just read an article that included statistics that would prove my father's point, so I ran up to my room to find it.

"My father/mother is wrong"[8]

It is disrespectful for a child to feel that he has to tip the scales in his father's favor. But it's obvious that it's **worse** — and prohibited — to tip them to his father's **disfavor** and agree with someone who has challenged his parent.

MY PARENTS HAVE MANAGED a bungalow colony for many years. My father is a jack-of-all-trades, so he's well qualified for the job. If you have ever been in a bungalow in the country, you understand why this is essential. The manager is hired by the owner and is called upon to handle major and minor emergencies and to field complaints, fix what he can, and call in an expert for the rest.

Having many years of experience, coupled with his natural abilities, my father can solve many of the problems on the spot. He fixes screens, chairs, and tables. He's pretty good at repairing roof leaks and has become quite an authority on plumbing. He's always on grounds, accessible and accommodating — a big plus and convenience for the tenants.

Over the years I've picked up a lot of information hanging around my father. Not all of it was about fixing things. Some of it was about fixing me.

This story happened when I was a young teen.

It was early Sunday morning when the phone rang. Leib Steiner, one of our tenants, was asking for my father. I handed over the phone and soon gathered from my father's answers that it was about a leak. Dad assured him he'd take care of it.

The following Sunday there was a knock on the door of our bungalow. It was Leib Steiner with a sour look on his face.

"What happened to your usual prompt service, Jake," he asked my father, obviously annoyed. "I called a week ago — as I'm sure you remember. Forecast this week is for rain, Jake," he finished, as he eyed the ceiling, seemingly imagining himself in a downpour.

"You called? I don't remember any such call, Leib," my father answered.

I, who was standing nearby, piped up, "Don't you remember, Dad? It was last Sunday. I answered and gave you the

phone. I heard you tell Mr. Steiner you'd take care of it."
*When Leib Steiner had left, with my father's assurance he'd
take care of the problem that morning, my father turned to me.
"I may have made a mistake," he told me, "but so did
you." And he taught me a halachah of* kibbud av va'eim *that I
remember to this very day — and that I teach my own children.*

Supporting a parent's stance in his absence[9]

While validating in a debate makes it seem like your parent
needs your backing, defending a parent's stance in his **absence**
is considered respectful.

> *"I know you feel strongly that my father is wrong. I can tell
> you firsthand that my dad would have accepted the chairmanship,
> but between his work and other communal responsibilities, he
> only gets three or four hours sleep a night."*

"Dad's right!" is wrong

When a father is disciplining a child, siblings should not
insinuate that the father needs their backing, as in the following
scenario:

> *The family is spending time together, and one of the children,
> Shmuel, misbehaves. Dad reprimands him. Shmuel protests and
> will not accept the blame.*
> *Shmuel's brother, Mendy, pipes up, "Dad's right, Shmuel."*

Branches, buds, and flowers

The obligations of sons and daughters to their parents
are more than can be listed and warrant a lengthy
discussion. Yet, [what *can* be said is that] these obligations
include two basic mitzvos, honor and reverence, and
we are given examples of each. Reverence: Don't sit
in your parent's place, don't stand in their place, and
don't contradict what they say. Honor: provide food and

drink, clothing and coverings, help them in and help them out. **These and anything of similar nature and benefit** are the obligations of all sons and daughters to their parents[10] (Rambam, *Peirush Mishnayos*).

Honoring parents — feeding, dressing, transporting, etc. — are merely examples of service that branch off into myriad offshoots. So it is with reverence. The three areas mentioned in the *Shulchan Aruch* (240:2) of **not standing or sitting** in a parent's place, **not calling** a parent by their first name, **not contradicting, not validating** in public, are also only examples. They also branch off to include many buds and flowers, giving us the delightful aroma of *yiras av va'eim.*[11]

To mention but a few...

Not interrupting a parent

שִׁבְעָה דְבָרִים בְּגוֹלֶם וְשִׁבְעָה בְּחָכָם...

There are seven attributes of an unrefined person (בּוּר) and seven of a wise person (חָכָם)... (*Pirkei Avos* 5:9).

One of the seven attributes of the wise is that a wise person does not interrupt the words of another.[12]

A wise person doesn't interrupt anyone, all the more so a parent.[13]

WHEN I VISITED my father in Florida last summer, I found out that the air conditioner was broken on the main floor. I don't remember my father mentioning it. I can't remember him ever complaining. But there were record-breaking temperatures the week I came, so I could experience firsthand how awful it was without AC. I convinced my father that now was the time to get a new unit.

When we went together to the store to pick it out, I tried very hard to keep quiet. I have a bad habit of interrupting, and I know it drives my father mad. I kept biting my lip, reminding myself to let my father have this conversation without my interrupting him every thirty seconds. I stood by, stifling the words that remained on the tip of my tongue. Uncharacteristically, I just observed as my father spoke to the salesman to clarify details that were important for him. We purchased the unit, and both left the store smiling, each one of us having accomplished his purpose.

When a parent is speaking with someone else in person or on the telephone, a son or daughter should only interrupt if important, and after quietly asking permission. Early on, parents should teach their children acceptable methods of interrupting them when they are in the middle of a conversation.

Not answering before or for a parent...

"What is considered *yirah*?" ask our Sages.

One answer given is: "Not to speak in his [parents'] stead"[14] (*Peah* 1:1).

Rashi comments on this: "When a parent is being asked a question and is expected to answer, a son or daughter should not be quick to answer instead of him."[15]

We learn this from *Bereishis*:

Eliezer, Avraham Avinu's messenger, asked Besuel to give his permission for his daughter, Rivkah, to marry Yitzchak Avinu. Lavan, Besuel's son, who was also present, spoke up before his father, Besuel, could answer, to give his opinion on the matter.[16]

...unless appreciated

When a parent is being addressed, and is expected to answer, a son/daughter may answer in his stead if the parent would appreciate it.[17] For instance, if the subject is one the father doesn't like talking about, such as questions about his background, wartime experiences, or finances, by entering the conversation, the son or daughter would be doing so to spare his father discomfort. Or, when a parent would be embarrassed because he is not familiar with the topic, the son's or daughter's answer covers for the parent's lack of information.

Correcting

The *Shulchan Aruch* (240:11) tells us that if a son or daughter sees a parent doing something **prohibited by the Torah** he should *not* say to him:

> *"That's not the way it's done!"*
> *"You did that all wrong!"*
> *"The halachah is like this, not like that."*
> *"You're not allowed to do that!"*
> *"You just made a very serious mistake."*

Since parents are human, even knowledgeable parents can make a mistake. Whether they weren't aware of a particular halachah, or out of negligence or error they failed to fulfill it, a son or daughter should respond in a respectful, nonaccusatory manner, rather than admonishing or correcting:

> *"Can I show you what it says about this?"*
> *"Can I tell you what I learned?"*
> *"Does it say...?" "Doesn't it say...?"*
> *"Can we look this up / ask a Rabbi about this?"*
> *"Could it be the acharonim pasken a different way?"*[18]

A response does not always have to take the form of a question, as long as it is said respectfully — "Perhaps we are supposed to...," "I once heard the preferred way is..."[19]

Correcting a misquote

The honor and reverence that a son and daughter must show parents is so paramount that even when a parent makes a mistake by misquoting or misinterpreting — for example, a verse in the Torah, a Torah source, interpretation, or insight, or even a halachic ruling — a correction should be made only when the child knows his parent wants to hear it and will appreciate it, or when someone will have a loss.

Using a tactful, indirect approach, by questioning rather than challenging, we make it possible for a parent to correct himself in a nondemeaning manner.

Another possibility is to indicate a written source for our

conclusion. Then a parent can come to his own conclusions.[20]

Corrections should not contain contradiction: "That's not what it says"; nor may they be delivered in a condescending manner: "That's the way you think it was said? Next time you should read it straight from a *Chumash.*"

The following should be kept in mind:

❖ Any correction that could be made privately should not be made publicly (unless a parent would want to be corrected on the spot).

❖ Whenever a correction can be made by someone other than a child, that is preferable.

❖ When a child knows his parent won't listen or doesn't want to hear, and will, in fact, be annoyed, the child is exempt from correcting.

A time to remain silent

WHEN MRS. KRAMER AND HER DAUGHTER, Meira, heard that their neighbor, Pinchas Fine, had passed away, they coordinated their schedules so that they could pay a condolence call to his wife, Toby Fine.

There were a handful of people gathered in the room when they walked in. At first, the discussion centered on the deceased's life and his many accomplishments. After a while, the conversation turned to other topics.

Mrs. Kramer reminded Toby about the marvelous time they had the previous winter when they unexpectedly met in Florida.

Knowing it was proper and beneficial to the deceased that the discussion be centered on his good and worthy deeds, Meira turned to her mother and said, "Now we should be speaking about the deceased."

Meira was correct in her assessment of the proper topics at a *shivah*, but she was wrong in correcting her mother, since her mother's conversation was not in violation of halachah.

If she could have done this in a respectful way, Meira could have subtly steered the conversation back to more appropriate topics.

MY FATHER WAS BEING honored with Maftir on the second day of Rosh Hashanah. The minyan consisted of members like my father, who had a limited knowledge of Judaism. They had never gone to yeshivah, and like many of their contemporaries in the 1920s, went to work as teenagers to help support their families. My father, who was orphaned at the age of 8, was in the work force by 16. Having inherited only poverty and loneliness, he was a self-made man. He had, to his credit, many accomplishments. One in which he took great pride was that despite limited skills he had taught himself to read the Haftarah.

I, his 17-year-old yeshivah bachur, whom he had sent to learn, was the baal koreh in that minyan on that Rosh Hashanah.

I'll tell you what happened that day, but it wasn't until years later that I really appreciated what had taken place

One of the shul members must have realized that if I stood next to my father while he was reading the Haftarah, being the big "expert" that I was, I would probably find mistakes to correct which were not essential. So my father's friend, this shul member, made sure that I was given the honor of holding the Sefer Torah, which automatically positioned me at a distance from my father.

He must have been thinking, "Here your father sent you to yeshivah, more than most of his friends did for their kids, and now you are going to embarrass him in front of his friends. Not in this shul!"

He must have credited me with enough brains not to call out a correction from where I was sitting, but wasn't sure what "damage" I might do if he, a loyal friend, hadn't watched out for my father's kavod on that Rosh Hashanah day.

Exercise. Its value has been pounded into our psyches. Weight-bearing. Crucial.

Another lesson to carry into the spiritual realm. Exercising deference. Exercising restraint. Yes, bearing the weight of a parent. Developing muscles to accept all mitzvos that require restraint — and deference to a Higher Authority.

Endurance. Perseverance. Sweating it out. Becoming a stronger person.

Chapter 21

We Aim to Please:
Parents' requests and children's responses

מוֹרָא אֵינוֹ אֶלָּא שֶׁלֹּא יְזַלְזֵל וְיַעֲבוֹר עַל רְצוֹנוֹ

What is *yirah*? It means primarily not to
slight [a parent] by disregarding his wishes

(Netziv, *Meromei Sadeh, Kiddushin* 30).

When a child is **aware** of a parent's need or is specifically
asked to be of assistance, it is part of the mitzvah of honor to
respond positively and cheerfully.

*MY DAUGHTER, SHEVY, came home from school,
deposited her briefcase, and made her announcement.*

"Ima, our class is learning about kibbud av va'eim. *The
teacher asked each girl to think of something she can do for
her parents that she hasn't been doing until now."*

*"So, Shevy, what did you pick?" I asked, privately
commending that teacher.*

*"If you watch me, you'll see," she said, as she skipped to
the kitchen.*

It didn't take me long.

(Let me preface this by telling you that Shevy is like a lot of kids. They help around the house. But until they do it, and how they do it, is another story.)

That afternoon, I asked Shevy to straighten up her room. Instead of the usual "uh-huh" followed by deafening silence and no action, I heard something else.

I thought to myself, Is this it? Is this her class assignment?

I waited for another chance to see if it wasn't just a fluke. But sure enough, she repeated it, once to me, and then, later in the day, again to my husband.

This was the scene:

"Shevy, could you please close the window in your room — it's raining."

And Shevy replies, flashing a full smile, "B'simchah! (I'll be happy to)."

This is major. That such a little girl could come up with such a big idea. Of all the things she could have chosen, she got to the core of this mitzvah.

But is a child obligated to do everything a parent asks of him, even if it's difficult for him?

Parental request for personal assistance

"The company is coming soon. Can you please vacuum the rug?"

"Oh Ma, not now. I'm in the middle of homework."

"My car is in for repairs. Would you drive me to the dentist tomorrow morning at nine?"

"Nine in the morning? Tomorrow is the only day I can sleep in."

"Can you help me bring in the groceries from the car?"

"I'm on the phone."

"Do you have time to pick up my shirts from the cleaners?"

"Not really. I have to go straight to practice, and it's not on the way."[1]

When the Torah tells us "Honor your father and mother" it is referring to requests like those above – offering personal assistance and benefit to parents, responding promptly and pleasantly. Disregarding such parental requests, making them inconsequential to us, is a lack of *yirah*, part of the mitzvah of לֹא לִסְתּוֹר דְּבָרָיו, not to "throw down their word." Only with compelling reasons should a child ask for a postponement or exemption.

"Is it okay if I do it later?"
"Can Shmuel do this now and I'll do his job tomorrow?"
"I want to help, but it's hard for me now because..."

For mothers and fathers:

A parent's job is to appreciate that these mitzvos of *kavod* and *yirah* are "difficult mitzvos to fulfill properly." In some homes, requests are flying fast and furious, making this a rather "constant" mitzvah. We have to *help* our children and beware of setting them up for failure. In this case, the failure would be a request that is too difficult for the child to obey, whether in scope or nature.

Compliment them when they are successful, hear them out when they are struggling, and climb into their shoes and appreciate the difficulty of the challenge from their perspective.

When it's not about the parents' direct physical needs

"I HAVE A CAMERA THAT I SAVED up for and bought with my own money. Recently one of my classmates asked if she could borrow it. When she returned the camera a few days later, I saw it was slightly damaged. When I pointed out the damage, she said it was like that when I gave it to her. I was very sure that it wasn't, but since I couldn't prove it, I felt that I had to let the matter drop.

"When my mother found out, she was insistent that I not lend out my camera again. My mother is a person who does a

*lot of favors, but she feels that an item like a camera that can
be easily damaged should not be lent.*

"Must I listen?"

*"FROM TIME TO TIME, FRIENDS ask me to sign as a
guarantor. I know times are rough, so I'm happy to do that
favor. But a few times I got stuck and had to pay for friends
who couldn't repay the loans.*

*"I have a good job, and I don't mind helping out friends. I
know they'll pay me back when they can.*

*"My father asked me not to sign anymore. He is afraid
that because of my generous nature I will be pulled into
something that will be over my head.*

*"I live at home and have a good relationship with my
parents. My father really feels strongly about this. On the
other hand, just because of a few disappointments, I don't
want to let down my friends who count on me.*

"What's the right thing to do?"[2]

When a son or daughter lives at home

Our Sages have expounded on these questions at length:
What if the parent's request does not provide the parent with a
direct benefit? What if the matter primarily concerns a son's or
daughter's personal benefit?*

The conclusion reached by the majority of Rabbinic authorities
in the responsa and also concluded by the two great luminaries
of our times, Harav Yosef Shalom Elyashiv, *ztz"l*, and *yblcht"a*
Harav Shmuel Wosner, *shlita*,[3] is that a son or daughter **should**
comply with a parent's request, even when that request primarily
affects the son or daughter (with qualifications, as discussed in
the following pages).[4]

This question is addressed in the contemporary *sefer*,
Vayevarech Dovid, by Rabbi Yisroel Dovid Harfenes:[5]

Q Is a son or daughter living at home obligated to comply with

---

* A detailed description of their discussions can be found in scholarly books on honoring parents (see Bibliography).

a parent's request when the matter is not directly connected to parental needs or other benefits to the parent, but rather a matter concerning the needs of the son or daughter?

A Sons and daughters living at home should respond agreeably even to such requests [based on the halachah cited above] and for the following reasons:

1. Out of gratitude for food, lodgings, medical attention, tuition...

   Do we dare write etcetera to cover decades of giving and sacrifice? *Chazal* tell us that even if a person did a small favor for us, we should feel indebted. How much more so to a parent, who sacrificed day and night for years, and took care of all our needs. [6]

2. When one moves to a new community (even if he doesn't plan to stay), he must comply with the new and different customs, and even stringencies, of that place so that unpleasant confrontations won't arise as a result of his inappropriate behavior.

   This would surely apply to a son or daughter in their parents' home. Children should follow the rules and customs of their home so that harmony reigns.

3. The Torah obligates a parent to provide for the needs of his dependent children. Once a child is able to be independent, all benefits a parent provides are considered *chessed*, not an obligation but *"hachnassas orchim"* on a huge scale.

   Our Sages tell us that when we are a guest in someone's home, it is proper to comply with the host's requests. He is the master of the house. It is his home, and he is in charge.

If your host tells you to be home at 11 p.m. because that's when he locks up, probably you wouldn't answer, "I'll be home at twelve." If it was very difficult for you to return by that time, at the very least you would explain your difficulty and try to work out something to your host's satisfaction. Likewise, a child should follow the routines of his home: mealtimes, bedtimes, and curfews.

When complying is very difficult, when a parent's request causes significant distress (צַעַר רַב),*¹it is in place for a son or daughter to explain his difficulty, concerns and misgivings, fear or pain:

> *"Chessed is so much a part of who I am that it's worth it for me to pay for the camera repairs."*
> *"How can I face my friends if I refuse to give a loan?"*
> *"I know you don't want me to get a license yet. If you tell me all your rules and regulations…would it make a difference?"*
> *"I know you want us home by ten, but the class party is going to last longer than that."*

Discussion is encouraged as long as it's done with *derech eretz*. Sons or daughters can negotiate (without contradicting or belittling), but when all is said and done, in every home, some things will be nonnegotiable.

When you can't agree…

When a son or daughter finds it extremely difficult to comply with a parental request (feeling that they will have a major loss if they go along), but the parent, on the other hand, feels it's not correct to concede on this issue, it is a fortunate home that has a Rav to whom to turn.

Some people feel that only *kashrus* questions or proper mourning procedures should be brought to a Rav's attention. But we see from Rabbinic responsa that throughout the millennia many questions related to honoring parents have been brought to Rabbanim.

When a son or daughter does not live at home

When a son or daughter is married and/or not living at home, a parental request is weighed differently. When a request primarily concerns a son's or daughter's personal conduct or preferences — such as how they invest their money and where they vacation, which job to take, where to shop — then, if complying with a parent's opinion or request would cause the the adult child a monetary loss (הֶפְסֵד) or significant distress

---

* *Teshuvos V'Hanhagos* 3:275: Rav Moshe Sternbuch, *shlita*, differentiates between צער רב — a significant, major *tza'ar*, and צער מעט — a minor *tza'ar*.

(צַעַר), and/or impinge on *shalom bayis*, halachah allows a son or daughter their preference. They are not obligated to comply.*²

IN OUR FAMILY, we have a history of a certain medical condition that has affected several of my siblings. Before I married, my mother told me that I must tell her if I ever have signs of this condition, since she has so much experience in this matter and would want to advise me as to the best course of action.

This warning settled in the back of my mind.

Until last month.

Despite her warning, I knew how my mother would react to my symptoms. I couldn't bring myself to cause her this anxiety. On the other hand, I knew very well that if I didn't tell her, she would find out one day and would be unforgiving.

To complicate matters, I also hesitated because I had investigated alternative methods of tackling this condition that I know my mother wouldn't approve of. She believes in conventional medicine all the way. Her disapproval, I felt, would be very difficult for me to deal with.

I was in a real quandary, so I brought my predicament to a Rav. He answered that I was not obligated to tell my mother because of the difficulties it would cause me (tza'ar rav). However, continued the Rav, if I felt I could manage with my mother's response, I should tell.

There are, however, parental requests that would *not* cause significant loss or distress, or interfere with *shalom bayis*. But they do require "sacrifices," because the child would prefer to do things differently. In these cases, sons and daughters should aim to please.

---

*A parent might be annoyed that his son didn't listen to him, feeling that by ignoring his opinion his son is somehow showing a lack of care for him. For some fathers and mothers, it is more painful for their request to be ignored than for their physical needs to be neglected.

Surely, sons and daughters should try not to annoy a parent. At the same time, a parent should not become annoyed!

Parents should not set themselves up to be aggravated. They do this when they demand a child's compliance in an area in which, according to halachah, he is not obligated to comply.

Aiming to please

Chumash Vayikra begins with a discussion of *korbanos*. We are told that when a *korban* is offered, it should ascend with a *rei'ach nichoach* (רֵיחַ נִיחוֹחַ), a pleasing fragrance for Hashem.

rei'ach: a fragrance

nichoach (נִיחוֹחַ): from the root *noach* (נֹחַ), to draw pleasure from

What is the pleasure?

Rashi answers: נַחַת רוּחַ לְפָנַי שֶׁאָמַרְתִּי וְנַעֲשָׂה רְצוֹנִי, "a fragrance that causes pleasure to Me, knowing that I speak and My will is done."

It is as if Hashem is saying, "I give mitzvos, and My children follow them. They do it the way I have asked of them."

The Chofetz Chaim tells us that *yiras Shamayim* is defined as not going against Hashem's *ratzon*, His will. Similarly, he says, *yirah* of parents means being concerned about a parent's *ratzon*, his wishes, preferences, opinions, and instructions.[7]

When our parents ask us to do something for ourselves in a certain way, and we acquiesce and do it the way they want, we give them the pleasure and satisfaction of knowing that we respect their opinion and defer to them. We are willing to do it *their* way.

> *MY FATHER WAS AN EASYGOING PERSON and asked very little of me. When he did offer advice, it was usually on the mark.*
>
> *I carried my papers together with cash and checks in a rather disorganized fashion in my jacket pocket. This disturbed my father greatly, and he asked me many times to put my cash in a wallet. I always smiled but never did anything about it.*
>
> *No question it was a more logical thing to do. It would even have been helpful to separate the money from the papers as I was always taking out my little papers, and the bills probably slipped out from time to time.*
>
> *Why didn't I listen? No special reason. Just too lazy to change. Got used to doing it my way.*
>
> *Now that my father is no longer alive, I think back to that*

request. It would have taken so little effort to go along, but it would have made him so happy that I was listening to his advice.

Rabbeinu Yonah in *Iggeres HaTeshuvah*[8] says: עִיקַר כִּיבּוּד אָב וָאֵם לַעֲשׂוֹת לָהֶם נַחַת רוּחַ בֵּין בְּדִיבּוּר וּבֵין בְּמַעֲשֶׂה, "At the heart of *kibbud av va'eim* is to give parents pleasure with both words and actions."

This is the pleasure of knowing "my child wants to please me."

***MY SON DANNY** and his family were visiting with us.*

I was busy in the kitchen preparing lunch for the family. Suddenly I realized that it was awfully quiet in the house. I knew my daughter-in-law had taken the baby to the doctor, but where was everyone else?

I found my son resting on the couch. He had been on a night shift, so it was no wonder. But where were the kids?

I was not anxious to disturb him, but was very concerned about the whereabouts of his brood. I waited a few moments and then saw Danny shift positions.

"Danny, where is everyone?" I asked in a loud whisper.

"In the park," he mumbled back.

Danny's family lives in a quiet rural area where safety is a non-issue. He was forgetting that in our town, children can't be on their own. At least that's how I feel.

With many apologies, I explained the danger to Danny and asked him to bring his children home.

Half asleep, he let me know that he understood my concern, but reassured me that they'd be fine.

Not convinced at all, I made a further apology but insisted that he bring them back.

Danny saw I was not backing down. Wearily, he pulled himself up from the couch, mustered a half smile, and went to fetch the children while I went back to my pots and the cake that was almost ready to come out of the oven.

When they returned, Danny went to lie down, and I gathered the children around me. I thought I would get some extra mileage out of this.

"You know your father was on duty last night, and he's

really zonked. But I asked him to go bring you all back. What do you think he wanted to do, lie down or get you?"

Even the 4-year-old knew the answer.

Looking down at these children whom I loved so dearly, I hoped that I would now be able to plant a seed that would take root in their minds.

"Your dad only went because I was worried. He saw it was important to me. He didn't want to go, but he went anyway."

They listened.

Then we sat down to eat lunch.

When parents show their children that they heed their own parents' requests, whether pleased or not, full of energy or very tired, hungry or satiated, tense or relaxed…no lesson is more powerful or convincing.

I INVITED MY PARENTS for the two days of Shavuos. We live in a large, lovely home, so when my mother suggested that I invite my three siblings and their families to join us as well, I told her it was no problem at all. She was excited thinking about how much fun it would be. And then my mother added one more request.

"I don't want to do this if it's going to mean a lot more work for you, Elisheva. I want to call in a caterer. We'll have the whole Yom Tov catered, we'll use paper goods, and I'll hire someone to clean up afterward."

I had a hard time with this second request. "Ma, when do my sisters and brother ever come to me? I want to show off a little bit with my milchig recipes and use my best china."

"But Elisheva," my mom said, "I won't enjoy the Yom Tov if I see you working so hard."

The discussion went back and forth, with me insisting and my mother insisting. In the end, I won.

Did she?

Chapter 22

Less Distress, More Success

It's a mitzvah not to cause *tza'ar* (distress, pain) to parents.*
This is part of the mitzvah of reverence (אִישׁ אִמּוֹ וְאָבִיו תִּירָאוּ).[1]
Chazal teach us what the Almighty Himself says about this subject.

> When a child honors his father and mother, Hashem says, "I consider it as though I am dwelling in their midst and they are honoring Me."[2] **

And the opposite...

> When a child pains his father and mother, Hashem says, "I have done well not to dwell in their midst, because if I had, they would have been causing Me pain."[3]

A startling equation is made by the Almighty Himself: *Tza'ar* to parents = *tza'ar* to the Creator.

---

* Throughout this book you will encounter other examples, as well as halachic qualifications of this principle.

** When we honor parents, we should have in mind that we are fulfilling two mitzvos: honoring parents and honoring Hashem! (*Rif*)

Travel through this chapter with us. Look around at these heroes, these people of distinction. Be inspired by their determination to guard their parents from any type of worry and woe. And discover some of the habits of highly successful children.

Remember our tour? Because this stop — causing distress to a parent — covers so much territory, we can't possibly explore its every detail. We'll take a brief look, then get back on the trail. There are more sights waiting.

Keeping peace with siblings

In addition to the intrinsic wrong of holding onto a *machlokes* and not attempting to reconcile, arguing siblings are turning a deaf ear to the mitzvah of *kibbud av va'eim* by causing their parents distress.

THIS YEAR, IT'S OUR TURN to go to my parents for Pesach. We're a bunch of siblings and we rotate. We'd all like to be there every year, but what can we do?

One evening, I got a phone call from my brother, Leib.

"Hi, Aviva. I'm going to say something now that's not going to make you happy, but I'm sure after you hear, you'll understand there's really no choice."

I was hoping it wasn't what I was thinking, but it was.

"It's about Pesach," he went on. "You know Etty's leg is in a cast. There's no way we can make Pesach."

I was thinking, dear brother, I know where you're heading, but don't go there. This year it's our turn. Don't do this to me and my family. We've looked forward to this all year. Roll up your sleeves and help your wife get through this tough time.

But Leib did not read my thoughts. "So?" I said, hoping he would hear the opposition in my voice.

He didn't.

"Okay then, Aviva, it's pretty clear that this year we'll have to change the order. You'll go next year."

I hung up fuming. What nerve! Extenuating circumstances always come up. If we're always going to break the rule, it's not going to be a fair rotation.

I was too upset to think clearly. I decided the best thing was to sleep on it.

But sleep I couldn't. I tossed and turned. Finding no peace, I got up and took my Tehillim. *Settling into a recliner, I felt tears of frustration sting my eyes.*

Sometime before dawn, two questions I had once heard at a lecture came to my mind. They impressed me then, and I had a feeling they would serve me well now.

I took a piece of paper and printed those two questions in large, bold letters. Then I folded the paper in four and stuck it into my apron pocket.

The days went by, and I got myself into pre-Pesach cleaning mode. Every once in a while, I thought about the Seder, and about how much I was going to miss being with my parents.

"Why? Why did I just give in?" I muttered dismally.

Then, I would fish in my pocket and pull out the paper. Unfolding it, I saw my neat letters staring back at me:

What will bring a smile to your parent's face? And what would bring a frown?

Each time I read it, I reminded myself "why" we were staying home.

True, for me this change of plans was a big disappointment. But much more important was that if this snowballed into an argument, and our parents got wind of it, as they surely would, it would ruin their simchas Yom Tov. *That far I wasn't willing to go.*

That's really why.

What could be a better reason for not arguing with a sibling than, "I don't want to hurt my parents"?[4]

As distressing as it is for parents when their young children fight, it can't compare to the anguish they have when their grown children, and certainly married children, quarrel among themselves. After decades of pouring their strength into their precious children, to see them not speaking to each other — and even carrying the contention to the next generation, when cousins won't speak to each other — is a heartache for parents.

"HOW CAN I ENJOY my grandson's bar-mitzvah when my own son won't be there?" Selma Lang was complaining to her son Jake, who refused to invite his brother to the simchah he was making. Although neither remember how it started, Jake hadn't spoken to his brother in years.

Looking perfectly miserable, Mrs. Lang's voice was pleading, "When we came out of the camps, we were overjoyed to find another Jew alive," she tried to explain to Jake. "To discover a family member was simply a taste of Gan Eden. To think I had to live to see two brothers, my own sons, not on speaking terms..."

But Jake wouldn't be moved.

In order to educate children in the value of peace, parents themselves should model proper behavior. How fortunate are those children who see parents backing down and giving in for the sake of peace.

WE TRAVELED A LONG DISTANCE to attend that wedding. Although it entailed considerable expense, as soon as we heard that Shaya's son was engaged, we booked tickets to make sure we would be there for my nephew's wedding.

I sat at the chuppah and listened carefully as the kibbudim were called out, waiting to hear my husband's name. They reached the seventh berachah and — you guessed it — the uncle of the chassan who traveled across country for the wedding was absolutely ignored.

We left after the chuppah and haven't spoken to my brother-in-law or his family since.

We parents must show children that when we're facing a challenge, we rise to the occasion, giving people the benefit of the doubt, a chance to explain. Do we dare allow our children to see this example, setting them up to protest, "Mommy doesn't talk to her sister/brother/sister-in-law, so what do you want from me?"

They don't have to know how hard it was!

When you do a favor for your parents, don't spoil it by telling them how hard it was for you.[5]

"You know how long I had to wait in line at the post office to mail your package? My boss was furious that I came late."

We usually want others to notice and appreciate the kindnesses we do for them. The more they feel indebted, the better. On a higher level, a *chessed* can be given so gracefully that the receiver feels "it was nothing."

We learn this elevated behavior from an interaction between our foremothers, Rachel and Leah.

Rachel asked her sister Leah for the mandrakes given to her by her son Reuven. Mandrakes were considered a *segulah* for the children for which Rachel longed.

"Was your taking my husband insignificant?" [Leah replied]. "And now to take even my son's mandrakes?" (*Bereishis* 30:15).[6]

This statement is a wonder. Rachel did not "take away" Yaakov. Just the opposite! She stepped aside so that Leah could be Yaakov's wife. Why didn't Leah feel indebted? What prompted Leah to make such an accusation?

One answer given[7] is that when Rachel made this sacrifice for her sister, she gave Leah the feeling that she was only giving her what rightfully belonged to her. Rachel never reminded Leah of that favor, and never made her feel like it even was a favor, never made her feel indebted, never threw it up to her — "You know, all your success is really due to me" — not at that moment and not in all the ensuing years.

We should aspire to treat our parents the same way. If a parent says, "I'm so sorry to bother you," a child should answer, "It's the least I can do," giving the parent the impression that it is really coming to him. Because it is.

"But," you might counter, "if I don't complain and I even do it with a smile, they'll really think that what I did was nothing. Then my parents won't realize the great sacrifice that I made."

That's the goal.

ON THE ONE HAND, they wanted me to do it and needed me to do it, and would admittedly appreciate if I did it. On the other hand, they were hesitating — and I knew why.

This year, I took on a 6th grade instead of my regular 3rd grade class that I have been teaching for years. This means working on a new curriculum. Not that I didn't create new material for every school year (as my family well knows). Still, a different class means completely *new. Add in a nursing baby and a husband with a promotion. Although Binyamin's increase in salary is slight, the position is prestigious and a good opening for further advancement. But the hours — at least for now — are, like, not real. These days, Binyamin only comes home at 10 p.m., which basically leaves me holding down the fort on my own. So my parents felt that to burden me with making a* sheva berachos *this time would be unreasonable.*

How could I do this to my sister? We are five girls, with me the oldest. When my younger sister married, I arranged a beautiful evening, and repeated this for my third and fourth sister as well. Now, it's our last — my baby sister's — turn. I didn't want to disappoint her. I have the largest home, all the chairs, and my parents have always taken off the biggest part of the preparation by having food catered. They order fifty portions of a main dish and fifty soups, while I contribute the first course and dessert.

When I spoke with my parents, I tried to make it seem like it would be a cinch, which I was hoping it would be. They agreed warily, reiterating that their agreement was conditional: They would be taking care of catering.

Two weeks before the wedding, I started to work on the dessert — or at least, started planning the dessert. I decided to do a chocolate mousse, which freezes well. The trouble was that the days passed and I wasn't getting to it. Time was marching on. Not wanting to wait any longer, I stayed up one night until 3 a.m. to get the whole thing over with in one shot.

With that done, I turned to the first course. I wanted something colorful and attractive that didn't need heating and could be on the table when everyone walked in. I decided to do a layered vegetable salad, with a dressing on the side. Now I just needed to get the tall glasses for the salad, and the special little pouring cups I had in mind for the dressing. But days passed, and I wasn't getting to the store.

It was a few days before the wedding. Now it was not a joke. I knew that I'd better get going. With school needs pulling, and family needs pressing, it wasn't easy, but somehow I managed to get it together.

The next day, my father called. He was checking to make sure I'd have room in my fridge and freezer when the caterer came.

"Sure, Ta. I'm keeping the fridge clear, so whatever needs to be refrigerated will go right in. But why the freezer?"

Then I hear my father saying, "The dessert will need to be frozen, and the caterer will be sending a first course that needs to be refrigerated until about an hour before the meal."

The dessert...? The first course...? "Now? Now you're telling me?! Now — after I —"

I caught the words in time.

The cups were still in the packaging and could be returned, at least for credit.

So...we'd be eating chocolate mousse for a while? What's so bad about that?

Withholding hurtful comments made by others (rechilus)

Our tongues have the awesome power to gladden, on one hand, and to strike a felling blow, on the other. One way to hurt people is by repeating to them what others have said about them in our presence and not theirs.

While much has been written about the transgression of *lashon hara*, less publicized is its partner in crime, *rechilus*: לֹא תֵלֵךְ רָכִיל בְּעַמֶּיךָ, "Don't go about as a talebearer among your people."[8]

A *rocheil* is a traveling salesman who peddles his "merchandise," a gossiper who collects comments made about people and brings this merchandise — these comments — back to the people who were the topic of the conversation, knowing they will be upset.

Applying this to *kibbud av va'eim*, it would mean a son or daughter telling a parent what someone said about him or did to him when they know that hearing it will be painful and lead to ill will.

Relaying hurtful comments from parent to parent

Stirring up a fight

If one parent makes a statement that would obviously hurt or distress the other parent, the child should not repeat it (to the second parent).[9] *

> *Daughter to mother: I heard Dad say that you will never host as well as his mother.*
>
> *Mom: Your grades on this report card are very disappointing.*
> *Daughter: Dad said it's your fault. He said if you wouldn't spend so much time on the phone, you'd have more time to check our homework.*

Fanning the flames

> *Dad is waiting impatiently for Mom who has not yet come home. His son, Baruch, knows that Dad is upset. If Baruch volunteers: "I see Mom down the street. She's walking like she has all the time in the world," he is fanning the flames of contention.*

This is *rechilus/machlokes* which often causes disruption in *shalom bayis*. The sooner children become sensitive toward these matters, the better.

The skill of being a peace seeker, rather than a contention monger, taught early on, will stand sons and daughters in good stead in every relationship throughout their lives.

Your parent asks you, "Who gave you permission to do that?"[10]

You answer: "Mom said it's okay." If Dad accepts that, well and good. But in a case when identifying the so-called culprit

---

* It's always good policy not to say something you don't want repeated.

(your other parent) will not go over well, you should find an alternative satisfactory response, such as, "I didn't realize it would upset you so much. I won't do it again," without incriminating the second parent.

The halachah of *rechilus* helps us stay out of hot water and prevents us from pushing others into it. Don't give your mother a reason to be angry at your father and vice versa.

To what degree is a child responsible for knowing whether his words will cause a blow-up or even a minor rift between parents? This is between the child and the Almighty, Who knows when we know…and also when we don't know. He also knows when, with a little bit of thought, we could have known.

Relaying hurtful comments made by others

If telling parents what other people said or did to them serves no purpose and would only cause pain and create animosity, don't!

> "Dad, you know that ad you worked so long on? Well, as soon as I hung it up, Saul Gold, your supposed friend, covered the whole thing with his own notice."

Even when the child's intention is to acknowledge the injustice of the remark, it is still rechilus.[11]

> "Mr. Bloom announced that he is volunteering to be on the shul building committee only because you are doing such a poor job. But, Daddy, that's so untrue!"

I think so, and so does he![12]

If you are thinking of adding support for your stance, for example, from a friend, a relative, or a neighbor — Don't go there!

> "Aunt Mindy agrees with me that a kid my age should be able to use her allowance any way she wants."

> "I discussed my idea with Uncle Gershon and he feels my way is more practical than yours."

Rechilus about parents' relatives[13]

Not only statements made about parents themselves, but also those made about a parent's relatives, can cause anger, anguish, and arguments.

> *"Mom, Mr. Fried said your brother overcharged and on top of it, did poor work."*

> *"Dad, I was standing right behind Mr. Abrams when he imitated Grandpa's shuffle."*

Why shouldn't they be told?

You're irritated because someone made a disparaging or critical remark about your parent. Shouldn't your parents know what others, especially family members, are thinking and saying about them?

Not if it will only vex and cause dissension!*

> *Daughter to mother: Aunt Fay said to Daddy that she knows you are hoping for a raise. Then she laughed and said, "You should be thankful that your boss doesn't fire you."*

Aunt Fay said something that shouldn't be repeated. Bury that comment.

> **I INVITED MY SON,** *Jonathan, his wife, Simi, and their darling baby to spend a week with us at our summer home. Since both of them have high-pressure jobs and long workdays, I tried hard to give them a nice vacation. It was worth all the effort. The get-away was a huge success. At least that's what I thought — until Jonathan called.*
>
> *He confided during our conversation that Simi was sorry she came. She resented the fact that I spent hours on the phone while she sat around with nothing to do. She was insulted that I hardly even looked at the baby and the meals were so skimpy she was starving most of the day.*

---

* If you think they need to hear the information in order to protect themselves from future harm, ask someone knowledgeable in the laws of *rechilus* if your assessment and halachic presumption is correct.

*I keep asking myself, "Why did Jonathan tell me? What
was he thinking?"*
The only answer I have is — he wasn't.

If Simi would be confronted with her remarks, she might
say, "I was just tired when I said that. All in all, it was a terrific
week." Or, she might say, "I never said those words. All I said is
that Mom didn't notice the baby's new headband, my appetite
was insatiable the whole week, and there were so many things I
wanted to discuss since we get together so seldom."

Or she might not.

Seven things are hidden from a person, and one of them is
other people's thoughts.[14] It's enough that we hear what they
say to our face! It's a *blessing* that we don't know what they're
thinking about us. If Hashem wanted to reveal to us other
people's thoughts, He would have made a little window in our
forehead where thoughts would appear tickertape style. Better
yet, He could have made them audible. In His wisdom, He
decided to keep thoughts hidden.

We have a mitzvah to emulate His ways, making ourselves
G-dlike. If Hashem doesn't give us access to thoughts, likewise
we should not be passing on other people's expressed thoughts,
i.e., what people say about others when not in their presence.
How hurtful it would be to tell your mother (or father), "I met
Mrs. Hershberg, and she said she is shocked how you have aged."

The image of people discussing us is always disquieting. The
rocheil delivers a double blow, one from the person he is quoting,
and a second swipe from himself when he delivers a statement
that is painful and will cause dissension. If we understand that
this "report" will not sit well with the listener, in this case our
parents, it is a Torah prohibition to repeat it.

How much ill will is generated because of *rechilus*! We keep
relationships within the family healthy when we walk away (לֹא
תֵלֵךְ רָכִיל) from such hurtful reporting.

Commitments

If you always do a certain favor for your parents, and they're counting on it, don't leave them in the lurch.

If your parents depend on you for certain assistance …

> *You always do their tax returns.*
> *They count on you to build their succah.*
> *They are expecting to be invited to your Purim seudah, like every year.*
> *You always drive them to a weekly appointment.*
> *Your mother depends on you for Thursday shopping.*

…they will be distressed if you no longer give that assistance or renege on an expected routine. If you can't do this favor, whether temporarily or permanently, let them know, when possible, in enough time to plan accordingly. Excuse yourself, offer an apology, express regret, and make an effort to find a substitute.

Resolving issues out of court

Though we must honor parents immeasurably, if a child has a financial claim against a parent, he is allowed to summon him to *beis din* to recover a loss. The *sefer Otzar Kibbud Av Va'eim* discusses this issue:

> Though according to the letter of the law, it is permissible to take one's father to *beis din* with a financial claim, one who guards his soul (*shomer nafsho*) will distance himself from this and anything like this that diminishes his father's honor.
>
> It is also preferable that the *beis din* speak to the son and convince him to distance himself from all this lest he stumble in his speech [in the heat of presenting his case] and be guilty, *chas veshalom*, of many transgressions.
>
> Therefore, he should be willing to bring in mediators between himself and his father, and should not allow himself to be burned in these hottest of waters.

If a son feels he must submit a claim against his father, he should consider well how to present his case respectfully so that his father not be humiliated and so that he [the son] will not become angry.

When a child feels he will not be able to remain in control of his emotions, he should hire someone else to present his case for him.

It is a *middas chassidus* (exemplary behavior) to refrain from calling a parent to a *din Torah*, even when we're sure we have a sound case.[15]* Even in such a case, it is always worthwhile to discuss the matter with a Rav.

Behaving in school

One of the best ways to give parents *nachas* and avoid causing them distress is to behave in school.

> *RABBI YAAKOV BENDER, Rosh Yeshivah of Yeshiva Darchei Torah in Far Rockaway, gives a yearly talk to the students on honoring parents:*
>
> *"When I must call up a parent, I begin the conversation, 'Hello, this is Bender. Everything is okay.' In those few seconds between the time a principal identifies himself, and then gives the reason for his call, five scenarios of doom flit through a parent's head. I care about your parents, and I don't want to cause them unnecessary anguish. Do you care about them?*
>
> *"One way you can show you care is by behaving in yeshivah. Don't act out to the point that your parents have to be brought in. When a child makes an effort not to destroy school property, not to instigate contention or rebellion against a teacher or the administration, not to ask teachers questions that he knows they can't answer with the intention of showing off or embarrassing them, not to read books, throw notes, keep his cell phone on, or eat in class —*

---

* Furthermore, if a father has a claim against someone, it is a mitzvah for the son to represent his father in court, sparing his father the distress that can accompany a court appearance (*Vayevarech Dovid* 85).

besides the intrinsic value of resisting the temptation, he is also fulfilling the mitzvah of kibbud av va'eim *by not being* metza'er *(aggravating) his parents."*

Guarding parents from (unnecessary) worry

שֶׁיֵּשׁ לַבֵּן לְכַבְּדָם "וּלְשָׁמְרָם" בְּכָל יְכָלְתּוֹ...

Sons and daughters should honor parents and "guard" them with all their ability/might.[16]

MY MOTHER IS IN A FACILITY *after having what the doctors think was a mild stroke. I try to go every day to make sure that she is well cared for and to keep her company.*

My father is at home with a severe infection in his foot, which must be elevated. Not being able to visit my mother, he depends on me for on-the-spot updates on her condition, and my mother depends on me to tell her how my father is "really" doing.

I want them both to be peaceful. I realize that any agitation can only impede their healing, so I always carefully consider what to say. I have to be careful, because they speak to each other on the telephone during the day, and conflicting accounts are not going to work.

So I stick to the part of the truth that will sit well with each. To my father, I say: "Today, Mommy was able to walk a little bit without her walker. This morning she had a hearty breakfast. Her room looks so cheery," without adding, "Mommy had a terrible night. She hardly slept, and woke up with a splitting headache," or "I found Mommy in a bad mood. She kept crying that she wants to go home already." To my mother, I say: "Dad had at least three visitors when I was there yesterday. The doctor told him he's being an excellent patient," and I don't add, "Dad's wound is not healing as fast as it should, and his sugar is up."

It's not always easy, so I daven that Hashem give me the right thoughts and words.

IT WAS THE KIND OF CALL we all dread.

My parents were vacationing when my mother was rushed to the hospital in the middle of the night with a heart attack. She was in a coma, and it looked bad. My panic-stricken father called all the children. In the middle of demanding professions, full calendars, and high-pressure lives, all of us, every single one — the doctor, the lawyer, the accountant, the architect, the computer programmer, and me, the social worker — dropped everything to rush to our mother's side. I stuffed some things into a bag and booked the next flight, leaving my husband in charge. It sounded bad enough that I wasn't sure whether I would find my mother still alive when I landed.

Meanwhile, back at home, my father-in-law had just been released from the hospital, still quite ill. Though he had aides caring for him, my mother-in-law needed my husband, Ari, their only son, to help.

So there I was, out of the country with my comatose mother and anxious father, with Ari left to care for the kids, his job, his parents, plus his other obligations. He did his usual best juggling all the responsibilities.

After two weeks, my mother woke up and slowly began to recover, and my siblings and I went home.

The night I returned, my husband said, "I'll tell my mother tomorrow where you were." "What?" I said in disbelief. "Your mother doesn't know that my mother was deathly ill? How were you able to keep it a secret, and why in the world would you want to?"

"As long as I could manage and the kids were safe, why tell?" said my husband, giving what he seemed to feel was a reasonable reply. "My mother was so busy with my father, she hardly noticed what else was going on around her."

"What do you mean, why tell? We were scared my mother wouldn't make it! You know it was that bad. You're with your mother every day for hours at a time. It never slipped out? And what about the kids? They never said why I was away?"

"Not a word," said Ari, sounding quite pleased. "I sat them down when you left and explained, 'We have two

sick grandparents, Savta and Zeidy, and two very worried grandparents, Saba and Bubby. Bubby has enough on her mind. If we tell her about Savta, sick in the hospital, first of all, she'll be aggravated. She certainly doesn't need that now, with Zeidy so sick. And second of all, if she knows, she won't let me come to help her.'

"You know," Ari continued, "if my mother had even an inkling, I wouldn't have been able to offer her any help. Every day, she's completely overwhelmed. I go to handle the doctors. Together we plan her day, give it structure, and spend time with my father. She would've thought a hundred times before picking up the phone to ask me for the help she needs if she'd known where you were. Tomorrow, at a relaxed moment, I'll explain at least part of what happened. Mostly, I'm going to emphasize that all is fine."

I was impressed. It took a lot of self-control on my husband's part to keep my mother's medical crisis, my absence, and the surrounding commotion a secret from his mother. He spent so many hours together with her, yet didn't even hint at any disruption in our home. I was also proud of the kids for their control, ingenuity, and understanding in keeping the secret.

What a lesson for my kids! Some difficulty, some sacrifice is okay for parents. It was a real hands-on experience.

Not wanting to aggravate parents is not what creates chasms in a family. Not wanting to cause unnecessary aggravation is not what distances child from parent. Thinking about our parents' peace of mind doesn't ruin closeness, it creates it.

I'M IN A DORM in Yerushalayim. It's Chanukah. I'm so lonesome for the festive Chanukah celebration in my parents' home. I can't get a taste of the latkes, and I can't see the dreidels spinning. But I could feel a little bit of their spirit by listening to my father's hadlakas neiros over the phone.

The problem is — when they light there, it's 1 a.m. here. If I call, they're surely going to worry. I can just hear my father saying, "What are you doing up at this hour?"

What about communication?

Children of any age still living at home, who are in constant contact with their parents, might ask, "If I have to withhold information in order not to distress my parents, won't this disturb the normal give and take of a healthy home? How can I share and unburden myself? How can I hide things? And maybe I shouldn't."

And, in fact, you shouldn't. When it's important for parents to know, it's important for a child to reveal — and the reverse: When it's important for a child to reveal, it's important for parents to know. In both instances, parents would and should want to listen.

KOL HALASHON IS an international organization that records live Torah lectures (later stored in accessible archives), and makes them available by telephone to the general public. One of the Rabbanim whose shiurim are recorded is Harav Yitzchak Zilberstein shlita, Rav of Shikun Ramat Elchanan in Bnei Brak, and son-in-law of Harav Yosef Shalom Elyashiv zt"l. At these shiurim, Rav Zilberstein reviews and dissects the halachic ramifications of the questions presented to him.

Questions come to the Rav from all over the world. This question came from a teacher in Europe who was teaching in a Jewish school for students with limited background in Judaism.

The teacher presented to Rav Zilberstein a question that was asked him by his 13-year-old student, "Shimon," who was orphaned of his mother.

Shimon's father had remarried, and it was a very successful marriage. One could see that the father was very happy. His second wife kept a clean, organized house, she was a good cook, and very pleasant to everyone. However, when Shimon's father wasn't home, she hit Shimon.

If Shimon tracked in mud on his shoes or spilled things, or dropped his jacket and briefcase in the hall, instead of patiently explaining her preferences, she gave him a slap. Presumably she realized that this was not proper, because she understood not to do this in front of her new husband.

Poor Shimon. It's not enough that he was missing h departed mother, but he had to suffer in this way, withou. the support of his loving father.

Shimon's question to his teacher was: "What does Hashem want from me?" (13 years old!) "On the one hand, my father is very happily married. If I tell him what is happening behind his back, it would cause my father terrible tza'ar. He would be very upset with his wife. My father loves me very much, and he knows how hard it is for me without my mother. He would not take kindly to this. How can I spoil his marriage and rob him of his happiness? But still...for me, it's so hard."

Hearing his story, said Shimon's teacher, he was humbled. He put his arm around the anguished child and shared his pain.

His teacher understood that a weighty decision lay on the shoulders of this incredibly sensitive son. To show Shimon that he grasped the implications, the teacher offered to bring the question to a world-renowned Rav.

Rav Zilberstein repeated the question to his audience, and paused, obviously overcome. "Some questions," he said in a piercing voice, "reach the Kisei HaKavod! And this is one of them."

Rav Zilberstein said that he brought this question to the attention of his illustrious father-in-law, Rav Elyashiv, ztz"l. The answer that was relayed back to Shimon by Rav Zilberstein in the name of Rav Elyashiv was, "Shimon, rest assured. You may tell your father.

"We have a principle that just as we don't have to contribute financially for kibbud av va'eim (i.e., suffer a financial loss) when parents have their own money, one need not compromise one's health (suffer physically or emotionally) in order to fulfill the mitzvah of kibbud horim.*

"Imagine this young, vulnerable boy. His main concern is the suffering he will cause his father — the disruption of his

---

* When a participant asked if telling the father would be *rechilus*, Rav Zilberstein said it is permitted because it would be *rechilus l'toeles*, *rechilus* whose purpose is to guard him from harm now and in the future.

father's happiness in a new marriage, to which he is willing to give equal status or maybe even greater consideration than his own heartache."

Three more times during the retelling of this story, Rav Zilberstein repeated with great wonderment in his voice, "There are some questions that go straight to the Kisei HaKavod!"

Even married children who are not at home may want to share with their parents the ups and downs of their lives, their hurdles and struggles. And, in fact, many parents want to be involved in their children's lives, whether to give advice, or just listen and share daily events. For these parents it would distress them more if their children didn't share this information with them. **Disclosure will very much depend on the nature, wishes, and inclinations of each parent.**

Still, during our married lives, there will be many things that we won't and shouldn't share with our parents for other reasons — like private issues our spouse does not want disclosed. This should not impact on our responsibility to view the situation from a parent's perspective. Think about their *tza'ar* and find the right words to give them peace of mind.

BEFORE MY WEDDING, an elderly man gave me a piece of advice: "Parents struggle many years raising children. Now that you are getting married, just make sure they hear mostly about the good stuff."

Withholding "bad" news

When it's not important for parents to know, and most likely they'll never find out, and hearing the news will only cause anguish or aggravation, a son or daughter should not relate upsetting, distressing news (שְׁמוּעוֹת רָעוֹת) to a parent.[17]

When there is bad news that *must* be relayed to a parent — because it's important for them to know and most likely, they'll find out — preferably someone other than a son or daughter should do the telling.* For example, if a parent will have to

---

* As we learned from the laws of waking a parent: If a parent must be woken, it should

attend a funeral, obviously he must be informed of the death, but a son or daughter should not be the one to tell him.

WHEN MY GRANDDAUGHTER was diagnosed with a devastating illness, the first one I wanted to turn to for comfort was my mother. Just considering the tza'ar she would have caused me to hold back.

It wasn't easy. Every time we talked, it was on the tip of my tongue to tell her.

As the days passed, I realized that my mother could easily hear about my granddaughter — her great-granddaughter — from anyone, even a person she hardly knew, since many people were davening for the child. How would my mother feel if she found out that a stranger knew and she didn't?

My husband and I weighed all the considerations and then added what we felt would be my mother's choice.

That evening, my husband went over and gently broke the news.

This is the correct approach, unless it is clear that the parent would prefer that the son or daughter do the telling directly.

What's the difference between the son-in-law and the daughter doing the telling? The *tza'ar* for the parent is the same, but the *source* of the *tza'ar* is not, and that says it all. This does not minimize the obligation in-law children have to parents-in-law, but stresses the uniqueness of the parent-child relationship. Sons and daughters should aim to be a source of pleasure, not pain. We are not allowed to cause pain to any living creature, how much more so not to a parent.

Informing a parent of his serious illness

If a parent is seriously ill or diagnosed with a terminal illness, and the doctors have not told the parent the extent of the condition, a child should not be the one to inform the parent, since the knowledge could affect the parent emotionally, even physically, and cause the condition to worsen.

---

be done by someone other than their son or daughter.

If it is decided that the parent must be informed, it should be done when possible and practical by someone other than the child.

MY FATHER ALWAYS TOLD US children while he was still healthy that should he ever be diagnosed with a terminal illness he wanted us to tell him about it so that he could put his affairs in order, financial and spiritual. Whenever he said this, I'd look at my strong, healthy father in surprise, hoping with all my heart that I would never have to be in that position.

But that was not to be. One day, I got the call. I sat there and cried my heart out.

I called my husband, who is a Rav. I knew he would know how to handle it.

My husband called my father and told him that it's a segulah for arichus yamim to say Vidui.

My father, being a very smart man, understood.

Call when you get there

When a child is traveling, and parents are worried, he fulfills the mitzvah of *kibbud horim* when he calls.[18]

MY HUSBAND AND I do a lot of traveling. Every time we land, he calls his mother to tell her that he's arrived safely. It always bothered me. I used to say to him, "You're not a baby. Why do you always have to check in with your mother?"

Once I learned the halachah, my attitude changed. I was shocked when I learned that this is part of kibbud av va'eim. I had thought that "calling in" was only for children. The halachah taught me that I was really off the mark, because we're really always someone's child!

Eliminating tza'ar of all dimensions

And if you say, "How far do we have to take this?" think of it this way: How far do we go to search for those tiny crumbs of *chametz* on Erev Pesach? Those who want to do this *mitzvah b'hiddur* want to eliminate all *tza'ar*, even the tiniest bit.

MY FATHER'S PARENTS were coming to visit us. Since they live far away, this was a big deal. We could all see how happy my father was since he hadn't seen his parents in over a year. My mother was filling up the freezer with things she knew they would enjoy. We kids were busy making signs to welcome them and trying to figure out who would double up so Opa and Oma could have their own room.

Two days before their arrival "a problem" was discovered. I heard about it when I saw my father slap his forehead and say to my mother, "Why didn't I think about this sooner, but what a mazel we noticed in time. I hope it's not too late to take care of this."

My father was in quite a dither and I still didn't know what the matter was.

I saw him go to the closet and take out his wedding album. "How will my parent's wedding album solve any problem?" I wondered. I knew it wasn't a time to pester them, so I just asked quietly if anyone knew what was going on.

Well, I was told it had to do with pictures. Hanging prominently in our dining room, we have a picture of Opa's father, which someone had sent us. However, there is no picture of my Oma's father, who recently died. My father was sure that his mother would feel slighted.

Where would we get a picture on such short notice?

Ah ha! The wedding album. I hurried along with my father as he dashed off with the album to the photo store. He asked the owner if he could crop the picture from the wedding album and enlarge it, since the album picture was so small. The result — still way too small. Then again — still not big enough. And then a third time, until my father was satisfied that it matched the size of the other picture exactly. No favoring one grandfather over the next in our house! Then we ran around trying to find a similar frame.

I made it a point to be around when my Oma came into the dining room. She noticed her father's picture right away, walked over to the wall and stood there a long time.

I thought to myself, Oma, you'll never know how much effort your son made not to cause you *tza'ar*.

Chapter 23

Damah ben Nesinah

Which child hasn't heard the story of Damah ben Nesinah? Often related in classrooms and a favorite at bedtime, children love to hear about this devoted son who was so careful not to wake up his father.

R' Eliezer was asked: How far does the obligation of *kibbud av va'eim* go? He told them: Go and see what Damah did for his father, Nesinah, in the city of Ashkelon. The Sages wanted to buy a precious stone for the *ephod* of the Kohen Gadol, on which Damah would have made a profit of 600,000 gold dinar. However, the key was under the head of his sleeping father, and Damah did not want to disturb him.[1]

Do not disturb!

A child may not wake up a sleeping parent. Disturbing a parent's sleep is included in the admonition not to cause *tza'ar* to parents. Therefore, children should be trained early on to tiptoe and whisper when parents are sleeping.

Please wake me!

If a parent would want to be awakened, and would be upset if not roused, it is a mitzvah to wake him.[2] How can a child make that decision?

When parents have specifically asked to be awakened, the decision has been made.

Even if you weren't asked, but as a son or daughter you are familiar with your parents' habits, preferences, and needs, and usually know when they would want to be awakened:

❖ You know your father would never miss a *minyan* or is punctual for his Daf Yomi *shiur.*

❖ It's the bank and your parents are waiting anxiously for a mortgage approval.

❖ Last time Uncle Gedalya came and your dad was sleeping, you weren't sure what to do. This time you know.

Even when a parent would want to be awakened, as in the above scenarios, it is preferable that it be done by someone else[3] (as long as this will not prove embarrassing for the parent), since a son or daughter should not be the source of *tza'ar* to his parents. If no one else is available, a son or daughter is allowed to wake a parent.

When parents have specifically asked not to be woken, a child should not wake them.[4]

Given this, the story of Damah ben Nesinah is a puzzlement. Wouldn't Damah think that his father would be upset when he woke up and discovered that his son had lost the chance of a 600,000-*dinar* profit — today equivalent to millions? Most parents would be delighted to have their sleep interrupted for this kind of a profit.

"A million dollars! I'll catch a nap later."

If their child would refrain from waking them, as did Damah, they would be greatly distressed (*tza'ar*). They would *want* to be woken and therefore it would be a mitzvah to wake them. Accordingly, it seems that Damah ben Nesinah acted improperly and does not set an example we should follow. Why, then, is this story used as a classic example and the source for not waking a parent? Why do *Chazal* say we learn correct behavior from this story?

This question is discussed by Harav Moshe Feinstein, *ztz"l*.[5]

It appears that the father, Nesinah, was not *"shafui b'da'ato,"* his mind was not clear, to the extent that he wouldn't have appreciated the value of 600,000 gold *dinar*. He wouldn't have had any pleasure from the announcement of that huge profit. He just would have been annoyed that he had been woken up.

According to this interpretation, we *do* learn the proper halachah from this Gemara. A father with a clear mind surely would have appreciated the value of this deal to his son and would have wanted to be wakened. But in this case, where there was no appreciation and only aggravation, *not* waking him was the proper thing to do.

There is another lesson here. Nesinah was not the typical father. The way he acted was not the way a father would generally act. Honoring his father required Damah's attention to Nesinah's peculiarities. *This* father did not appreciate being awakened, no matter what the reason.[6]

When our parents are "atypical" — if they have ways of doing things out of the ordinary, an attitude seldom encountered, unconventional habits, uncommon preferences and unusual requests — our responses should be weighed in the light of and adjusted to their individual perspectives and ideas.

This is our unique parent. This is our unique situation. This is our unique *kibbud av va'eim*.

No pressure!

From the story of Damah ben Nesinah, we derive this halachah: For a profit, i.e., one's own personal benefit, we are not allowed to cause *tza'ar* to a parent. It follows that a son or daughter is allowed to *request*, but not *pressure*, a parent to provide the child with money, services, or any other personal benefit against the parent's will.*

---

* Note that we are speaking of profit, not loss. Damah is not *losing*. He is forfeiting a profit. A loss is taking away what I already have. מְנִיעַת רֶוַח — withholding a gain — is a situation when I don't get what I feel I could have had.

The *sefer Otzar Kibbud Av Va'eim* expands on this:

A child who pressures a parent against his will, besides violating the mitzvos of *kibbud* and *yirah*, violates many other mitzvos of the Torah...[7]

If the son or daughter pressures to the extent that it makes a parent ill, other positive and negative mitzvos are violated as well. If we have an obligation to preserve and enhance the health of our parents, certainly we wouldn't be allowed to do something to endanger or compromise their well-being...[8]

WE'VE BASICALLY OUTGROWN the house we're living in now. It's a buyer's market, so my wife and I agree that this is the time to make a move. We found something perfect. The trouble is, we don't have enough for the down payment. I asked my father, who is well off, if he can loan me the money.

I got back a speech from him about how we're young, can manage where we are, and how the house we want is overpriced. And as far as a mortgage, he feels that we're biting off more than we can chew.

A few days later, I called again, hoping he'd be in a better mood and change his mind. Even over the phone, I could tell that he was getting annoyed.

By my third phone call, I guess he probably felt it was harassment. But I figured, he's got it, we need it, and after all, we're his children. So why not?

Asking is okay. Getting your father "annoyed" is not.*

I CAN'T SEE ANYTHING wrong with one man on a keyboard. I've been to many weddings that were lively and loud with a one-man band.

My son said that none of his friends do that. He claims that he hardly knows anyone who took a keyboard alone. "The

---

* If a child is needy to the extent that he is entitled to charity, his wealthy father is obligated to contribute to his expenses before giving to strangers (see Ch. 6 for priorities in *tzedakah*). If the father is reluctant, the child should ask a Rav about approaching his father since it is still prohibited to pressure him, even in such a case.

music is the most important part of a wedding," he told me. "Even if other people do it, I'm not."

This wedding entails so many expenses, many more than I anticipated. I feel this is one way we can cut down, and still keep it nice.

How valuable it would be if this son was aware that he is not allowed to pressure his father for a band — his personal "gain" — at the expense of his father's distress. It's okay for the son to ask or suggest ways of making it work. He can offer to cut corners in other areas.

Chazal used the extreme example of Damah ben Nesinah, where we see an extraordinary profit forfeited, to bring home this point: certainly for a lesser profit a son or daughter should avoid causing *tza'ar*.

MY DAUGHTER CALLED last week and asked if she and her darling family can come for Pesach this year as they do every year. Oh, how I would love to have them.

But I thought this out carefully and answered honestly, "Tammy, I would love to have you, but it's too much for me this year. I don't feel I'm up to it."

I was shocked at Tammy's reaction: "Ma, you have a whole month still. What's too much about this? If you pace yourself, you'll make it fine."

While it is true that most parents are anxious to give children whatever they can — and even what they can't — sons and daughters should avoid pushing and coercing their parents beyond their capacity.

Though these deeper lessons can certainly be learned from Damah ben Nesinah's concern not to cause *tza'ar* to his father, let us not diminish the importance of the basic lesson: guarding a parent's sleep.

UNDER THE BEST OF CIRCUMSTANCES, travel can be exhausting. When it involves a long airplane trip, the "aftershocks" can linger in what is famously known as jetlag. On a recent trip, I not only had my share of those nights waiting for sleep to overtake me, but also a bout of dehydration that made me good and sick. Splitting headaches and nausea descended upon me relentlessly.

So, here I was, a guest in the home of my daughter Mimi and son-in-law, Aharon, and my rambunctious granddaughter. Totally exhausted, I needed nothing more and nothing less than a few night's sleep.

I curled up in my bed, ready for early retirement. Mimi was as anxious to see me rested and feeling good as I was myself.

Just as I was safely under the covers, I heard loud noises outside. Curiosity propelled my weary bones to get up and peek out the window. Next door, on a patio, tables were set, lighting was arranged, and a screen was being put up. I groaned in disbelief. Of all nights, the neighbors had to make a party when I needed sleep so badly.

In no time at all, guests started arriving and the music began.

Whether the music was tasteful or not was beside the point, which was that they played the songs at an ear-splitting volume. I had nowhere to run or hide.

I couldn't get over it. Why would anyone do this when so many families lived in this family-friendly neighborhood? Since my bedroom faced the party, I got the full blast of the musical presentation.

Miserable, I sat in bed, inserting and reinserting earplugs that didn't work against the racket that filtered through.

Not hearing any movement outside my door, I assumed my daughter and her family — whose rooms did not face the noise — had gone to sleep early.

I tried to lose myself in a book. Just then, I heard the door to the apartment open, and my daughter saying to her husband something like, "He just kept saying this was a once-in-a-lifetime party because he was turning fifty."

I couldn't sleep anyway, so I got up to join them.

"What happened, Mimi?" I asked. "Where were you?"

She told me about her escapade.

"I was really anxious for you to get a good night's sleep," Mimi told me. "I wanted you to enjoy this trip. How could

you with all that noise? When I realized the noise was not letting up, I called some of the neighbors to ask if they'd be willing to complain about the music, but no one wanted to be the one to make the call."

There are those who just complain, and those who make a stand. Being the latter, Mimi went next door — unbeknownst to me — and asked the party's host to lower the volume.

He told her, "This is my party. A once-in-a-lifetime party. I'm turning fifty!" Then he added, "Why don't you and your husband join the festivities?"

Mimi explained to him that her mother was visiting, and that the music was making it impossible for me to fall asleep. "Let my mother sleep!" she pleaded, despite the obvious fact that no one cared about her dear mother. Mimi left, defeated, feeling the stares of some of the guests, who had, in all likelihood, invested personally in this celebration. "No one cares..." or so she thought.

What Mimi didn't know as she left the party — but was now obvious to the three of us — was that the host had, in fact, kindly lowered the music.

There have been a handful of times in my life when people have kept me up with loud music. Each time, I would tolerate the problem, and wish wistfully for someone else to make it go away. Well, there was no knight in shining armor in this story, but there was a loving daughter, determined to do the mitzvah of kibbud av va'eim. When these partygoers ruined her efforts, she brought all her love to the moment, and risked ridicule and resistance to try and help me.

I couldn't believe what she had done, and Mimi was a bit surprised herself. Laughing merrily at her bravado, we gave each other a quick hug.

I fell asleep quickly, less from the need to sleep than the deep calm that wafted through me as I realized how much she cared about my well-being.

Chapter 24

Slights, Stings, and Slurs

כָּל הַמְבַזֶּה אָבִיו וְאִמּוֹ אֲפִילוּ אֲפִילוּ בִדְבָרִים
בִרְמִיזָה הֲרֵי זֶה בִּכְלַל אָרוּר מִפִּי הַגְּבוּרָה

One who degrades his father or mother [with his actions or] **even verbally, and even with only a discourteous gesture,** brings upon himself a Divine curse [i.e., Divine wrath] (*Shulchan Aruch* 241:6).

Who does not need Hashem's blessing? People travel great distances to seek a blessing from a *tzaddik*, spend considerable sums of money, and put forth tremendous effort to procure a *segulah* — all to access Hashem's blessing.

When we degrade our parents, we bring upon ourselves the *exact opposite*!

Degrading would include:

❖ The prohibition to **strike** a parent (*Shemos* 21:15)*

---

* Hitting and wounding (causing bleeding), which is prohibited, impinges on the circumstances under which a child may administer medical treatment to a parent and the issues in restraining a violent mentally-ill parent. This is the subject of extensive discussion in halachic responsa.

❖ The prohibition to **curse** a parent (*Shemos* 21:17)*

❖ **And specifically, the prohibition: "Cursed is he who demeans or belittles his father or mother"** (אָרוּר מַקְלֶה אָבִיו וְאִמּוֹ) (*Devarim* 27:16).[1]

The Sages tell us that every time the word אָרוּר, "cursed," is used, it indicates that we are being "chased away." The Almighty distances Himself from us and we cause ourselves misfortune (אָרוּר בּוֹ נִידוּי, בּוֹ קְלָלָה) (*Shevuos* 36a).

Honoring in speech teaches us to speak in ways that increase our parents' honor — the many additions and inclusions we discussed in Chapter 12: "It's What You Say *and* How You Say It."

Reverence in speech teaches us to avoid and omit words that detract from parental honor.

Two major Torah prohibitions assist us in weeding out noxious words. The first is: לֹא תוֹנוּ אִישׁ אֶת עֲמִיתוֹ, "Do not aggrieve your fellowman" (*Vayikra* 25:17).

Do not aggrieve

The Torah prohibits us from saying things to people that cause them pain.

The Torah speaks about two types of *ona'ah* (לֹא תוֹנוּ), depriving people of what is rightfully theirs. One is *ona'as mamon*, stealing their money, and the second is *ona'as devarim*, stealing their dignity. The second is considered a more serious crime than the first.

We have to be careful with everyone. The laws of *kibbud av va'eim* add that we must be exceptionally careful with our words to parents.

> *SHE WAS ON A PLATFORM. Though it was only four inches from the ground, you could see that this girl was in the clouds. Draped in chiffon and silk, she looked her part as a radiant bride-to-be.*

---

* In halachic terms, this means expressing a desire that the Almighty bring some misfortune on a parent. This prohibition applies even after a parent's death (to wish harm to his soul).

This was it. She had tried on at least ten other gowns, but none compared to this. I stuck in a pin here and a pin there. Then we all stood back — me, my assistant, and the mother — admiring the almost finished product. The mother, obviously quite thrilled with the outcome — probably equally thrilled that the treks from salon to salon were finally over — was taking out her checkbook, eager to put down a deposit.

"Wait a minute!"

We all turned to the girl in white who was calling a halt to something.

"We are not finalizing anything here until I bring at least two friends to hear their opinion."

My assistant quietly left the room. I busied myself with my pin box. The mother slowly put her checkbook back into her purse. It would have been nice if she could have put some of her shame inside also.

They left together. I wanted to call after them, "Did you forget something?" But I held my peace.

I felt a little bit of motherhood had been forgotten somewhere in that room that evening.

Just a small introductory phrase could have saved the day — "Could we...?" "Would you mind if...?" — especially if said privately.

It's understandable that young people want input from contemporaries who might be more in tune with current fashion. The same thing could be accomplished, however, without compromising the mother's place and her dignity, without leaving the parent — and the salon owner and her assistant — with the message, "Mom, you're just here to write the checks."

Offensive, hurtful words are not to be excused as a "generational thing." There are clear guidelines in our Torah and from our Sages defining kosher speech and giving it no less status than kosher food.

This chapter will not address statements made by sons and daughters that clearly never should have been said and certainly should not be printed.

On the other hand, Torah guidelines for avoiding hurtful

words, especially to parents — and the gradations are many — certainly need to be addressed.

Using words to hurt a parent would include:

Words that breed discouragement

> *"You're not going back to school, are you? Do you really think you can keep up with students so much younger?"*
> *"Now you're going to start making challos, after all these years? You know how long it will take you to get it right?"*
> *"Remarry? At your age?"*
> *"Computers? You must be kidding!"*

Words that create anxiety

Whether it's their war experiences or teenage years they'd rather not discuss, if we see parents don't want to go there, stay away. Maybe someone else feels it's important to coax them to discuss those hard years, but it's not the job for a son or daughter.

Words that vex, provoke, or offend

> *"How come Daddy understands it right away and you don't?"*
> *"Who are you trying to impress anyway?"*
> *"Ma, I heard that story twenty times."*
> *"Okay, Dad. Talk it into yourself."*
> *"Yuck! What did you put into this soup?!"*

Or words that embarrass

> *"You asked that already, and I already answered you."*

Think how disturbing and humiliating it would be for a parent to hear this. It is disrespectful to any human being, all the more so to a parent. Why not just answer again? Ten times would be ten mitzvos. If it were a customer, wouldn't you find the patience to answer as many times as it took to make a sale — and with a smile![2] Every repetition offered *b'seiver panim yafos* (pleasantly) earns us eternal reward.

To some, a son or daughter speaking this way would be termed "rude." To others, it would be considered ill bred. To still others, just plain fresh. But when we use the words *ona'as devarim*, we put these statements in their proper category: a transgression of the Torah.

And rationalizations don't help:

> "Oh, come on… It was just a joke."
> "It's not what I say. It's just that my mother is too sensitive."
> "I'm just being honest!"

Regardless, *ona'as devarim* remains *ona'as devarim*. And the transgression is severely compounded when directed toward parents.

THE TRADITION IN OUR FAMILY was that my parents would come to us for the Seder. They had a wonderful time with the grandchildren, and the story of Yetzias Mitzrayim was passed down from generation to generation with my father's divrei Torah *that he had heard from his father.*

After the Seder was over, some of my students would come over to fulfill the mitzvah of כָּל הַמַּרְבֶּה לְסַפֵּר בִּיצִיאַת מִצְרַיִם הֲרֵי זֶה מְשׁוּבָּח, *"Everyone who expands on telling the story of Yetzias Mitzrayim is to be lauded." I had prepared many topics to share with my students — each one penetrating and reflective of the kedushah we tried to attain this unique night of the year. This year, my father decided to stay up and participate with us. Though it was two in the morning, I think he was invigorated by the young, lively crowd, and he had his own ideas to share. And share he did. But the subjects were not especially connected to Leil HaSeder.*

Every time my father began with a subject that was not to my liking, I quickly eased us back to the matter at hand.

He tried again. Before he got too far, there I was again, directing the discussion back to something pertinent.

Of course, it was obvious to everyone around the table what was going on.

Sad to say, it took me many years before I was able to revisit that Seder night with a new perspective — and to feel ashamed of having shamed my father.

I could have taught my students an important lesson that evening, and my actions could have spoken louder than any of those inspirational comments I made that night.

Special delivery — CANCELLED

Anyone, but especially a parent, is the wrong address for these types of deliveries:

Comparing...
"*I never have to help when I go to my mother-in-law's house.*"
"*Laya's mom always brings something when she comes to visit.*"

Sarcasm...
"*Great job!*"

Demeaning gestures...
Like raising eyebrows, pointing with your finger to your forehead...

Silence...
Not responding or giving parents the cold shoulder can scream disrespect as loud as any hurtful interchange.

Mimicking...
It surely can be humorous to imitate mannerisms and idiosyncrasies. In private, this would be *ona'as devarim*, and if done in public, would involve still other prohibitions, as is true for all the above.

It's important that a father not make fun of or ridicule a mother in front of the children and vice versa. Aside from the intrinsic wrong, if the children take up this line of mimicking and belittling, the father will have encouraged his children to "belittle a parent," thereby causing loss of Hashem's blessing to his children, *r"l*![3]

Parents who want respectful speech from their children must model it, showing them what respectful speech looks like from spouse to spouse, from parent to child, and to all other people.

Do not be a talebearer

Another Torah prohibition that assists us in weeding out noxious words is the warning not to be a talebearer, לֹא תֵלֵךְ רָכִיל בְּעַמֶּךָ (*Kedoshim* 19:16), which includes the transgression of *lashon hara* (and *rechilus*).

A son or daughter who speaks *lashon hara* about his parents certainly transgresses the mitzvah *of kibbud av va'eim*. In addition, he transgresses the prohibition of belittling parents... (Chofetz Chaim, *Hilchos Lashon Hara*, Positive Mitzvah 10).[4]

What is lashon hara?

Lashon hara is a true statement about someone (in our context, a parent) that:

Demeans (גְּנוּת)

While some people are careful when speaking about outsiders, they might not take the same precaution with close relatives.[5] Nonetheless, a parent is not supposed to be put on the table for dissection. Many sons and daughters are not aware that analyzing a parent's attributes and painting an unflattering picture to others is *lashon hara*.

Saying that a parent is "arrogant," "stingy," "dull," "gluttonous," "irrational," "meddlesome," "neurotic," "phony," "shallow," "selfish," "lazy," "dumb" is prohibited.

Or telling a story that illustrates a failing, such as: "It's not that my father is tightfisted. He spends a lot of money — but only on himself" (even if it's true).

Even if we include ourselves — "I'm also a shallow person."

And even if said in jest.

Because all of the above are demeaning words spoken for no halachically condoned purpose.

Causes a loss (נֶזֶק)

If a son or daughter were to discredit a parent's skills or merchandise — "If I needed a travel agent, I'd never use my father" — and as a result, people wouldn't use those services or buy that merchandise, the child has caused his parent a loss.

Or a comment that causes a parent to lose social standing — "If you take my mother as committee chairman, this evening will never get off the ground."*

---

* Unless permitted according to the laws of *lashon hara le'to'eles*.

Critical but constructive (to'eles)

While the Torah prohibits demeaning and damaging speech, relating negative information for **constructive purposes** — to correct a damage or to prevent future damage — is not *lashon hara*, as long as we avoid unnecessary damage or derision and our intention is for that constructive purpose only.

The best scenario is when not only we benefit, but the person we are discussing has benefit from our discussion as well. For example, a parent will benefit because we are relating the issue to a sibling, a Rav, or someone in a counseling or advisory capacity in an attempt to come up with practical solutions, develop a better attitude, or brainstorm for helpful reactions. The goal for both speaker and listener is to improve the parent-child connection.

If a son or daughter simply takes pleasure in casting his parent in a bad light, he is traveling in the wrong direction.

Listening to lashon hara

WHENEVER WE SISTERS GET TOGETHER, some part of our discussion is always about our parents and the things we don't like about them. This has been going on for years and years. Truth is, I really feel sick after every conversation. I know it's not right, yet somehow the pattern keeps repeating itself.

Just as it is prohibited to speak about the weaknesses of parents for no purpose (no *to'eles*), it is wrong to serve as a listener. Listening is a transgression in its own right.[6] When others are speaking about our parents, it is our responsibility to defend them and protect their reputation.

Still, just as speech can be beneficial, listening can be beneficial.[7] If your sibling or spouse has difficulty in his dealings with your parent, it is permitted to listen to their complaints — under certain conditions.[8]

A fly? Or a bee?

A statement is considered *lashon hara* if we have lowered our parent's esteem in the eyes of others, or caused him damage or embarrassment.

But what if that doesn't happen?

Would this still be considered *lashon hara* even if the derogatory implications are not accepted and even if no damage occurs?

Yes, answers the Chofetz Chaim, quoting Rabbeinu Yonah in *Shaarei Teshuvah*,[9] because the Torah does not want a Jew to use his power of speech for lowly things.

> Two things happen when we speak *lashon hara*. The first is the damage or shame that we cause the person we're speaking about. The second is the decision to make the other person look bad and our happiness at his disgrace or loss. Even if no possible harm could come, we still have made the decision to use our tongues to condemn and malign.

Quoting Rabbeinu Yonah, the Chofetz Chaim continues:

> "Foolish people (אֱוִילִים) heap condemnation, but righteous people (יְשָׁרִים) are satisfied" (*Mishlei* 14:9). [The root of the word אֱוִיל (*evil*) is אַל (*al*), "nothing," meaning "empty people."] It is the way of a fool to seek out weaknesses in others, never to praise or to look for the good in other people. Upright people, on the other hand, conceal the shortcomings of others and praise a person for his strengths.[10]

Rabbeinu Yonah compares this fool to a fly. If you want to find a fly, where are you sure to find him? Go to the garbage. A fly is always looking for garbage. That's what he lives on. That's what sustains him. Unfortunately, some people have the nature of a fly. They are always headed for the garbage. They land there and stay there. It is what sustains them.

Be a bee. She takes the nectar, the sweet liquid secreted by the flower, and gives the world honey.

> A wise man was walking with his students when they came upon a carcass. "What a foul odor," said the students. The wise man said, "How white are its teeth" (*Chovos HaLevavos, Shaar HaKeniah*, Ch. 6).

The odor was pervasive. One need not have been clever to notice it. The white teeth were much less obvious and easy to overlook. They needed the wise man's focus.

If this can be said about a dead animal, how much more should we try to find the virtues of human beings, and certainly our parents.

There you go! That's the choice. Will we choose to be a fly or a bee?

Will we choose to be a fool or a wise man?

Chapter 25

When Following Orders Is Against the Law

Though we are commanded to be loyal and devoted children, and please our parents in every way we can, a parental request that involves a violation of the Torah is weighed differently.

אִישׁ אִמּוֹ וְאָבִיו תִּירָאוּ וְאֶת שַׁבְּתֹתַי תִּשְׁמֹרוּ אֲנִי ה' אֱלֹקֵיכֶם

Every man shall revere his mother and father, and keep My Shabbos, I am Hashem (*Vayikra* 19:3).

Chazal explain that the mitzvah of Shabbos is placed immediately after that of reverence for parents to teach us: "Though I [Hashem] have commanded you to revere your parents, if they tell you to desecrate Shabbos, or any of the mitzvos, a child may not comply." The primary loyalty and reverence of both parent and child is to Hashem and His Torah.[1]

Torah law, Rabbinic law, and accepted custom

אָמַר לוֹ אָבִיו לַעֲבוֹר עַל דִּבְרֵי תוֹרָה, בֵּין בְּמִצְוַת
עֲשֵׂה בֵּין בְּמִצְוַת לֹא תַעֲשֶׂה, וַאֲפִילוּ מִצְוָה שֶׁל
דִּבְרֵיהֶם לֹא יִשְׁמַע לוֹ...

[If] his father told him to transgress a Torah mitzvah, whether a positive commandment or a negative command-ment, even a Rabbinic mitzvah, he shouldn't listen to him... (*Shulchan Aruch* 240:15).

If a parent were to ask a child to perform a personal service (which is a Torah obligation of *kibbud av va'eim*) that involves a transgression of the Torah, the child would not be allowed to do so.

> *A very hungry father asked his daughter, Yael, to cook hot cereal for breakfast on Shabbos, since his nutritionist said that oatmeal is a perfect way to start the day.*
>
> *On any other day, Yael would prepare her father his preference. But because cooking is not permitted on Shabbos, she would have to respectfully decline and offer a suitable substitute.*
>
> *Then Yael could plan ahead to circumvent this problem before the next Shabbos.*

Not only personal service, but any behavior that involves transgressing a positive or negative commandment, a Rabbinic law, or an accepted custom...[2]

> *Mrs. Fried just heard that her daughter Aliza's sister-in-law is divorcing. On her next visit, Mrs. Fried remarks, "Aliza, I heard your sister-in-law is getting a divorce, and I heard it was quite messy. They are married so many years. What could have gone wrong?"*
>
> *"Mom, I really have no idea. No one has told me."*
>
> *"But, Aliza, didn't you notice anything?"*

Mrs. Fried is asking Aliza questions that will inevitably lead to *lashon hara*. Aliza is not allowed to reveal negative information even if pressured.[3]

> *Mr. Schwartz and his son Meyer are in business together. They manufacture pocketbooks. Mr. Schwartz asked Meyer to arrange to have labels made that say "genuine leather." Meyer knows that the pocketbooks are not made of genuine leather.*

> *Meyer should try to convince his father that honesty is the best policy.*
>
> *Mr. Schwartz should be proud that he has a son who can't go along.*

When "following orders" is against Torah law, how do we keep reverence in place?

We are only faulted for lack of reverence when our behavior reflects *chutzpah* and arrogance (*azus*).

Yael, Aliza, and Meyer are not lacking reverence for their parents. Rather, in a case of conflict, loyalty to Hashem takes precedence.

> *In my parents' home, they were sure to use up all the bread products before Pesach, but that was about the extent of their preparation for the holiday.*
>
> *So, when I came home for spring vacation, I knew that anything needed to be done for Pesach would be my responsibility. When my mother saw me cleaning pockets one afternoon, she raised an eyebrow. But when she saw me going to check the rooms with a candle the night before the Seder, she put her foot down.*
>
> *To avoid a blowup, I waited until she went to sleep. Then I began my search.*

Returning to the Source
(without forgetting our source)

Kibbud horim is called "among the most difficult mitzvos to fulfill properly."[4] The difficulty is compounded when parents and children have conflicting value systems, beliefs, and lifestyles.

The challenge facing a son or daughter raised in a nontraditional home who subsequently returns to a life of Torah is formidable, but not insurmountable.

What are his obligations?

Certainly, if a parent was raised in a non-Torah environment and grew up without the benefit of a Torah education, his nonobservance is due to lack of knowledge, and a son or daughter is obligated in the mitzvos of honor and reverence: care and concern for his parents' health and well-being; speaking respectfully; zeroing in on their strengths, and realizing that much of what he is is in their merit; not contradicting; correcting with deference — just to mention a few of the many obligations we have explored in previous chapters.

Nonetheless, the line is drawn at requests that would involve Torah violations. If we are asked by our parents, for instance, to purchase nonkosher food / to attend an interfaith ceremony / to accompany them in a car on Shabbos / or any other behavior that would involve a transgression, we must respectfully decline.*

This, however, does not exempt a son or daughter from all the mitzvos of *kibbud* or *yirah* that are possible and permissible. For example: If a father asks his son to fix a leak on Friday night, the son can't make the repair on Shabbos. But he can show his respect for his father's wishes and fulfill the mitzvah by making the repair right after *Havdalah*.

What are some of the concerns of the parents of children who have become Torah observant?

After decades of dedication and sacrifice and often a significant investment in education, parents are understandably hurt by the rejection of their values and lifestyle. They are concerned that all they invested will be lost, and that their child's love, respect, and loyalty to them will be diminished.

Many are sincerely worried about this new, unfamiliar lifestyle and wonder, how will this affect them? How will this affect the family unity?

A son or daughter should demonstrate that religion isn't a form of rebellion against parental authority, that it will not alienate him from the family, and that his parents will benefit more from his becoming a committed Jew than from his remaining an uncommitted one.

Self-damaging requests

If a parent asks his son or daughter to give him an item that his doctors have stated to be harmful for him, what is the child to do?

---

* In cases which are not as clear as these, one should consult a Rav.

❖ A diabetic parent asks his child for a piece of cake

❖ A parent who is not allowed to have salt asks his child to salt the food

❖ A parent with an alcohol problem asks for a drink

❖ A parent who was told to stop smoking asks for a cigarette

The Torah obligation to guard one's health (וְנִשְׁמַרְתֶּם מְאֹד לְנַפְשֹׁתֵיכֶם) overrides a parent's request for a harmful item.[5] Were a child to obey, he would be abetting the violation of this positive mitzvah.

A child must refuse to honor a parent's request if medical authorities say it is **"life-threatening."**

If the item is **harmful** to the parent's health — but not dangerous to life — yet the parent insists on being served the food or drink or given the item, opinions vary as to whether the son or daughter must comply. In general, it will depend on the medical evaluation of the extent of the potential harm or damage.

When in doubt, a child should not act until he can clarify the health effects.

What should a child say to a parent when he can't serve him? Best is some variation of: "Dad/Mom, I want to do as you wish, but I have to heed the doctor's instructions."

MY FATHER'S MEDICAL STATUS became increasingly complex during the final five years of his life. Treating one ailment often caused another, and side effects of medication brought their own discomforts.

About six months before my father passed away, he suffered a stroke. Though he regained many functions, he needed a walker, his hearing and sight worsened, and his cognitive functions were impaired.

In the course of a new treatment for heart failure, my father was diagnosed with suspected renal failure and rushed to the hospital. Just over a week into his hospitalization, my siblings and I were asked to give our consent to our father being intubated.

We quickly called our Rav for guidance.

Halachah gave us our answer. The procedure was carried

out immediately, and my father remained under sedation.

The following morning, the doctors decided to slowly wean my father off the sedation. I was scared. How would my father react to waking up and finding a long tube down his throat?

True to my fears, my father was terribly agitated over what had happened.

The tube was very uncomfortable for him, maybe even painful, and it was very distressing to see my father in so much torment. Furthermore, he couldn't hear properly (his hearing aids had been removed for safety's sake) and he was, obviously, unable to talk with a large tube in his throat. I felt sick to my stomach seeing my father suffering like this, and at certain points I rushed out of the room to heave and shed some pent-up tears.

I gently and calmly tried to explain to my father what was going on, that this was a temporary medical procedure until his lungs were clear of fluid and more capable of functioning on their own. I reassured him that, hopefully fairly soon, the doctors would remove all the tubes. I empathized with him at how uncomfortable it must be, but told him that it was absolutely necessary for his speedy recovery, adding, "because, Daddy, we all want you back home and better as soon as possible."

My father was having none of this sweet talk. He was furious at my attempts to calm him. He wanted that tube out NOW. He signaled me with his fingers (his hands had been tied to the bars of the bed) to either untie him or to remove the tube from his mouth. He was giving me a mix of imploring and disapproving looks: imploring me to do his will, and disapproving that I could watch him suffer and be complicit in going along with the hospital, who were obviously "incompetent and uncaring."

I found myself facing a torturous dilemma. This was a no win. I knew I couldn't remove the breathing tube. Even though my father was pleading with me to pull it out, I had to disobey.

My siblings and I never ceased advocating — actually, that's the wrong word — nudging endlessly would be a better description of what went on. We raised our voices louder than we would have ordinarily. Finally, a doctor came, *reassessed the situation, and adjusted the tube — alleviating my father's pain.*

We had passed this test, but I was filled with dread thinking about the long road ahead of us.

Doing what is right isn't necessarily easy or comfortable. I beseeched Hashem to help me make the right decisions to help me care for my father in accordance with His will.

Joining disputes

הָאָב שֶׁצִּוָּה אֶת בְּנוֹ שֶׁלֹּא יְדַבֵּר עִם פְּלוֹנִי וְשֶׁלֹּא
יִמְחוֹל לוֹ עַד זְמַן קָצוּב וְהַבֵּן הָיָה רוֹצֶה לְהִתְפַּיֵּיס
מִיָּד לוּלֵא צַוָּואת אָבִיו — אֵין לוֹ לָחוּשׁ לְצַוָּואתוֹ

A father demands that his son or daughter refrain from speaking to *"Ploni"** and not forgive him until a specific time. The son, for his part, would be willing to end this argument immediately if not for his father's command. [In such an instance], he need not fear disobeying (*Shulchan Aruch* 240:16).

Since instigating or encouraging the continuation of a quarrel is a Torah transgression (לֹא יִהְיֶה כְקֹרַח וְכַעֲדָתוֹ, "that he not be like Korach and his assembly"; *Bamidbar* 17:5), why is it singled out here? Wasn't it already addressed in the previous section of the *Shulchan Aruch*, where we are told that a child may not accede to a request that necessitates transgressing the Torah?

One lesson is that *sinas chinam* (baseless hatred) and *machlokes* (dispute) are such serious transgressions that they are singled out for independent discussion and warning.[6]

What should a son or daughter do when placed in such a situation?

The father himself is acting in violation of the Torah and asking his son to be a partner in crime. The son should not make this a

---

* *Sefer Chareidim:* אֵיזֶהוּ שׂוֹנֵא? כָּל שֶׁלֹּא דִבֶּר עִמּוֹ שְׁלֹשָׁה יָמִים מִתּוֹךְ אֵיבָה — An "enemy" is defined as one with whom one has not spoken for three days out of anger.

family feud. All the more so when the father's opponent is not altogether at fault and/or has asked the parent for forgiveness. Still, in the presence of his father, the son should avoid obvious gestures or public displays of friendship toward his father's rival, so as not to arouse his father's ire.[7]

> *OUR NEIGHBORS THE LEVINES are making a wedding. My mother hasn't spoken to these neighbors for years, after a fallout over a tree of theirs that juts onto our property. She expects us all to follow suit.*
>
> *I grew up with these children, and I personally have no problem with the Levines. I think it's only right to participate in this* simchah. *But I'm not going to announce my plans to my mother. What would be the point? She would be furious and take it as a personal slight.*

If such a response wouldn't work for you, look for a different one. The main thing is to find a solution whereby you avoid quarreling with a third party and at the same time avoid angering your parent.

Out of loyalty to our parents, we tend to take their side in a dispute. Our anger is fueled by righteous indignation that our parent was wronged, and we lose our objectivity. Nonetheless, though we may be convinced our parents are right, we should encourage them to end the argument. It's a special *zechus* if a child can be the one to bring that peace.[8]*

Quarreling with family members

If a parent asks you to do something that will cause friction with your spouse or an in-law, you must ignore the request, since in effect, the parent is asking you to transgress a Torah law.

> *From day one, my mother didn't like my wife, Ruth. Her greatest pleasure would be if I divorced her. My mother has more than hinted to this on many occasions.*

---

* If the other person caused your parents serious damage, major loss, or extreme anguish, your pain will obviously be very great. Clarify and pursue a Torah approach and proper response for such a painful occurrence.

I know what bothers my mother about Ruth. Though I may agree with some of my mother's criticisms, still, I'm not ready to ruin my marriage because of it.

My mother and I had a long talk, and it wasn't pleasant. But I had to make it very clear that Ruth just can't come up in our conversations.

My father had a run-in with my in-laws. It was some kind of a disagreement about monies that were promised. My father got so angry over what he sees as my father-in-law's lack of integrity that he forbade me to go to my in-laws' house.

I hope he'll calm down. Can you imagine what would happen in our home if my wife heard that I wouldn't be coming with her to her parents' house?

My father is really upset. I'll just have to tiptoe around this one, and make sure not to mention our visits.[9]

Stringencies

A child has obligations to the Almighty that even parents cannot override, but a stringency (*chumrah*) is a different matter. A child must be wary when adopting a stringency, a behavior beyond that which halachah requires. If this behavior distresses parents, if they are adamantly opposed, and particularly if they have a reasonable objection, a Rav should decide if this behavior should be continued.

> *A YOUNG MAN CAME to the Chazon Ish.*[10] *He said that he wanted to follow the most preferable behavior (לְכַתְּחִילָה) in a certain matter. However, it greatly distressed his mother. The Chazon Ish encouraged him to accept a lenient approach.*
>
> *"But I want to do this in the most preferable way," was his argument.*
>
> *Advised the Chazon Ish: "For you, the b'dieved is a lechatchilah (in this case, a leniency is what is preferable)."*

From the responsa of Harav Moshe Sternbuch:

[If a son or daughter wishes to adopt a stringency (מִילֵי דַחֲסִידוּת), and the father is opposed because he feels that if his son or daughter were to take this on, he or she would exude an air of superiority and undermine the father as head of the household, a son or daughter should not ignore the father's wishes.]

Therefore, if a son or daughter wants to take on a stringency, they should make every effort to see that their father does not feel slighted. Certainly they should not cause anguish to their father or answer him rudely, flippantly, or behave arrogantly.

Instead of receiving blessings for his "exemplary actions," he would bring upon himself the opposite, אָרוּר מַקְלֶה אָבִיו וְאִמּוֹ, "Cursed is he who belittles his father and mother." Any gain would be outweighed by the loss.[11]

Before accepting upon oneself a stringency that will cause a family disturbance, and to ensure that you are, in fact, bringing the Almighty pleasure, a Rabbinic authority should be consulted, as was done in the following instance.

MY PARENTS ASKED ME TO MAKE the bris of our newborn son after midday, this being easier for them as well as their guests. Since we are told, זְרִיזִין מַקְדִּימִים לְמִצְוֹת — mitzvos should be done promptly and energetically, I wanted to make the bris at the most preferable time, first thing in the morning.

This question was brought to Harav Elyashiv, *ztz"l,* who responded:

True, a bris should be done first thing in the morning. However, since it is permissible to do the mitzvah at any time during the day, the son must (חַיָּיב) listen to his father.

He may ask close friends to intercede with his parents on his behalf.

If his parents still aren't convinced, he should go along with their request.[12]

THE FIRST ELEVEN YEARS of my life were uneventful, beyond the usual occasions and milestones. My relationship with my parents was typical. I was a conscientious child, very responsible, with a strong desire to please. Our home was traditional.

My mother's sister and her family were what we referred to as "more right wing." Living not too far apart, our families visited often. I was intrigued by whatever was going on in my aunt's home, and slowly felt myself being pulled in that direction. My parents were aware of my leanings, so they were not altogether caught by surprise when, at the age of 14, I asked to transfer to the school my cousins attended.

My parents must have experienced reservations, but they allowed me to make such a monumental decision. To this day, I admire their ability to see past themselves and to parent me in the way they understood suited my needs and temperament.

Being in a more observant environment influenced me profoundly. I had wonderful teachers, and felt invigorated by the intense study of Chumash, Navi, Yahadus *and* Halachah.

I began taking upon myself certain mitzvos that I had not seen in my home. I was struggling with my mother, who felt that I was becoming too fanatical and extreme. I lacked the maturity to deal with the situation appropriately, and often found myself feeling "holier than thou."

My principal was a very influential personality in my journey, and this disrespectful attitude did not escape him. He gave me solutions that appeased my mother. He said that I should take things slowly, one step at a time. He was very insistent that my growth be a healthy process, and emphasized that one of the Aseres HaDibros was kabbed es avicha v'es imecha.

My parents, again to their credit, let me go to camp with my cousins. One summer, I asked the Rav of the camp if I should take it upon myself to eat only chalav Yisrael *products. I was sure that he would be impressed by my piety and tell me, at the very least, to be careful with this outside my parents' home.*

His answer put me firmly in my place. With a slightly annoyed expression, he told me in no uncertain terms that I was not to take this chumrah *upon myself.*

"But why?" I stammered. "I want to be makpid."

"Maybe," he answered. "But not for the right reasons. Your hakpadah *will make you feel superior to your parents, and*

no child should feel that way toward a parent. It leads to chutzpah. If your future husband is makpid *on* chalav Yisrael, *then, and only then should you take it upon yourself."*

With time, I learned the value of asking she'eilos *regarding* kibbud av va'eim. *I had assumed that "the more stringent the better," and that being* machmir *certainly superseded my parents' wishes. Thankfully, I was repeatedly reminded of my proper place in the parent-child hierarchy. The battle against haughtiness was, and continues to be, a struggle.*

I constantly remind myself of the crucial foundation my parents gave me and their encouragement of my initial transfer. Without them, I would not be alive, and without the education they funded, I would not have experienced the growth that I did.

There were challenges right up to my wedding, through the birth of my first child, and until today. As long as there is a relationship, there will surely be situations that challenge that relationship.

Fortunately, the man I married is amazing in his respect for his parents — and mine.

The lessons I was fortunate to learn from my rebbeim and my husband is that a child who wishes to foster a stronger relationship with Hashem and His Torah (i.e., all the stringencies that we think will do it) should certainly embrace the mitzvah of kibbud av va'eim *with the very same enthusiasm as* kashrus, tzenius, *and Torah learning.*

Potential areas of parent-child conflict

A son or daughter is looking toward spiritual growth and personal fulfillment. The circumstances in which he feels he can accomplish his goals do not meet with his parents' approval. **Halachah recognizes these aspirations and ambitions as legitimate, and therefore limits parental coercion.**

Four areas of potential conflict are discussed extensively in classic and contemporary Rabbinic responsa: (1) settling in Eretz Yisrael; (2) marriage; (3) *talmud Torah*; and (4) *tefillah*.

One must tread very carefully before making this type of life-altering decision. Every family will have its own dynamic. With all the information in hand, parents and children in conflict should — together — seek Rabbinic guidance in order to reach a halachically correct conclusion.

We now stand in front of one of those "towering edifices" we mentioned at the beginning of this book. Take a quick look. There are benches filled with some of our greatest sages deeply studying and ruling on these complex issues of *kibbud av va'eim.* Mark the spot. You can return at your leisure for a more in-depth exploration, which is beyond the scope of this tour.

With that said, let's look at some questions that can come up.

Settling in Eretz Yisrael

- "May one move to Eretz Yisrael over parental objections?"

- "Can parents insist on a son or daughter returning if they merit living in Eretz Yisrael?"

- "May one influence others to move to Eretz Yisrael when it is known to be against their parents' wishes?"

> *MY HUSBAND AND I always had our hearts set on living in Eretz Yisrael. A year and a half after our marriage and four months after the birth of our daughter, plane tickets in hand, we were on our way to realizing our dream.*
>
> *Though we often spoke about moving, my mother was devastated when it finally happened. I am her oldest child, and our daughter is her first grandchild. This was the 60s. Israel was just after a major war. How safe was the Middle East? Besides, Israel in those years was sooo far.*
>
> *We didn't have a telephone for three-and-a-half years. To make an international call, we had to make an appointment at the central post office. When we did manage to speak, the connection was not always clear and the call was so*

*expensive we really couldn't enjoy the conversation. So we
rarely spoke. Flying home was an extravagance that we could
ill afford.*

*When I think back to those years, I am so ashamed of how
shallow and self-absorbed I was. Though our decision turned
out to be a good one, my mother suffered terribly. My new
life enveloped me, and I didn't trouble myself to consider my
mother's deep hurt and heartache.*

*It took me years to understand her thoughts at that time,
which she hinted to me many years later:*

*"Was my daughter **going** someplace or **running away** from
some place? Did I fail her? There is finally a grandchild to
pamper. So much to share. So much nachas to be had. Why
am I being deprived of all this?"*

And the very worst was that I didn't seem to care a hoot.

*If my husband and I could do this over (if!), we would still
make the same decision — but surely not with the same
callousness. I would take the time to embrace my mother
physically and emotionally, to assure her how much I love
her, will miss her, would stay in touch come what may. I
would have written more, sent more long, detailed letters,
more pictures, and looked for more ways to "send" our love.*

*Probably my mother still would not have been at peace with
our decision. However, hindsight tells me that even though I
was young and insensitive, with some prompting and a little
knowledge of hilchos kibbud av va'eim I could have done
much (as opposed to the nothing I actually did do). I could
have been a proactively loving and devoted daughter in the
many ways that were available to me and so have reduced the
sadness my mother experienced in those years.*

We learn (*Megillah* 16b) that Yaakov Avinu was faulted for
leaving his parents for twenty-two years, thereby forfeiting the
opportunity to serve them.

The question is asked: Weren't his parents, Yitzchak and
Rivkah, responsible for sending him away to find a wife?

Though there are many answers to this question, here is one
thought: Yaakov Avinu was not censured for leaving. His parents

had to send him away, for several reasons, and Yaakov had to go. He was faulted for not sufficiently feeling his parents' *tza'ar* at his absence.[13]

Marriage

- A child wishes to marry and the parents object to his choice...
- Parents are encouraging the child to marry when his heart is not in the match...
- Parents claim that the child's choice of a mate will bring them shame and anguish...
- Can't a parent legitimately object if the proposed mate suffers from a flawed character / physical and/or emotional limitations / health complications?

When there is a difference of opinion as to the suitability of a match, it is critical for parents and children to consult their Rav for a Torah perspective.

The following incident is recorded:[14]

I ONCE WENT TO SEE Harav Shlomo Zalman Auerbach with a young man who was about to finalize a shidduch. He posed the following question:

"Both the girl and I would like to finalize the shidduch," the young man said, "but my father is opposed to the match. Can I go ahead with the shidduch without my father's agreement, in accordance with the opinion of the Rema, that in matters of a marriage partner one need not yield to his parents' opinion?"

Harav Shlomo Zalman became very serious. He then addressed the young man, saying forcefully, "Indeed, there is such a halachah, but under no circumstances will I have a hand in this. One does not do such a thing!"

To emphasize his point, the Rav repeated himself several times.

"Practically," said Harav Shlomo Zalman, "I suggest speaking with your father, using divrei chachmah *(words of wisdom)."* *He then gave very specific advice as to what to say.*

And that's exactly what happened. When he did as the Rav advised, the father changed his mind, and even participated heartily in the engagement celebration.

Talmud Torah

When our Sages say that Torah study takes precedence over *kibbud av va'eim*, they are referring to long-range progress in learning, maximizing spiritual growth, and acquisition of Torah wisdom.[15] This is a legitimate need. However, one whose progress in learning is such that it does not preclude paying attention to his parents' physical needs, must temporarily interrupt his studies to ensure this care.

Even when a son leaves his parents' locale in order to strengthen his learning, his eyes and heart should be directed toward his parents... asking, checking, and probing as to their well-being.[16]

 Must a son listen if...

...he wants to learn in a location his parents feel is not safe?

...he is very studious and learns until the early hours of the morning, but Mother insists that he get more sleep, since he gets up early?

...his parents want him to leave Torah learning to pursue a career?

...his parents want him to come home for Shabbos, but he feels he'll gain more if he stays in the yeshivah dorm?

...his father asks him to help build a succah, and he has study partners lined up for the whole vacation?

...his parents want him to attend a family Chanukah party that will interfere with his evening learning session?

Answers to these questions are not based on whim or mood, but rather the Torah's guidelines for situations where *talmud Torah* conflicts with *kibbud av va'eim*.

Tefillah

The conflict: A father wants his son to daven in the same shul as he does, but the son prefers a different shul.

From the father's perspective, he enjoys his son's company and closeness. Another consideration might be that in his community, it is customary for parents and children to daven together. It's a slight for him if the son doesn't come.

Though it is surely a mitzvah if the son complies with his father's request, halachah takes into consideration a son's preferences.

For instance, he may prefer:

❖ An earlier *minyan*

❖ Another shul's pace, decorum, and intensity, so that he can hear and concentrate on the davening and *krias haTorah*

❖ *Tefillah* and/or *shaliach tzibbur* more to his taste

❖ A *tzibbur* more his age

From the responsa of Harav Avraham Pam, *ztz"l*:

> ...True, the son's motivations are justified, and some of his considerations are even halachic requirements. Still, the son should be wary about exercising his prerogative ...
>
> A wise son will carefully weigh the advantages against the disadvantages. If his decision leads to confrontation, and even heated arguments, he is bound to transgress several Torah prohibitions. Then he will have lost more than he gained. It is in reference to this and similar situations that it says, "Woe to one whose defense attorney becomes his prosecutor." Sometimes the very action that we feel will be a great merit for us, will, in fact, become a "prosecutor."

Therefore, one should try to come up with an idea to appease and please his parent, and also fulfill his obligation of *tefillah* and *krias haTorah*.* One who comes to purify himself receives Heavenly assistance.[17]

Rav Pam's wisdom is pertinent to all of the situations mentioned in this chapter.

The Torah acknowledges certain filial aspirations as valid, with the potential to overrule parental objection. Each of these decisions needs great deliberation, and a wise person will act with caution. A son or daughter should daven to Hashem to plant the right thoughts in his mind and give him the right words so that he can strive for *kavod veyiras Hashem* without forfeiting *kavod veyiras av va'eim*.

When we speak about pursuing peace, the expression used is רְדִיפַת שָׁלוֹם, running after it, not just meandering down the path.

---

* For example, a son might get up very early to daven at a *minyan* of his choice for *Shacharis* and *krias haTorah*. Then, he could return home to join his father, accompany him to shul, remain for *Mussaf*, greet his father's friends afterward, and accompany his father home.

REVERENCE:
A Final Thought

Hashem spoke to Moshe, saying, "Speak to *Klal Yisrael*, and say to them, 'Be holy.'"[18]

The mitzvah to "be holy" is immediately followed by the warning: "Revere your mother and father."

Why this sequence?

First, it reminds us that it is our parents who enabled us to come into this world to become holy. If we have merited climbing the ladder toward *kedushah*, we recognize that it was our parents who brought us into the world, the place where it is possible to work our way up.

Here's a second way to understand the connection between these two mitzvos. This *parashah, Kedoshim Tehiyu,* "You should be holy," is our source for many mitzvos, particularly pivotal mitzvos of *bein adam lachaveiro.* Among them:

❖ Don't take from the produce of the field that must be left for the poor

❖ Don't steal

❖ Don't withhold wages

❖ Don't curse

❖ Don't put a stumbling block in front of someone who can't see

❖ Don't pervert justice and don't show favoritism in the courtroom

❖ Don't be a talebearer

❖ Don't sit back while your friend suffers a loss

❖ Don't harbor hatred in your heart

❖ Don't embarrass

❖ Don't take revenge

❖ Don't hold a grudge

❖ Don't cheat in weights and measurements

So many "don'ts"! — which teaches us that in order to be *kedoshim*, holy, we have to be able to control our natural inclinations and say no to ourselves on many occasions.

We'd like to gossip a little, but we have to clamp our mouths shut and switch the dial to "off."

We are asked for advice. We'd like to suggest something that is to our benefit, but it would not be beneficial to the person who is asking. Rein in and curb those self-interests.

We want to be a little lazy. Get up and help that person in distress.

We feel the urge to pad an expense account?

All of these mitzvos require self-discipline and self-control, reminding us that we can't do whatever we want.

How can we be prepared for all these nos and don'ts?

By being trained in our early years to accept a no. By growing up knowing that certain behaviors and responses are out of bounds.

From his earliest years, a child steeped in the atmosphere of *yiras av va'eim* is telling himself, "Find another seat. This one is reserved. It belongs to my mother/father."

Your father is having a disagreement with your uncle. You know your father is right. You're itching to butt in. Zip your lip — he'll manage without you.

Your mother just broke your umbrella. It was an expensive one. You're ready to say something about negligence. Then, you catch yourself.

Rav Shamshon Raphael Hirsch comments on this mitzvah:

In *Parashas Kedoshim*, the Torah gives us the mitzvah of reverence for one's mother and father as opposed to the mitzvah of honor, which is given elsewhere. This is because reverence for parents is the preparation for a life of *kedushah*. As is known, a person is born a פֶּרֶא אָדָם, in a crude, unpolished state. The deference that a child develops for his parents in his early years is the root of all future strength he will have to rule over his desires. It will give him the capacity and control to accede to others. Placing one's parents' will before his own, as a child, is a practice in humility and will enable him, in his adulthood, to place Hashem's will before his own. In this way, reverence for parents is the initial preparation for a life of *kedushah*.[19]

In-credibly *In*-spiring

Portraits of steadfast devotion

Chapter 26

Special Connections

Here are sons and daughters who triumphed in turning their challenges into a special connection.

I WORKED IN A FAMILY BUSINESS with my father, of blessed memory, for thirty years. The main lesson I learned: if you make it about the business, it becomes about the family. If you make it about the family, it becomes about the business. Here's what I mean:

You're in a family business. You say to yourself, this business, like any business, exists to make a profit. Therefore, we will make all our decisions based on what is most profitable for the business. The fact that it is a family business is secondary. Sounds logical, right?

The problem is that a family business is not like other businesses. In a non-family business, legitimate business disagreements about how you best make a profit get decided by whoever is in charge. If you don't agree with the decision, you're free to leave, and if you disagree too vehemently, you get shown the door. In a family business, those aren't reasonable alternatives. Unless you are a fool or heartless, *you can't fire your family member (though unfortunately it certainly happens). Simple business disagreements can become personal family struggles. Minor family dysfunctions become major business roadblocks.*

But if you begin with the family — in my case if you begin with the relationship between yourself and your father — and you decide that relationship is the most important thing, if you make the hard decision that short-term profits might suffer because you don't want to turn a business disagreement into a personal fight, in the end you will become an effective team, working toward a common goal.

Let's begin with the basic relationship. In most family businesses, the father has established the business, and brings in his children. So in addition to the usual respect a child owes a father, there is the fact that the father has given the child an initial boost in business. If you are the child, get used to that fact. I am now 60 years old; I have been working at my job for forty years, running my company for almost twenty. Still, on those thankfully rare instances where I get into arguments with especially nasty people, one of the first things they say if they want to hurt me is "Your father gave you this business; you built nothing on your own." If you have a problem with dealing with that attitude, just get over it. Personally, my response when people say that to me, and this comes from my own deep appreciation for what I have, is "You bet my father gave me a boost. He gave me a great home life, lots of love, and a good business. How lucky am I?"

My father and I, toward the end of his life, had a common refrain we would tell each other. I told him he did the hard part — starting a business from scratch. He told me that I took the business to heights he never could have. Frankly, I think he was just saying it because he loved me and he was a good father and it was a nice thing to say. But I can tell you I was absolutely 100 percent honest in what I was saying to him — I think creating a business from scratch is harder than taking a successful business and making it more successful. I never wanted to be one of those guys who was born on third base, thinking he had hit a triple.

I never spent one minute of my life trying to show myself or anyone else I had outdone my father, and frankly, I don't understand people who do. I remember one day there was an article in the Wall Street Journal about a prominent family in the retail business. The article was an interview with the son, who was exactly my age, talking about how he had taken the business in a different direction than his father, the founder, because his father didn't have his "vision." His father, almost exactly the same age as my father, reacted vehemently against this public humiliation. This very prominent retail business wound up going very publicly bankrupt, amid fights and recriminations within the family, but especially between this father and son. And over what? Because the son wanted to show that he was smarter than his father? Whatever ego issue there was between father and son became a business issue, which ruined the business and ultimately ruined the family.

Interestingly, when my father and I read that story that morning, I criticized the son for taking public credit and questioning his father's vision. My father criticized the father for reacting so vehemently against his son.

My father created an entire industry almost from scratch. He was, therefore, entirely confident in the superiority of his judgment. But we all know where that story winds up. Inevitably, competition appears on the horizon. In our case, it was a company that was lowering their commission, and raising the standard of their customer service. They began to take away much of our market share. In the business world, we would say they began "eating our lunch." But we didn't change. My father had a certain way of doing business, which had been successful for decades, and he was vehemently against changing to meet this new competition. I saw what was happening, and had many conversations with my father about changing our commission structure, or improving the way we handled customer service. He was unbendable on these issues. I made the decision that I would, for the short term, allow business to suffer, and back my father even internally against doubters.

Eventually, we were saved by what they call in business management "the burning platform." It's hard to get people to change, but if the platform upon which they are standing begins to burn, they will know it's time to take the leap into the water. So when our competitor beat us time and time again, and my father on his own could see that we had no choice, we held hands and jumped together. I could have pushed earlier, I could have told my father he was being blinded by his own past success. But instead, I waited until he could see it for himself. Might that have cost us some business? In the short run, undoubtedly. But in the long run we were stronger, because after we jumped we were swimming together.

For years, when my father and I would travel together on business, my father would do almost all the talking, and I would have a briefcase full of supporting material.

Once in a while, my father would subtly signal me to begin talking about something, to pick up the thread of where he left off, just so he could rest and have time to collect his thoughts. But the key was that I always made sure that the potential customer saw that we were a team, and that I was the supporting member giving full respect and backing to my father. That was good not only for my relationship with my father, which is why I did it, but also, less importantly, it was good for business. No one wants to go into business with a company full of internal conflict. People saw my father and me as a team, the two of us rowing in one direction, speaking with one voice.

It's also important to pay attention to "the geography of respect." As he grew older my father spent winters in Miami and summers in the Catskills. He only used his office a few months of the year. My father asked me, many times, to move to his office during the times when he was away, so I would have a more comfortable place to work. I never did. I think it was an important signal to send to everyone in the company — that though my father was not there physically, he was there in spirit; that while I may have been running things on a day-to-day basis, my father was still the guiding force of the company. My not sitting at his desk was a physical manifestation of that. Even when my father ceased coming into the office altogether, I never sat at his desk. I bought a new desk, and rearranged his former office so that I was not sitting in his place. It was a way I found of compromising between our desire not to waste office space but my desire not to appear to be supplanting my father.

When my father was out of the office, which was at least half the year, he would call in to check what was going on. He and my mother would go for walks, for instance, on the boardwalk in Miami Beach, and when they got to the end of the boardwalk, my father would go over to the pay phone (these were the days before cell phones) and call the office. I sat with each of my key colleagues and told them to expect these phone calls. These people were in sales, working largely on commission, and this was valuable time from their day. But I told them it was important to the company to give my father the respect of their time and attention, and to answer his questions. As for me, I kept a special pad on my desk, and when something interesting happened during the day, I would jot it down on that pad, so that when my father called I always had something to tell him. Certainly, it was time-consuming, but I never wanted my father to feel as if he were bothering me; I wanted him to feel that I was waiting for his call to give him good news, and to get his advice and guidance on whatever business challenges we were facing.

Family businesses are a powerful force. Ninety percent of all U.S. firms are family owned or controlled, and 33 percent of Fortune 500 corporations are family businesses. One half of the total wages paid within the U.S. are paid by family businesses. But roughly one third won't make it from first to the second generation, half of those won't make it from the second to the third, and from the third to fourth is merely a 5 percent success rate. I think that is because many of those businesses are making the fundamental mistake of not putting family cohesiveness first. Running a family business without putting family cohesion first is like planting cut flowers. No matter how hard you work, they will not grow and blossom.

Measuring the success of a family business by profits alone is a sure recipe for turning money into problems. Success is not the key to family happiness. In a family business especially, family happiness is the key to success.

———•◦•———

"WHO WAS THAT WHO CALLED, HONEY?" *my mother asked as I returned the phone to its place on the kitchen counter.*

"It was Chani," I said, already anticipating the questions that would surely follow. I kept my face pleasant, making sure my smile didn't waver.

"And what did she have to say?" my mother asked, completely unaware of my discomfort.

I felt myself tensing as I told my mother all about my friend's new job and her upcoming trip to Europe, carefully sidestepping other details of our conversation that were confidential.

I returned to my room and fell onto my bed. I took a deep breath and exhaled slowly, then again.

They do so, so much for me, *I reminded myself.* I am so incredibly lucky to have them and grateful to be back in their home.

Which of course I was. It had been a tremendous relief to know that after my divorce, I had a loving, devoted pair of parents who welcomed me and my two little sons into their home without conditions or hesitation.

As you may imagine, I had gotten used to a certain level of independence during my married years. The independence marriage offers slips onto one's shoulders with the ease and comfort of a favorite old sweater. Giving up that newfound independence and sliding back into the role of a daughter in her parent's home was not simple.

For one thing, my privacy was gone. Not just in terms of phone calls, but even an impromptu trip to the store was no longer just a matter of deciding and then heading out. Now it was important to my parents to know where I was going, why I was going, and when I'd return.

Then there were Shabbasos and Yamim Tovim when I had to move out of my room to a foldout bed in the living room, to make space for my married siblings. I did this voluntarily, yet the privacy I enjoyed and still needed, the feeling of stability of having a place to call my own, was disrupted.

It wasn't just not having my own physical space, but every aspect of my life — the brands and foods I liked to buy; the way I enjoyed cooking; the days on which I did my laundry — my own way, at my own convenience and pace — the way I strategically placed items around my own home — were things of the past. When I offered to help out, I needed to do things my mother's way, rather than the way I'd gotten used to, so that I wouldn't invade my mother's space and place.

Though I had kept my job, and my paycheck provided for most of my children's needs, it did not cover all of our expenses, and I was very much aware — though my parents never said a word to me about this — that we were a financial burden on my parents, albeit a burden that they accepted with open arms. But I, who had already tasted independence, felt that everything I ate was nahama d'chisufa *— bread of shame.*

Will I never again have that contentment of being my own self in my own place? *I thought. I felt my eyes moisten, but willed myself not to cry.*

I blinked the almost-tears away and then lay very still. I remembered a saying my father had repeated often when I was growing up, one that would become my guiding light throughout the next few years.

"There is a tiny difference between חֶסֶד *and* חָסֵר*,"* he *would say, "a tiny turn that reshapes a* ר *into a* ד*, but a huge difference in perspective. Are we going to focus on the* חֶסֶד *— what we have, or the* חָסֵר *— what is lacking?*

"But not only that," said my wise father. "We can choose to see the חֶסֶד *in the* חָסֵר *— the kindness in the lacking, to see all the good that is truly there."*

That is what I'm going to do, *I decided. My privacy and*

independence are compromised, yes, but I still have so very, very much. I have a home for myself and my children, parents who love and care for me, and siblings who are wonderful and incredibly supportive. I have so much chessed — from my parents, and from Hashem. I would focus on all that I do have instead of dwelling on what is lacking. After all, as they say, happiness is a decision, not a situation.

And I would also focus on my parents' perspective.

No doubt, it was a challenge for them — taking in a daughter with two little children — after they had gotten used to having their privacy and a quiet, organized home, for the past years. If the divorce was painful for me, was it not so for my father and mother? Their hopes for their daughter to build a bayis ne'eman *— all they invested, including a major financial input — dashed. But there was no question. Their home and hearts were open to us, as they always had been.*

It was with that thought in mind that I slipped into a deep sleep. When I awoke in the morning, the sun was bright, the morning air crisp and fresh.

With the new morning came a new idea. An idea that would allow me to savor the taste of independence and at the same time, honor my parents and express my gratitude to them.

I worked most of the week, but Tuesday was my day off. I decided to tell my mother that I wanted to give her a break in the kitchen one day a week, and that every Tuesday I would prepare dinner. I told my mother my idea, watching with pleasure as the emotions flitted across her face; first surprise, then gratitude, and then a sweet blend of excitement and pride that stayed on her face the rest of the night.

"Are you sure about this?" she asked me on Monday night. I assured her that indeed I was.

The next morning, while my mother went out to a shiur, *I headed to the store to buy the ingredients I needed. I spent the morning in the kitchen, singing along with my favorite CD, and cooking up a gourmet, four-course meal (and of course, cleaning up after myself).*

When we sat down at the table, I felt so...contented. My

whole being was buzzing with creativity and independence, and the look on my parents' faces told me they were equally pleased.

The shift in my outlook made a tremendous difference, but there were still very real challenges, particularly as my boys grew older.

I grew up in a wonderful home, but still, every person takes their own path in ruchniyus, and, inspired by my parents' commitment to Yiddishkeit, I had taken on my own chumros as an adult, choosing to be more careful about what I exposed myself and my children to.

Now that I was back in my parents' home, I no longer had control of these things. I reminded myself that our job is to do ratzon Hashem, and when it comes to a choice between a mitzvah — that of kibbud av va'eim — or a chumrah, the ratzon Hashem is clearly to go with the mitzvah. I could not make the mistake of hurting my parents by insisting on the chumros I had accepted when building my own home. Here too, I focused on the ruchniyus that was there — the beautiful divrei Torah at the Shabbos table, the special way my parents prepared for Shabbos, the tzedakah my parents so generously gave — pointing these out to my boys as they got older.

After a few years, it was time for us to move into our own home. I knew that this was what my children and I needed, but I also knew that telling my parents we were leaving would be very hurtful for them. I didn't want them to feel that I was ungrateful. They had invested much and had grown extremely attached to my children. Once I reached a decision that this move was right for us, I carefully chose an opportune time to speak to them. I was very emotional as I told them how much I appreciated everything that they had done for me all through my life, and especially during these years, despite the hardship it entailed for them. I explained why I felt we needed to move on. With siyata d'Shmaya, they were able to accept my decision.

After all these years, there was no way that I could just leave. I made my last day in my parents' home a truly special one. That day, Tuesday though it was not, I made a special, gourmet meal, choosing all of their favorite dishes that I had made during the past few years. I then asked them to walk through the house with me, to see what I had prepared.

My mother's eyes welled up with tears as we began our tour. In each room I had left a memento with a short note, something referring to the time we had shared together as a family, and as my mother fingered each one, I could see in her face that she knew I understood how she felt. Our moving out would leave a void in every room, and in the house as a whole.

By the time we finished, none of our eyes were dry. But they were tears of love and connection, and I was grateful that despite the hardships that these years presented, I was able to make choices that had brought our hearts even closer than before.

———◆———

"...AND FROM MY STUDENTS, [I learned] most of all..."

And from my students... When I hear that Chazal, a nearly endless stream of faces comes to mind. After all, as the principal of a boarding school like Beit Elisheva, I've seen so many children rise above challenges you and I can barely fathom.

But the faces that stand out the most in that brilliant, inspiring stream are the faces of Leora and Odelia, two little orphan girls who blossomed into tenaciously strong young women. The girls who made me realize that despite the pain, adversity can truly bring out the best in a person.

Yes, I see the shining, determined faces of those two extraordinary sisters, Leora and Odelia Devor.

They came to our school as little girls, entering second and third grade. Mrs. Devor, their mother, brought them to my office to register them for the coming year.

The story of the Devor family was similar to many stories I have heard in my years as principal. Father died. Mother has responsibility of support, long hours away from home, still can't make ends meet, worried about the girls without proper after-school supervision.

So, when Mrs. Devor overheard two women lauding "Beit Elisheva," our well-known boarding school, an idea took root in her mind. She asked around and the more she heard, the more she was convinced that Beit Elisheva would provide what her girls were lacking. In our dorm, they would have food and shelter, caring counselors, and help with clothing that was beyond her means. Most important to Mrs. Devor, the girls would have a supervised, structured day — classes with dedicated teachers plus a full afternoon program.

Weighing the options, the scale tipped heavily to one side. Still, the decision could not have been easy for this loving mother. All her warmth and love would be saved for weekends, holidays, vacations, or brief visits.

Leora and Odelia, like so many others, grew up in Beit Elisheva. As principal, I got to know these sweet girls well. We all watched them grow and mature. We saw that they were stars. Another thing we saw was their special devotion to their mother. Whatever they could present to her — a picture made in an art class, a cloth pocketbook designed in an arts-and-crafts lesson — was always made with their mother in mind.

"Look, Mrs. Roth," Leora would say, pointing. "Do you think our mother will like this apron I sewed for her?"

"Mrs. Roth" — this from Odelia — "I just took this vase from the kiln. When I go home this week, I'm going to surprise my mother."

Anything they thought would bring a spark of joy was lovingly presented to their beloved mother.

Mrs. Devor suffered from more than the loss of her husband and separation from her children. Over the years, her health deteriorated. Unable to afford proper medical care, when she needed expensive dental work, there was simply no way she could afford it.

I had to swallow my gasp when I saw her. There she was, standing in the courtyard — with no front teeth!

One afternoon, not long after, they knocked on my office door. As I waved them into the seats opposite my desk, I searched my mind for words of comfort and encouragement, for something to help them come to terms with their mother's difficult situation.

But that wasn't what they had come for.

"Mrs. Roth," said Leora, "we wanted to know if you could help us find a job."

"A job?" I blinked at her, my mind furiously working to shift gears. Why was she asking about a job? As principal, I did often help our girls find afternoon jobs doing babysitting or light housework to make some pocket money, but when I saw the Devor girls, I'd expected them to want to speak about their —

"We want to buy our mother dentures," explained Odelia. "It's so hard for her since she lost her teeth. She feels so bad about herself, so embarrassed."

Dentures? But dentures were so expensive, far beyond what these girls could ever afford. My mind reeled at the impossibility of Odelia's plan.

"We've worked it out." Odelia's eyes were matter-of-fact. And determined. "The dentures cost seven thousand shekel. If Leora and I both take jobs, we can raise it. It might take a while, but we'll make it."

And they did. For nearly a year, those girls spent hours every afternoon scrubbing floors, changing diapers, washing dishes...for the love of their mother.

To be honest, I didn't expect them to make it. Seven thousand shekel is a princely sum. When I found those girls their first jobs, I never thought they would keep them for more than a couple of weeks, a month at most.

Nearly a year to the day they'd told me their plan, they burst through the door to share their joy. They'd achieved their goal. They'd given their mother new teeth, renewed self-respect...and some of their own driven perseverance.

I saw how right they'd been. Mrs. Devor's beautiful new smile rejuvenated her shriveled self-respect, rekindling the desire and the will to take care of herself. A new dress, and then new shoes (bought by guess who) — her girls delighted in each purchase. The change was a powerful one, and gave the girls tremendous peace of mind.

Until the day their mother lost her dentures.

I still don't know how it happened. No one does, I think. But they disappeared.

The girls were devastated.

Leora sat opposite me and described their search. She had looked everywhere — everywhere — torn the house apart with her mother and Odelia, opened every drawer three times, emptied every closet, crawled under the beds, returned to each corner and every inch of space again and again and again.

But they were gone. The dentures they had forfeited a year's worth of afternoons for, the precious gift of normalcy they'd so joyously attained for their mother — had vanished.

I sat opposite Leora as she described their search. How my heart broke for her. "Leora?" I ventured. "What are you going to tell yourself to get through this?"

She lifted her eyes to meet mine, and I could see the brilliance of her strength shining in them.

"Mrs. Roth," she responded unhesitatingly, "I just keep telling myself over and over: the teeth are lost, it's true. But the mitzvah isn't. Mitzvos don't get lost."

Chapter 27

Sunset

The sky is awash with color: iridescent pink-and-purple streaks brightened occasionally by fiery orange highlights with a yellow glow.

It is a time filled with awe-inspiring beauty, as the shining sun, a luminescent ball in full splendor and glory, sinks below the horizon, and its brilliant colors fade.

Sunset — a magnificent painting, the Master Artist's very own handiwork.

Sunset — a time, also, that hints at the oncoming darkness.

The sun, ruler of the daytime sky, is allowed a final display of beauty.

And those to whom we owe infinite amounts for their life-giving sunlight, shall they be deprived of this grandeur?

Shall we not grant them the glowing sunset that is surely their due? Must we not help them shine these later rays — and days — through a wash of color, warmth, and glory?

"I'M SURE EVEN THE QUEEN OF ENGLAND doesn't get more respect than your grandmother," a neighbor once marveled. And it is for sure true.

When my grandfather passed away seventeen years ago, my grandmother's two sons, my father and his brother, Uncle Shlomo, both invited her to live with them. Uncle Shlomo lives in Brooklyn and my parents live in Monsey. My grandmother, who is affectionately called "Babu," said that she left the city twenty years ago and didn't want to move back, so our home in Monsey was her first choice.

Babu sold her spacious home and relocated to Monsey. My parents built her a comfortable home attached to theirs, keeping the layout as similar as possible to her previous home. The rooms were planned architecturally to accommodate as much of her beautiful furniture as possible.

The care and devotion my mother has shown would be remarkable even for a daughter, but it is magnified by virtue of my mother being a daughter-in-law. When I commented on this, my mother said wistfully, "Adina, it has always been painful for me that my parents died young. I feel blessed to be able to care for a parent."

It's one thing to say it. But I watched my mother mean it. Here is a case in point.

Having grown up as a city girl, my mother reveled in the comparative country living of Monsey. She thoroughly enjoyed the grassy, open space of her front yard. Exercising a green thumb she never knew she had back in the city, our lawn gradually blossomed into a miniature botanical garden. Yet, she and my father had no problem building Babu the addition, though it covered most of that lawn.

"That's apparently what the space is meant to be used for," my mother said simply, and she proceeded to plant flowers outside my grandmother's bedroom window so that Babu could enjoy the view.

Privacy was always important to our grandmother, so my parents are very careful about that. Even when family comes and we're short of sleeping space, we carefully consider before we ask if a couple can sleep in Babu's second bedroom. For years, the connecting door between our homes was kept locked. We knocked and waited for an answer before entering.

Babu always has her meals with us. Once, before the

Shabbos seudah, one of the grandchildren ran to tell Babu, "It's time for Kiddush!"

"No, not that way," my father corrected her. "We say, 'Babu, we'd like to invite you to join us for the seudah.'"

Babu always accepts our invitation with a smile. She is escorted to the meal like royalty. With her attendants alongside, she takes her place beside my father. If you were there, you would see my father doting on his mother, offering this and that, taking special care to speak slowly and clearly, repeating conversations when necessary, making sure that his mother feels included and happy.

Babu has some beautiful clothes that she no longer wears. Most have gone out of style, but one fake fur coat caught my eye, and I asked my mother if I could have it. She wouldn't hear of it, claiming that my grandmother might one day need it. I wondered where Babu would be going that would warrant wearing fur. Well, I found out soon enough.

My parents were going to visit a new grandchild in the hospital, and Babu was going along. I happened to be visiting at the time. It was a cold afternoon. I watched my mother hand Babu her fur coat, and saw Babu's delight as she smiled and patted her fake fur. My mother had understood that there are no age constraints on looking good.

Over the years, my grandmother has had various health complaints and ailments. "Well that's how it is when one is old," one might say dismissively. Not my parents. They go with her to numerous specialists in Manhattan to get to the bottom of each problem, taking test after test to make sure they aren't overlooking anything that could help Babu feel comfortable.

As the years pass, Babu needs more and more of a helping hand. Once, when my mother was helping Babu dress, she asked me to hand her Babu's jewelry. She then told me the following, a statement I had heard before and one that was repeated many times in our home.

"Our wonderful Babu is the matriarch of the family. She always took care of everyone, and now it's our turn to take care of her."

My mother fastened Babu's necklace, then stood back to admire the rubies set in gold. Nodding an approval, she smiled at Babu and said with conviction, "You deserve to look like a queen."

Basic to honoring parents of any age is caring for their physical needs. Since aging will commonly go hand in hand with an increased need for assistance, parents' senior years will demand more availability on the part of children. We will often be on call, our ears carefully attuned to requests, our steps responding with alacrity with a heightened sensitivity to parents' desire for independence and special concern for their dignity. Reverence for our parents should also not slacken — and if their patience lessens, ours must only increase.

Where does this "child" find himself when his parents need him most? Usually running a demanding household, dealing with *chinuch* issues, paying tuition, holding down a job, and dealing with other pressures pulling in all directions. Just then, responsibilities to parents loom large.

Nonetheless, the Torah assures the elderly parent: You will not face these years alone. Though your strength may wane, your children's care and respect for you will not diminish.

SHE IS BITING HER LOWER LIP *every time I walk into the nursing home. There are unusual habits. She taps her foot, which makes it fall off the wheelchair's footrest. She holds her head to the side.*

And the biting.

It's five years since my mom's diagnosis of dementia — five years and much turmoil between us siblings regarding the caregiving. Finally, it's agreed that I'll bring my mom to live near me. We calculated that Mom's money would last longer where the cost of care is lower.

It's supposed to be a trial year, but we all know there's no turning back. She'll stay in an apartment very close to us, with a fulltime caregiver. My family, with six children, will be able to visit her and take her places. My siblings have done their share. Now it's my turn.

After five years of living near us, first in her own apart-

ment and then a nursing home, Mom has a stroke. It paralyzes her right side, making chewing and swallowing nearly impossible. While in the hospital, with time against us, a decision has to be made. I contact my Rav, we receive advice from doctors, and research the issues. With lots of emotional upheaval, disagreements, and uncertainty, we allow the doctors to place a stomach feeding tube to keep my mom alive.

On one of my many visits to the home, I notice that she bites her lower lip to the point that it bleeds. I look more closely and see that her lip is swollen. It pains me to see this, but I am told by the staff that there is nothing to be done. "Old people with illnesses have quirks," they assure me.

"But maybe something is hurting her," I insist.

After two weeks of advocating for her, the floor nurse, the head nurse, and the doctor sit together looking at photos of my mom and evaluate her through a pain assessment chart especially designed for patients who are unable to speak. This assessment is done by rating facial expressions, screams, or unusual movements.

"She has 2 on a level of 0-10," the doctor tells me. "She is being given antianxiety medicine after the convulsion she had a few months ago. She is okay. We can do nothing else for her."

I'm still worried. It just doesn't feel right.

A week later, I was at the dentist with tooth pain.

"You've got an old filling here that needs replacing," my dentist said after an examination and X-ray. "Good thing you came in now or you would have needed a root canal."

Biting my lower lip as I experience the numbness from the anesthesia, I think of my mom. Teeth! Oh my! I haven't taken care of Mom's teeth in two and a half years, since she had the stomach tube inserted.

I head straight for the nursing home, where the social worker, who is in charge of the residents' dental care, accompanies me to see my mom.

One look is all we need: red swollen gums and what looks like an infection. The social worker informs me that my mom *might need dental surgery, perhaps even in a hospital setting.*

I immediately make an appointment at a hospital dental clinic, which provides sedation for patients who need it.

Each day that passes, I wonder how much pain my mom is in. I know what a serious toothache is like.

Fasting, Mom is examined by the head of the department. Full X-rays are done as I wait patiently outside.

The dentist's assessment is as follows: "She has two bridges that need to be removed. That involves four teeth. They are so full of pus that I want to do them immediately. There are another four teeth that need filling."

I am stunned. Why didn't I think of this earlier?

I beg Mom's forgiveness. "You were biting your lip to tell me something is wrong. This was your only way of talking. Please forgive me for not thinking of it sooner. All those months, you were in pain. I am so sorry, Mom. So, so sorry."

The dentist allows me to stay there as he works on Mom, despite the tears trickling down my face. I tell him I am a doula, and have been in delivery rooms and even operating rooms many times. I must admit, though, that this is more harrowing.

Afterward, we wait while vital signs are being observed. I sit there quietly, unable to answer my ringing phone. I feel as if the anesthesia has flowed into me as well.

While gently stroking my mom's forehead, I promise myself that I will tell my story to everyone I know who has a parent who cannot speak up for himself. I want them to understand that our parents are depending on us to be their advocate. They need us to be their voice.

As our parents spend their final years in less-than-optimal health, it is we who must daven for siyata d'Shmaya to give them the respect and comfort that is their due.

TO MANY, IT'S A frequented tourist attraction. For students here for a year or so, it's a place away from the dorm to munch on Uri's Pizza, buy a book, or find that perfect gift.

To us, it's home.

Geulah — whose alleyways and hidden courtyards branch out from the main street, Rechov Malchei Yisrael.

We know most of the shopkeepers, who have served us for more than two decades. And while tourists and visitors may know the storefront and interiors rather superficially, our family has gotten a glimpse into what really lies inside, not only in the tiny stores, but also in the shopkeepers and merchants who man them.

There is much greatness in that small stretch of road — and much humility. For these fine people attribute none of this greatness to themselves.

Follow me to one of its corners and you will notice the metal shutter pulled down over the storefront. Many of us still remember the store as it used to be, run by a father and his son. But where are they now? Why is the store closed? And for how long?

The answer was simply stated by the son, when I met him on the street. "My father's health was failing. At first, he could still come to the store. But eventually, even that was too much for him. He needed full-time care at home so I closed the store to give him that."

No drum roll. No fanfare.

Now, let's walk further down the street. Sandwiched between a bakery and a candy store is a bustling family shop run by a father and three sons who work non-stop to handle the constant crowd.

I've been in this store on many occasions over the years and couldn't help but notice the father's decline. What started with confused behavior and sharp orders to the sons soon deteriorated into loud arguments with customers. It never took more than a minute, though, for a son to appear on the scene — calming his father, appeasing a buyer — and business returned to usual.

Their father was once the balabus — *efficient, energetic, dependable. Although he is still present in the store daily, his mind is sometimes far away. I watch with admiration the tremendous patience the sons demonstrate, even at the expense of having customers wait while their father is searching for an item, often not able to remember what he is looking for.*

Surprisingly — or maybe unsurprisingly — business flourishes. I thought to myself, I'm not the only one watching. We must all feel the same.

Now and then, the father wanders off. Because of his confusion, he sometimes walks out of the store and in a second, he could disappear into the crowded street. More than once was I eye-witness to the following. The son who was manning the store at the time, always keeping an eye out for his father, immediately noticed that he wasn't there. He dropped everything to rush after his father, leaving the cash register unattended and customers waiting. I would see him put his arm around his father, his head lowered close to his cheek, as he softly spoke to him, gently urging him back into the store, and then with a little more coaxing, back to his place behind the counter.

No matter how many times I witness this scene, it never fails to make an impact. It doesn't matter which son is there to come to the rescue. All three children are clearly of the same mind: As long as we can make this work, Abba stays at his post in this store, the family business he established so many years ago.

These are the unsung heroes whose stories are often known only to close family, maybe some neighbors (and customers) and a handful of friends.

But the One Above, Who knows all, watches and records. Nothing is lost.

These children are running lucrative businesses. This is business big time.

MY MOTHER WAS in Columbia Presbyterian Hospital for open-heart surgery. Within hours after surgery, Mommy suffered a massive stroke. She was in a coma for four weeks.

Although Mommy was not conscious, my sisters and I took turns sitting by her side saying Tehillim, *singing and reading to her, on the chance that she sensed our presence.*

One day, as I was saying the Shema with Mommy, it's hard

to describe what I saw, but for the first time I felt there was some reaction. From then on, she slowly began to come out of the coma.

Two weeks later Mommy was transferred to a nursing home.

Although Mommy was barely responding, we continued to do whatever we could to stimulate her. We felt that if we hadn't been there the staff would surely have given up. We were not going to give up or give in.

Among those long days that promised little, there were some extraordinary ones.

I was sitting next to my mother on one of my visits. I remember feeling a heaviness, as if a thick blanket had been thrown over me. I must have leaned over a bit and fallen asleep on my mother's shoulder. I awoke with a start — I had only slept a few minutes — and realized what had happened. The thought brought a smile to my face. Spontaneously, I burst out, "Oh Mommy! Could there be a better place in the world to fall asleep than on your mother's shoulder?"

It was a comment unbidden and unplanned, straight from my heart. But what those words did for my mother! I will never forget the glow I saw on my mother's face. My mother, who had so little to give, was able to see herself again in her once familiar role. I, her daughter, needed her, needed her shoulder.

The stroke had left my mother unable to communicate. It was heartbreaking for us. Our dear mother couldn't tell us how she was feeling, what she wanted, that she loved us, or whether she was pleased with our care.

Now that glow spoke volumes. I knew my mother's heart was full of joy, sensing that my words had risen from a deep well of love.

Another scene comes to mind. My mother had a virus. It was of course not pleasant for her. I was sitting next to her holding her hand. I said, "Mammaleh, your stomach hurts you?"

She nodded.

"Mommy," I said, leaning toward her, "you know, Mommy dear, your pain is my pain."

Wonder of wonders, my mother answered me. "Oh...do I know!"

Please understand how momentous this was. I can't say that Mommy had never responded, but in all the seven and a half years that we had been taking care of Mommy, I can count on my fingers the responses we've heard. At better times, Mommy might squeeze my hand. On the best days, we might hear, "Ya." And even those were few and far between. I took those words, "Oh, do I know," those loving words from my mother who could not express her feelings to us, and kept them in a special place close by, where I could reach for them often.

It's so easy to stop being enthusiastic when there is seldom a reaction. So much perseverance is needed not to give up. It is rare moments like these that give us the strength to go on.

Here's an additional way to offer invaluable help...

***TEARS FLOWED FREELY** when my father told us the diagnosis. Our dear father, to whom we turned for everything, was informed that his illness had returned. Five pained voices rang out in unison, "What can we do for Abba?"*

The next morning, I was on my way to Suri Fisher's house, where women in our neighborhood gather weekly to say Tehillim *for people facing medical or other serious challenges. The 150 chapters of* Tehillim *are divided into thirty small booklets of approximately equal size.* It's called* Tehillim Mechulak *(Divided* Tehillim*). In this way, in five minutes (we have been doing this for years, so we are pretty fluent), thirty women finish the whole* Sefer Tehillim.

Bleary-eyed after tossing and turning most of the night, my mind was, of course, on my father. As I reached for the handle of Suri's door, the words flew out of my mouth — "Of course — Tehillim Mechulak.*"*

Every day, we could finish the whole Sefer Tehillim *for a* refuah sheleimah, *a complete and speedy recovery for our father.*

---

* One book for each day of the month, for those who complete *Sefer Tehillim* every month.

As soon as I got home, I prepared a list. We are five siblings and their families — sons and daughters, sons- and daughters-in-law, grandsons and granddaughters.

I started the calls, and by the end of the day, the thirty booklets were assigned.

It's been five years now. All five families are still going full force, still beseeching for continued rachamei Shamayim, *Heavenly mercy, for Abba, with the power and merit of Dovid HaMelech's words.*

Of course, devotion to parents embraces much more than just their physical well-being…

"IF YOU'RE PLANNING TO CHANGE THEM, Ahuva, now is surely the right time. But I can't imagine who will be willing to do this two and a half weeks before Pesach."

My mother and I had been discussing my dining room chairs and their well-worn, well-torn plastic covers. I could practically hear them shouting, "We've served you well, but we're old and ripped and have crumbs in our seams. So, if you are planning to change us in the near future, don't put us through the wringer. We won't make it. Just change us now!"

Procrastination is me. But once the decision was made, I realized I'd have to step on it if I wanted the job done before Pesach.

A neighbor gave me the number of the workers who'd covered her chairs. She said they did a good job, were pleasant to work with and kept their promise on the delivery date. So, armed with two cell phone numbers and a home number for Mr. Parness, I was hopeful. I reached him on my first try.

It was Sunday, two days before Rosh Chodesh Nissan.

"Mrs. Davis, I'm really sorry. If you would have called me a few weeks ago. But you realize…"

I did realize, as he went on patiently to explain, that I had joined a long list of customers who reminded themselves at the last minute that it would be lovely to change their plastic coverings before Yom Tov.

"I'll try to fit you in, Mrs. Davis, but I can't promise."

"But Mr. Parness, where does that leave me?"

"Mrs. Davis, try to understand — "

"But what would you say the chances are, though?" I asked.

"You know what? Call me in two days and I'll give you an idea."

The next time I called, Mr. Parness wrote down the order, my name and address.

"And which floor is it?"

"Third," I answered.

"Is there an elevator?"

I replied in the affirmative, but wondered, What does it matter? This is not a delivery.

I didn't dwell on it, because his last words were, "I'll really try," and at that moment, that was all that interested me.

It was now Monday morning, a week before Pesach, and I hadn't heard a word. I called his cell.

"Mr. Parness, I know you're extremely backlogged, and I'm really sorry to pester you, but is there still a chance to fit me in?"

"Mrs. Davis, I understand you. I really do. I just don't know what to say."

Mr. Parness must have heard my groan, because then he said, "Your best bet is to call my house number. Tell the person who answers that this is the third time you are calling and explain that it's important for you to have the order before Yom Tov. Maybe he'll agree to fit you in."

I assumed this person that I was going to call was a partner, or a secretary who takes the orders, while Mr. Parness does the actual cutting and sewing himself.

With just a week to go, I was happy finally to have gotten to the right person. Isn't that the way it is with everything? The right address? Whoever this person was, he was obviously the decision maker. His word, Mr. Parness affirmed, would do it.

I called immediately. A thick, heavy voice answered. I explained my dilemma. The person asked for my information once again, which I, a drop impatiently, supplied. Impatiently, because he kept asking me to repeat the details. Once, he couldn't hear what I said. Once, he heard incorrectly, and was obviously writing it down very, very slowly.

Funny way to run a business, *I thought.* Wouldn't it make more sense to hire a younger, energetic partner or helper if you want your business to thrive?

Finally, whoever he was had gotten all the information he needed and then told me that he would try to get me in for the next day. Well, that was an unexpected surprise!

It was now a few days to Yom Tov. We were up to our elbows in Pesach cleaning. So, when the doorbell rang, no one rushed to answer. Eventually, my daughter went to the door and returned to tell me that "the man for the plastics is here."

I wiped my hands and hurried to the front hall, then stopped in my tracks. At the threshold was standing an elderly man, bent over, clutching a walker. Attached to the side of the walker was an oversized bag, bulging with its contents.

I had still not recovered from my shock when he asked if he could come in.

With obvious effort and difficulty, he moved the walker forward, taking small, measured steps. Only after he had advanced a bit did I see that behind him followed another man, much younger, his arms wrapped around a giant, cylindrical role of plastic.

The younger man introduced his father, Mr. Zalman Parness, and then identified himself as his son. They both followed me into the dining room. The son rushed to bring one of the chairs near his father and helped "Abba," as he referred to his father, get settled. Without further ado, he reached into his father's bag hanging from the walker, and pulled out a pair of scissors, pins, and measuring tape. Maneuvering the roll of plastic, his eyes measured the inches. His skilled fingers snipped a piece that he handed to Abba. His father placed the piece of plastic on the chair's seat, then meticulously began folding and bending it this way and that, tucking and untucking — a little tighter, then looser. Satisfied with the fit, those seasoned hands pinned it secure. The son then turned the chair to the other side. The father carefully measured, tucked, and pinned. On cue, the son turned the chair to the front, same with the back, where the procedure was repeated. And then, are you listening to this? He lifted the chair, which was by no means lightweight, and held it high in the air while his father put in pins around its legs with the same precision, turning the chair this way and that so his father wouldn't have to bend, and could work on all four chair legs without straining.

It was quite something to see. The plastic, with all its folds and pins, had been transformed into a perfectly fitted cover, which only had to be stitched.

The son pulled the chair aside and replaced it with one with arms. The whole process was repeated with no change of pace. First one side, then the other, on to the front, then the back, finally raising the chair, standing ever so patiently while "Abba" pinned around the legs — now one, now the other. Father and son, working rhythmically, in unison.

All this time, my children were standing by the side watching. Pesach cleaning could wait. This was not to be missed.

After the second chair was pinned, the son folded the two samples into a bag.

Their work completed, I asked the son how he wanted the payment. He pointed to his father, as if to say, "Why ask me? He's the boss."

Mr. Parness senior quoted a final price, adding that it would be preferable to give half the money then, and the other half on delivery.

When I asked the son when it would be ready — I should have known better by then — he again pointed in his father's direction.

The father answered, "Two days."

Mr. Parness senior then gave me an explanation of the quality of the plastic he uses, and his unique method of fitting, which we had witnessed with no small amount of wonder. He finished with detailed directions on how to care for the covers, a list of dos and don'ts attesting to his expertise in plastics. In a relaxed moment, he told us that he

*had been in the business for forty years, and how happy he
was that his son has joined him.*

*Meanwhile, the son was packing up all the materials and
equipment neatly into the bag. Then he helped his father
to the walker, adjusted the bag and its contents, and slowly
they walked out together.*

*When the door closed, my children gathered around me,
from the little to the big. Each one had something to say
about what they had witnessed.*

*From Shimmy, "Mommy, he worried so much about his
father."*

*From Chavi, "Did you see how he lifted it so high, so his
father wouldn't have to stretch?"*

All the children were amazed at the son's patience.

*Our teenager, Sruly, commented, "He could probably do
more business if he did it himself."*

*At that moment, it came to me. Of course! It was Mr.
Parness senior who had answered the phone at home. The
son had directed me to his father, the decision-maker, the
last word. "If he fits you in, I'll be there."*

*Two days later, the son brought me the covers. I gave
him the balance of the payment and he gave me a receipt.
ZALMAN PARNASS PLASTICS was printed prominently on
the top. Of course.*

*This had been his father's business for over forty years. For
all intents and purposes, I later learned, the son had taken
over the lion's share of the business, leaving to his father that
which he enjoyed and was able to do. He made sure, however,
that everyone, including his father, understood who was boss.*

*Truthfully, he gave us much more than plastic covers for
Yom Tov, and much more than a receipt. He gave our family
something that will remain with us even after our shiny new
plastics need replacing once more.*

Everyone wants to be seen as an אִישׁ הָגוּן, someone worthy of
respect.[1] While it is an ongoing assignment to give this dignity
to all people, it is of paramount importance in later years when
independence slips away and skills are compromised.[2]

IT MIGHT BE A BOOK or a lecture. But it could also be a few words shared by an acquaintance that could be life altering. For me, it was the latter. It was my friend, Leeba, who took me down this new path.

My parents have reached the time when they could use our help — our, being their married sons and daughters.

No problem — for any of us. Having been raised in a family and community where that's what children are doing, we perk up our ears, ready for any request. Actually, it's really much more than that. We are always poking around, looking to fill in the gaps.

Being well organized, my sisters equally inclined, we march in to our parent's house with our lists of "To Dos." We clean the fridge, organize the kitchen cupboards and bedroom closets. We fold laundry and make sure it is put away, shop and unload groceries. Errands needed? Meds to be picked up at the pharmacy? We are there on the button — always on the alert... Time for a new fridge? We are all involved in consumer reports.

Until Leeba entered the picture.

Sharing a seat on an intercity bus trip, we had plenty of time to chat. Since my parents were always at the forefront in my life, the conversation naturally turned to them.

Leeba only needed a minute or two to hear me describe what she calls my "takeover" to issue her warning.

"Mirel," she said sternly, "this is not good. Not at all. Children should not be invading, taking over, pushing a parent aside. Whatever you do — ask first."

It hit me like a bucket of cold water — not a sprinkle or a spray, but a startling splash! Yes, that was us. "Invading" and "taking over."

How come I bought this so quickly, without objecting, without a counter-attack, without a sparring match with Leeba?

That's because, immediately, scenes from my parents' house popped up. They had been there, but they had been mentally eclipsed. Now they came up full force.

Mummy looking bewildered after closets had been rearranged...Remembering Daddy's expression as I put the *food I had cooked on the table. Maybe he didn't want that kind of food?...*

Since then, Leeba's five words have become my motto —
"WHATEVER YOU DO, ASK FIRST."

Mrs. Take Charge (me) no longer charges ahead, micromanaging, thinking that my parents are tickled pink. I used to just glance through the fridge to see what was missing. Now, before I make a fruit and vegetable order, Mummy tells me exactly what to put on the list and how much of each. When I give Mummy a shoulder rub, I ask first, "Mummy, how does this feel? More on this side? Is this enough? A little to the left?" After a recent snow, I wanted to damp mop the floor. Request denied.

And the fridge?

When we finally understood that we should ask Daddy for his opinion on the matter, we found out that our father was perfectly happy with the one he has.

Whatever you do, ask first.

This may not work for everybody, but it's working for us. And most important, it's working for my parents.

Helping parents hold onto their self-sufficiency (read: dignity) is not an "extra" aspect of the mitzvah. If we compromise on that vital aspect of their life — of everyone's life — we miss the inner core of *kibbud av va'eim.*

THE FOGEL FAMILY IS RENOWNED for their exceptional devotion to their parents, and now that their father passed away, for their kibbud eim.

There isn't a thing they wouldn't — and don't — do for their mother. You name it, they are on the spot. Mom asks, and it's as good as done.

With all these great efforts, one daughter shares her frustration: "Since Mom doesn't drive, we children drive her wherever she needs to go. And we're all fine with that. Whatever she has to do, she lets us know the night before. Then we arrange or rearrange our schedules. If one sibling can't make it, another will jump in, and we are at her doorstep promptly.

"Problem is, Mom doesn't agree to this arrangement. She allows us to do things for her only if we are... 'anyway.'

"We can bring food to her if we are 'anyway' preparing.

"We can drive her to the dentist if we are 'anyway' going in that direction.

"You can't imagine how this complicates everything. It would be so much easier for all of us if our mother would just let us do it for her without having to give excuses like, 'Mom, I was in the neighborhood anyway...' Or, 'We have extra that would just go to waste anyway...'"

She sighed, "We would do anything for our mother. But this...this seems like such a waste of time and energy."

The mother in the above story let her children in on her preference, saying in effect: "Although I must receive from you, I need to feel that my imposition is minimal, not interfering with your routine, not a yoke or burden." Not only should children be there for parents, as much as possible it should be on the parents' terms. Even someone who takes *kibbud av va'eim* so seriously can sometimes lose sight of this vital point.

Kibbud av va'eim is surely about *what* we do, and crucially about *how* we do it.

I WISH I HADN'T BEEN PRIVY to the following conversation. It still grates on me when I remember it. I was on the train, coming home from work. I thought I'd use the time to rest, but the fellow sitting next to me was on his cell. I guess he didn't care who was listening, because he was speaking loud enough that you could hear him a few seats away. And laughing.

"I told Dad," he said into the phone, "that if he doesn't eat, we're going to put him in a place where they'll force him to eat. And I let him know that one thing is for sure. If he doesn't start eating, he won't be staying in my house anymore."

Then, I heard him say in a voice of mild amusement, "I know, I know. He's doing this to get attention. He wants us all to stand around and beg him to eat."

I flinched as he repeated, "Ya, all Dad wants is some attention."

Were you one of those children who didn't want to eat? Do you remember how your parents danced in front of you, willing to do headstands until you slowly took one bite, two bites, three bites? They read to you, sang to you, entertained you with helicopters and airplanes, depositing the food in your little, stubbornly closed, mouth. This is a model for the patient, solicitous care a wise child will return to his aging father and mother.

The *sefer Meah Shearim*[3] writes that a wise person will act toward his elderly parents similarly to the way he acts toward his young children. He worries about his children, attempts to foresee any and every minor need — and gives to them even before they ask! — just the way his parents treated him in his youth, striving for the delicate balance between offering assistance "even before they ask" and the sensitivity not to "jump in" without their consent.

Centuries ago, a rough-handed approach, like the one in the story above, was taken to task.

A son or daughter may be caring for elderly parents… and still be greatly remiss in fulfilling the mitzvah of *kibbud av va'eim.*

For example, an elderly father wakes up early in the morning. Although the household is still slumbering, he is feeling weak and hungry. He hears his son moving about and asks if there is something for him to eat.

"It's not even morning, and you're already hungry?" the son answers. "It's not time for breakfast now. Do you see anyone else eating? Now is the time to sleep, not eat."

Although this son will provide his father with three sumptuous meals later in the day, because he shamed him, degraded him, and had no consideration for the altered needs of his age, in Heaven, those three sumptuous meals are of no importance[4] (*Sefer HaMussar* by Rav Y. Kaltz, *Perek* 5).

Even if this son or daughter provides his parent with the finest material benefits this world has to offer — mansions and gardens, cars and vacations, gourmet food, silk and satin apparel — if it is accompanied by insulting, unkind gestures,[5] in Hashem's book, it's all worth nothing.[6]

Nothing?

Even if we have given someone the finest gifts in the world, but it is done with an unpleasant demeanor, it is considered as if we have given him nothing — כְּאִילוּ לֹא נָתַן כְּלוּם. On the other hand, if we show him a caring and cheerful expression, even though we have not given him anything of material value, it is as if we have given him the best gifts this world has to offer[7] (*Avos D'Rebbi Nosson, Perek* 13).

Food for the body…and nourishment for the soul…

MY HOME AWAY from home for almost two months of my father's illness was the Bikur Cholim lounge, generously designed for families of patients who need to spend Shabbos, Yom Tov, or any extended time at the hospital.

Now, I'm not one to toot my own horn, especially since my mother taught us, "Self-praise is no praise." But when I had a few minutes just to think, I felt that I was doing a pretty good job as a daughter. If I would have to rate myself on a scale of 1 to 10, I felt I would do okay.

On to my story.

I was in the lounge, getting ready to grab a bite before going back to my father's room, when I heard a knock at the door. A second later, the door was pushed open. My attention turned to a tall gentleman standing on the threshold.

"Would you happen to know in which room I can find Rabbi Moshe Stein of Brooklyn?"

"Room 710," I volunteered, identifying myself as Rabbi Stein's daughter. To the best of my knowledge, I had never met this person. My curiosity was piqued, but soon obscured by the many concerns for my father crowding my mind.

I was just finishing my sandwich, when I again heard a knock. It was the same tall fellow, who this time introduced himself.

"I'm Shimshon Goldstein, an acquaintance of your father." Hesitating for a second, he continued with just a hint of disapproval in his voice, *"I hope you don't mind my offering some advice concerning your father."*

"Not at all." I was really curious what he had seen in that short time that I might have missed.

"I've known your father for years. We even learned together. He is a tremendous talmid chacham, *who always fills his time meaningfully. You children know that, even more than I."*

I nodded vigorously at the apt description of my illustrious father.

"Why don't you buy him an MP3 so he can keep his mind occupied with shiurei Torah?*"*

Quickly defending myself, I replied, *"Things get lost easily in a hospital,"* to which Mr. Goldstein gently chided, *"You can buy a MP3 for fifteen dollars."*

As I cleaned up the remnants of my lunch, I was left with much food for thought. Of course. Fifteen dollars would be a small investment for whatever amount of time it would enhance my father's hospital stay. It would give him quality hours, a chance to use his day constructively, as he has been doing for close to 90 years.

Um...

Mr. Goldstein, on a scale of 1 to 10...

I'M NOT SURE WHEN I REALIZED that Daddy and Mommy really ought to move near us. The idea probably sprouted when my mother started showing symptoms of dementia at age 70. It was frightful to watch the deterioration in my formerly hardworking mother, heartrending to see her life fall apart, and she still so young. It soon became clear that Daddy and Mommy needed more help than the "seven hours a day, five days a week" aide they had hired.

My parents were facing some big changes, and we wanted to help as much as possible. My husband and I both felt that they would be best off moving near us. The clincher was when the apartment directly across from us became available for rent with an option to buy.

We knew that we were certainly not the ones to call the shots. My father would be making the decision. Still, I felt a responsibility to actively campaign for what I believed was the best solution and would make my parents happiest. On a practical note, I felt we had a lot to offer, including:

1. A busy household. Never one to sit still, stimulation was just what my mother needed.

2. Two apartments on one level. This meant we could break through the common wall, and with all of us living on the same level, we'd be able to keep our finger on the pulse, supervising and assisting Mommy without it being obvious.

3. The right household schedule. I still had young children and I was serving three meals a day anyway, so my parents wouldn't feel that I was going to extra trouble for them.

4. A nearby shul. A friendly local shul was only a stone's throw away. For my father, whose daily schedule revolved around going to shul three times a day, this would be perfect.

5. Extended family nearby. We have a lot of family members living nearby who could provide much-needed company.

Armed with the above arguments, I began my campaign in earnest. I called my parents several times a week, pleading with my father to consider the idea. The standard response was that they did not want to be a burden on us. However, as my mother's situation worsened, my parents accepted our offer.

All the above reasoning did not mean that the cost (and I don't mean monetary) of having my parents live with us would be negligible. I was aware that there would be extra stress to our family in many areas and that our new living circumstances would present potential problems, but I was optimistic that Hashem would help us find creative solutions to issues.

Now I will share with you how my parents' living with us actually worked out.

The first months

My parents, Saba and Savta, moved into the rented apartment adjacent to ours. This being a trial period, we had not yet made any renovations.

Savta was disoriented, as we predicted, but it soon passed. Saba immediately adjusted to his three-times-a-day walk to and from shul, where he was greeted with warmth and respect. In addition, he participated in a Gemara shiur *for retired men. The* maggid shiur *was a friend, and he saw to it that Saba was well integrated.*

Savta, meanwhile, became a fixture in her seat in the kitchen. We now had unlimited amounts of peeled vegetables — onions, garlic, carrots, zucchini, potatoes, you name it. Laundry was being folded as quickly as it came out of the dryer. Savta also accompanied me on trips to the local fruit-and-vegetable store and supermarket. On nice days we went on outings.

After some research, we pre-selected a general practitioner for my parents' approval, and we were grateful that they felt very comfortable in his care.

Slowly, things were falling into place.

After only two months, my father decided to make the move permanent. Work began on renovations to their apartment to enable my parents to live more comfortably. Our occupational therapist gave us expert advice on safety. Our interior designer creatively figured out how to ensure both convenience and tasteful design.

My husband and one of my brothers organized the move of my parents' prized possessions. I believe it gave my parents much comfort to be surrounded by familiar objects.

Before long, my parents were settled in their new home. My mother enrolled in a program for elderly people with memory loss. She was picked up each morning around 9 a.m. and returned at about 3 p.m. During those six hours, she enjoyed a wonderful, stimulating program as well as breakfast and lunch. She returned home in a cheerful mood, often commenting on the camaraderie that prevailed. She couldn't really remember what she had done in the program, but the warmth and caring stayed with her.

We settled into a happy routine, but the zechus *of having my parents live with us also included many challenges.*

Our responsibilities

If Saba doesn't feel like taking pills, how much should we push?

If Savta doesn't want to change her clothing, and we feel it's absolutely necessary, can we force the issue?

If Savta's knees hurt and she declares that she isn't going to her program in the morning, should we push her to go? We know that shortly after missing the ride, her knees will feel better, she will have no recollection of the problem, and she will be upset at missing her activities that day, and might even accuse us of not letting her go.

Basic decisions, such as attending late-night simchahs, became complex issues. Savta might really want to go at the moment, but she wasn't remembering how uncomfortable she found such rides or her discomfort at not recognizing the baalei simchah. It was hard to limit Saba's salt intake at simchahs, and with his kidney issues, this was problematic. Given these realities, should I deny my parents the so-called pleasure of going to the simchah?

These were real decisions for us, and not easy ones at all. It was very hard to decide when to push and when not to. My measuring rod became, "What would they really want in this situation?" Sometimes we asked she'eilos and sometimes we made gut decisions. We might never be sure what the right choice was, but we tried to do our best.

Our parents' needs versus our own family's needs

Though we sought to provide my parents with an environment ideally suited to them, challenges were bound to arise, and they did.

Noise: What we considered "normal" noise, such as pots clanging, grandchildren crying, typical family disagreements and the like, bothered Savta.

Going away: My husband and I occasionally went away for Shabbos or one meal to participate in a simchah. Though we left my parents with appropriate company and supervision, they preferred us.

Family privacy: To meet my parents' needs, we had to

hire additional helpers to serve as caretakers and com-
panions. Some family members felt that their privacy was
compromised.

Depriving the children: I'll give you one example. In our
house, soda is a Shabbos treat the kids look forward to. For
my parents, soda created stomach problems and couldn't be
on the table.

Guests: It was hard for Savta to see us having our usual
number of guests on Shabbos. Do we stop inviting?

Questions: The same questions could be repeated an
unlimited number of times at one meal. For some family
members, the frustration was enormous.*

It was important to reiterate time and again that kibbud av
va'eim is a mitzvah d'Oraisa. That sets the tone for priorities,
but doesn't necessarily alleviate the frustration. Personally, I
found it helpful to keep in mind, "Whatever difficulties one
has during the year were decreed on Rosh Hashanah, so let it
be this — (the frustration incurred in the course of fulfilling the
mitzvah of kibbud av va'eim) — rather than something else."

I found myself compensating different family members
when I was aware that they had really stretched themselves.

Some days, whether due to time constraints, lack of
patience, or sometimes simply mind overload, I felt I couldn't
spend time with my mother. To forestall the inevitable guilt,
I tried, rather, to concentrate on all the time we did spend
together, reminding myself that if my mother had been in a
nursing home or other facility, she might not see me all day,
every day either.

What a balance we had to strive for!

In short, we all needed to work continuously on ourselves
and our middos. This is perhaps the hardest of all the
challenges.

Difference of opinion among siblings

Our handling of my parents' finances, health, and schedule
was fair game for criticism from siblings. Sometimes after

---

* Note: Each and every time we answer a question is a *mitzvah d'Oraisa.*

considering the other point of view, we willingly agreed to change our direction and decisions. Sometimes, just for the purpose of peace, we altered our stance. At times, we felt that our way was truly the best way for our parents and that it would be counterproductive to shift gears. This led, now and then, to uncomfortable situations. Sad, but true.

It was hard when there wasn't agreement on what was clear to me: my parents were in our care so it was fair and reasonable for us to have jurisdiction. I davened to Hashem to help me understand another perspective. I prayed that there would be more unity in our handling of my parents' well-being, knowing that's what my parents would surely want.

Perks

In conclusion, I'd like to add that we've seen incredible berachah *in our family since my parents moved in. I know this is not coincidental.*

It is said in the name of the Chazon Ish that the measure of a person's *yiras Shamayim* can be seen by the type of care he gives to his elderly parents.[8]

—————◆—————

The *sefer Meah Shearim* (*Shaar* 32) directs our attention to the difficulties of the sunset years with this poignant description: "[T]hey, who were once the rulers and providers of their home, are now dependent on others and must turn to their offspring to sustain them. Though they are needy, they are ashamed and cannot bring themselves to ask. They yearn for their children's attentiveness, but do not reveal their longing."

It is up to sons and daughters to ease their parents' discomfort by not only attending to their needs but even anticipating them: וְהָיָה טֶרֶם יִקְרָאוּ וַאֲנִי אֶעֱנֶה עוֹד הֵם מְדַבְּרִים וַאֲנִי אֶשְׁמָע, "It will be that before they call I will answer; while they yet speak I will hear" (*Yeshayahu* 65:24).

AN ACCOMPLISHED AND TALENTED WOMAN, Mrs. R., has led an exemplary, full life. Now, in her golden years, she is not alone. Her many children and grandchildren tend to her every need. She mused during a recent visit:

"As I am growing older, my health is deteriorating. I'm not what I used to be, which, of course, can be distressing. My friends tell me the same thing.

"All my life, I've had the privilege to be in touch with gedolei Yisrael, so I asked this question, which is on my mind now, more than ever: 'What is the purpose of a person growing old, with all its hardships?'

"They answered me: So that your children will have the zechus to take care of you."

Children devoted to parents...adding days to their life and life to their days.

In the Family

Chapter 28

Stepparents

חַיָּב אָדָם לְכַבֵּד אֵשֶׁת אָבִיו אַף עַל פִּי שֶׁאֵינָהּ אִמּוֹ
כָּל זְמַן שֶׁאָבִיו קַיָּים וְחַיָּב לְכַבֵּד בַּעַל אִמּוֹ כָּל זְמַן
שֶׁאִמּוֹ קַיֶּמֶת

One must honor his father's wife and his
mother's husband [though they are not
biological parents] as long as the parent is
alive (*Shulchan Aruch* 240:21).

In addition to the honor we give parents, we are obligated to
honor other relatives. The first mentioned in the *Shulchan Aruch*
is a stepparent.

This conversation took place between two friends. It was
retold to us by "Miri."

> **"MIRI, MY MOTHER'S** engaged."
>
> *"Mazel tov!"* I beamed at her.
>
> *"Miri!"* Tammy shrank into the cushions behind her, as
> *if trying to jump out of the reach of my words. Her eyes*
> *narrowed, and two deep creases cut between her eyebrows.*

"I thought," she said, clearly hurt, "that of all people, you would understand."

I knew what she was getting at — what she wanted from me. I also knew how I felt...now. But how could I explain that to her? My mother's remarriage was something I rarely spoke about.

"You don't want her to get remarried," I said, hoping she'd take off from there.

"Exactly," Tammy said heatedly. "It's not like there are still kids at home, that she'd need a —" she choked out the word — "father-figure to help raise us. She was doing fine. Our neighbors have been there for her, and she has tons of friends. So why on earth does she need to get married again?"

I knew that it was up to me to begin.

"I remember when our mother told us she was planning to marry." "Sure, I knew my father was really and truly gone, but this kind of —"

"Sealed it." Tammy finished the sentence for me.

"Exactly. It's like it reinforces your loss and makes it fresh all over again. Till now, we had talked about our father freely. The house ran the way it did when he was alive. His pictures were all over. And then — poof! — everything changed. Now we'd have to fight to keep his memory alive."

Tammy sighed. "It's just so wrong...thinking of him, this *stranger, sitting on our couch or at the head of the table saying Kiddush. It's like, what on earth is he doing here?"*

I winced at her description. Who knew better than I?

"Miri," Tammy pleaded with me, "tell me how you do it. Please. You seem to have adjusted so well to your mother's new husband. Wasn't it hard?"

I saw she was desperate for me to throw her a rope, but I hesitated. "I don't know what will work for you. I can only tell you what helped me."

Tammy's eyes were begging me, Tell me something. Help me.

I took a deep breath. "If you love your mother, you'll want it to be good for her. That's what I tell myself, Tammy.

Maybe a child can't see how remarrying is the best thing for his parent. But if a parent chooses this path, our job is to go along."

"That's it?" Tammy asked skeptically. "That's what did it for you?"

"No, not right away. At first, I was too caught up with my own sorry plight. And anyway, kids can't be expected to see that their mother is missing anything, can't see any reason for their mother to remarry and — here's the big one — replace their father."

The room was quiet, our shared burden weighing heavily. I sipped my coffee, letting Tammy swim with her emotions.

"You know, Tammy?" I said after a while. "In my mind, my mother's new husband was not only stealing my mother — after all, she had been ours alone and we weren't ready to share her — he was also stealing my father from me. He was stealing my father's memory, the memory, no matter how unrealistic, of him as the perfect human being and the perfect husband and father. Instead of appreciating this stranger's strengths, I resented him for being nice. The nicer he was, the more I disliked him. I'd think to myself, you know why he's being nice? To win us over, so we'll like him more than my father."

"I'm not even up to that yet, Miri, but I can hear what you're saying."

"When I caught my stepfather being 'nicer' than my father, more considerate in certain ways, having a better sense of humor, being handier around the house, it killed. You know why it killed? Because I was afraid my mother would like him more. I couldn't stand seeing my mother enjoying his company. To me, that was being disloyal to my father. So the happier my mother was, the more hurt I was."

"But Miri, didn't you say you wanted your mother to have the best?"

"I said it, and at a certain level I surely meant it. But it was only later that my heart caught up with my mind.

"Meanwhile, it was really bad. I knew that what I was doing wasn't fair or reasonable. The poor man could never do anything right. If he didn't greet us as soon as he came home, that wasn't good. If he said hello right away, I also found a reason to pout. I mean, what on earth was he supposed to do, not exist?"

Tammy smiled. "You're right. It does seem a bit ridiculous when you spell it out like that." Then she grew serious. "But that's the thing. Even though this man is a good person, or so my mother says, I still do sort of wish he didn't exist. At least, not as the person to be married to my mother." She smiled wryly. "I wish my father still existed for that."

"Don't we all? I don't think you ever grow out of that fantasy that one day your father will knock at the door and say, 'Hi everyone, it was all just a mistake. I'm home!'"

"No, I guess we don't ever outgrow that dream," Tammy said, taking a deep breath. "But it's not going to happen. And my mother's remarrying really drives that home."

"It's true. But I think that once we recognize the emotions, realize where these feelings are coming from, it's easier to accept a stepfather."

"I know you're right," Tammy said with a frown, "but it's like there's this big disconnect. Even though it all makes sense here," she tapped her forehead, "I just feel like…like I can't."

I nodded. "I really understand you. I felt the same way. And for me, in some ways it was even worse because I wasn't married, and I was living in the same house. At every turn there was a collision. I was so mean to my stepfather. I won't repeat some of the things I said. It was horrendous, Tammy. I was making him miserable, and I was making my mother miserable. And it had to be affecting their marriage."

"Oh, Miri, it's all so complicated…and scary. When I think about all the new ways of doing things he's bound to bring in and force on us… I like the way our house is running now. I'm used to it. It's the way my father wanted it, and we still follow all his customs. If we have to change now, I feel there's a mega-message. It's like throwing out everything my father believed in."

"Oh, how I know that feeling, Tammy. That's exactly what

happened in our house. It hurt me that my mother so easily slipped into his new ways, although I knew it was the right thing to do, and everyone said my mother was amazing for doing it. But as far as I was concerned, he was trampling on my father's memory, disgracing what my father stood for and the path he forged for us."

"So, what did you do?" Tammy asked me. "How did you get from there to here?"

"It took a long time, a very long time, and a lot of work. I had a few mentors who guided and encouraged me. One of them was a teacher at school. Another was a former camp counselor. She had gotten married and moved nearby, and when things got tough, I would go over to her house and we'd talk till I felt I could handle the situation. I slowly collected thoughts that kept me afloat.

"I think the biggest thing was to keep at the forefront of my mind that I really didn't want to make it hard for my mother. I wanted to make it good. And I knew that anything I did to show disapproval of her new husband was just making it harder for her.

"I also davened, Tammy. A lot. 'Hashem, please help me,' I would say over and over. 'I can't do this myself. It's too big for me alone.'

"And He did. One day I thought of something that I think was the clincher for me. I asked myself what if my father had had a chance to give us a speech before he died.

"I'm sure he would have said that he wanted my mother to remarry, to build a new life. And that he wanted us kids — those still at home and those already married — to be nice to whomever that person would be. I can hear his booming voice saying, 'Miri, you make sure that Mommy is happy.'"

I paused, watching Tammy's face as my words filtered into her heart. From her expression, it seemed to me she was picturing her own father saying the very same things.

"If my father were alive to hear the mean things I was saying to my stepfather, I know he'd say, 'Miri, do you realize how much you are aggravating your mother?' And he'd surely add, 'Have rachmanus on this man who is taking responsibility for

Mommy and the family. And remember, he has feelings...'
And maybe my father, who loved us deeply, would also say,
'Miri, look what you're doing to yourself. I know you can do
better.'

"I cried bitterly from those imagined words. I so wanted to
prove my father right, but it took time for that voice to reach
my heart to the point that I was able to stop my disgusting
behavior by telling myself, 'You are hurting your mother and
your father, alav hashalom, your stepfather, and your Father
in Heaven' — and believe it enough to have the strength to
do something about it.

"I kept speaking to people. I'll tell you what one Rebbetzin
told me. 'When you all leave the house, then what? Do you
want your mother to make her own coffee and drink it alone?
Now she's found someone compatible. If she passes this up
and waits until her children are ready for her to remarry, who
knows what will be then?'

"Those were some of the thoughts that were shared with
me, and I in turn repeated them to my yetzer hara. I really
wanted to make it good for my mother. I knew what she
wanted most. The answer blasted in my ears: Just be nice
and respectful of our new father. And of course, her dream
was that I would call him Abba.

"This is my story, Tammy. This is what worked for me.
I couldn't have done it without Hashem's help. The Avi
Hayesomim gave me special siyata d'Shmaya to get this right.
I felt I had help from my father, a"h, as well.

"After my marriage, it became important that my husband
wanted this to work, and encouraged me. He gets along well
with the step-shver, if there is such a term."

"Just remember in the long run, we're the winners. Our
children have a grandmother and a grandfather. My mother
is cared for, and she is a 'we.'

"Now when I visit them and see Abba — yes, it took time,
but I actually do call him that — prepare that cup of coffee
for my mother, my heart swells with happiness. I love when
my mother calls and leaves a message on my machine saying,
'Hi, Miri. Mazel tov on the upsherin. We love you. You give

us so much nachas. Grampa and Gramma.' I feel like singing and dancing. She said we! She said us!

"I can see my father nodding from on high. And I know what he's saying. He's saying, 'Miri, my dear Miri. Keep up the good work. You are doing a tremendous mitzvah. You are also giving me a lot of nachas.'"

We learn about our obligations to stepparents from the verse, כַּבֵּד אֶת אָבִיךָ וְאֶת אִמֶּךָ, "Honor your father and your mother." From the first אֶת, we learn the obligation to honor one's stepmother (אֶת אָבִיךָ — she who is with your father), and from the second אֶת, one's stepfather (אֶת אִמֶּךָ — he who is with your mother). Though we derive this from a textual interpretation, it is considered a full Torah obligation.[1]

When a divorced or widowed parent remarries, often there are painful and unfamiliar changes for the children. They may find it distressing to see their parent marry someone very different from what they would have expected or hoped for, or they may be displeased with the decision for other reasons. Despite this, the obligation of filial honor to their birth parent remains unchanged and must now be extended to include the new spouse.

Even if a child was not raised by the stepparent, he is still obligated to honor him/her. If the stepparent also raised him, he has the additional obligation of gratitude for all that his stepparent did for him.[2]

The *Shulchan Aruch* stresses *as long as the parent is alive.* Since honoring stepparents is a form of honoring parents, the obligation applies specifically during the lifetime of the biological parent. Nevertheless, continues the *Shulchan Aruch*, it is proper to continue to honor a stepparent even after the parent's death.[3]

What does honoring stepparents entail? Stepparents should be treated with all aspects of honor required for parents.[4] For example, a stepparent should be assisted with anything directly connected to his personal needs.[5] Included in the mitzvah is anything connected to household maintenance, such as shopping and errands, putting things in order, and cleaning up.[6]

Part of honoring is showing concern for their dignity, things like extending greetings and farewells, and giving preferential seating at *simchahs*. Also included is standing.*

There is an obligation to speak and act respectfully to stepparents, and to be careful about *ona'as devarim* (hurtful words) *to* them or *lashon hara* (demeaning, damaging words) *about* them.

> Many unknowledgeable children (*amei ha'aretz*) arrogantly demean and rudely address their stepparents, and even feel justified in what they are doing. They feel that by doing so they are honoring the memory of their deceased parent, showing their loyalty by taking up arms against the stepparent who has replaced him.
>
> This is not the Torah way, the way of G-d-fearing people… Such children are transgressing the mitzvos of the Master of the Universe, Who commanded us to be concerned about the honor of stepparents (*Meah Shearim, Shaar 67*).

Stepparent is a word associated with the ache of death or divorce. It spells a major life upset, whether a child is still at home or married.

It is not difficult to understand those children who, in their own pain, cause pain to a stepparent, but that doesn't make such behavior right. We can acknowledge their pain. We can offer support. We can help them see that while life will never be the same, there is still good to be found. But we can never say that *ona'as devarim* and the like is permissible — because the Torah says it's wrong.

Being respectful and helpful to stepparents is a mitzvah. Seeing a child performing a mitzvah, especially when it's difficult, can only bring *nachas* to the deceased parent.

Every child can turn to the Almighty and ask for the strength and extra Heavenly assistance to meet this great challenge.

---

* Opinions differ. Some say it's enough to raise oneself slightly (הִידּוּר), and some say one should rise to a full standing position when the stepparent passes nearby (קִימָה מְלֵאָה).

In the case of a divorce, one must honor a stepparent even if his biological parent resents it and protests, e.g., if one's mother resents the attention given to the stepmother, or one's father opposes assistance to the stepfather. By asking the child to limit the honor he gives to the stepparent, the biological parent is, in effect, asking him to transgress a mitzvah of the Torah.

MY PARENTS GOT DIVORCED three years ago when I was 12. My mother got custody of the children, and we visit our father every other week. My sister is getting married in a few weeks, and I don't know what to do. My mother never remarried, but my father did. His new wife does everything she can to make us comfortable in their home. She makes all our favorite foods, and the house is stocked with all kinds of books and games. We feel she really cares.

Here's the dilemma: Our father said he's counting on us kids to make sure his wife feels comfortable at the wedding. But then our mother warned us, "You can say hello, but that's it."

We were shocked and didn't know what to say — or what to do.

"It's bad enough that I'm still alone," my mother said bitterly. "Do I also have to be alone at this wedding while you are entertaining her? Where's your kibbud eim?"

When a situation of conflict arises, both parents and children should seek the advice of a Torah authority on this complex question and attempt to align their emotions as closely as possible to Torah directives. And of course, it's up to parents to act wisely and not put a child in this and similar painful situations.

HE WAS A SHINING STAR, an accomplished young man with a promising future. She — well, her friends were waiting to see who would be the lucky one to get the catch of their class.

Yitzchak Goldman and Rivki Brand became "the" couple everyone was raving about.

They settled near Rivki's parents and good years followed. Shimmy was born, and then Leah'le. Everyone was happy.

Except for Rivki's father. Mr. Brand began noticing things about his son-in-law that bothered him. True, they were small incidents, and Mrs. Brand warned her husband not to look for trouble. But Mr. Brand couldn't be swayed. He kept noticing.

The biggest problem was that Mr. Brand couldn't keep his dissatisfaction to himself, and started sharing his reservations with his daughter. Week after week, month after month, Rivki heard all about her husband's shortcomings.

Even the best marriages won't always weather that type of constant pounding.

As much as Rivki wanted to plug her ears, she couldn't. In time, all this negativity came tumbling out of her own mouth.

Yitzchak felt his father-in-law's critical eyes, his disdain. When his wife turned against him too, he reacted in kind. And when Mr. Brand enlisted other family members to join the fray, both Rivki's and Yitzchak's defenses were broken completely.

More details are surely not necessary, first, because this story is probably similar to other marriages that have been destroyed by taking this route, and second, because there is another part of this story that is simply amazing, and that's where I'd rather take you.

Sad to say, the couple separated. Rivki returned to her parents' home with the two children. Yitzchak went back to his parents.

Then came the separation terms. It was decided in court that the children would spend time with their father every other week.

Now picture this. Shimmy and Leah'le are living with their mother and her parents, their grandparents, who encouraged this separation. The grandparents now want to justify themselves, and they do so by letting everyone — including the children — know what a no-goodnik Yitzchak is.

The Brands did a good job. The children were buying it. If Mr. Brand had complaints even in the good times, he had much more "evidence" for his campaign now.

Yitzchak was crushed by the separation from his wife and

children. His health suffered, his skills suffered, and soon he was out of a job. Yitzchak Goldman was no longer a shining star.

As time passed, the children's faces were more and more sour when Yitzchak's brother came to pick them up for their biweekly visit with their father, until it reached a point where it became a real hassle to convince them to come along.

Finally, seeing that there would never be a reconciliation, Yitzchak gave Rivki a get.

Yitzchak struggled to rebuild his life. He remarried and achieved a measure of calm in still-rough waters.

For the children, their father's remarriage only complicated matters. Now their visits were to a new house and a new mother. Yitzchak's wife, Tziporah, wasn't comfortable with her new son and daughter or they with her, and so the connection between father and children steadily weakened. Yitzchak was losing his son and daughter, and there didn't seem to be anything he could do about it.

Rivki also remarried. Binyamin Fine was a smart, sensitive man, a widower with two little girls. He was not only a caring partner for Rivki, but proved to be a loving stepfather to Shimmy and Leah'le.

Though Binyamin was aware that the children's relationship with their father was "chilly," only after the marriage did he see the situation for what it really was.

He was utterly amazed at the way the children spoke about their father, the derogatory comments dropped here and there, and how they tried to wriggle out of visits.

What in the world is going on here? *he wondered.* He's their father. How can we let them trample this mitzvah and completely disregard kibbud av?

He took it upon himself to set this right, pleading with the Almighty for siyata d'Shmaya.

First, he approached Rivki. He knew there had been hard years, but he begged her — with anguish that she knew was deep and real — to stop bad-mouthing Yitzchak. Then he spoke to his in-laws, who already adored him, entreating them to desist. Lastly, he turned his attention to the children.

Hashem helped, and he found the right words. After speaking with Yitzchak's brothers, he was able to paint for Shimmy and Leah a more truthful, kinder picture of their father.

It didn't happen overnight. Binyamin was planting seeds. He was both patient and determined to see them sprout.

Maybe because of his sincerity, surely because of his tefillos, and no doubt due to Heavenly assistance, the children's attitude toward their father slowly changed.

With their stepfather's encouragement, Shimmy and Leah started visiting Yitzchak more often and more willingly. When Yitzchak and Tziporah were blessed with more children, Shimmy and Leah joined them for the celebrations.

As Yitzchak's family expanded, Binyamin urged the children to lend a hand in that busy household. He explained in what ways they could be helpful, and sent them time and again to pitch in.

As if that wasn't enough, when he knew that things were hectic in the Goldman home, he even sent his own girls to help.

Binyamin hit a home run with bases loaded. But listen to the cheers as he bats one out of the stadium for an all-time record.

Binyamin encouraged Rivki to be in touch with Tziporah to coordinate the children's visits, and from this a workable relationship between the two women was created.

Inevitably, the subject of last names came up. Wouldn't it be easier and raise less questions if Shimmy and Leah, who were being raised by Binyamin Fine, took on the name of their beloved stepfather?

Maybe. But Binyamin encouraged them to keep the name Goldman.

At Shimmy's bar mitzvah, the extended Goldman family participated. I'm sure you can guess who was seated at the dais next to the bar mitzvah boy.

A bitter divorce
plus confused children
plus an aching father

plus a "new" father who insisted on following Torah rules —
equals two children who were able to fulfill the mitzvah of
kibbud av b'hiddur and *simchah*.

*MY MOM DIED when I was 3 years old, and my brother
only 18 months. My dad was an exceptional father who made
sure my brother and I had everything we needed, including
his enveloping love.*

*My dad remarried when I was 6 years old. Being considered
very eligible, he had many marriage proposals over the
years. No one told us outright, but I overheard enough
conversations to know that those prospective wives made
the marriage contingent on our being sent to an orphanage.
My new mom took us on "willingly," if not with great displays
of love. She cared for us devotedly, speaking her language of
devotion.*

*During those three years before the marriage, I had become
a bit of a spoiled Daddy's little girl. I was precocious, and
probably felt very threatened by this new woman wanting
me to share my devoted father.*

*My stepmom was a real disciplinarian, determined to
make mentchen out of my brother and me. From the day
my dad remarried, we called Trudy "Mommy." It was not up
for discussion, though I resented it and wanted to call her
anything but.*

*My stepmom would not tolerate disrespectful behavior or
chutzpah. I was definitely somewhat scared of her. I don't
remember her being very affectionate and loving. She was
not the hugging, motherly type. My dad was the nurturing,
loving, affectionate father. She was more practical, and
simply did what needed to be done, meaning that we were
well groomed, dressed nicely, and definitely, on the outside,
perfectly cared for children.*

*I cannot remember my stepmom ever referring to us as her
stepchildren. Her extended family, her parents and siblings,
automatically became our Granny and Grandpa, aunts and
uncles. They completely accepted us as her children. In that
respect, we had a very normal upbringing. On the other*

*hand, maybe because I wanted attention and sympathy, I
wanted people to know that she was my stepmom.*

*When I say that my mom was strict, I mean very strict.
The truth is, she herself was brought up with an iron
hand. Disrespectful behavior, or what some think of as
"typical naughty children" things, sometimes got serious
punishments like having to stay long hours in my bedroom,
lengthy grounding, and no phone time for a week.*

*My mom made sure we did well in school. She was firm
and uncompromising when it came to homework and exams.
As a result, my brother and I always came home with good
report cards.*

*As much as I felt my mom was unjust and unfair, I know
that I didn't make it easy for her at all. I had a rebellious streak
and I knowingly provoked her. I looked for every reason not
to go home, spent long hours at friends — friends my parents
were not keen on — and didn't tell her where I was going. I
didn't actually say anything fresh, mostly I simply didn't talk
to her.*

I still let everyone know that she was my stepmom.

*Looking back, I realize it must have been difficult for my
dad trying to keep the equilibrium between my mom and me.*

*With all my complaints, I credit my mom with saving my
life.*

*We thought of our home as traditional, sort of a pick-
and-choose your mitzvos. Some things, though, were
nonnegotiable. Mom lit candles, there was a Friday night
meal, we went to shul, our home was kosher, and there was
no writing on Shabbos.*

*We lived in a little farming town with a small percentage
of Jews, who, for the most part, knew almost nothing about
their heritage. Eighty-five percent of my friends intermarried.
My mom saw the way things were moving. She strongly
disapproved of my friends. Due to their influence, she felt,
my grades were dropping. That alone was intolerable to her.
She pressed my father: "If you don't get your children out of
this town, they'll go the way of their friends." My father, who,
on his own, would have stayed put, let himself be convinced.*

At first, my brother and I were very upset about the move. I didn't speak to my mom for weeks. I was forever running back to my hometown and old friends, which irritated my parents and resulted in more discontent in the house.

Our new school was open and liberal, as opposed to our old hometown school, where rules were enforced. It was a lot of freedom for me, and I didn't do well with the long leash. My marks plummeted. My parents didn't approve of my new friends either.

The community rabbi, who welcomed us to town, took an interest in our family. Hearing about my tenacious nature, he suggested to my parents that a different educational setting might help me. He felt it would be good for my brother as well, so we both switched schools — and a fortunate move it was.

We were now enrolled in a Jewish day school. It was small, so my classmates welcomed every new face, and I slid right in. My teachers and the administration were warm and encouraging. I got a lot of (badly needed) positive attention.

I was encouraged by the school to join a youth group, which provided me with social activities like Shabbatons. I was running back to my old hometown and former friends less and less. Chosen for a leadership position in the school, I ran programs and headed activities. I also became close to several families, where I saw new models.

My life started settling down. As I became more successful and happy, things improved at home. Because there were fewer issues to fight about, my mom was less disapproving and less strict, which did much to reduce stress in the house.

I was fortunate to be surrounded by caring teachers and rabbis with whom I spoke often, still carrying that chip on my shoulder of having a stepmom. They were sympathetic. They heard me out, and I felt I was getting advice from people I had come to trust. Through these relationships, I developed tools to deal with what was going on in my life.

I would describe my relationship with my mom at this point as civil, which was a big step forward.

I married young and successfully. Once I started having a family and interacting with my own children, I felt I was now looking at my mom through new glasses. I started to see and accept my mom for who she is, and began to realize what she wanted to do for my dad, my brother, and me. I realized and accepted that she never purposely wanted to hurt or upset me, but more that the things that I wanted or expected were just not part of who she is.

Honestly, now that I am older, I choose not to go down that road anymore. Areas that I felt I lacked growing up have become an active avodah *that I have worked on in my relationship with my own children, such as giving them physical affection, confiding and sharing things, and raising them with unstinting love.*

In retrospect, now I can say that despite the tremendous chip on my shoulder because I had a stepmom, she really did a good job at bringing us up with good values.

I give my mom credit for what my brother and I became. She pushed us to excellence, to do better than our best, and she gave us a lot of practical skills for life.

At some point in my life, I discovered that my own mom had not been a well woman mentally. As an adult, I realized what this would have meant for me and my brother growing up.

Today, after almost twenty-seven years of being married and a mother, my relationship with my mom has changed. Two situations brought that about.

The first was the birth of my special needs child. By then, my parents had moved to the city in which we live. My mom was at my side, offering me support in every way.

The second was my father's decline. My sweet-natured father took a dive financially and couldn't recoup his losses. He became a broken man, and fell into a depression from which he couldn't seem to climb out. His general health deteriorated. Now my mom was taking care of a sick, difficult husband. How much gratitude we have to her!

For those and other reasons, my mom and I are very close today. I don't dwell on the past, except to pick out the ways

in which she helped me get to where I am today. Since I have
lost my father's closeness, she is today my confidante. I turn
to her for advice, and we share our lives.

We look back and feel great appreciation to our mom for
saving our family and building it.

Who knows where we would be today if our mom had not
come into our lives.

Keeping the peace

In a *baraisa* in the name of Rabbi Yishmael, we read: "Thirteen
things are especially beloved to *HaKadosh Baruch Hu,* among them
Kohanim, Levi'im…Eretz Yisrael, Yerushalayim, and the *Beis
HaMikdash…*[7] The proof that they are beloved is that for each of
the thirteen a verse is cited where it appears with the word "*Li,*"
to Me, an expression of endearment. Tellingly, when the virtue of
peace, *shalom,* is mentioned, the word "*Li*" appears twice. *Chazal*
say this is to teach us that *shalom* is the most beloved of all.

This source, together with many other sources brought in our
sefarim, teaches us the importance of loving peace and pursuing
it. Resolving conflict between two people, הֲבָאַת שָׁלוֹם בֵּין אָדָם
לַחֲבֵרוֹ, is a mitzvah we mention every morning at the beginning
of davening. What happens when one of those two people is
you?

How can you honor those that you're obligated to honor when
you're not talking to them?

"HER NAME IS ROSE," my father said simply.

I had been walking with the phone from the hall to the
kitchen, but I ground to a stop. If my father wanted my
attention, he surely had it. It was the first time I was hearing
about my new stepmother-to-be. I wasn't exactly sure how
to react.

Tragedy had hit my father's life when my mother suddenly
died. We three children were off at school, and our father was
terribly lonely. That's when this phone call came. My father
told us he had only recently been introduced to Rose, but it
looked promising. It seemed he wanted to prepare us for an

announcement he must have been confident was coming. It was not hard to hear from his voice that he was happy with this decision.

They married soon after, and my father and his new wife decided to remain in his home in Canada. Our relations with his wife were cordial, but never really deepened beyond that.

My sister and I moved to New York, and my brother, Seth, to the Midwest. We each found our mates, with my father and stepmother honored guests at all three weddings.

During one summer vacation, my sister and I returned to Canada to visit my father and his wife.

Until today, I'm not exactly sure how we offended Rose, but deeply offended she was. So much so that following that summer, she was unwilling to visit either me or my sister in our homes, or even my brother if we were also there. Although a few attempts at reconciliation via the telephone were made, they were rejected. So, with no other option, my father would come to visit us on his own. To me, this was always a great pity.

Two years ago, my father and stepmother came to New York for a holiday. My father planned to spend one Shabbos with me and the other with my sister. Rose opted to stay in the hotel.

How long is this going to go on? I thought miserably. How long am I going to let this go on? This second thought was prompted by my realization that the following Pesach there would be a bar mitzvah in my brother's family, and the following Rosh Hashanah, the bar mitzvah of my eldest son. My father promised to come to both simchahs, leaving Rose to decide if she wanted to join him or not.

I found this situation intolerable, that any wife should be left by herself both at Pesach and at Rosh Hashanah, and I decided I had to do something. I felt very strongly that when I come to the beis din shel maalah, I will be asked, "Did you do all in your power to make shalom?" What would I answer, that I was in New York and they were in Canada?

Perhaps years ago I should have flown to Canada to broker a peace and end this cold war. But, now Rose was in New

York, an hour and a half away from my home. I felt that this was the time to do something.

"Go. Now," I commanded myself. "Before you change your mind. Before there is a snowstorm or some other good excuse and before you chicken out."

My husband agreed to watch the kids while I drove to Manhattan. I left at five — of course, the worst hour. I hit very heavy traffic and very strong rain. A trip that should have taken one and a half hours took three.

Hashem has His reasons for everything. I arrived when my father and his wife were just finishing their evening meal. Had I arrived earlier, they might have been in their room, and Rose might not have agreed to meet with me at all.

As I started to cross the dining room, I still had no idea what I would say. I just knew that I had to make my effort. I was determined to give this my best shot.

When I was halfway across the room, my father looked up and saw me. He was literally speechless. I walked slowly, deliberately, mouthing a prayer that Hashem should bless my good intentions. Rose watched me approach, but I could not read her expression.

I reached their table. Fortunately, they were sitting by themselves. I mustered all my courage, and with a voice I hope conveyed sincerity, I said to my stepmother: "Hello. I'd like us to be friends."

She answered quietly, "Okay."

By the time I left, "they" (!) promised to visit me during the week.

I drove back home in very heavy rain, but I had a sunny smile on my face that I couldn't keep off. During that holiday, my father and his wife spent a Shabbos with my sister and her family, and we also had a grand family Shabbos at my home — my father and his wife, my sister and brother, and all the children and grandchildren.

The consequences of this reconciliation were far reaching. Both my father and his wife came for the bar mitzvah of my nephew. They have been present at chassunas, bar mitzvahs and brissin. Recently, we made a surprise 80th birthday party for my father, with his wife's knowledge and participation.

And there have been even more far-reaching and surprising results.

When I told the story to a former neighbor, she was moved to contact her in-laws from whom both she and her husband had been estranged for some years. Now they, too, are reconciled.

I hope this story will inspire others and have a continued ripple effect, and that many more family members have the courage and strength to achieve peace.

Older brothers

חַיָּיב אָדָם בִּכְבוֹד אָחִיו הַגָּדוֹל

A person is obligated to honor his older brother (*Shulchan Aruch* 240:22–23).

Another relative to whom we must show extra respect is an older brother.[8] We learn this from the additional vav in *"v'es"* — כַּבֵּד אֶת אָבִיךָ וְאֶת אִמֶּךָ. Some authorities interpret this as referring to the oldest brother, while other sources say this includes any older siblings, brothers, and sisters.[9]

"Honoring" would mean speaking respectfully and deferentially and giving precedence in food and drink.[10] For example, when food is brought to the table, it would be a mitzvah to pass the food to an oldest brother first, or elder sibling according to age — or any other expressions of honor appropriate for an older sibling.[10*]

While we should not speak disparagingly about anyone or to anyone, special mention is made of the older sibling.[11] Certainly one should not insult or embarrass him.

Though many are unaware of this halachah, this is Torah wisdom that when put into practice will enhance the home.

---

* It is important to underscore that those to whom the Torah affords honor should act in an honorable, exemplary way.

Sefer Chassidim[12] reveals to us an encouraging teaching: If a child was orphaned of parents when he was young, there is still a way to fulfill the mitzvah of *kibbud av va'eim* through a living "substitute." If one has an older brother and shows him proper respect, it is considered as if he is fulfilling the mitzvah of honoring his parents. The same is said of grandparents.

Like the honor due to stepparents, the Torah tells us that honoring older siblings is another aspect of honoring parents.

Chapter 29

In-Laws

חַיָּיב אָדָם בִּכְבוֹד חָמִיו [וַחֲמוֹתוֹ]

A person is obligated to honor his father-in-law [and mother-in-law]

(*Shulchan Aruch* 240:24).

THE WEDDING HALL was alive with sounds of laughter, joyous chatter, and lilting wedding music. My niece Ayala, the daughter of my brother, Reuven, was the radiant bride. I glanced at my mother, sitting right beside me at the table, and smiled. I knew that Josh had been right.

Not that I realized it right away. When he first suggested the idea, I was shocked.

It was in the morning, just as I had started to clear the breakfast dishes.

"Devorah," he said, "I've been thinking about this wedding."

"Me, too. It's just so, so exciting. It'll be the first time everyone's together in I don't know how long — all the cousins and —"

"Devorah." There was something in his voice that made my heart beat just a drop faster. "I was thinking that I shouldn't go."

I almost dropped the plates. I actually let go for a second, but I caught them, set them down on the edge of the kitchen counter.

"What? What are you saying — Josh, are you joking with me?"

"No, I'm serious." He looked up, and I could see in his eyes that he was.

"But — how could you not go? You and Reuven are so close! You're his only brother-in-law. I don't understand — why wouldn't you go?"

"Because of your mother."

"My mother?"

He nodded. "Think about what it will be like for her. To be there, alone."

My heart constricted as he spoke, as the full force of my mother's situation hit me. It was my mother he was talking about. Yet it was her perceptive, sensitive son-in-law who got it before me, her daughter.

He was right. My mother would be alone, even while surrounded by her children and grandchildren, her nieces and nephews. So alone.

She had taken my father's passing two years ago especially hard. They were two halves of one neshamah, and so beautifully in tune. My parents' connection was profound.

The pain of his absence was equally profound.

"I still buy all his favorite foods," she told me one day. "I can't eat them without crying over my plate, but I can't pass them by in the store, either."

Yes, it was hard enough for her to tread through life without her beloved husband by her side. But to be at that wedding — the first family simchah since he's gone — to feel such joy, such nachas at seeing her grandchild wed...and to be unable to share it with my father? The loneliness, the pain, the still fresh, aching absence —

"If I don't go, you can share a hotel room with her, eat with

her, stay by her side," Josh told me. "You'll be her partner. She won't be alone."

"But you don't have to stay home for that! You could come and I could stay with Mommy, instead of with you."

He shook his head. "You know your mother. She would never allow it."

He was right. My intuitive husband knew my mother well. She was the ever-thoughtful mother-in-law, taking care to never come between her children and their spouses. If I told her that I would stay with her instead of Josh, she would dismiss the idea. But if Josh wasn't able to make it...

I nodded and told Josh I understood what he was saying.

So Josh made some excuse and stayed home from the wedding he truly longed to attend. And I came alone. So that my mother wouldn't be.

As I sat there at the table, I thought about the last couple of days.

I was together with my mother nearly every second of the day. We giggled together over the luxuries in the hotel room, thrilled at the gorgeous scenery on a leisurely mid-morning walk, played one of the board games I brought along after everyone had gone off to their rooms. My focus had been entirely on her, on being by her side, never leaving her alone long enough to allow her joy to be marred.

Josh's words returned to me. "Your mother will have someone she can be with, someone she can rely on, someone she belongs to. If I come, that won't happen — at least not in the same way."

The music changed, its easy cadence deepening, quickening, the volume rising and filling the room.

"Oh, Devorah!" My mother, her face glowing with delight, reached over and squeezed my hand. "It's time to dance again!"

And so I took her hand in mine, and we headed off to the dance floor. Together.

MY HUSBAND, YAAKOV, AND I LIVED with his parents in a two-family house. This "together" wasn't always simple to achieve. My mother-in-law is strong-willed, of definite opinions, and a perfectionist in everything she does.

This story that I am about to tell you happened many years ago. Despite the lapse in time, some things you just don't forget.

It was a really cold winter. My in-laws were invited by cousins to spend a few weeks in balmy southern California. Glad to have a reprieve from the snowdrifts, slush, and ice, they took them up on the offer.

Two days after they left, a neighbor suggested Naava Pollack, her niece from England, as a match for our son, Rafi.

Rafi and Naava met. He liked her. She liked him. We liked her. Before we knew it, the Pollacks were flying in to meet Rafi.

Rafi is our bechor. We were newcomers to this scene. Wasn't this supposed to take some time? But everything was rolling along at a fast pace — maybe just a bit too fast for my liking.

Tuesday morning, the Pollacks met Rafi and suggested that since everyone liked everyone else, why didn't we drink a l'chaim that night?

"Tonight?" I gasped.

"Well, I don't want to rush anyone, but if we're all in agreement, I see no reason to delay," Mr. Pollack said, and then announced apologetically, "I need to be in England first thing tomorrow morning for an important business meeting. We're flying out tonight at eleven. This is the height of the season for us. I probably won't be able to return for at least four weeks."

So, really, why not?

Because my dear in-laws are in California, I almost screamed! I surely wasn't doing anything without them.

I called California. They were ecstatic. Rafi is their first grandchild. I could feel their happiness over the wires.

After the first few minutes of excited conversation, I mentioned that the bride's parents were flying back to England that night, so we would have to drink the l'chaim that very evening.

"What should we do?" I asked dismally, knowing Yaakov had just spent a disappointing half hour on the phone with our travel agent. "Even if we could get you on the earliest available flight, you won't make it."

My head was swimming from excitement and no small amount of the jitters, so the next thing I said — with no malicious intent but without much forethought — was: "You can listen in on the phone. We'll put you on speaker, and you'll hear everything. It'll be almost like you're here."

No response.

It took a second for me to realize that they were not on the phone.

I redialed.

They would not answer.

A little too late, I realized the gravity of my mistake.

Where were my brains and where was my heart? Shouldn't I have realized that having gone through the horrors of Auschwitz and Bergen-Belsen they could not fathom not being present for their first grandchild's engagement? It was everything they had dreamed about. It was what kept them going.

The engagement party that night was a bittersweet occasion, especially for me. I could not believe my father-in-law and mother-in-law were not with us to share this momentous occasion. Their pained silence weighed heavily on my heart.

When it was all over and the guests had left, I turned my full attention to my husband's parents. I knew I had to come up with something quick to prevent it from escalating into a full-blown machlokes, if it hadn't already.

I tossed and turned that night, racking my brains, asking Hashem to help me out of this mess. Toward morning, I had an inspiration.

Now, I hoped it would work.

My in-laws were due to arrive on Sunday. We planned a welcome that would set the tone.

Who do you think met them at the airport?

No less than Rafi and their new granddaughter-to-be,

Naava. Holding a giant bouquet of pricey flowers, Naava, who had never laid eyes on them before, smothered my mother-in-law with kisses, squeezing out at least some of her resentment with tight hugs.

We didn't leave it at that.

Rafi drove them to the house. With their bags and parcels in grip, he ushered them up the stairs, suggesting that they stop in our house first for some light refreshments.

My in-laws stepped over the threshold to see a room full of friends, neighbors, and family, and tables set up for a simchah. Platters of cake, delicately carved fruit arrangements — a full spread.

The musician, stationed on the side, began his music. The photographer captured the magic moments — my mother-in-law's look of surprise and delight, my father-in-law's quiet dignity and look of satisfaction, the smiling faces of the crowd greeting them. Nothing, but nothing, was missing.

Except the Pollacks.

That evening, the winter snow still covered our front lawn, but the hurt feelings had thawed.

The snow came back that winter, in full force, but this incident never came up again.

The following story describes one exemplary act. Even if it were an isolated incident in this daughter-in-law/father-in-law relationship, it would be worthy of note for its depth of insight. How much the more so because it is only a snapshot in a full album of sacrifice, caring, and wisdom.

As you might imagine, and you would be correct, the same can surely be said of the special in-law children in the two previous stories. Indeed isolated incidents, but truly indicative of their lifelong devotion.

I WAS STIFLING A YAWN with one hand, and looking at my watch with the other. The face showed 2 a.m.

The music is playing, the badchan is in rare form, and it looks like this mitzvah tantz is far from over.

I had expected a long night, but what I didn't expect was to see Shoshana Rosen sitting among the guests.

My neighbor Shoshana is a real early bird. I see her from my window, like clockwork, leaving her house at 7:30 a.m. for her bumper-to-bumper commute to work. "Early to bed, early to rise," is the motto in her house. I know it's true. I've seen it consistently.

When we neighbors are sitting together at a simchah, *we know that at ten, Shoshana will excuse herself, with her regrets; tomorrow is an early morning.*

So I'm surprised to see her there in the wee hours of the morning. Is she related to either side? Even if she is, what is so crucial that's prompting her to uncharacteristically forfeit her sleep?

Maybe it wasn't my business, but Shoshana is not the type to take offense. My curiosity gaining the better of me, I asked her.

I was thrown for a loop when she explained, "My father-in-law is going to be called to be part of this mitzvah tantz. *Since my mother-in-law's gone, my father-in-law lost his companion, his friend, his listening ear. Tomorrow, we'll talk about the wedding. He'll tell me that he danced, and I'll be able to tell him that I was sitting there, watching. And he'll smile, knowing that it mattered to someone."*

A word to parents-in-law

There is much to say about a parent's role in establishing and maintaining a healthy, peaceful relationship with children-in-law. Although a parent's obligations are not our focus, a few words are in place:

A parent-in-law's obligation to sons- and daughters-in-law is no less than to all other people.

It is forbidden to embarrass anyone especially in public. This **also** applies to children-in-law.

It is forbidden to say hurtful words to anyone. This **also** includes sons- and daughters-in-law.

Grudge bearing and revenge are Torah prohibitions. This applies to children-in-law as well.

The prohibitions of *rechilus*, *lashon hara*, maintaining a fight ("be not like Korach and his assembly"),[1] concealed hatred ("you shall not hate your brother in your heart"),[2] and words spoken insensitively (*ona'as devarim*) all **also** apply to in-law children. Caring about a person's dignity ("you shall love your fellow as yourself"),[3] and judging favorably ("with righteousness shall you judge your fellow"),[4] were meant to include those children who join our family through marriage.

MY SON MOSHE came home from shul, and to my dismay, I noticed that his tallis was stained in several places. This was quite a surprise to me, because Moshe has always been immaculate. Since his recent marriage, he has someone new taking care of his wardrobe — his newlywed wife. This, too, was a puzzle to me, since I can attest to the fact that my new daughter-in-law, is, herself, immaculate, and very particular about cleanliness.

Okay. Let's try this: He puts on the tallis in the morning, goes to shul, takes it off before she even sees the stains. There you go, *I told myself.* The world's best shvigger.

But you know what? Deep down, and not so deep down, I was a little put off at the thought of my son being neglected, embarrassed that he should have been seen so slovenly attired, and a tiny bit disappointed in my daughter-in-law's care of her husband — my son.

Should I say something to her or not? I know it's against the rules — a real no-no. But maybe, I rationalized, Esti would be thankful to me for bringing it to her attention.

Sure.

I decided to drop it and follow the rules, to zip my lip.

A minute later, Moshe interrupted this silent conversation I had been having with myself.

"Good Shabbos, Ma. Hope you don't mind, I left my tallis at home, so I borrowed Dad's."

Remember, as parents-in-law, you are older and hopefully wiser, more experienced, and hopefully more in control, and therefore, expected to take an active role in promoting and ensuring peaceful relationships.

The *Pele Yo'etz* gives parents-in-law this advice:

If we find ourselves with a daughter-in-law who has a difficult nature, it is the parents' obligation to act patiently and to speak pleasantly, without demands. If you feel you must speak up, it should only be done privately. Never speak about her shortcomings, only praise her to others. Certainly never complain to her parents about her or quarrel with them. The most care must be taken not to complain about her to your son, lest you plant seeds of discontent. Woe to those who would cause such a tragedy. The Almighty Himself allows His Name to be erased in order to maintain peace between man and wife.

It is better to suffer a thousand wrongs (רָעוֹת) rather than cause dissension between a husband and wife.[5]

Acquiring children-in-law gives us an opportunity to develop our character. We should prepare for this experience by davening in *Shemoneh Esreh*, in *Atah Chonen*, that Hashem give us the wisdom to say the right things and to act appropriately, and in *Sim Shalom*, that He bless the relationships — both the marriage, and with us (his/her mother- and father-in-law) — with peace.

WE WERE LIVING in my in-laws' basement at the time. Or, more precisely, we were sleeping in their basement, and sharing the rest of the house.

One day, my mother-in-law and I decided to bake chocolate cupcakes together.

We took out all the ingredients, amiably measuring, pouring, and mixing side by side.

Finally, we placed the paper inserts into the muffin tins. We were almost ready.

My mother-in-law went to preheat the oven, and I began spooning the rich brown batter into the tins. I was careful to fill each one three quarters of the way.

"Shaina — "

It was my mother-in-law peering over my shoulder.

"I think," she said, "that you should fill them up only half-way. I make this recipe all the time, and they rise quite a bit."

"But I want them to be nice and tall — with a real 'cupcake' top," I explained. Always the one to care about aesthetics, and a perfectionist in my baking, I wanted these cupcakes to look "just right."

"If I fill them only halfway," I continued, "they won't rise enough and they'll be flat on the top."

"I think they'll be fine," my mother-in-law gently restated her opinion. "I always do them that way. And I'm just afraid that if you fill them higher, we'll have a big mess to clean up.

"But, honey," she went on, as she turned to the sink full of dishes, "do whatever makes you happy."

She said it, and she meant it. And I knew it.

So, of course, expert baker that (I felt) I was, with my vast — all of 22 years' worth, compared to her at least double that — amount of knowledge, I went ahead and did it my own way.

Before long, the house was filled with the delicious aroma of warm chocolate cake.

And...not much later...

The smoke alarm went off.

My mother-in-law ran to fan the smoke away from the alarm. Meanwhile, I ran to investigate the source of the billows of smoke, which were so quickly smothering the delicious chocolaty smell.

I opened the oven and to my utter dismay and embarrassment found that my mother-in-law had been right.

There were my beautiful cupcakes, risen well past the top of the tins — plus some. Actually, plus a lot. They sort of looked like volcanoes that continued to erupt and spill their gooey brown contents over the sides of the pans and down onto the oven racks and the oven floor.

Meanwhile, I didn't know quite what to say or do. I just wanted to sink into the tiled kitchen floor and disappear.

No chance of that happening, I turned to face my mother-in-law. I thought she'd be furious. I deserved for her to be furious. I had ignored her warnings, and now we had a grand mess to clean.

*But in that moment of trepidation and guilt, I underes-
timated who I was dealing with.*

*She did not say one word about the mess. She did not
say "I told you so," and did not even hint to it. She wouldn't
even tell me how to clean up my "handiwork" when I finally
swallowed my pride and asked for advice.*

*Instead, we cleaned up together, side by side, with her
smiling and calm, putting me at ease.*

My dear mother-in-law, always the keeper of peace.

Married children's obligations to in-laws

A person is obligated to honor his father-in-
law [and mother-in-law]
(*Shulchan Aruch* 240:24).

The *Shulchan Aruch* and its commentators[6] clearly state a
son's and a daughter's obligation to in-laws. In addition, it
is a wife's responsibility as a helpmate to assist her husband
in fulfilling his obligations to his parents which remain after
marriage.[7]

Where in the Torah do we learn that one has obligations to
in-laws?

When Moshe Rabbeinu went out to greet his father-in-law,
Yisro, he bowed before him, kissed him, asked about his welfare,
and invited him into his home.[8] The *Midrash* tells us: From this
we learn that a person should give honor to his parent-in-law.[9]

Among the many lessons we learn from our great teacher,
Moshe Rabbeinu, is the way he models outstanding *derech eretz*
for an in-law.

וַיֹּאמֶר חֹתֵן מֹשֶׁה אֵלָיו לֹא טוֹב הַדָּבָר אֲשֶׁר אַתָּה עֹשֶׂה — When
Yisro, Moshe Rabbeinu's father-in-law, saw how Moshe
was instructing *Klal Yisrael* and rendering decisions, he
offered some unsolicited — and blunt — advice: "What
you are doing is not good" (*Shemos* 18:17).

A few verses later, we read Moshe's reaction:

וַיִּשְׁמַע מֹשֶׁה לְקוֹל חֹתְנוֹ וַיַּעַשׂ כֹּל אֲשֶׁר אָמָר — Moshe listened to the voice of his father-in-law and did all that he said (*Shemos* 18:24).

Consider a present-day rendition of this encounter: "Chaim," says his father-in-law, "I see the way you're handling your business and it's not good. Sit down and I'll tell you how to do it more efficiently." Or, "Sarah, I've noticed the way you deal with bedtime, and there's pandemonium here. Let me give you some advice based on my years of experience…"

How would Chaim and Sarah react?

Even if a son or daughter is not able to implement the advice completely, exactly, or at all, certainly humility and deference for age and experience is in order.

Moshe Rabbeinu bowing to the advice of Yisro? In his great humility, he understood that if the advice is helpful — take it.

Respect for in-laws is expressed in the following ways:

❖ Extending the same honor and deference one would give prestigious elders (כְּמוֹ שְׁאָר זְקֵנִים חֲשׁוּבִים)[10]

❖ Speaking respectfully and deferentially[11]

❖ Serving them food and drink[12]

❖ Serving them preferentially[13]

❖ Assisting them with their needs[14]

❖ Standing for them[15]

❖ Preferential seating at the table and at a *simchah*[16]

❖ Visiting from time to time, especially on Yom Tov[17]

❖ A son-in-law should give his needy in-laws priority in charity distribution if there are no sons available to provide support.[18]

❖ Not calling them by their first name or sitting in their seat[19]

❖ Not causing them *tza'ar* or demeaning them; all dealings should be with a concern to avoid quarreling[20]

How much toil and effort, how many days, nights, and expenses did one's father-in-law and mother-in-law invest in raising their son or daughter until they saw them married. Thus, it seems that included in the honor for one's in-laws is the repayment of a debt, just as with honoring one's own parents... And, if, *chas veshalom*, one does not honor them, but instead causes them *tza'ar*, aside from transgressing the instructions of *Chazal* and many prohibitions and positive commandments, he also falls under the category of one who repays good with bad.

Therefore, it is incumbent upon sons- and daughters-in-law to honor their in-laws with all types of honor, both during their lifetimes and posthumously. It's especially important to encourage the woman to be careful with the honor of her father-in-law and mother-in-law[21] (*Sefer Cheshbon Pirtei HaMitzvos*).

To be or not to be...
a successful daughter-in-law

For some women, getting along with a mother-in-law is a daunting task. Indeed, our Sages state that there is a natural antagonism between a mother-in-law and a daughter-in-law.[22]

So is there any hope? Is this combination doomed to failure?

We can take heart when we hear the words of the Chofetz Chaim.[23] *Chazal* tell us: וְכוּלָּן בַּאֲבַק לְשׁוֹן הָרַע — "All people speak [at least] *avak lashon hara* (an indirect form of *lashon hara*)."[24]

Could it be that *Klal Yisrael* is obligated in a law that no one can fulfill?

The Chofetz Chaim (quoting the *Maharsha*) explains this to mean that without any effort at watching our tongues, just spouting whatever comes to mind, we will all easily fall into the trap of hurtful, damaging statements. Whereas if we put thought into what we say — יִתֵּן עֵינָיו וְלִבּוֹ עַל דִּבּוּרוֹ — we surely can avoid even nuances of improper speech.

So it is with the mother-in-law/daughter-in-law bond. If we just hope for the best, without any significant effort, the best might not happen.

I WENT INTO *SHIDDUCHIM* DREAMING of a wonderful husband, home, and family. I looked forward to the new constellation of relationships that marriage brings. Always considered a very friendly, relaxed person who got along well with many different types of people, I had friends of all ages and stages in life and assumed this would continue. It was only natural for me to envision myself as the type of daughter-in-law who would walk arm in arm with her mother-in-law as we strolled or shopped. I had a hard time with all the negative talk about mother-in-laws, and just knew I'd have a really special, close relationship with mine.

How little I knew...

During the engagement period, I picked up on little signs of her displeasure here and there, but I can't say I was really paying attention. In the whirlwind of preparations, there was enough to distract me.

It only hit me full force after the wedding.

My mother-in-law and I were total opposites. We had different outlooks on almost everything, and really different sensitivities. She didn't seem to understand a thing about me, not the way I thought, felt, or acted — and the feeling was mutual.

I was being scrutinized and dissected. My words and actions were being picked apart. Slowly, the old me was disappearing and a new me was emerging — a person who couldn't do anything right. What was happening? Here I had been swimming in peaceful waters, and now I felt I was being pulled into a whirlpool, being dragged down, down, down... I was literally drowning — drowning in the anger and the pain of being so misunderstood.

The teacher in her graded me for housekeeping — 0; kitchen skills — 0; caring for her son — 0; and in later years, child raising — 0 minus. Whatever I did, the right way to do it was the other way.

I wished she wasn't part of my life. I wanted to have nothing to do with someone who seemed to dislike everything about me.

I cried endlessly. I would walk around in a daze, constantly *thinking about what was happening, pushing myself to get through the day. I would walk and think, lie in bed and think, sit in the hospital with my newborn and think, go through Elul and Rosh Hashanah and think. I would daven for shalom, but I couldn't imagine how it would happen. I felt like I was climbing a huge mountain carrying a sack of stones on my back. How was I going to do this? Be good? Be nice, kind, caring, and respectful to a person who was hurting me terribly? Be sensitive, warm, and understanding to a person who had no sensitivity to me?*

I could fill a book with details of the horrible things she said, the snide comments delivered to me and about me, and the offensive things done to me. I could replay vivid scenes from those dark, stormy years.

But I choose not to go there.

I don't want to remember and relive that torment and shame. Anytime I do, my husband knows right away where I'd been, and begs me to stay away. He is so proud of me and so grateful for what I've accomplished, for where I am now.

So I'll share with you a different part of my story, the story of how I climbed the mountain.

It took years and years. I shed enough tears to fill a small pond. That's how it seems to me, at least. But today I'm a different person, and my relationship with my mother-in-law is something I never thought it could be. This is how I think I got here, with Hashem's help.

I started by asking myself, "What does Hashem want from me?" Why did He put me in this situation when I'm a person who is (was?) so well liked? How could it happen? Why did it happen?

Those classes in emunah I heard all my life came to my aid.

We believe Hashem runs every detail of our lives, that there is a master plan so perfectly designed for us — from the smallest detail to the biggest. Hashem decided that this mother-in-law is fit for me. She is exactly what is good for me and for my growth. This must be "an opportunity of a lifetime" — of my lifetime.

I was forced to do some introspection. I kept repeating

to myself, "You can't change other people." (That's not even what Hashem wants from me!) I had to change myself.

This is the mashal I used all the time. It goes like this: There is the chocolate cake and the chocolate chip cookies. Each of these are made with the exact same ingredients: flour, eggs, oil, sugar, vanilla, cocoa or chocolate chips, baking powder, and salt. Why, then, do they look so different in texture and taste?

Because the ingredients come in different amounts.

We are all made of the same ingredients: a neshamah and a body at odds with each other. We all face life's challenges. But our character traits come in varying amounts. Some people are born with a half a cup of sensitivity, while others were given two heaping cupsful. One person has two cups of negativity or anger, while the other has only a smidgen. Here's a person with a quart of patience, and another with half a teaspoon. Did we choose our mix?

Two people may have similar features, but they're really totally different in "taste" and "texture."

This imagery helped me a lot. I now look at it like, "It's really hard for her. She was given a heaping measure of faultfinding. It must be so hard to live with such strong emotions. She's not trying purposely to hurt me. This is her personality. If I were she, with her mix, maybe I would act the same way."

Slowly, I learned not to internalize. The more I introspected, the more I realized what I needed to do. I had a mission, a huge challenge. I felt Hashem was waiting and watching to see if I would pass the test, and I knew that He was rooting for me.

So began the inner work.

I began complimenting, first pointing out positive qualities to my husband about his mother. To say he was shocked is an understatement.

I expanded this and started complimenting her. That was probably also a shocker. But undoubtedly not too hard to get used to.

I went out of my way to let her spend time privately with her son, even when it was sometimes "my time" that was being sacrificed.

I bent over backward to give her more time with the (grand)children.

My mother-in-law voices her opinion about almost everything, and likes to run the show. I learned not to be an immediate naysayer. I thought through the nonnegotiables together with my husband, and negotiated wherever I could.

The harder the challenge, the harder I worked, the greater was my satisfaction. I started feeling stronger and more confident.

I could be excluded from a family event with a wave, "I'm sure you wouldn't want to come." On the other hand, I was made to understand that my mother-in-law would be devastated if she were excluded from any birthday party or outing. This double standard used to drive me nuts. Now, I pictured Hashem smiling down at me, saying, "My daughter, My child, I'm proud of you. I know how hard you are trying. You are doing great — all l'sheim Shamayim." That was my inspiration and what kept me going.

Another idea that worked for me was, "No expectations." Expect nothing from your mother-in-law, but loads from yourself. Because if I expect, I'm bound to be disappointed. Give kavod, don't expect kavod. This is the biggest, and I guess it covers almost everything. Give compliments, and don't expect them back. Give presents, and don't expect any in return.

So that's what I did. I decided I would enjoy — yes, enjoy — giving to my mother-in-law. Before chagim, on her birthday: "Just thinking of you, thought you could use it." I try not to look for anything in return, or expect anything coming to me.

I slowly came to realize that it is a chessed to hear my mother-in-law talk out her feelings. She is criticizing my chinuch. I'm too easy-going, not strict enough. She goes on to explain how concerned she is about the children. Of course, it's not easy to sit and listen to her say, "I have thirty years' experience teaching. You must be more strict, punish, potch" and so on.

Now, I talk to myself and say, "How hard it would be for her to just swallow so many worrisome feelings." I think about how utterly irritating and annoying it must be for her to see me acting totally the opposite of how she would act. Then I am able to say, "Mommy, I feel so good that you are *open enough to tell me what's on your mind." I learned to say things like, "That's interesting. I have to think about it," and add, "I know you are saying this because you really care about us and the children." Or, "I care about your opinion and I realize you have more experience." Even if I have to say, "I'd like to, but I'm not sure it's going to work for us," or, "In theory, I agree, but practically...," I'm making her feel good. I'm listening to her and we are communicating.*

Maybe she even has some good points that I can learn from. Whenever I can, why not give her the kavod *of accepting her ideas and opinions? Wouldn't I want the same if our roles were switched? And I think, "What if my daughter-in-law is selfish or cold, without any warmth to her children, not knowing how to respond to their tantrums or feelings? How happy I would be if my daughter-in-law would hear me out and even consider my ideas."*

It was a long path with a lot of sweat and tears along the way, many ups and downs, but I was determined to keep plodding ahead.

I can hardly believe that I'm writing this, that I'm penning words that I always dreamed of but never thought would be. After many years of struggle, my mother-in-law and I are...

Friends.

I know what she is, and I know what she isn't. And I try to work with what is.

And, hey, you know what? She probably feels the same way about me.

"Water reflects back what is shown to it" (*Mishlei* 27:19). Why is water used in this parable and not a mirror? Because you can look into a mirror while you are standing upright, but when looking into a body of water, you have to bend down. If you reflect goodwill, and if you're willing to bend, it will usually be reflected back.[25]

Drowning in resentment

What happens when a daughter-in-law feels grossly mistreated, slandered, belittled, like the young wife in the above story? When she is drowning in resentment and bitterness and she is not able to work this out herself like our heroine, what should she do?

The Torah tells us, לֹא תִשְׂנָא אֶת אָחִיךָ בִּלְבָבֶךָ, "Do not hate your brother in your heart." This is the transgression of concealed hatred. [26]

If a person has wronged us, **according to the Torah definition of a wrongdoing,** things like "damage," "slander," or" "shame" (we are not talking about forgetting a birthday or not inviting for Yom Tov), it is improper to bottle up this anger and remain with ill will.

Chazal tells us that concealed hatred is considered more insidious than revealed hatred. [27] The Torah emphatically warns against bottling up this bitterness. Seething and fuming is harmful to our health, can easily lead to speaking *lashon hara* or harming our "enemy" in other ways. When hidden in the recesses of our heart, there is no chance of coming to understanding, no opening to work things out, undermining the Torah's objective of a harmonious society. Rather, the Rambam teaches us, it is a mitzvah to reveal our complaint in a calm, respectful way, in order to restore peace. [28]

Reveal to whom?

Parents-in-law:

A husband and wife may choose to go together to his parents or decide that the husband may go alone to present his wife's position. The intention is **to reveal in order to resolve**; the message is, "I care enough about this relationship to make it work."

While a direct meeting may work, and surely has worked for some, this option can be a tricky choice. The sting of the complaint will often override any attempts at peacemaking, and importantly, the well-known adage warns us: if you're thinking of changing anyone but yourself, the chances are slight.

So then what?

A listening ear can help. That listening ear might be…

A husband:

Familiar with his parents' idiosyncrasies, he can help his wife judge favorably, give her a different perspective, and help her work out solutions. (This is called *lashon hara l'toeles*. [29])

If a wife complains to her husband about her in-laws, he should be there for her emotionally and feel her pain. His message to her should be, "We are in this marriage together, and I am here to protect you. Your hurt is my hurt."

That's his message in private. However, he must remind his wife that she cannot be disrespectful to his parents.[30]

An outside party:

Or, the listening ear may be a helpful outside party. It could be a wise trusted friend. Sometimes professional help is recommended. And of course we should always seek *daas Torah*.

A wife can be encouraged to keep peace even when she is right. When that is not possible, and the harmony in the home is severely threatened, contact with in-laws would require limitations. This last resort should only be considered with Rabbinic approval.

Winning over in-laws

Most relationships don't develop automatically. We have to make them work. (The daughter-in-law and mother-in-law who adore each other at first sight are the exception.) Given the unfamiliarity of a new situation, the differing habits and customs of mothers-and daughters-in law, and a lack of history of constant giving like we have with parents, for most people, this garden needs tending.

The role of the daughter-in-law in creating harmonious relations with her in-laws is facilitated by the right attitude and some basic skills.

Particularly…

…*being appreciative*

MY MOTHER-IN-LAW bought me a stunning velvet robe for my birthday. I was in total shock when later I heard her claim that I never thanked her. I couldn't understand why she would say such a thing.

I distinctly remember the scene. She handed me an impressively wrapped gift box, gracefully adorned with a satin bow. I returned a big smile, a hug, and a warm "thank you so much, what a nice surprise."

Bewildered, I discussed this with my good friend Ruth as we were riding home from a class. She usually has some wisdom to offer that just sits right.

"That's funny," Ruth laughed. "You know, Atara, the same thing happened to me. When I finally got my M.A., my mother-in-law brought over a box — silver papered matching bow, quite elegant. I hugged her, pecked her on both cheeks, and effusively expressed my appreciation. She was late for an appointment, so she hurried off.

"When I opened the box, I saw a gorgeous sweater. It was obviously expensive, and, knowing my mother-in-law, she probably spent hours choosing just what she felt I would like."

We stopped at a red light, and Ruth turned to see my expression. She could see I was listening with both ears.

"Days later," Ruth continued, "I understood from something my mother-in-law said that she felt she hadn't been thanked. I tried to figure it out but was completely stumped. With a little coaxing from my husband, I finally got it.

"He explained to me that holding a closed box in my hands, I could only be thanking my mother-in-law for her thoughtfulness. She wanted me to open the present, ooh and aah, and let her know how much I liked it...the rich quality ('Oh Ma, cashmere! You shouldn't have'), the color ('You remembered I loved blue...how considerate')...the unusual buttons...the perfect fit."

I listened. What was left to say but, "Of course."

If the gift is something ongoing that we use all the time, it's "permissible" to thank more than once. A husband is a rather ongoing gift. Don't forget to call on your anniversary to thank your in-laws for what they presented to you.

...being willing to share

❖ Share your husband, her son.

MY IN-LAWS COME TO VISIT US TWICE A year, Pesach and Succos. They rent an apartment nearby. Either we visit them

*where they are staying, or they come to us. This year, I was
home with two sick kids, so my husband Chezky went by
himself.*

*When he came home, he was greeted by aromas of the
meal I had prepared.*

*"Hi, Deb, smells good," he said, and then he continued,
"Since I was there already, my parents wanted me to stay
for the* seudah. *Mom made one of my favorites." He ended
apologetically, "I'm really full. Can you save it for tomorrow?"*

"No!" I stormed. "This kind of food doesn't save."

After I had worked so hard, where was his consideration?

It took me three days to get over it.

*Several weeks later, I was sitting in a class when I heard
the teacher say, "A person is obligated to honor his parents-
in-law." I winced.* Where was that hiding? *I thought grimly.
I looked around at the others in the room. It was clear from
their faces that this was a new idea for most of us. I listened
intently to the rest of the presentation. It was all new.*

When I got home, I had plenty to think about. What was
that quote? I reread my notes: *"How much effort do parents
invest and how much* tza'ar gidul banim *do they experience
until they see their sons married? At that point, they just hope
for a little* nachas. *Instead, their new daughter-in-law fans the
flames of dissension. As if this isn't enough, she drags her
husband into the fray against his parents..."*[31]

Dreadful, *I thought to myself.* I don't want to be one of
those.

*I pictured that Chol HaMoed fiasco — but now, much to
my surprise, it looked so different. My in-laws see us two
and a half weeks out of fifty-two, and we always come as a
family. It was probably nice for my mother-in-law to spend
time with her son one on one, and serve him his favorite
dishes.*

And maybe Chezky enjoyed it too.

And what about his kibbud av va'eim *that he hardly has a
chance to do, with them living so far away?*

*I'm obligated to honor my in-laws! If only I had heard this
before. My mindset would have been so, so different.*

❖ Share some of your life.

Because it's her life too. Especially when there are children — the *nachas* that your in-laws have waited for so long.

❖ Share time with both families.

THE HARRIS FAMILY lives in New York. A match was suggested for their daughter, Shuli. The young man is from London, but is willing to move to the States if everything works out.

"Terrific," says Mommy to Shuli, as she claps her hands in delight. "Now I won't have to share you with anyone."

What message is Mrs. Harris giving to her daughter? "Shuli, dear, think only of us." The wise mother prepares her daughter and encourages her to share time with her in-laws.

In many homes, the wife's side "wins," since she is more comfortable in her parents' home. In doing so, she creates a hurtful imbalance. For such a daughter-in-law, it is important to find other ways to include her in-laws. This is part of her respect for her husband and for them.

...aiming to please

"A G-d-fearing woman, she shall be praised." Her goal should be to discover what pleases her in-laws, making an effort to make their will hers (*Pele Yo'etz*).[32]

A daughter-in-law is entering an established family with its unique customs and habits. Taking an interest, learning how they like things done, and being sensitive to their needs — is her "praise."

When one marries, it is helpful to picture a large sign on her in-laws' door:

WELCOME TO A NEW HOME!

COME IN
AND
FIND THINGS TO ENJOY!

...judging favorably

BALANCING A CHOCOLATE TRIFLE in one hand and a plate of miniatures in the other, I hurried up the walk to my in-laws' home. I could already hear the tumult inside — and why not? My husband's youngest brother, the mazhinka, was engaged — and to none other than my cousin, Atara.

After that gala engagement party, we swung into wedding mode. We all wanted to make this grand finale something memorable.

Three months wasn't a lot of time. My mother-in-law — "Ima" to all of us — took on most of the planning. A stickler for detail, she was at it all day and half the night.

We four sisters-in-law were busy coordinating gowns, arranging shtick, and planning combined sheva berachos.

Before you knew it, there we were, standing with the frilly rose-tinted arches, waiting for the music to herald Atara's entrance.

And there she was — the kallah herself — flying through, and into her mother's awaiting arms.

Isn't it a moment to treasure? A warm embrace, a few happy tears. The culmination of almost two decades is what we saw as they whirled hand in hand. Hardly could my aunt release her daughter to the next in line, her new machateneste.

My spunky mother-in-law kicked up her heels, and she and Atara spun around endlessly. Then the savtas, then Atara's sisters stepped into the circle, each one in her turn celebrating a private dance with their sister, the beautiful kallah.

Now it was our turn — me first as the oldest — until I gave my place to my younger sister-in-law, and she in turn to the next in line. Left was Batya, the youngest of us, and the peppiest. Batya grabbed Atara and they took off. With each leap, Batya's sneakers peeked out from under her gown. She was having a blast.

I'll tell you what happened next. See if you can picture this. Suddenly Ima appeared in the middle of the circle. She put her hand on Batya's shoulder. In mid-dance, Batya spun around, only to find herself being pulled out of the circle. My mother-in-law deposited Batya on a chair, and then quickly rejoined the circle of her dancing guests.

"What was that all about?" I said a little too loudly. Equally bewildered, the woman beside me answered, "We'll never know."

I was feeling so sorry for Batya. If it had happened to me, I would be mortified. Who drags a daughter-in-law out like that? What are people thinking? What is Batya thinking?

Not sure if misery wanted company, I decided to try to cheer her up. But when I looked at her, Batya seemed totally relaxed.

"Um...Batya... You okay?"

"Uh-huh. Just taking a break." She smiled. "A long one, I guess."

"What happened? You're sure you're okay?"

"I'm fine. Ima can't forget about my bout with pneumonia last month. She feels I should be taking it easy for at least another few weeks."

Batya saw my eyes widen. I was getting ready to say, "Batya, you are married now. You can make those decisions yourself." But Batya didn't wait for my response.

"You know this is Ima's big night," she continued. "We all know what she invested — months of planning every detail so that it would all be just right. She's running a big event. She's like...tense."

"But, Batya, we all waited so long for this wedding and — "

"Let it go. You know Ima likes to 'mommy' us. If my jumping bothers her, so I won't jump. Tell me, do you think it's worth aggravating her so I can have some fun?"

I sat down next to her — this young sister-in-law — and considered whether I should share my thoughts with her: Batya, you really jumped high right now.

...a sincere prayer

Our efforts should be accompanied by a heartfelt *tefillah* to the Almighty to give us the wisdom and the will to make the right choices. Choices that will bring our in-laws *nachas* and help us to find favor in their eyes so that we will merit to achieve the uplifting words of the *Chareidim*: "Father and mother of one are like father and mother of the other."[33]

———————•••————————

From the wisdom of Harav Avigdor Miller:

> Don't look for a perfect husband. You won't find him. Be a perfect wife, and then make your husband perfect in your eyes.
>
> Don't expect a perfect mother-in-law. Be a perfect daughter-in-law, and then make your mother-in-law perfect in your eyes.

How do you make your mother-in-law "perfect" in your eyes?

Part of believing in Hashem is believing that not only did He create the world, but that He runs it purposefully, with no mistakes. Every *neshamah* comes into this world with a particular mission and the ability to accomplish it. All of our social and familial circumstances are tailor-made for that purpose.

This includes not only parents, but in-laws.

From the trillions of *neshamos* that could have been chosen for us as in-laws, Hashem, in His wisdom, chose the ones exactly right for us — a perfect match, a match made in heaven.

In Addition

Chapter 30

Mending the Fifth

At the end of a fiscal year, stores, factories and companies take stock to see how the business is faring. Is there more coming in than going out?

Every Jew is supposed to take time from his hectic life to see how his "business" is doing: a spiritual inventory to review his behavior, to drop old non-profitable patterns and incorporate new ones with better returns, to come up with a plan to maximize profits.

The specific time allotted for this inventory check is the month of Elul and the Ten Days of Repentance. But, really, any time is the right time. This introspection is called "the *teshuvah* process."

What does it entail?

If a person transgressed in a matter that is between him and the Almighty (בֵּין אָדָם לַמָּקוֹם), the way to make amends is: (1) to stop the behavior; (2) to sincerely regret the mistake; (3) to come up with a viable plan not to stumble again; and (4) to make a verbal acknowledgement of the failing to Hashem.

However, if the wrongdoing involved another person (בֵּין אָדָם לַחֲבֵרוֹ), there are several extra factors that are necessary to make proper amends:[1]

1. **Compensation** (when appropriate). If you stole, for example, you have to return or repay.

2. Still, compensation is not enough. We might think, "I paid him. That's it." Not so. Even after we've paid up, an **apology** is still due.[2] (On the other hand, "I'm sorry" won't help if we still owe the other person money and refuse to pay.)

3. One might well think, "Okay, I paid *and* I said I'm sorry. Now, the matter is behind me." Halachah says differently. The person who was wrong must be **appeased**.

   What does "to appease?" mean? The dictionary would tell you it means to pacify, to satisfy, to restore harmony. We wronged someone. We would like him to swallow it and move on. The Almighty wants more than that. He wants the hurt undone. Even if we are on speaking terms with the other party, and feel *we* have moved on, were *they* able to move on? If we wronged someone, it's our job to set it right.

This is the formula: Compensation…apology…and appeasement, making sure that we have really gotten the annoyance out of his heart.

Just as we must ask any fellow Jew for forgiveness, we must make amends to our parents. You might call it an in-house inventory.

> MY SON YECHIEL and his family are a terrific team. We love them dearly. But everyone is human (including me). This year, there was a situation involving them that hurt me. They knew I was upset. When Yechiel made his annual Erev Yom Kippur call to ask for mechilah,[3] the way he chose to do it just hit the spot.
>
> "Ma, I want to apologize for the things I didn't do that I should have done, and I want to apologize for the things I did do that I shouldn't have done."
>
> We both knew what he was referring to. He handled it with just the right balance of sincerity and wit.

Sincerity and wit. Most times that will do it.

The bigger stuff

"Please forgive me." "I'm sorry." Will that always do it? Maybe for the smaller stuff, but for the bigger stuff, it will usually take something more.

MANY YEARS AGO, when I was a seminary student, I decided to stay for a third year. My parents were very against the idea, and forbade me. I didn't listen. I did try, in what I thought was a respectful way, to explain my reasons for wanting to remain, but the results were disastrous. My parents, especially my mother, refused to speak or write to me that entire year.

I am ashamed to say that I did not discuss my decision with a Rav.

When I decided to return to the States the following year, we made up. My mother started speaking to me again, and all was forgiven, or so I thought.

Twenty-five years later, I attended a shiur on the laws of asking and accepting mechilah. In the course of the shiur, it was mentioned that a son or daughter should ask parents for mechilah before every Yom Kippur. And you should be specific. A generic "sorry" may be okay for the daily oversights, but if there were significant incidents of disrespect, it's important to single them out so your parents know that you understand what you're apologizing for.

I had always asked my parents for mechilah every year before Yom Kippur, and of course, they always said yes. But I was never specific. After this shiur, though, I knew what I had to do. I had to ask my parents for mechilah for what happened twenty-five years before. I figured my parents would forgive me, and I thought it might be a little emotional. I was not, however, prepared for what did transpire.

First, I spoke to my father. I think he was touched that I had made this sincere effort to ask mechilah, and he said he forgave me.

Then I went in to talk to my mother. At first she was speechless. Then she said she was so happy that I was bringing this up, but that "happy" is too trite a word. My mother said that

it took a few years for her to get over this incident, but still
there has always been something there — a lingering hurt —
like a demon that she felt was always hovering between us.

   She asked why I was coming now for mechilah *after all*
this time. I told her about the class. I learned you have to
go with a broken heart, and I was. I was so sorry for causing
her anguish, and I was asking her to please, please forgive
me. My mother was surely blown away by this long overdue
acknowledgement of that terrible hurt of just ignoring her
for a year. She needed time to digest this apology that she
had surely despaired of receiving.

   Well, my mother eventually told me that she forgave me
with her whole heart. She recognized how difficult it was for
me to do this — since apologizing is not my forte! She gave
me a berachah *that in the* zechus *of my tremendous effort,*
the nisyonos *I was currently experiencing should become*
null and void.

   May Hashem will it so!

If we want our apology to be accepted,[4] if we are sincere about
making amends and really "getting the annoyance out of their
heart," the *Sefer HaTeshuvah* gives us the recipe for success:

   When we are apologizing, the main thing is to
   come contritely, to recognize and admit that we did
   something wrong, and to ask to be forgiven for our
   misconduct because we sincerely regret the offense we
   committed [which, though it might not seem serious to
   you, is *very* serious to the other person].

Checklist

4 Be specific.

   This way, parents will hear that you realize exactly what
   you did and the repercussions. (Unless being specific will
   add to the original humiliation/aggravation.)

4 Don't come with excuses.[5]

   Sometimes it *is* good to excuse ourselves and show why
   it wasn't as it seemed. The other side of the coin is that

if we come with excuses and defenses, it may seem like we are attempting to absolve ourselves of blame. This can provoke even greater anger and ruin what we have set out to accomplish. In this case (of a significant hurt), parents want to hear that you recognize that you did something wrong, even if it wasn't on purpose, and that you feel bad for the *tza'ar* you caused them.

4 Approach contritely, with humility…

4 …and with the recognition that you acted improperly.

4 Express unqualified regret…

4 …and ask to be forgiven for the wrong you committed and the aggravation you caused.[6]

Such an apology is hard to turn down.[7]

Get ready for a speech

"After all that, I still need to listen to a speech?"

Maybe.

Even after you've apologized, and seemingly the apology was accepted, a parent may want to tell you how hurt he was. Might be you didn't exactly understand the implications of what you did or said.

Try to listen. Try to hear. This, too, is part of appeasing.

Sending an intermediary

If a son or daughter has tried and failed to appease a parent — for instance, the parent is too angry to listen to him, if the child himself is not able to get to the root of the hurt, or if he doesn't express himself well — then he can send someone in his stead who will be more successful at restoring peace.[8]

Even if "all we did" was say something that offended [our parent], he must be appeased — repeatedly, persistently — until he is able to forgive (Rambam).[9]

"HE'S NOT AVAILABLE RIGHT NOW," my mother-in-law said. But there was a hint of anxiety in her voice, a blend of discomfort and sadness that made it clear to both Zev and me just why my father-in-law hadn't gotten on the phone.

"I don't know what I'm going to do." Zev sank down into

the couch as soon as we hung up the phone, burying his head in his hands.

I sat beside him, trying to offer silent support. I didn't know what I could possibly say to make my husband feel better. And in truth, I felt nearly as wretched as he did.

The situation was awful. Really, really awful. Like Zev, I was starting to despair that there was anything he could do to rectify those terrible words he'd said, lashing out at his father that Shabbos.

Zev is normally fairly soft-spoken, but everyone has their sensitive spots, the ones that transform us from level-headed adults to injured, defensive children. And the conversation was headed down a dangerous track that day. I could feel him tensing up, his responses coming faster and sharper, his father's demeanor mirroring his own, and then — snap!

I gasped when I heard the words he said.

My father-in-law blanched.

My mother-in-law's hand flew to her mouth.

Zev sat there, shaking.

No one said a word. I don't think any of us even could have; we were frozen, as if a heavy cloud of doom had descended upon the table, immobilizing us all. The harrowing silence stretched out, becoming increasingly thunderous as the seconds ticked away.

A scraping sound pierced the cloud, thrusting us back into the moment, into the horror of reality. My father-in-law had pushed his chair away from the table. He stood up.

"I'm sorry, Dad." Zev was standing, too.

But his father made no sign that he'd heard him. He left the room, the sound of his slow, steady footsteps echoing around us as he walked into the hall and up the steps.

My mother-in-law rushed after him. After a few minutes she returned to the table.

"He's not coming down as long as you're still here," she said heavily, avoiding our eyes. "I think you should just bentch and go home."

"I'll go talk to him," Zev said, "tell him I'm sorry again."

She shook her head. "Not now."

We did go home, shaken and subdued. That night, Zev dialed his parents as soon as we finished Havdalah. He apologized again, but it was clear that his father hadn't forgiven him.

When he awoke the next morning, he looked haggard, drained.

"I couldn't sleep," he said when he saw my concern. "I can't believe I said that... I can't believe I hurt my father that way."

That morning I davened with Zev and his father in mind, asking Hashem for this horrible breach to be repaired.

But instead of the reconciliation we hoped for, as the next three and a half weeks passed, the tension only increased.

Whether my father-in-law was just too hurt to forgive, or whether he felt my husband was insincere, I wasn't certain.

And now, here we were: it was my father-in-law's birthday, and he refused to speak with us. "Let's go see him," I said.

"It won't make any difference," Zev said. He was still staring at the floor, slowly shaking his head.

"But let's try. Maybe...maybe we can somehow fix it."

Zev sighed again, then nodded and stood up.

We didn't talk much on the ride over. There was a tremor of anxiety in the air, but also — I thought, at least — a whisper of hope. Surely if his father saw how sincere we were...surely that would make a difference...

But my hope began to dissolve when my father-in-law stepped out of his bedroom. He was clearly agitated, the lines of his face drawn taut.

"Mazel tov, Dad," Zev said. "Happy Birthday."

I echoed his greeting.

My father-in-law nodded slightly, acknowledging our words. But his stiff expression had not thawed at all.

"I — I wanted to show you the present I'm making you," I said, taking a nearly finished scarf out of my bag. "Mom told us that your favorite scarf got snagged on some bushes, and so I started this one for you, with the same colors."

He gave a small wave with his hand, not even turning to look at the scarf. "I don't need presents," he said. "Just a bit of kavod. Kibbud av va'eim *is much more important than trinkets."*

I swallowed, nodded, and let the scarf drop back into the bag.

I sneaked a glance at Zev. He looked miserable.

"Dad, is this going to go on forever?" he asked.* But his father just pursed his lips until they became a thin, impassable line.

And suddenly I understood. My father-in-law's words shouted in my ear: Just a bit of kavod... Kibbud av va'eim is more important...

His dignity had been ripped away from him that Shabbos. It wasn't just that Zev had spoken those words, but that he had been able to do so, that there was such a chasm in his inherent kibbud av va'eim, *in the way he viewed and related to his father, that it was even possible for him to speak to him in such a way.*

It was his sense of being a father, of someone looked up to and respected, that Zev had shattered, and I could see all of Zev's apologies from my father-in-law's perspective, as flimsy words that missed the point, that couldn't fix the problem because they didn't really address the problem.

I took a small step forward. "Dad, I want to try and tell you how upset Zev has been since that Shabbos. He's been walking around, agonizing over what he did. 'How could I do such a thing to my father?' he keeps repeating. 'What was I thinking? Where was my sechel?' He's devastated, and not just because you're upset with him, but because he truly regrets what he did. He can't believe he did it, that he was even capable of saying those words. And to you, to his father!

"Dad, you know how much Zev looks up to you. He thinks the world of you. He is so ashamed that he could have spoken that way when all he wants to do is show you how much he loves you."

---

* Review material presented earlier in the chapter to discover the Torah evaluation of this statement.

I stopped for a moment and took a breath. As I did, I became more aware of my surroundings, the way my father-in-law's expression seemed to have softened, of Zev standing beside me, his face twisted in pain that reflected my words, and of how I must have looked, as well. Tears were pouring down my cheeks.

"Please," I begged. "Please forgive Zev. He knows he owes you so much more than an apology."

The room was silent, as it had been that Shabbos nearly a month before. But this time it was a peaceful quiet.

Zev sensed it. He walked over to his father and held out his hand. His father grasped it, and they embraced.

———•◆•———

You put your foot in your mouth. You ignored their pain. You broke a promise. You broke their heart. And you broke one of the commandments.

Apologize.

This is the placation, the conciliation, the restoration of harmony that we, as sons and daughters, should aim to achieve.

Chapter 31

Seizing the Power From Eisav

Eisav was a *rasha*, a wicked man who was involved in the lowliest, most depraved behavior. He was a *rasha* who never regretted his actions — yet in the mitzvah of *kibbud av* he excelled!

When *Chazal* wanted to use an example of filial devotion, they chose Eisav as the ultimate role model for *kibbud av*.

אָמַר רַבָּן שִׁמְעוֹן בֶּן גַּמְלִיאֵל: כָּל יְמֵי הָיִיתִי מְכַבֵּד אֶת אָבִי וְלֹא הִגַּעְתִּי לְחֵלֶק הַמֵּאָה מִן הַכָּבוֹד שֶׁעָשָׂה עֵשָׂו לְאָבִיו.

Rabban Shimon ben Gamliel said: My entire life I tried to honor my father, yet I did not achieve even one percent of what Eisav achieved in his service of his father (*Bereishis Rabbah* 65:16).

פָּתַח רַב יֵיסָא וְאָמַר: בֵּן יְכַבֵּד אָב ...בֵּן זֶה עֵשָׂו...

Rav Yasa began and said, "A son will honor his father..." (*Malachi* 1:6). *Chazal* tell us the son they are referring to is Eisav (*Zohar* 206).

Chazal tell us the reward Eisav received for his *kibbud av*:

וְכִיבּוּד הַהוּא שֶׁכִּיבֵּד אוֹתוֹ הִשְׁלִיט אוֹתוֹ בָּעוֹלָם
הַזֶּה...

All the power and greatness that Eisav and
his descendants achieved in this world is
a result of the honor he showed his father
(ibid. 206).

אֵין לְךָ קָשָׁה בְּכָל הַמַּלְכוּיוֹת כּוּלָם כֶּאֱדוֹם וְהַאֲרִיכוּ
שָׁנִים עַל כּוּלָם וּמִי גָרַם לָהֶם לְהַאֲרִיךְ שָׁנִים בָּעוֹלָם
הַזֶּה? כִּבּוּד שֶׁכִּיבֵּד עֵשָׂו אֶת אָבִיו לְהַאֲכִילוֹ
וּלְהַשְׁקוֹתוֹ וּלְשַׁמְּשׁוֹ...

The most difficult of the exiles is *Galus
Edom* (Eisav). It is the longest of all. What is
the reason for the kingdom of Eisav's long
years [of success and strength]? The honor
that Eisav gave his father (*Meah Shearim,
Shaar* 206).

...אַף עַל פִּי שֶׁהָיָה רָשָׁע גָּמוּר וּבַעַל עֲבֵירוֹת
גְּדוֹלוֹת...לְפִי שֶׁהָיָה מְכַבֵּד אֶת אָבִיו מְאֹד,
אוֹתוֹ זְכוּת עָמַד לוֹ וּלְזַרְעוֹ וּלְזֶרַע זַרְעוֹ אַחֲרָיו...

Even though Eisav was a total *rasha*, and
committed the most serious sins…because
he honored his father exceedingly, that
merit was extended and remained for his
children and all his future descendants
(ibid.).

What exactly were the dimensions of Eisav's *kibbud av* that
earned him such exuberant praise? What did he do that gained
him such great reward?

Here are some of the praises Eisav earned:

1. *Chazal* tell us that Eisav had a garment that he had taken
   from Nimrod, who had received it from Adam HaRishon,

which looked like clothes of royalty (בִּגְדֵי מַלְכוּת), and he donned it especially when he served his father.

אֲנִי בְּשָׁעָה שֶׁהָיִיתִי מְשַׁמֵּשׁ אֶת אַבָּא הָיִיתִי מְשַׁמְּשׁוֹ
בִּבְגָדִים מְלֻכְלָכִים, וּבְשָׁעָה שֶׁהָיִיתִי יוֹצֵא לַדֶּרֶךְ,
הָיִיתִי יוֹצֵא בִבְגָדִים נְקִיִּים, אֲבָל עֵשָׂו בְּשָׁעָה שֶׁהָיָה
מְשַׁמֵּשׁ אֶת אָבִיו, לֹא הָיָה מְשַׁמְּשׁוֹ אֶלָּא בְּבִגְדֵי
מַלְכוּת. אָמַר, אֵין כְּבוֹדוֹ שֶׁל אַבָּא לִהְיוֹת מְשַׁמְּשׁוֹ
אֶלָּא בְּבִגְדֵי מַלְכוּת.

[Rabban Shimon ben Gamliel said,] "When I served my father, I wore soiled clothing [in order not to stain clothing while caring for my father]. Then, when I went out in public, I changed into my clean clothing. But when Eisav served Yitzchak Avinu, he wore special, regal clothing. He would say 'It's not respectful to serve my father in anything but royal garments'" (*Bereishis Rabbah* 65:16).

Nowhere in halachah do we see that a child must wear elegant clothing when he is with his parents. Is it possible that *this* was Eisav's greatness in *kibbud av*, that he thought of *original* ways to honor his father?

2. In fact, Eisav even endangered his life to honor his father.

שֶׁכִּבֵּד אָבִיו הַרְבֵּה, שֶׁיָּצָא לַשָּׂדוֹת וְצָד צַיִד, וּמֵבִיא
וּמְבַשֵּׁל וּמַכְנִיס וּמַאֲכִיל לְאָבִיו בְּכָל יוֹם.[1]

[Eisav] regularly endangered himself to hunt animals for his father. He not only caught them, but he brought them home and cooked them, and then offered the food and served it to his father. He did this every day (*Shemos Rabbah* 46:3).

3. Eisav looked for things that particularly pleased his father spiritually.

וְהָיָה אוֹמֵר לוֹ אָבִיו בְּנִי הֵיכָן הָיִיתָ הַיּוֹם הַזֶּה. וְהוּא
אוֹמֵר לוֹ בְּבֵית הַתַּלְמוּד. לֹא כָךְ הוּא הֲלָכָה מִן כָּךְ
וְכָךְ? לֹא כָךְ אִיסוּרוֹ לֹא כָךְ הֶתֵּירוֹ?

Eisav would go to the Yeshivah of Shem
and Ever and hear words of Torah. He
would then go and repeat these to his father
(*Midrash Tanchuma, Bereishis* 27:8).

Though *divrei Torah* were not important to him, he knew that
they were important to his father. From this we see that Eisav
looked for things that particularly pleased his father.

4. Eisav sought to please his father in material matters as well.

קוּפְרָא טָבָא לְפוּמֵיה וְכָסָא טָבָא לְפוּמֵיה פֵּירוּשׁ:
כָּל דָּבָר יָפֶה וָטוֹב שֶׁהָיָה רוֹאֶה בֵּין בְּמַאֲכָל בֵּין
בְּמִשְׁתֶּה הָיָה מִשְׁתַּדֵּל לְהָבִיא בְּפִי אָבִיו. כָּל זֶה
מֵרוֹב הַכָּבוֹד שֶׁהָיָה עוֹשֶׂה לוֹ. (קוּפְרָא לְשׁוֹן כָּל
מִינֵי בָּשָׂר.)

Eisav tried his utmost to bring to his father
every beautiful and good thing, any type of
delicious food or drink he saw. All this was
part of the great respect that he always gave
to Yitzchak (*Meah Shearim, Shaar* 69).

Even though *Chazal* say that Eisav had ulterior motives for
all he did for his father, nonetheless, Yitzchak Avinu was the
recipient of unparalleled *kibbud av*.

5. Eisav showed that his father's words were precious to him.

"...וַיִּשָּׂא עֵשָׂו קֹלוֹ וַיֵּבְךְּ" אָמַר רַב חִיָּיא: כַּמָּה רָעוֹת
עָשׂוּ אֵלּוּ הַדְּמָעוֹת לְיִשְׂרָאֵל שֶׁבָּכָה עֵשָׂו וְהוֹצִיאָן
לִפְנֵי אָבִיו כְּדֵי שֶׁיִּתְבָּרֵךְ מִמֶּנּוּ עַל שֵׁם שֶׁדִּבְרֵי אָבִיו
הָיוּ חֲשׁוּבִים אֶצְלוֹ בְּיוֹתֵר.

And Eisav said to his father, "Do you have
only one *berachah*, my father? Bless me
too, my father. And Eisav raised his voice
and wept." Rav Chiya said: ...Eisav cried...

because his father's words (blessings) were
of utmost importance to him (*Zohar* 175).

6. Not only did Eisav think of ways of honoring and bringing
nachas to his father, but he was also careful to avoid causing
his father *tza'ar*.

וַיַּרְא עֵשָׂו כִּי בֵרַךְ יִצְחָק אֶת יַעֲקֹב וְשִׁלַּח אֹתוֹ...
וַיְצַו עָלָיו לֵאמֹר לֹא תִקַּח אִשָּׁה מִבְּנוֹת כְּנָעַן.

Eisav saw that Yitzchak blessed Yaakov and
sent him to Padan Aram to take a wife...
and warned him not to take a wife from the
daughters of Canaan... (*Bereishis* 28:6).

Eisav overheard a conversation in which his father told Yaakov
not to choose a wife from Bnos Canaan. Immediately following,
the Torah says, וַיֵּלֶךְ עֵשָׂו אֶל יִשְׁמָעֵאל, "[right away], Eisav went to
seek a wife from Bnos Yishmael" (*Bereishis* 28:9).

Sifsei Chachamim comments on this verse:

אַף עַל פִּי שֶׁהָיָה רָשָׁע, אֶת זֶה לֹא עָשָׂה שֶׁיְּהֵא
מְצַעֵר אֶת אָבִיו כִּי הָיָה נוֹהֵג בּוֹ כָּבוֹד בְּאָבִיו.
וְהָרְאָיָה מִמַּה שֶׁנֶּאֱמַר: וַיַּרְא עֵשָׂו כִּי רָעוֹת בְּנוֹת
כְּנַעַן בְּעֵינֵי יִצְחָק אָבִיו.

Though Eisav was a *rasha*, *this* he would
not do. He would not distress his father,
because he always acted respectfully. The
proof is that as soon as he heard that the
Canaanite daughters displeased his father,
he desisted from going against his father's
wishes.

The above statements of *Chazal* certainly give us a picture of a
son who went all out for his father. However, it is the next *Chazal*
that is perhaps the clue to the extraordinary praise lavished on
Eisav.

וַיִּשְׂטֹם עֵשָׂו אֶת יַעֲקֹב...וַיֹּאמֶר עֵשָׂו בְּלִבּוֹ יִקְרְבוּ
יְמֵי אֵבֶל אָבִי וְאַהַרְגָה אֶת יַעֲקֹב אָחִי
רש"י: שֶׁלֹּא אֲצַעֵר אֶת אַבָּא.
רד"ק: כְּלוֹמַר, שֶׁיָּמוּת אָבִי וְנֶאֱבֵל עָלָיו, וְאַחַר כָּךְ
אֶהֱרֹג אֶת יַעֲקֹב אָחִי כִּי בְחַיֵּי אָבִי לֹא אֶעֱשֶׂה, כְּדֵי
שֶׁלֹּא אֶגְרֹם לְאָבִי שֵׂיבָה רָעָה.

Eisav hated Yaakov…and said in his heart:
"I will control myself until my father is no
longer alive before taking revenge against
my brother. I won't do anything in my
father's lifetime to cause him a שֵׂיבָה רָעָה,
to embitter his last years" (Radak, *Bereishis*
27:41).

The *Sifsei Chachamim* stresses that though Eisav was a *rasha*,
this he would not do. Why stress that Eisav was a *rasha*?

It is important to remember that Eisav was seething with
hatred toward his brother and bitterly jealous of him. The
Midrash tells us that Eisav was a murderer. Yet his eagerness to
please his father and not to cause Yitzchak Avinu *tza'ar* gave him
the intense desire, and therefore the willpower, to overcome his
lusts and passions, to seemingly change the very essence of who
he was — שֶׁלֹּא אֲצַעֵר אֶת אַבָּא (Rashi).

This was the ultimate *kibbud av* that Eisav embodied.

Many of us go to great lengths to care for parents and show
them exceptional deference, but who can claim that he has made
or is willing to make a substantial personality change that would
require almost superhuman effort solely to honor his parents?

Could *this* have been his great merit?

———•◦•———

In the well-known *sefer*, *Rachamei Av*, by Rav Yaakov Kittaina,
it says:

אִם אֲנַחְנוּ בְּנֵי יִשְׂרָאֵל הָיִינוּ מְקַיְּימִין הַמִּצְוָה כִּיבּוּד
אָב וָאֵם בִּמְסִירַת נֶפֶשׁ בִּשְׁלֵמוּת, אָז הָיָה כְּבָר עֵשָׂו
נוֹפֵל לְפָנֵינוּ וּכְבָר הָיָה הַגְּאוּלָה, אֲבָל הַבַּעַל דָּבָר
הוּא הַשָּׂטָן הַיֵּצֶר הָרַע מִתְאַמֵּץ לְהַכְשִׁיל אֶת יִשְׂרָאֵל

וּלְהַכְבִּיד עֲלֵיהֶם שֶׁלֹּא יְקַיְּימוּ מִצְוַת כִּיבּוּד אָב וָאֵם
כָּהוֹגֶן, לְפִי שֶׁבִּנְפִילַת עֵשָׂו יִהְיֶה הַגְּאוּלָה וְאָז הוּא
קִצּוֹ שֶׁל הַשָּׂטָן (כמ"ש הַתּוֹסָפוֹת (בר"ה ט"ז ע"ב,
בד"ה כדי) בְּשֵׁם הַיְרוּשַׁלְמִי), לָכֵן קָשֶׁה לְקַיְּימָהּ
כָּהוֹגֶן. (רחמי אב ב', בהערות ההגה"צ משאמלוי
הי"ד)

If *Klal Yisrael* were to practice the mitzvah
of honoring parents with great self-sacrifice
and with all that it demands, then Eisav
would be toppled and the *Geulah* would
arrive. That is why the Evil Inclination
exerts great effort to trip *Klal Yisrael* and to
ensure that the mitzvah of honoring parents
weighs heavily upon us and we do not
fulfill it properly. He knows full well that
the mitzvah of honoring parents is the key
to the downfall of Eisav and his descendants
and the *Geulah* that will follow.

כֵּן אָמְרוּ בָּאֲגָדָה, אָמַר רַב אֲלֶכְּסַנְדְּרִי אָמַר רַבִּי
שִׁמְעוֹן בֶּן לָקִישׁ, בֹּא וּרְאֵה כַּמָּה גְדוֹלָה הִיא זְכוּתוֹ
שֶׁל מְכַבֵּד אֲבוֹתָיו...הוּא מְקָרֵב גְּאוּלָה לְיִשְׂרָאֵל
שֶׁנֶּאֱמַר "הִנֵּה אָנֹכִי שֹׁלֵחַ לָכֶם אֵת אֵלִיָּה הַנָּבִיא
לִפְנֵי בּוֹא יוֹם ה' הַגָּדוֹל וְהַנּוֹרָא וְהֵשִׁיב לֵב אָבוֹת עַל
בָּנִים וְלֵב בָּנִים עַל אֲבוֹתָם."

R' Alexandri said [in the name] of R' Shimon
ben Lakish: Look how great is the merit of
those who honor their parents. They are
hastening the Redemption. As we are told
(*Malachi* 3:23,24), in preparation for the great
and awesome day when Hashem's honor
will fill the world, the Almighty says, "I will
send Eliyahu HaNavi for this purpose — to
reconcile the hearts of fathers to the sons,
and the hearts of sons to fathers"
(*Meah Shearim, Shaar* 68).

There has to be a flourishing of *kibbud av va'eim* before the *Geulah*.

Now we know why the *yetzer hara* will provide us with every kind of excuse to be lax in this mitzvah. The way for *Klal Yisrael* to weaken Eisav's grip is through strengthening their commitment to this pivotal and consequential mitzvah.

Every act of disrespect to parents gives power to Eisav, and every act of honoring parents lessens the power and success of the enemies of the Jewish people and brings the Final Redemption closer.

Chapter 32

The Reward

REB MENDEL GEFNER is a legend in Yerushalayim. A book, Olamo shel Chosid, was written about his fascinating and productive life. Arriving from Russia in 1920, he initiated many projects over the years to benefit the Yishuv, besides heading an illustrious family of seventeen children.

The most publicized of his projects began in 1971. He discovered in Sefer Rokeach, *in the name of Rav Hai Gaon, a source that said: If three hundred Kohanim would give their special blessing נֶגֶד מְקוֹם הַמִּקְדָּשׁ, near the Western Wall, blessing would come to Klal Yisrael.*

Reb Mendel went to the leading Rabbanim of the time, among them the Steipler Gaon in Bnei Brak, the Beis Yisrael of Gur, the Imrei Chaim of Vizhnitz, and asked if this should be publicized. Receiving their approval, he posted large signs inviting all Kohanim to gather for this great event, "Birkas Kohanim," on Chol HaMoed.

Over the years, this has grown to a massive assemblage of hundreds of Kohanim, plus tens of thousands of residents and tourists who come to be blessed.

Reb Mendel was also among the pioneers who purchased a plot of land in what is now the neighborhood of Kiryat

Sanz, Yerushalayim. Years later, when his wife, Esther Mirel, became ill, the Gefners moved to this community to be near their children, who were within walking distance or an easy commute. Sons and daughters flocked daily to their parents' home, taking care of their every need, particularly making sure that their father and mother were well nourished. After Mrs. Gefner passed away, the children continued their devoted care of their father.

The following story was told by one of Reb Gefner's daughters, Chaya Sarah.

As the children walked in throughout the day, the first thing each child asked was, "Tatte, could we bring you a drink?" or, "Please, please eat this delicious _____ (whatever it was they had brought)." With a large family, that spelled a lot of drinks and snacks. Reb Mendel always accepted what was offered.

During her visits, Chaya Sara watched the comings and goings of her siblings and was concerned. She asked her father, "Tatte, why do you always take what the children offer? Maybe it's not healthy for you."

"Chaya Sara," he answered, "if you notice, I only take a little of this and a bit of that. But to stop, I can't. I want each one of my children to have a long life."

The mitzvah of *kibbud av va'eim* is unique among the mitzvos, along with *shiluach hakan*,[1] in that its reward is revealed to us in the Torah.

"Honor your father and mother as Hashem commanded, **so that your days will be lengthened, and it shall be good for you...**" (*Devarim* 5:16).

What is the meaning of this remarkable reward of "lengthened days" (אֲרִיכַת יָמִים) and "so that it will be good for you" (לְמַעַן יִיטַב לָךְ)?

Chazal teach us: the reward for mitzvos is reserved for the World to Come.[2] As we learn from the verse (*Devarim* 7:11): וְשָׁמַרְתָּ אֶת הַמִּצְוָה וְאֶת הַחֻקִּים וְאֶת הַמִּשְׁפָּטִים אֲשֶׁר אָנֹכִי מְצַוְּךָ הַיּוֹם לַעֲשׂוֹתָם — "You shall keep the mitzvos...that I command you today, to do them." On this *Chazal* say, "***Today*** to do them, and ***tomorrow*** [in the World to Come] to receive their reward."[3]

This applies to the mitzvos of *kibbud av va'eim* as well:

לְמַעַן יִיטַב לָךְ – לְעוֹלָם שֶׁכּוּלוֹ טוֹב

"So that it will be good for you" — in a world of only good

לְמַעַן יַאֲרִיכֻן יָמֶיךָ – לְעוֹלָם שֶׁכּוּלוֹ אָרוֹךְ

"Your days will be lengthened (without an end)" — in a world where there is no end to time (*Kiddushin* 39b)

We find a hint to this in the mitzvah itself. In the phrase לְמַעַן יַאֲרִכֻן יָמֶיךָ (*Shemos* 20:12), the second *yud* is missing in the word יַאֲרִכֻן (unlike its usual spelling, יַאֲרִיכֻן; *Devarim* 5:16). Just as the *yud* is hidden from us, so too is the Next World hidden from us, affirming that the reward of "lengthened days" is designated for the World to Come (*Baal HaTurim*).[4]

Still, we have a principle: אֵין מִקְרָא יוֹצֵא מִידֵי פְּשׁוּטוֹ, "We should not overlook the plain meaning of a verse in the Torah." Here, the verse seems to be saying that the reward is in the here and now. Does this mean that *lengthened days* is referring to this world as well?

This question is answered in the morning davening.

> "*Eilu devarim*... Of the following things, one eats the fruits in this world, while the principal reward remains in the World to Come: honoring one's father and mother, acts of loving-kindness...bringing peace between man and his fellow...and Talmud Torah, which is equivalent to them all."[5]

While the principle, "the reward for all mitzvos is reserved for the World to Come," is true for all mitzvos, the mitzvos listed in *Eilu Devarim* are singled out. Although their main reward is set aside in the Next World, there is a bonus in this world as well. There are dividends ("fruits") given in this world that do not diminish the principal ("*keren*") in the World to Come.

The dividends

Rabbeinu Bachya tells us: The power of the mitzvah of *kibbud av va'eim* is great... We can see the fruits in this world...at times we see Hashem's blessing of **serenity** (שַׁלְוָה) **and success** (הַצְלָחָה) (לְמַעַן יִיטַב לָךְ)...and at times **lengthened days** (אֲרִיכַת יָמִים), the rewards specified in the Torah for this mitzvah (*Kad HaKemach*).[6]

Serenity and success (לְמַעַן יִיטַב לָךְ) ... bestowed and revealed in numerous ways

EVERYONE MUST BE GRATEFUL to their parents, but I have to say that I must be super grateful to my mother.

My mother is a wonderful person who almost never asks any of us children to do anything for her. We grew up in a home where my mother's biggest pleasure was to help us.

After my father passed away from colon cancer, my mother asked all of us to take a colonoscopy.

Since I am a person who tries to eat healthfully, exercises regularly, basically goes to sleep on time and davens every day, I was sure that I, of everyone in the family, wouldn't really have to worry about polyps.

Still, I decided to do my mother a favor and take the test. She so rarely asks anything of any of us that I figured the one time she did, I would get an easy mitzvah.

Surprise, surprise! I ended up being the sibling that had polyps. The doctor told me that I was very lucky that it was detected early.

HOW MANY TIMES have I read the line, "I hung up the phone, and I knew my life would never be the same."

Did I ever really believe that one short phone call can turn your world upside-down? Did I even understand just what "upside-down" could mean? And did I ever dream that it would happen to me?

I'm a 33-year-old single woman living in New York, having emigrated from my native England years ago, freelancing as an interior designer. If I fill in that I have two older, married brothers living in the Midwest, and a father and mother back home, you now have some of my basic data.

It was my brother's voice I heard when, unsuspectingly,

I picked up the phone. My father had been in a serious car accident, had been badly hurt, and was in a coma. I booked a ticket, and within hours was on a plane.

At the hospital, they announced, "Critical condition." There was no time for hand wringing. We — my brothers and I — had immediate concerns that needed our attention, primarily our mother.

She was also ill, and had been throughout our childhood. Mismanaged medication exacerbated her severe emotional disorder. My father had been her caregiver. Now, with my father hospitalized, what would happen to her?

My brothers and I were left to figure out how we were to care for two sick parents.

We found a facility that seemed to be suitable for my mother. After seeing her settled, my brothers arranged the many legalities and technicalities that were beyond me. They remained as long as they could, and did as much as they were able. Although I knew they had business and family obligations, still it was traumatic when after three weeks, the first, and then the second brother, said that he wasn't able to stay on.

My father was still in a coma when they left. And I was on my own.

I felt like the world was caving in. I was the youngest. It was a big jump for me to have to take a responsibility that I wanted to throw onto my big brothers. I didn't know what I was doing, or how I was going to do what I couldn't do. One thing, though, was very clear. I had just left my life behind me. All of a sudden, I was back home in London, and I had this big yoke on my shoulders.

The truth is, I had never been close with my parents. Moving across the ocean was also, maybe…let's call it a bit of an escape. Now I was in charge of both my father and mother, with no skills to do anything I was expected to do.

The first morning was really, really challenging. It was hard to get up. I was simply frightened to face the day. Somehow, I pulled myself together, put one foot in front of the other, and set out.

So there I was, learning how to communicate with doctors and understand diagnoses, learning hospital jargon and protocol. Keeping daily records of what the doctors were saying, deciphering prognosis reports. Learning to navigate the system, trying to hold on.

My father awoke from the coma after 5 weeks. He was left paralyzed and could barely speak. Recovery was a very slow process. After nine months, my father was admitted to an assisted living facility near that of my Mom.

If you can, imagine having to liaise with two different facilities and all their social workers, physiotherapists, physicians, opthalmologists, dentists, psychiatrists, and neurologists. Trying to remember everybody's names and remain on their good side so that there would be some sliver of a hope to turn their grace toward my father and mother. Why should they treat them any differently than the other hundreds of residents — especially when I would return to New York, and be thousands of miles away? I was nervous even to think about leaving.

Coming from a dysfunctional home and not having had a smooth relationship with my parents to begin with, it did not come as second nature to me to care for them. Still, I felt a tremendous responsibility to make sure that they were taken care of. I was and still am trying to be devoted and as involved as I possibly can be while trying to take care of myself as well.

I tied up some logistical and financial things, sorted out legal matters, and flew back. Back to New York, back to work... and tried to pick up where I had left off.

But even with a deep ocean in-between, a strong rope was still tied very tightly from me to my parents.

I now have three full-time jobs. Since I am self-employed, and freelancing, my day is not structured. It's not a nine-to-five job, where I clock in and out. I am constantly involved in my business and in touch with my clients.

And of course, I have to make sure that my parents are cared for and getting the proper attention.

The first thing I did was hire a private companion for each of my parents. The agency I used is responsible for checking up on these aides, and sometimes it's really helpful, and sometimes it's just another person to have to communicate with and take care of.

Before I left, I set up my parents' finances. Now I can pay their bills from New York and handle most of their care via e-mail. I have a list of ten to twelve professionals per parent. I have their doctors' e-mails, and I'm constantly in touch with them — probably my mom's doctors more regularly than my father's. Since my mother is more active, she tends to require more involvement on a more regular basis. Her doctor and I e-mail several times a week, depending on what is going on. Usually I check in with my father's doctors once a week if everything is okay. If either parent has an appointment, the private companion goes along.

I also maintain contact with their speech therapist, rec-reational therapist, and the unit clerk who does all the book-ings for the appointments. They e-mail me and I respond. My mom has bad arthritis and problems with her vision. I frequently conference with her physiotherapist and ophthalmologist.

Every three months for the last five years, I have flown home. I try to stay at least a week, meeting with the professional members of our team, so they don't forget who I am.

Most important, of course, is the time I spend with each of my parents. After the first year, there was not much more that they could do for my father. They just try to keep him comfortable. He is in a wheelchair. We read together, listen to music. He loves kids. It would be great to get my brothers' families to come more often...but it would be a big financial strain to bring their children over from the Midwest.

I also try to go out with my mother. She loves to shop, so sometimes we go together. It depends. My last trip, she had bad arthritis and was not able to walk, and was in bed basically the whole time. That made it a bit of a challenging visit.

One of my big projects on these trips has been my parents' home. Once my parents were both in facilities, we had to dismantle the house. My brothers helped with that, and we have an aunt who also helped. We had sales, and some open-house charity events, where most of what remained was given away.

During these times, there were lots of strangers walking through our home. On one of those afternoons, a tall, well-dressed woman came over to me. She had somehow figured out that it was my house. I remember that she had very kind eyes and offered her hand warmly. When she spoke to me, it was not only with her words, but with her kindness and warmth. I can just picture myself there right now. I was in the garage, which was kind of an unlikely place for such a pivotal moment.

"I know that I am a stranger to you," she began softly, "and who am I to say this? But I am sure that you are going through a very trying time. I wanted to share a thought with you."

I nodded, curious as to where her introduction was leading.

"If all of us were to stand in a circle," she said, "take our pekalach and put them into the center, I can guarantee you each one of us would go running back to pick up our own."

Why was what she said helpful?

I think it was an opportunity for me to digest that Hashem had catered this challenge to my specific tikkun, the job my neshamah was sent here to do. It was about accepting it and knowing that this is what I need in order to fulfill my tafkid in the world. In fact, I wouldn't want someone else's tafkid. I felt that was the message this kind woman gave me, the message HaKadosh Baruch Hu helped me to hear.

I can't say I always felt like this. In the past, I would say, "Why me, Hashem? And why can't my brothers be more involved? I am the only girl and it doesn't make sense for me to have to carry this myself." But I've grown tremendously as a person and am a completely different human being because of this experience.

It turned me into a giver.

ACTUALLY, THIS STORY HAS TWO PARTS that seem not to be connected at all. In the final analysis I think you will see just how related they are.

Our 10-year-old son, Yoni, our eldest, is a quiet child. He wasn't always like this. When he was younger he was full of life. Over the last year, he became more withdrawn. His ever-present smile was seen less often. Still, he was our sweet Yoni. So we weren't prepared when his teacher told us he thought our child suffered from an emotional problem. In class, he wasn't interacting with the other boys. He hardly participated and sat with a solemn face through most of the lessons.

On the teacher's advice, we took him for an evaluation. A battery of tests came out inconclusive. The experts couldn't put their finger on the problem. Despite our persistent efforts to get to the root of the problem, our dear, delightful Yoni remained quiet and very much a loner.

The second half of my story begins from the moment I got married. My parents wanted me to live near them. As a girl born after three boys, I was extremely close with them. However, the prices in their neighborhood were prohibitive. So my husband and I moved to a community where housing was affordable. There we raised our family, our bechor Yoni and his three younger sisters.

One day, without any prior signs, my healthy and active mother suddenly died. The pain was terrible for all of us. But for my father, the sun had set. He was shrouded in darkness.

After the shivah, my brothers and I had a family meeting to discuss what would happen to our father. The best option seemed to be that he would come to live in my home. But when we offered him that choice, he said it would be hard for him to get used to a new neighborhood and he would rather manage on his own.

When I came to visit him several days later, I saw what "managing" meant. The fridge was almost empty, the laundry wasn't done, and the house was neglected.

Again, I urged him to come to live with us, but my father had not changed his mind. Yet to leave him alone didn't seem to be an option either. "Abba," I begged, "please come to us." He didn't answer. He seemed to be looking around at his familiar surroundings and saying, I'm not ready for any more changes. When I left that day, I cried all the way home.

What could I do? Let's say I would make the hour trip (each way) twice a week. My brothers also agreed to come. But what about the rest of the lonely hours? My mother had been such a bright light for our father. I felt that without her, he would shrivel.

It was then that I came up with a bizarre idea: If Abba wouldn't move in with us, we would have to move in with him. I say bizarre because it surely made no sense just to pick up and move a family that was established in every way. Both my husband and I had good jobs, the children were in good schools. It made no sense, and I was sure that the idea would be vetoed by my husband.

Which it was.

"You're seriously considering leaving all that we built up here?" Zvi asked me

So much for that idea. I attempted to resign myself to his reasonable conclusion.

Much to my surprise, a few days later my husband had a change of heart, "I was thinking about it," he said to me one morning. "This is the kind of mitzvah that can slip through your hands too fast if you don't catch it." He was willing to give it a try.

I then presented my ambitious plan to my father. I suggested that we renovate his house, making two separate apartments with two separate entrances so that we would be right next door to one another, and yet Abba would have his own space and privacy. My father picked up on the idea right away and agreed to finance the move.

When I told Yoni about our plan, he looked thoughtful.

"What do you think, Yoni?" I asked.

"Well, it's an idea."

"Good idea or bad idea?" I pressed.

"Good."

My brothers were overjoyed with this plan; now our father would be properly cared for.

I'm not going to say that it was easy for us to get used to Abba's house. It was much smaller than the home we had lived in. We were the only young family in the neighborhood. The schools were far. I was getting a lower salary in my new job, and Zvi had a long commute. It wasn't easy, but it was also not terrible.

For my father it was also a big adjustment. At first he spent much of his time alone in his apartment. Slowly we learned what he preferred, what he liked more and what he liked less. It didn't take long before Abba was satisfied with this arrangement, and my brothers didn't stop thanking me when they saw how Abba thrived.

Eventually we all settled in. But the biggest change happened to Yoni. Like the other children, he was now in a new school. We were not sure what to do. In the end we made the decision not to tell the school about his "problems" right away. We wanted him to start off on the right foot. Of course we were waiting nervously for a phone call that would inform us of Yoni's difficulties.

The phone call never came.

Meanwhile, we noticed that Yoni seemed happier. We didn't have to wake him up in the morning again and again. He smiled much more. He also started to talk with my husband about his schoolwork and his friends. One day Michali told me merrily, "Yoni told me a joke." Yoni is telling jokes? I had tears in my eyes.

We were bewildered. What had happened?

"It is true, the school didn't call," I said to Zvi, "but sometimes teachers don't like telling bad news. It's really negligent if we don't call to find out how Yoni is doing."

Holding our breaths, we decided to speak to his teacher, hoping that his school day would reflect his improved behavior at home.

After the call, Zvi repeated to me the teacher's words: "Your son is a wonderful boy."

"I started to speak to the teacher about Yoni's difficulties," Zvi said, still shaken, "but he didn't understand what I was talking about. Every question I asked brought a positive

answer. He has friends? Yes. He participates? Yes."

We were stymied. What had happened? We knew pieces were missing from the puzzle. Was Yoni holding (withholding) them? Zvi wasn't sure, but decided to speak to Yoni directly. We were not at all prepared for Yoni's response.

At first, Yoni didn't want to talk about it. My husband was patient and gave him space and time. It didn't take long before it came tumbling out. A group of boys in his old class, the big shots. It seems that they had their friends and enemies — and Yoni was on the wrong side. They made fun of him, what he wore, what he ate, and never let him join in the games. Whatever he did, Yoni was the target for their taunts. Without him having to say too much more, it was clear that our sweet Yoni preferred to crawl into a cocoon so that they would leave him alone.

Till now. New school. New friends. New life.

We lived with my father for two more years. The week before my father died we were sitting together. He thanked me for our decision to move in together with him, stemming the loneliness that would have been if we hadn't come.

After his death we returned to our home, but not the way we had left.

If we hadn't made the choice to move, we might not have found out that our son does not have an emotional problem, just a problem with the environment, that in the merit of kibbud av *had been solved.*[7]

Serenity and success…bestowed but not revealed

It's not only what we get, it's also from what we were saved. If we could scan celestial accounts, we would undoubtedly be privy to the *non*-revealed stories — the many difficulties, misfortunes, and headaches that we were spared, gifting us with a greater portion of serenity and success. We can't illustrate this kind of reward with a story — since we don't *know* the full story — but undoubtedly in *Shamayim* there are some terrific tales…

Lengthened days (אֲרִיכַת יָמִים)

Full days

The Ramban teaches us that one aspect of "that your days should be lengthened" is a promise that *each* of our days will be lengthened.[8]

…More productive hours … more accomplished … more energy…

> MANY YEARS AGO, my mother had a heel spur. Those who have experienced this know it's very painful. She was advised by her doctor to buy orthotics — shoe inserts that are molded especially for each individual. She took this advice, and in a short time, experienced considerable relief.
>
> My mother was so delighted with the results, she started to recommend this cure to others. She was convinced it would cure not only this but multiple ills.
>
> Who were her first customers? We, her beloved children, whom she wanted to protect from any harm.
>
> I had a debilitating back problem. I was on my feet all day at work, and by early evening, at low ebb. In great pain, I couldn't make it past six. Although I saw no connection, I listened to my mother and bought the orthotics.
>
> Let me tell you, those little things changed my life. I can now stand and walk and bend and function until late hours.

Added days

A son or daughter who honors his parents may have to spend a significant amount of time, especially when the parent is older and needs assistance. Although the child may be happy to do the mitzvah, at the same time, he may feel a little "cheated" that he is not free to pursue his own interests. Therefore, the Torah promises that the reward for **kibbud av va'eim** is lengthened days — a guarantee that in return for the time that this child has dedicated to his parents, HaKadosh Baruch Hu will give him additional years for that "lost time."

How exactly is this calculated?

All the sacrifices will be tallied and added up [minute for minute, hour for hour, day for day, week for week, year for year!] and all the days of *mesiras nefesh* will be added on to the original lifespan decreed for that person (in the name of Harav Yosef Chaim Sonnenfeld cited in *Vayevarech Dovid* page 33).

> *I SPOTTED NECHAMA at a mutual friend's engagement party and invited her to sit with me. I hadn't seen her for ages.*
>
> *"I'm only here for a few minutes, and only because it's in the neighborhood."*
>
> *Noting my puzzled expression, Nechama was quick to add, "My father lives with us."*
>
> *"Oh, I didn't know," I said, giving her an opening to say more if she wished.*
>
> *"Even with our aide, I try not to leave unless I must. And then, not for too long. His medical condition is too complex."*
>
> *"How long has he been with you?" I asked.*
>
> *"Seven years."*
>
> *I tried to digest her answer. It was inconceivable to me that a person could be so completely devoted to a parent for seven years, to the extent that she felt she could only stay at a* simchah *for a few minutes. I wanted to say something. I was impressed with what she was doing in her typical quiet way, but any response seemed so puny for something so big.*
>
> *As Nechama was finishing her drink, I remembered something I had learned that seemed to fit. "Nechama..." I reached out to touch her sleeve. "I heard that all this time that you are devoting to your father will be repaid to you."*
>
> *Her face lit up. She shook my hand warmly, and whispered, "Thank you."*
>
> *Her kind eyes locked with mine. "Can you get me that source?"*

Of course, this daughter's devotion to her father was done without a second thought to any payback. Nonetheless, most of us can use encouragement to energize our pace and help us go on.

Why "lengthened days"?

❖ A son and daughter may feel that they lost out. They may wish that they had different, "better" parents. Despite their disappointment, they are willing to keep uppermost in their minds that these parents gave them life, the most valuable of all gifts, and in return, they extend honor and respectful behavior. Says *HaKadosh Baruch Hu*: "You have shown Me how much you value life — I will reward you with more" (based on the *Abarbanel*).

❖ The exact wording of the mitzvah is יַאֲרִיכֻן, "your days will be lengthened," and not "I (Hashem) will lengthen," to stress that it is in our own hands to work to deserve this (*Ohr HaChaim HaKadosh*).[9] This is based on the principle that a person is measured the way he measures (בְּמִידָה שֶׁאָדָם מוֹדֵד בָּהּ מוֹדְדִין לוֹ).[10] When we care for our parents, we lengthen their days, we help them live long, and measure for measure, we deserve to have our lives lengthened.

AS I APPROACHED OMA AND OPA'S HOUSE, my heart skipped a beat. I hadn't been here in so long.

The warm yellow light shining through the curtained windows was the first sign of this place that had always been a second home to me, a place I loved, home to people who I loved.

We sat together and talked. They asked me about my flight. I told them about the children and showed them the latest photos as we munched on Oma's cookies.

Before I left, Opa asked me to do him a favor.

"On my desk, right on the top, there are piles of paper, and a few pads. There are two with the same brown cover. Open them both, and see which one has a letter started on the first page. If you could bring that to me, with a pen, I would be very grateful."

I walked into the study. There was the desk. In another minute, I had both brown pads in my hand. Now...which of the two pads? I opened up the first one — "To Do." Nope. Next.

I opened the second. Opa hadn't gotten very far in his letter, but what I saw will remain etched in my mind. In his bold handwriting was the following:

To Our Dearest Children,

You are our true treasures. You have enriched and enlengthed our days.

I never found enlengthed *in the dictionary. But that didn't stop my Opa from clearly and poignantly defining his longevity and enhanced days, and his children's' share in it.*

An incentive

Hashem wants to give us a huge incentive that will keep us on track when the road gets bumpy, a powerful motivation and encouragement to keep us moving forward despite difficulties. Therefore, Hashem takes from His storehouse of blessings His very best gift of all: Life.

MY HUSBAND TRIES TO VISIT his parents almost every day. He has been doing this for many years. As they grow older and more issues arise, he is even more attentive to their needs.

He is a very devoted husband and father, and equally conscientious about his work, but sometimes his devotion to his parents seems a bit much to me. If I ever mention it, he answers with a smile, "Don't you want me around for a long time?"

More on lengthened days

When we assist our parents, give care and show concern, we lengthen our *own* days (לְמַעַן יַאֲרִיכֻן יָמֶיךָ), add years to *our* lives.

The Chasam Sofer tells us how to add years to our *parents'* lives, based on the verse: "And then Hashem will give you extra good because of your children" (*Devarim* 28:11).

Every person has a certain amount to accomplish in this world.

When he finishes his task, he finishes "his days." But if he has children or others over whom he has influence, then Hashem will allow him to live longer so that he can continue to guide them on the right path.[11]

We learn in *Mishlei*:

בֵּן חָכָם מוּסַר אָב וְלֵץ לֹא שָׁמַע גְּעָרָה

A wise son (בֵּן חָכָם) wants to hear parental rebuke (מוּסַר אָב), while a foolish son (לֵץ) shuts himself off to reproof (לֹא שָׁמַע גְּעָרָה) (*Mishlei* 13:1).

Fortunate are children who have parents who can give instruction. Though it's not easy to hear criticism, a wise son understands the benefit of his parents' *mussar*. A parent, who knows his son inside and out, is in a position to offer insights that others will miss or not care enough to notice.

When a wise son listens to *mussar av* (מוּסַר אָב), he is showing the *Ribbono shel Olam* that it is necessary for his parents to remain in this world, since their children need and heed their instructions.

In this way, the wise son is buying additional "life assurance" for his parents.

Chapter 33

It's Not Over
When It's Over

I had just finished a seminar presentation, "Seizing the Power from Eisav: Recapturing the Treasures of *Kibbud Av Va'eim*." The Q & A session had ended, and most of the participants had left the room. As I was gathering my books and papers, I noticed a woman standing at the side of the room, hands covering her face, her shoulders shaking. I put down my things and hurried over to her.

"Excuse me," I ventured. "Can I be of help?"

She lowered her hands to reveal a suffering expression. Without meeting my eyes, almost as if she were talking to herself, she said, "Where was this information when I needed it twenty years ago?"

Her thoughts were echoed by others.

> **WHEN MY PARENTS WERE ALIVE,** I was indifferent to even what I knew I should be doing, let alone what I had never done because I didn't know. Although I was always right there for a friend in need, I seemed to have a blind spot when it came to my parents. And now, for me, it's too late.

Yes. And no.

Yes, you were remiss. Opportunity knocked, and you didn't answer.

But no, it's not too late. Even if our parents have passed on, the mitzvah is not over.

מְכַבְּדוֹ בְּחַיָּיו מְכַבְּדוֹ בְּמוֹתוֹ

A son and daughter are obligated to honor
parents while they are alive, and this
obligation continues even after they have
passed on to the Next World[1]

(*Kiddushin* 31b).

The mitzvah of *kibbud horim* does not cease when a parent passes on.

When parents are alive, honor is expressed by caring for their needs. Similar obligations are relevant to a deceased father and mother.

When parents are alive, we have a mitzvah to revere them — to refer to them with titles, not to cause them anguish, not to belittle or embarrass them. These obligations also apply posthumously.

Our tour now takes us to the World Beyond.

Our parents still need us — even in the Next World

A basic principle of our Torah is that a person is responsible for his actions.[2] No positive action goes unrewarded, and no action will be without an accounting and a judgment. Although the difficulties and suffering we confront in this world serve to atone for many of our misdeeds, a person will undergo a judgment for those that have not been atoned for.[3] This is what the deceased will experience — before he enters *Gan Eden*.

The Chofetz Chaim writes about the proper perspective of a son and daughter at this time:

A person should consider it as if, *chas veshalom*,
he himself were trapped in burning flames or facing

painful suffering. He would surely want his children to rush to his rescue, to save him in any way they possibly could...[4]

Would a son or daughter stand by passively? Surely not. A child would do whatever he could to save his parents.

How can a child help? How can he rescue his parents?

A child's power to benefit a parent

As we learned, children must care for needy parents. They may not be left to manage on their own. In the Next World, *all* parents are in the category of "needy." *All* depend on their children for their welfare no less — and maybe even more.

Why are they needy and what are they needy of?

The answer is based on the fundamental truth that this world is the world of accomplishing, of doing mitzvos, and the Next, of reaping the benefits. This opportunity to accrue merit through fulfilling mitzvos ends with a person's passing.

While this is true, *Chazal* tell us another truth that opens a wide window of opportunity for our parents *and* for us: בְּרָא מְזַכֶּה אַבָּא, "A child can benefit his parents [in the Next World]."[5]

A child is referred to as the "legs" of his parent.[6] In this world, a person is a *holeich* — one who walks, one who makes strides, an accomplisher with potential for growth. This potential ends with his demise. But through the merit of children who serve as their parents' "legs," a father and mother can continue moving upward spiritually.

Through this remarkable reality, children keep their parents walking, climbing, ascending. The deceased once again can gain merit. "When children are occupied with mitzvos," Rabbeinu Yonah tells us, "it is considered as if the parent is alive and performing these deeds himself."[7]

Chazal are explaining the unique link that exists between children and parents. A child's accomplishments are passed to his parents — automatically. This is because a child is the extension of his parent. He is only in this world because of his parents, and therefore, his accomplishments are everlastingly credited to those who gave him his existence.*

When a father and mother give a child not only his life, but also proper values and tools for purposeful living, his contributions are truly theirs. What is more extraordinary is that even if parents had no input in his child's *maasim tovim*, they are also credited! We see this with Avraham Avinu and his father, Terach. Although Terach put many obstacles in Avraham's path, Hashem told Avraham that Terach had earned a portion in the World to Come. This is based on the principle בְּרָא מְזַכֶּה אַבָּא, "a son's merit passes to his father."[8]

In the Next World, when a parent can't help himself, a child can provide assistance. Even if parents were exceptionally righteous, a child can better his parent's status, increasing his reward and happiness.[9]

> The mitzvos that a child does after a parent's passing are an atonement and a benefit for the *neshamah* of his parent…
>
> Not only do a child's mitzvos provide a parent with additional merit that offsets the judgment (*din*) of the afterlife, but they enable the parent to advance and enter the most elevated places in *Gan Eden*… (*Ahavas Chessed*).[10]

The Parallel

The obligation to care for needy parents in the Next World parallels the obligation to care for them in this world.

מַאֲכִיל — to feed: The mitzvos that we do are credited to our parents. They are the "food" that nourishes their souls.[11]

---

* This concept is not limited to child and parent. Mitzvos can be dedicated for the merit of any relative or non-relative (*Sefer Ahavas Chessed, Chelek* 2, Chapter 15) .The difference is that in the second instance, it must be specified that the mitzvah is being done לעילוי נשמת פלוני בן פלוני, for the elevation of the soul of ___ the son/daughter of ___ (*Sefer L'ilui Nishmas*, p. 26). With parent and child, the transfer is automatic, specifying is only preferable (*Pele Yo'etz, Kibbud Av Va'eim*).

With each mitzvah we do, we should imagine that we are presenting our parents with the best delicacies, delighting their *neshamah* (*Pele Yo'etz*).[12]

מוֹצִיא — These mitzvos "bring them out," rescuing (*matzil*) and releasing (*matir*) them from harsh judgment...

מַכְנִיס — ...and bring them into *Gan Eden*, even allowing them to be seated among the righteous, elevating them to higher and higher levels of *kedushah*.

מַלְבִּישׁ — Certain mitzvos are of such value that in their merit, a parent receives special honor. In fact, he is "crowned" in *Gan Eden*. In that way, a child fulfills "clothing" his parent in a dignified way — posthumously.[13]

כָּל צָרְכֵיהֶם — Just like it is a mitzvah to "supply all their needs" when they are alive, it is a mitzvah to do so posthumously. Therefore, when children are able, it is a mitzvah to pay a parent's outstanding debts.* This brings peace (מְנוּחָה) to their *neshamah*.

Honoring parents posthumously includes both acts of intrinsic honor and acts that provide spiritual benefit to the *neshamah*, giving the *neshamah* an *aliyah*. Both are a fulfillment of מְכַבְּדוֹ בְּמוֹתוֹ.

Honor in Speech

חַיָּיב לְכַבְּדוֹ אֲפִילוּ אַחַר מוֹתוֹ, כֵּיצַד? הָיָה אוֹמֵר דְּבַר שְׁמוּעָה מִפִּיו, אוֹמֵר: "כָּךְ אָמַר אַבָּא מָארִי, הֲרֵינִי כַּפָּרַת מִשְׁכָּבוֹ," אִם הוּא תוֹךְ י"ב חוֹדֶשׁ. וְאִם לְאַחַר י"ב חוֹדֶשׁ, אוֹמֵר: "זִכְרוֹנוֹ לִבְרָכָה."

A child is obligated to honor his parents posthumously. How is this accomplished? When repeating a Torah thought of his parent, he should say, "My father, may I

---

* Under certain circumstances this is an obligation (when there are funds from an inheritance). While a child is not obligated to use his own money to pay this debt, if he is able it is a mitzvah (*Shulchan Aruch, Choshen Misphat,* 107:1-2).

serve as an atonement for him ..." After twelve months, one should add זִכְרוֹנוֹ לִבְרָכָה when mentioning a parent. (*Shulchan Aruch* 240:9).

An aspect of intrinsic honor and reverence is the way we speak to and about our parents. One may not refer to a parent by his first name when he is alive, and the same restriction applies after he has passed on.

One must title a parent in his lifetime with a prefix like "Rav," "Mr.," "Dr.," "Professor." After his passing, we add yet a "second title," a memorial suffix. During the first twelve months, we say הֲרֵינִי כַּפָּרַת מִשְׁכָּבוֹ/מִשְׁכָּבָה, "May I be an atonement for his soul."[14]* After twelve months, acknowledging the completion of the judgment, the memorial suffix is changed to זִכְרוֹנוֹ לִבְרָכָה/זִכְרוֹנָה לִבְרָכָה, "May his/her memory be for a blessing" (some add לְחַיֵּי הָעוֹלָם הַבָּא), or alternatively, עָלָיו הַשָּׁלוֹם/עָלֶיהָ הַשָּׁלוֹם.

There are many halachos and customs concerning posthumous honor. Why did the *Shulchan Aruch* choose to mention only this one aspect of honoring a deceased parent, "may I serve as an atonement for him/her"?

In fact the obligation of posthumous honor is encapsulated in this phrase.

Every positive action, word, or even thought of a son and daughter can improve a parent's position in the Next World. A child's mitzvos are in place of what a parent can no longer do. This expression, "May I be an atonement for his soul," is reminding a child not to neglect his responsibility to offer a parent merit. He should feel that his "needy" parent's welfare is dependent on him.

When we say "may I serve as an atonement for my parent," a son and daughter reminds himself during the first twelve months — over and over — "My good deeds will benefit my parents. Now, let me get going."[15]

---

* Some say this suffix is only added when quoting a parent on halachic matters or *divrei Torah*. Others say after any statement quoting a parent. Still others say even just when mentioning the deceased parent. (See *Otzer Kibbud Av Va'eim* 405–412.)

Honor in thought

When a parent is alive, we fulfill the mitzvah of honoring in our thoughts, *kavod b'machshavah*, by viewing parents with an *ayin tovah*, focusing on their strengths and **judging favorably**. Honoring a parent posthumously in our thoughts would primarily mean considering always: "What can I do to earn for my parents a **favorable judgment**? How can I benefit their *neshamos*?"

Honor in deed

"Honor your father and your mother" obligates us to care for our parents' physical needs. This applies to living parents. If one concludes that once a parent has passed away he is no longer obligated in this mitzvah, he would be mistaken. Then, a child is even more obligated (*Zohar*).[16]

Commencement of mourning

The Berachah

With the passing of any family member for whom one is obligated to mourn, one recites the blessing: בָּרוּךְ אַתָּה ... דַּיַן הָאֱמֶת, "Blessed are You...the true Judge." Accepting the Almighty's judgment is a source of merit for the *deceased*.

The Kri'ah

In addition, the mourner performs *kri'ah*, tearing his clothing. The halachos for *kri'ah* for a parent underscore our understanding that the child-parent relationship is unlike any other. This is sensed and expressed in the tearing.[17]

For family members for whom we are required to mourn, we tear in private.

For parents, we tear in public.

For others, we can tear by hand or with the aid of an instrument.
FOR PARENTS, one must tear by hand (when difficult, one may begin the cut with a knife or sharp instrument, and then continue tearing).

For all other family members, we tear on the right side.
FOR PARENTS, we tear on the left, the side of the heart.

For everyone else, the tear should be a *tefach* in length (about 3.5 inches).
FOR PARENTS, the tear must be made עַד שֶׁמְּגַלֶּה לִבּוֹ, until it reaches over the heart.

For everyone else, we tear only the outermost garment.*
FOR PARENTS, we tear all outer garments.

For everyone else, if we change clothing during the *shivah* (under the conditions when it is permissible), we need not tear the garment we have changed into.
FOR PARENTS, a child must tear any garment he has changed into during the *shivah.*

For all family members, one is permitted to baste the tear after *shivah* and, after thirty days, to mend it properly.
FOR PARENTS, basting is permitted after thirty days, but a proper mending is forbidden forever.

For all others, if we hear about the death after thirty days, we don't tear.
FOR PARENTS, there is no time limit.

An extended mourning

The period of formal mourning begins after the deceased is buried: the seven days of *shivah*, and an additional twenty-three days, which complete *sheloshim*. Thirty days marks the end of mourning for all relatives except with regard to parents. An additional eleven months is extended for a father and mother, as a sign of respect.

---

* For women, for reasons of modesty, the tear should immediately be adjusted.

When a child observes the restrictions of *shivah* (seven days), *sheloshim* (thirty days), and an additional eleven months, he is also fulfilling the mitzvah of *kibbud av va'eim*.

Throughout these additional eleven months, out of respect for his parent, a child is expected to refrain from certain behavior. We therefore restrict: new clothing, participation in joyous occasions, festive meals, social gatherings, and musical presentations. There are also restrictions on haircutting and excursions. When a question arises, as they invariably do, these laws and customs, their details and exceptions, should be presented to a Rav for clarification.

This refraining acknowledges our awareness of our parent's needs during this first year of accounting and judgment, ensuring that not only *we* remain focused and maintain this awareness, but that others see our concern for our parents, which is an honor for them.[18]

Just as we may not belittle a parent in his lifetime, we should not do so after his passing. Disregarding the restrictions of mourning gives the appearance of disrespect to deceased parents.

Merit-producing laws and customs

From the Gemara, *Midrash*, and *poskim*, we learn various ways of honoring parents posthumously, giving assistance, protection, and *nachas ruach* to their *neshamos*.[19] They are crucial during the first twelve months after a parent's passing and on every *yartzeit*. Many will be a *zechus* for the *neshamah* at any time.

The following is a brief overview of merit-producing laws and customs.

PRAYERS

Kaddish

The *Midrash Tanchuma, Parashas Noach*, describes the benefit of saying *Kaddish* for a parent. *Kaddish* has the power to shield the *neshamah* from the trials of judgment (of the first twelve months) and brings the *neshamah* into *Gan Eden*.[20]

The custom is for a son to recite *Kaddish* for his parents for the first eleven months of the twelve-month mourning period. The *minhag* of *Bnei Sefarad* is to continue a week into the twelfth month. Others continue until a week before the end of the twelfth month.[21]

Kaddish is recited publicly (in the presence of a *minyan*), declaring that Hashem's Name be exalted and sanctified (*Yisgadal v'Yiskadesh*). Leading the congregants to respond, "*Amen, Yehei Shemei rabbah*," is considered both a public sanctification of Hashem's Name (*kiddush Hashem b'rabbim*), as well as acknowledging the righteousness of Hashem's decrees (*tzidduk hadin*). The merit of both generates benefit for the *neshamah* of the *deceased*.

When there are no sons to say *Kaddish*, halachah speaks of other options, such as grandchildren, sons-in-law, or hiring a substitute.

"If a daughter wishes to benefit the soul of her parent," says the *Matteh Efraim*, "she should be careful at all times, whether praying at the synagogue or a prayer service in her home, to listen attentively to *Kaddish* and answer *Amen* with proper concentration. He Who knows the thoughts of all will consider this as if she had recited *Kaddish*...*"[22]

Another suggestion, lauded in the *Kitzur Shulchan Aruch* as more powerful than only saying *Kaddish*, is for sons — and he stresses that this applies to daughters as well — to "adopt" one particular mitzvah to meticulously and conscientiously fulfill. This should be dedicated *l'ilui nishmas* the parent.[23]

Maftir

Another observance that benefits the *deceased* is for a son to be called for the last *aliyah*,[24] reciting the *berachos* before and after the Torah reading, and reciting the *berachos* on the *Haftarah*. The *berachos* after the *Haftarah* resemble *Kaddish*.[25] By repeating the *Haftarah* blessings throughout the twelve months, the mourner is constantly reinforcing *tzidduk hadin*, our acceptance of Hashem's decrees.

Leading the congregation in tefillah

More beneficial than the *Kaddish* is leading the *tefillah*.*[26] If a son cannot *daven* all the *tefillah* (for example, he cannot properly

---

* according to minhag Ashkenaz.

pronounce the words), it is also beneficial for him to lead whatever part(s) he can.

Although these mitzvos are of great benefit to the deceased, it is important not to argue over the privilege, because instead of merit and pleasure, the *neshamah* will be shamed.

> A dedicated son could be upset that he missed the chance to honor his parent, a chance to give merit to the *neshamah*. But if he has priority (according to the halachah regarding mourners) and instead of standing on his rights gives up this merit solely to avoid an argument, the *tefillah* is credited to his parent's *neshamah* — and the person who incorrectly grabbed the honor has not benefited his loved one.[27] (!)

Yizkor

It is customary to remember the deceased after the Torah reading on the *Shalosh Regalim* (Succos, Pesach, and Shavuos), and on Yom Kippur. At this time, the mourner recites the memorial prayer, *Yizkor*.

There are four aspects to the *Yizkor* service that benefit the deceased:

1. Mentioning the name
2. Davening for the welfare (בְּגַן עֵדֶן תְּהֵא מְנוּחָתוֹ/מְנוּחָתוֹ/מְנוּחָתָהּ)
3. Pledging *tzedakah*
4. The actual giving of charity

The principal merit of *Yizkor* is the contribution of charity on behalf of the deceased. Through the merit of *tzedakah*, we recall the departed and ask Hashem to remember him/her favorably.

Although *Yizkor* is primarily intended to be recited in a *minyan*, on the appropriate days one may recite *Yizkor* even at home.[28]

MITZVOS

> The mitzvos that a child does after a parent's passing are an atonement and a benefit for the *neshamah* of his parent...[29]

Tzedakah

If a child makes a charitable contribution for his parent's *zechus*, it will surely benefit his parent to ameliorate judgment (*Mishnah Berurah*).[30]

A child should not neglect — even one day of his life — to give *tzedakah* for the *aliyah* of his parent's *neshamah* (*Pele Yo'etz*).[31]

Harav Avigdor Miller suggests that "every person should have a *tzedakah* box and every day give a small amount, even a nickel. In this way, he is remembering his parents and giving them the *zechus* of *tzedakah*, fulfilling the mitzvah of posthumous honor daily."[32]

Aside from actual money contributed to the poor, we can use money to buy items to donate in our parent's memory, for example, *sefarim* used by the community, which should be inscribed: donated לְעִילוּי נִשְׁמַת (name of deceased). *Siddurim, Chumashim, Tehillim* donated to a shul, or a *Shas* donated to a *beis medrash* are considered everlasting memorials.[33] When people use them throughout the years, it is an ongoing benefit for the *neshamah* of the deceased.

Pursuing peace

The mitzvah of "Do not be like Korach and his cohorts," is a warning not to maintain a fight, to do all we can to end a quarrel.

WE GREW UP in a house filled with the deep, melodious voice of our father, who was a chazzan and famed ba'al tefillah. We were moved to tears as he led the services. He had a way of making the words of the davening come alive, leap from the pages, and embed themselves in your heart. When he passed away suddenly, my sister and I were devastated.

I think we both felt the same way. We wanted him back so much, and that's what was behind our fight over his beloved siddur. Among the things my father left was his siddur. It was so much a part of our father's life. For both my sister and me, it was a part of him we could hold onto physically, and we both wanted it.

We fought. We stopped talking to each other.

I don't know how long this would have gone on and how far apart we would have drifted, if not for my friend, Rachelle. I spewed out my anger one morning as Rachelle and I were driving to our class. She heard me out, and then basically told me that I was way off.

"Two sisters stop talking, break up a family, because you want a part of the father you both loved so dearly?! That's some great way to show your love."

She didn't stop there.

I went home and had a good cry. I always prided myself on being a straight thinker. In my heart, I knew that what my friend was saying was straight.

My sister and I had been at this for a long time. How exactly was I going to back down?

I picked up the phone to call my sister before I could change my mind. I apologized for the unkind things I had been saying, and told her that the siddur was hers.

I hung up the phone. The world was brighter. I could feel my father smiling down and saying, "Good job."

The *Sefer Chassidim* tells us, "The *neshamah* is aware of the happenings of this world. Thus, fighting among siblings causes great distress to the *neshamos* of deceased parents."

How heartwrenching to see families destroyed because of inheritance. Some sons and daughters will fight until the end, even eating up most of their inheritance in lawyers' fees.

Is this the way to express gratitude to parents — by causing *tza'ar* to their *neshamah,* and shaming them in Heaven because of the quarreling of children and the many transgressions it involves? [34]

What an injustice to the Almighty, Who blessed parents with enough wealth to keep them comfortable in their lifetime, and still have enough left to apportion to descendants.

Unfortunately, it is not uncommon, upon the passing of a parent, to see quarreling among siblings concerning the division of the inheritance. As our *sefarim* tell us, the *neshamah* has no peace when children are quarreling. Therefore, if there is a difference of opinion among the siblings or the widow, all parties involved should, without delay, present their claim to a *talmid chacham*, expert in these laws, so that peace can be quickly restored.[35]

Just as we have an obligation to lessen their distress during their lifetime, we should make an effort to lessen their distress after their passing, especially since it is primarily in *our* hands to do so.

> If a child pursues an unworthy path, he surely disgraces his parents in the Next World.
>
> If a child's deeds are worthy, he brings honor to his parent, both in this world and the next. In this world, people would admire his parent for raising such upright offspring, and in the Higher Realms, he will be honored by the Almighty Himself.
>
> Then, the Almighty will have compassion on the parent (in the merit of his child). He will be given a place of honor (*Zohar, Bechukosai*).[36]

Chessed

By performing acts of *chessed*, we awaken the Divine attributes of *chessed* and *rachamim* (compassion) in Heaven, and Hashem "uses" that compassion measure for measure for the benefit of our parent's *neshamah*. The deceased is then spared the trials of judgment and merits an *aliyah* to *Gan Eden* and within *Gan Eden*.[37]

Interest-free loans

The Chofetz Chaim stresses the great merit of providing interest-free loans.[38] A lending fund, where loans are given on a continual basis, provides a flow of merit for the deceased parent.

> A person should establish a loan fund. Since each and every loan is a mitzvah of the Torah, and each and every loan is a benefit to his parents, in this way he will enable the *neshamah* to rise to great heights.

Gemach

A *gemach* (lending fund) can also include items that are a benefit to the community. Anyone can start his own *gemach l'ilui nishmas* a parent, providing ongoing merit with each lending.[39]

"SO WHAT DO YOU THINK? Any ideas?" is what my mother asked me a few weeks after her father, Zeidy Berman, passed away.

"I have something in mind," I answered. *"But let me run it by Penina. She'll be very involved in this decision."* I told my mother I'd get back to her the next day.

After the shivah for her father, my mother was very intent on doing whatever she could for her father's merit. She herself initiated several projects. The phone call for suggestions of ideas was made to each of my sisters and brothers. My mother asked each of us to house a gemach dedicated to Zeidy's memory. We considered the many different options and then made our decisions based on what was suitable for our households.

I decided on a bed gemach (lending folding beds free of charge), based on several considerations. First, I had available storage space. Second, our community in Elad needed it, and third, no other gemach of beds existed in our area.

If you're not familiar with the concept of a gemach, I'll tell you what it means and how it's run. The word gemach is an acronym for gemilus chessed. It's a free lending service to benefit people who need anything from a portacrib to a wheelchair, from a blood pressure monitor to a loudspeaker or a projector, or an apartment close to a hospital. It involves an initial outlay of money and continued availability to borrowers. But most of all, you need good will and a ready smile.

Once we decided on the bed gemach, we put in an order for twenty-five beds. The legs fold, so the beds can be stacked like boards. Our storage area is 6 x 15 feet. I organized all of our personal belongings in 1/3 of the area, and the 25 beds and 25 mattresses stand vertically in the other 2/3's.

In addition, we bought a large dolly to help the borrowers transport the beds from the storage room to their car, or even directly home for those who live nearby. We then ordered 25 small metal plates, which we attached to each bed, and one large one for the door of the storeroom, which read: *"This gemach is dedicated l'ilui nishmas Reb Aryeh Leib Berman."*

We advertised in our local phone directory, which has a special section for gemachim, specifying our hours — evenings and Fridays. Then we swung into action.

Word spread quickly. Calls came in, and soon we became quite well known.

Now almost every week, all 25 beds are out on loan. All week long people call to reserve the number of beds they want and the day they would like them. While some people take beds for weekdays, most of the callers want one or more for Shabbos when they host guests. That means most of the people pick up the beds on Friday, leaving an open check as security. The rule is, the bed should be returned by Monday, or whenever they're finished using it.

Beds are needed not only on happy occasions. Over the last 10 years, during the difficult time of ongoing missile attacks, Elad has hosted people fleeing from both the north and the south of Israel. Having to evacuate their homes to a city in the center of the country, they arrived in Elad to stay with relatives or friends.

The whole family — me, my wife, and the children old enough to open the storage room to accommodate borrowers — participate in this mitzvah, which is actually counted for two. It's the mitzvah of chessed and also the mitzvah of hachnassas orchim, since borrowers could not do this mitzvah without our beds. Both of these mitzvos are dedicated to Zeidy.

Once, we got a call from a city near Herzliya. "This is Gadi Ben David," the deep voice said. "My friend Ehud told me his cousin got some beds from you. In another six months, I'm making a bar mitzvah. Can you help me out?"

That was a little earlier than usual to put in an order, but I wrote the date on our calendar and told Gadi we would reserve all 25 beds as per his request.

Every month for the next 5 months, Gadi called to make sure our offer was still good.

Finally, the week of the bar mitzvah arrived. Gadi pulled up to our building with a truck. I brought him to the storage room and helped him stack the beds on the dolly. When we finished and all the beds were loaded onto the truck, Gadi thanked me profusely, handed me a check as collateral, and then asked how much he owed.

"No charge," I said with a smile.

"Not even a small charge?" he asked. "I mean…nothing?"

"Just enjoy, and mazel tov on the simchah," I answered, offering a handshake.

Gadi took my hand and shook it…for a long time, all the while looking at me — how can I describe it — totally dumbfounded, not getting it at all.

After a while he released his grip, hesitated a moment, and then blurted out, "Why are you doing this? Why are you working so hard for nothing?"

I motioned him to follow me. We walked over to the door of the storage room. Pointing to the plaque, I said, "That's why I'm doing it."

He still didn't get it, so I explained that my grandfather had passed away and that I was doing it for an elevation for his soul. "And for me," I told him with a smile, "that's not 'nothing.'"

I walked Gadi back to his truck. We shook hands again. He climbed behind the wheel, and then looked back at me. It seemed like he wanted to say something, but I guess he changed his mind.

With my beds in the back, and probably a lot of questions on his mind, he buckled up, turned the key in the ignition, and drove off.

"Praiseworthy is the person who purchases an item, even a small item, that can benefit the community," says the *Pele Yo'etz*, "and then lends it. With it, he can earn for himself a blessing from the borrower and a blessing from Above."[40]

And a merit for those in whose name it is dedicated.

YOU MIGHT BE ACQUAINTED with the internationally acclaimed organization Yad Sarah. With its headquarters in Jerusalem and 101 branches, it loans out more than 250,000 pieces of medical and rehabilitation equipment every year, has 6,000 people registered as volunteer workers, uses 40 vans, and has an annual operating budget of approximately

$18 million. It is estimated that every second family in Israel has been helped by Yad Sarah at some time.

In addition, it runs day rehabilitation centers, a play center for special children, a geriatric dental clinic, an equipment repair center that handles over 90,000 repairs per year, and offers legal aid to the elderly.

While Yad Sarah is probably the biggest free loan service in the world, are you familiar with its humble beginnings and the origin of its name?

When former Jerusalem mayor R' Uri Lupolianski was a young man, he purchased a vaporizer for his sick child. It took a chunk of his modest salary, so when he finished using it, he felt it would be a waste to have it sit in storage. Instead, he started lending it out. When people heard that he was lending the machine, he received donations of other medical items. The supply grew.

At first, everything was stored in his home. When that wasn't practical due to space considerations, the equipment was moved to a storage room nearby. As the supply grew to overflow, he was given the use of a small structure on the grounds of Bikur Cholim hospital.

At the time, his father, Jacob Lupolianski, retired and sold his business. He offered to give that money to expand the lending services.

In 1976, Yad Sarah was incorporated as a non-profit organization. It was named for Jacob Lupolianski's mother Sarah. The word "yad," which means hand, is also used to mean "memorial."

Just think! Each and every loan of equipment is a mitzvah in and of itself. Each and every loan is a merit. Yad Sarah is benefiting more than 400,000 people every year while at the same time providing benefit, *nachas ruach,* and continued merit for Sarah Lupolianski, *a"h,* due to her son R' Jacob and her grandson R' Uri, who established and dedicated this fund in her memory.

Even young children can participate in giving merit to parents or grandparents by collecting *siddurim* and *sefarim* in shul and putting them back in the proper place at the end of the day and on Shabbos to facilitate future use.

TORAH STUDY

The most important way to achieve an *aliyah* for a parent's *neshamah* is through Torah learning.[41]

We honor parents posthumously by repeating their *divrei Torah*, particularly when the listeners are inspired.

Another way is to publish or promote a parent's writings.

Still another way is to dedicate a *sefer*. This would include authoring a *sefer* and dedicating it; having a share in publishing or reprinting a *sefer*, and dedicating it; or purchasing a *sefer*, putting in a dedication sticker, and donating it for public learning. Consider donating the *sefarim* owned by your parents to places where they will be learned from.

In addition, one could promote Torah learning by delivering a *shiur* or sponsoring a lecture or event.

Among the most important ways of honoring a parent posthumously are setting aside times for learning (קוֹבֵעַ עִתִּים לַתּוֹרָה); increasing the time we are already learning; supporting *talmidei chachamim* who will learn *l'ilui nishmas* (saying out loud, "This learning is dedicated to..."); and supporting yeshivos.

Torah learning in a group setting generates more *zechus* for the deceased since a group doing a mitzvah is greater than an individual. When at least ten men assemble for *limud haTorah*, it is a tremendous *aliyah* for the *neshamah*.

Learning Mishnayos

Mishnah study has a special power to bring merit to the *neshamah*. The letters of *Mishnah* and *neshamah* are the same, alluding to the unique ability of *Mishnah* study to elevate the *neshamah*.

Our greatest Rabbanim asked their descendants to learn *Mishnayos* for them after they passed on.

It is recorded that when his wife passed away, the Steipler Gaon instructed his daughters to learn *Pirkei Avos* as a *zechus* of Mishnayos learning for their mother (personally corroborated by his son, Rav Chaim Kanievsky).

Those families who are not able to complete *Mishnayos* themselves can commission a Torah scholar to learn on behalf of the deceased.

Chiddushei Torah

"When a son discovers a new Torah insight (particularly on Shabbos), achieves a clear understanding of his learning, or learns something new, it is a special *zechus* for the *neshamah* of his parent."[42]

A son-in-law can give the same *zechus* to his father-in-law.[43]

The *Yesod VeShoresh HaAvodah* elaborates on the topic of *chiddushei Torah*:

> It seems clear to me that if a person spends some time on Shabbos Kodesh contemplating new ways to improve his service of the Creator in the coming week in order to bring *nachas ruach* to the Almighty, whether it be elevating his thoughts, refraining from improper speech, increasing his diligence in Torah study, improving his concentration in davening or *berachos*, or conducting his business dealings in a scrupulously honest way, it is clear that these plans for improvement are in the category of *chiddushei Torah*.[44]

In this way, both men and women can offer their parents the merit of *chiddushei Torah*.

To create a plan to improve our behavior — can there be a greater "Torah insight" than that?

Additional customs and memorials that benefit the deceased

It is a mitzvah to take care of the **burial needs** of any person, how much the more so for parents. It is the responsibility of the children to **erect a monument**, which is a benefit to the deceased.

Eulogizing the deceased is a *zechus* for the person when we praise him and especially if the listeners learn from his good ways.

Visiting the graveside and saying special prayers brings *nachas ruach* to the deceased.

Lighting a candle for seven days of *shivah*, on each *yartzeit*, and the four times of *Yizkor* brings benefit to the *neshamah*.[45] Some light by the graveside. When the candle is lit, the following should be said: הֲרֵינִי מַדְלִיק נֵר זֶה לִמְנוּחַת וּלְעִלּוּי נִשְׁמַת אָבִי מוֹרִי פב״פ, אִמִּי מוֹרָתִי פב״פ, "I am lighting this candle for the eternal rest and ascent of the soul of my father, my teacher, (Hebrew name son of Hebrew name), or my mother, my teacher, (Hebrew name, daughter of Hebrew name)."

Naming a child after a parent gives *nachas ruach* and benefit to the *deceased*.

All are a fulfillment of the commandment to honor a parent after his passing (מְכַבְּדוֹ בְּמוֹתוֹ).*

Observing the yartzeit
(the yearly marking of the day of passing)

At the time of the first *yartzeit*, the *neshamah* resides in *Gan Eden*. At that time, and on every subsequent *yartzeit*, the *neshamah* stands in judgment once again, with an opportunity to move to higher levels in *Gan Eden*, based on the continued merits engendered by his life's accomplishments and the merits of his offspring that have been credited to him.[46] Therefore, especially on that day, a child should do as much as possible to help his parent achieve an *aliyah* in *Gan Eden*.

Before any act done on behalf of a parent, it is proper to state explicitly that this is being done to give merit to *avi mori* _____ *ben* _____ (my father, my teacher, _____ son of _____) or *imi morasi* _____*bas*_____ (my mother, my teacher, _____ daughter of _____). Or, at the commencement of the *yartzeit* day to say, "I am dedicating all the *maasim tovim* (good deeds) I do today for the *zechus* (merit) of (include here the name of the parent)."[47]

What are some of the ways that we can benefit a parent on a *yartzeit*?

---

* For a complete guide to mourning, see *Mourning in Halachah* (ArtScroll/Mesorah).

❖ *Tefillos.* These begin the Shabbos before the *yartzeit*. Some sons have the custom to be called for *Maftir* and/or lead the *Mussaf tefillah*. Some customarily lead the *tefillos*, beginning from *Kabbalas Shabbos* through (and including) *Maariv* of Motza'ei Shabbos.[48]

On the day of the *yartzeit*, the one who has *yartzeit* says *Kaddish*, and if possible leads the davening for all three *tefillos*, including *Keil malei rachamim*.

❖ Learning *Mishnayos*

❖ Making a *siyum* and/or a *seudah* upon completion of *Mishnayos*

❖ Giving or organizing *shiurim* for the merit of the deceased

❖ Increasing charity contributions

❖ Lighting a *yartzeit* candle

❖ Visiting the graveside

❖ Supplying a *"tikkun"* after the morning *tefillah*. The mourner provides the congregation with beverages and cake. The numerous accompanying blessings and *Amens* are a merit for the deceased.

❖ Fasting[49]

❖ Since the deceased undergoes judgment every year on the *yartzeit*, it is proper for a child to direct his thoughts as to how he can benefit his parents with minimum distractions and maintain a proper demeanor befitting the day.

> A child who sincerely wants to honor his father and mother should involve himself in Torah and good deeds because that is the greatest honor to his parents, when people say how fortunate is he/she to have raised such a child... (*Kitzur Shulchan Aruch*).[50]

Double benefits

Every mitzvah that a child performs after his parent's passing is a benefit to his parents. Therefore, besides being credited with the mitzvah itself, he is also fulfilling the mitzvah of *kibbud av va'eim*.

For every one mitzvah performed, he reaps the benefits of having performed two mitzvos.

This is even if he has no intention. Yet, with intention to benefit, the deed is more valuable. The following text is given to us by the *Pele Yo'etz*:

טוֹב שֶׁיְּהֵא שָׁגוּר בְּפִיו לוֹמַר מִדֵּי יוֹם:

How good it is for a child to say the following text each day:

יְהִי רָצוֹן מִלְּפָנֶיךָ ה' אֱלֹקֵינוּ וֵאלֹקֵי אֲבוֹתֵינוּ שֶׁתְּקַבֵּל בְּרַחֲמִים וּבְרָצוֹן כָּל מַעֲשֶׂה הַטּוֹב אֲשֶׁר אֲנִי עוֹשֶׂה בֵּין בְּמַחְשָׁבָה בֵּין בְּדִבּוּר בֵּין בְּמַעֲשֶׂה וְיִהְיֶה הַכֹּל לִזְכוּת וְלִמְנוּחַת וּלְעִלּוּי נֶפֶשׁ רוּחַ וּנְשָׁמָה שֶׁל אָבִי/וְאִמִּי/ וְחָמִי/וַחֲמוֹתִי וכו׳. יְהִי רָצוֹן שֶׁתְּהֵא נַפְשׁוֹ צְרוּרָה בִּצְרוֹר הַחַיִּים.

May it be Your will, Hashem, our G-d, and G-d of our fathers, to accept with compassion every good deed that I do, whether it be in thought, in speech, or in action. May all the good that I do serve as merit, eternal rest and ascent for the soul of (insert names of parents/in-laws). May his/their soul be bound up in the bond of life.

וּבָזֶה יִשָּׂא בְרָכָה מֵאֵת ה' וּמִנֶּפֶשׁ הוֹרָיו.

By saying this we will be blessed by the Almighty and by our parents in Heaven.[51]

I'D HEARD THAT IT IS a great comfort for the soul to have family members close by at the time of passing, so I was glad that my brothers and I were all there together to say Vidui and Shema at our father's bedside during his last moments.

I wasn't ready to let him go. I still had a yearning to express my love and appreciation for him. I wanted to find a way to live this year with my father's memory very much alive.

I soon discovered that there were many ways I could continue to honor and care for my father after his death. I decided that during that first year I would devote myself to doing whatever it took to elevate his neshamah.

I'm comforted by the knowledge that while my father was alive I seized the moments and gave him honor and nachas, and consoled that the possibility of continuing to give honor and nachas is not over.

Epilogue
Who Says Children Are for Nachas?

A word to parents

Who says children are for *nachas*?

The question was the title of a speech given by Harav Yaakov Reisman, Mara D'asra of Agudas Yisrael of Long Island. It was given at the *bar mitzvah* celebration of his son, a special needs child. I received his permission to share some of his thoughts.

Rav Reisman told a story he had heard from Harav Moshe Shapiro of Yerushalayim, a true story that took place in Bnei Brak in the early 1950s.

A FATHER WAS AT HOME with his children. His wife was away and he was in charge of his lively brood. A knock at the door and in comes his uncle, who sees his nephew, the father, caring for the children. He is being patient and gentle, doing his best to multi-task.

Surveying the scene, the uncle turns to his nephew and asks, "Do the children realize how devoted you are? Do they realize how much you do for them?"

And then, he hits him with a second question. "When do you think you'll be paid back for this?" ["This," meaning "your devotion." "Being paid back" meaning, "When will you see the fruits of your labor — when will you have nachas?"]

The father paused for a minute, and replied, "B'ezras Hashem, in the years ahead."

But the father was struck by the question. The more he thought about it, the more he realized how unsure he was of the answer. He turned it over in his mind and knew that this question was big. He said to his uncle, "Next week, I'm going to Yerushalayim. I'll go in to the Brisker Rav and ask him."

The following week, he went in to see the great Rav of Brisk and asked his question: "Ven vet men tzurik tzolen? When will a person be paid back [for his years of devotion to his children]?"

The Brisker Rav heard the question and answered, "Di kasha shmekt fun apikorsus — This question is tinged with apikorsus" [meaning, there is something improper about the question itself. It expresses an approach contrary to the Torah].

When the Brisker Rav saw that the father was shaken by the response and confused as to its meaning, he explained with these words:

"Olam chessed yibaneh [Hashem created the world in order to do chessed]."

Rav Reisman went on to discuss the cryptic answer of the Brisker Rav.

We could ask the question, Why did Hashem create a world and all its needs? Before the creation of the world, nothing was lacking. There was no need for benevolence or philanthropy. There were no sick people, no poor people, no brides who needed to get married. Why create a world and all that would be required to sustain its needs? Why not leave things the way they were?

The answer is: דֶּרֶךְ הַטּוֹב לְהֵטִיב — Hashem's essence is hatavah, a desire to bestow kindness. And so He created the entire world, with its rivers, mountains, valleys, continents, vegetation, animals, constellations, jungles, and deep seas — which we will never see or even know about — all to create situations to do chessed.

He created something from nothing in order to do chessed.

What is the closest we can come to emulating this attribute of Hashem, "creating something from nothing to do chessed"?

In truth, we usually are not creating situations for chessed. *Mostly, the need is there. People come to us and we try to be helpful, or we go to places where there is a need. I agree to put myself in a position to do* chessed, *but the need is already there.*

But to create a situation for no other reason than to do chessed? *Where do we see that most clearly?*

Children.

Before there was nothing, and then we created a situation where we must do chessed.

That's what the Brisker Rav meant when he told the yungerman *that day in Yerushalayim, "Olam chessed yibaneh." Who says there has to be a payback? Children give us the opportunity to exercise the* middah *of* chessed. *They are not for payback.*

Rav Reisman continued:

Does Hashem have nachas *from us?*

Do we see a direct correlation between Hashem's chessed *and the* nachas *He has from the recipients of this* chessed? *Do we see that if we get more, we give back more?*

Lamentably, we often do not.

The sefer Tomer Devorah *tells us: Without Hashem, we can't do anything. All our abilities are only because Hashem gave them to us. Our hand moves because Hashem allows us to move. We can only speak because of the ability Hashem gave us and continues to give. And yet, we take the abilities that Hashem gives and misuse them. At any moment, He could take that ability away. Yet He doesn't, hoping that we will reconsider and improve. Hashem continues giving to us, even when we disappoint Him, even when we use His gifts* to go against His will! Even though He sometimes has no nachas, He keeps on giving. And He says, מַה אֲנִי אַף אַתָּה — "Copy me. I created, from nothing, a big world, the purpose being to do chessed. You created, with My partnership, little worlds [children] from nothing — for the purpose and the opportunity to practice the middah of ahavas chessed. Like My chessed, your chessed should not be contingent upon return.

"Results" are not an obligation. "Having nachas" is not an obligation — it's a gift.

This is true in all areas of our life. For example, we have an obligation to earn a living. We have an obligation to maintain our health. Hashem asks us to make an effort, but who will be wealthy and who will be healthy is totally in His hands. It is not in our power to ensure results. We do, and Hashem decides.

Why would we think otherwise?

Because after the Creation, Hashem asks us to live according to His cause-and-effect laws that govern the world. We have to act as if everything depends on our actions, while realizing that nothing does.

Generally, we do not think this applies to raising children. Yet the Gemara (Moed Katan 28a) tells us: חַיֵּי בְּנֵי וּמְזוֹנֵי לֹא בִּזְכוּתָא תַּלְיָא מִילְתָא אֶלָּא בְּמַזְּלָא תַּלְיָא מִילְתָא — Life [who will be born, and how long they will live], children [who will be blessed with them and if they will be a source of nachas] and sustenance, do not depend on the efforts we make, but on Hashgachah Pratis (Divine Providence).[1]

We are obligated to put into our children everything we have. Will there be nachas? That's up to Hashem.

This is the message Rav Reisman conveyed on that bar mitzvah morning.

Meriting the gift of nachas

If nachas is a gift from Hashem, is there anything we can do to merit this gift? What is considered a worthy effort?

This question was posed to the Steipler Gaon. His answer was: *tefillah* (prayer) and *dugma* (personal example).

Tefillah

Rav Mattisyahu Solomon, the Lakewood Mashgiach, writes about the importance of *tefillah* in raising children in his *sefer*, *With Hearts Full of Love*:

> Of course, there is also a place for ideas and strategies [in *chinuch*], but it all begins with *tefillah* — a sincere and heartfelt *tefillah*... We have to make our *hishtadlus* — an effort toward achieving our goals — but we have to realize that the actual achievement of those goals is entirely in the hands of the *Ribbono shel Olam*...
>
> If we want success, we have to daven for it with all our heart...

Great leaders throughout the generations were posed this same question:

The Chasam Sofer was asked in what merit he raised a Ksav Sofer. He answered: "Do you know how many tears I shed for my son's success?"

When the Brisker Rav was asked the same question about his progeny, he answered, "*Tehillim* and tears."

And when they asked the Steipler Gaon himself for a *berachah* for success in raising children, he answered, "Daven! Until this day, I daven for my son's success." At that time, his son, Reb Chaim Kanievsky, was 52 years old!

The Chofetz Chaim was known to say:

> Success with children is 100 percent *siyata d'Shmaya* (Heavenly assistance). One must expend maximum effort so that after 120 years, when he appears before the Heavenly tribunal, he may legitimately claim that he tried his best.
>
> Ultimately, however, it is all from Hashem. Therefore, one must continually pray for the spiritual success of his children.

Personal example

Dugma (דּוּגְמָא) means being an example of what we want our children to be. *Chinuch* is not what we preach, it's who we are.

If we want our children to be honest, we ourselves must be scrupulously honest. If we want our children to be generous, the best way is for them to see generosity in all its glory — from us.[2]

If we want our children to understand what honor and reverence for parents really means, they should watch us hosting, visiting, calling, rising, not contradicting, showing gratitude, and the many other facets of this mitzvah. Nowadays, we complain that children are ungrateful. Are *we* sufficiently grateful?

Rav Chaim Volozhin explains that Avraham Avinu was given ten tests. Each test was given to set a path for us, i.e., to make it easier for subsequent generations to pass similar tests.

What the Avos strived for with great sacrifice will be implanted in their descendants and can be acquired with a small effort (בְּקְצָת יְגִיעָה).

Whatever a parent does with *mesiras nefesh* is implanted in his children. They will be able to access this with minimal effort.[3]

We can't force our children to give us *nachas*. And there is no way that we can forcibly pull this gift of *nachas* from Hashem. But we can show our children what it looks like (דּוּגְמָא) by giving it to our own parents, and we can daven (תְּפִילָה) that the lesson is passed from generation to generation.

Appendix A

Outline of 34 Se'ifim —
Shulchan Aruch, Yoreh Deah

Siman 240:1-25

Se'if 1 — The two major obligations of honor and reverence and their severity
Se'if 2 — Parameters of reverence—a parent's place, name, and statement
Se'if 3 — How far must we go to fulfill the mitzvah of reverence?
Se'if 4 — Defining the parameters of כְּבוּד בְּמַעֲשֶׂה, pleasant assistance
Se'if 5 — Child's financial responsibility to parents
Se'if 6 — Honoring in speech
Se'if 7 — Obligation to stand
Se'if 8 — How far does the obligation of honor go? (parents who have caused a child a loss)
Se'if 9 — Posthumous honor
Se'if 10 — Care of parents suffering from mental illness
Se'if 11 — How to correct a parent
Se'if 12 — Availability
Se'if 13 — Conflicts between learning Torah and caring for parents
Se'if 14 — Conflict of interests between father and mother
Se'if 15 — When a parent's request would require a violation of the Torah
Se'if 16 — If parents tell a child not to visit, speak to, or forgive someone
Se'if 17 — Obligations of married, divorced, or widowed women
Se'if 18 — Are filial responsibilities subject to the fluctuation of parental virtue?
Se'if 19 — Advice to parents
Se'if 20 — Parameters of punishing children
Se'if 21 — Honor due stepparents
Se'if 22-23 — Honoring older siblings/eldest brother
Se'if 24 — Honor due in-laws and grandparents
Se'if 25 — When parental preferences are binding and when not

Siman 241:1-9

Se'if 1 — Cursing parents
Se'if 2-5 — Striking parents (medical treatment)
Se'if 6 — Demeaning or belittling parents
Se'if 7-9 — Problems of questionable lineage

Classic Rabbinical Sources Quoted

R' Shlomo Yitzchaki (*Rashi*) — France (1040-1105)

R' Moshe ben Maimon (*Rambam*) — Spain/Egypt (1135-1204)

R' Yehuda HaChassid (*Sefer Chassidim*) — Germany (1150-1217)

Rabbeinu Bachya ben Asher (*Kad HaKemach*) — Spain (1263-1340)

R' Menachem HaMeiri — Spain (1249-1306)

Rabbeinu Yona Gerondi (*Shaarei Teshuvah*) — Spain (d. 1263)

R' Aharon HaLevi (*Sefer HaChinuch*) — Barcelona (c. 1235-1290)

R' Levi ben Gershom (*Ralbag*) — France (1288-1344)

R' Yitzchak Alnakava (*Menoras HaMaor*) — Spain (d.1391)

R' Yitzchak Abarbanel — Spain/Italy (1437-1508)

R' Yehuda Kaltz (*Sefer HaMussar* published 1537) — Turkey (c. 1500)

R' Yosef Karo (*Shulchan Aruch*) — Spain/Tzefas (1488-1575)

R' Moshe Isserlis (*Rema*) — Poland (1525-1572)

R' Elazar Azkari (*Sefer Chareidim*) — Tzefas (1533-1600)

R' Yeshaya HaLevi Hurvitz (*Shelah HaKadosh*) — Poland/Frankfurt/Prague/Jerusalem (1560-1630)

R' Chaim ibn Attar (*Ohr HaChaim*) — Morocco/Jerusalem (1696-1743)

R' Moshe Chaim Luzzatto (*Ramchal/Mesillas Yesharim*) — Italy/Acre (1707-1746)

R' Chaim Palagi (*Tochachas Chaim*) — Turkey (1788-1869)

R' Alexander Ziskind (*Yesod VeShoresh HaAvodah)* — Lithuania (d. 1794)

R' Moshe Sofer (*Chasam Sofer*) — Hungary (1762-1839)

R' Eliezer Pappo (*Pele Yo'etz*) — Bulgaria (1785-1828)

R' Avrohom Danzig (*Chayei Adam*) — Vilna (1747-1820)

R' Yechiel Epstein (*Aruch HaShulchan*) — Lithuania (1835-1905)

R' Shamshon Raphael Hirsch — Germany (1808-1886)

R' Yisrael Meir Kagan (*Chofetz Chaim*) — Radin (1839-1933)

R' Meir Simcha HaCohen (*Meshech Chochmah*) — Dvinsk (1843-1926)

Bibliography

Otzar Kibbud Av Va'eim, Rav Tzuriel Taasah, תשס"ט

Vayevarech Dovid, Rav Yisroel Dovid Harfenes, תשס"ה

Mora Horim V'Kibbudam, Rav Naftali Shmuel Yona, תשנ"ב

Simchas Naftali: Maalas Kibbud Horim, Rav Naftalia Shmuel Yona, תשנ"ח

Kibbud Horim B'Halachah U'b'aggadah, Rav Zev Greenwald, תשס"ג

Kibbud Av Va'eim, Rav Yaakov Pinchas Feldman, תש"מ

Kibbud Horim, Rav Moshe A. Peniri, תשמ"ו

Ben Yechabed Av, Rav Yoel Shvartz, תש"מ

Lema'an Ya'arichun Yamecha, Rav Mordechai Shlomo Apter, תשע"א

Meah Shearim, Rav Eliyahu Capsali

The *sefer Meah Shearim* was written over 500 years ago by the Kabbalist and historian, Eliyahu Capsali (1490-1550).

Rav Capsali was Chief Rabbi of Candiah, in the Greek Aisles. He was acknowledged as a leading Torah authority of his times, and his influence stretched far and wide. He was a prolific writer of halachah, *aggadah*, *kabbalah* and ethics. He had an extensive library (which was destroyed) and had knowledge of little-known Midrashic sources.

Meah Shearim was the only major work written exclusively on honoring parents until recent times. His works remained in manuscript form until recently. It was published for the first time from the manuscript with source notes and commentary, introductions and indexes by Rabbi Avraham Shoshana, Ofeq Institute, Jerusalem 5761.

Kimah V'Hiddur, Rav Yitzchak Eliyahu Stesman, תשע"א

Veyikarei Shemo B'Yisrael, Rav Avraham Levi, תשס"ח

The Fifth Commandment, Rav Moshe Leiber, Artscroll/Mesorah, 1998

Appreciating Parents, Rabbi Moshe Goldberger, 1987

Mourning in Halachah, Rabbi Chaim Binyamin Goldberg, Artscroll/Mesorah 1991.

Glossary

a"h — acronym for *alav hashalom* — peace unto him

abba — father

acharonim — later authoritative commentators on the Talmud (16th century to the present)

agunah — a woman whose unresolved marital status prevents her from remarrying

ahavah — love

ahavas chessed — love of kindness

alav hashalom — peace unto him

aliyah [pl. *aliyos*] — being called up to the Torah (in the synagogue)

amei ha'aretz — unlearned people

Amen — "So be it" — the word recited after hearing a blessing or *Kaddish*

arichus yamim — lengthened days

Aseres HaDibros — The 10 Commandments

avak lashon hara — a tinge of derogatory, hurtful speech; a statement that can lead to actual *lashon hara*

Avi Hayesomim — Father of orphans

avi mori — my father, my teacher

Avodah — (1) the service of G-d, whether in sacrifice, prayer or self-refinement; (2) work, effort

ayin tovah — a good eye; a positive outlook

azus — impudence

b'dieved — after the fact (not preferable)

B'ezras Hashem — with Hashem's help

b'hiddur — by enhancing; beautifying

b'seiver panim yafos — with an interested, pleasant face

baal koreh — one who reads the weekly Torah portion aloud at prayer services

baal simchah [pl. *baalei simchah*] — host(s) of a joyous occasion

badchan — [Yid.] — one who amuses those gathered for a joyous occasion with humorous verses and antics

balabus [Yid.] — master of the house

balabusta — the woman of the house; a capable housewife

baraisa — statements of Tannaim not included in the Mishnah.

bar mitzvah — the occasion at which a 13-year-old boy becomes responsible for observing the Commandments

baruch Hashem — Blessed is G-d; thank G-d

bayis ne'eman — a loyal home (referring to loyalty to the Almighty)

be'er — source of water

bechor — firstborn son

bein adam laMakom — between man and the Almighty

bein adam lachaveiro — between man and his fellow

beis din — rabbinic court

beis din shel maalah — The Heavenly Court

beis medrash — study hall

berachah [pl. *berachos*] — blessing(s)

bimah — platform in the synagogue on which the Torah is opened and read

Bircas HaMazon — the blessings recited after eating a bread meal

Birkas Kohanim — The Priestly Blessing — recited by Kohanim on holidays in the Diaspora, and daily in the Land of Israel

bli ayin hara — may there be no [effect from an] "evil eye."

brit / bris [pl. *brissin*] — circumcision(s)

bubby/bobba [Yid.] — grandmother

chagim — holidays

chalav Yisrael — milk that has been supervised by a Jew from the time of milking

challah — special bread (usually braided) eaten on Sabbath and Festivals

chametz — leavened food, forbidden to Jews on Passover

chanoch lana'ar al pi darko — educating a child according to his needs

chas veshalom — G-d forbid

chassan — bridegroom

chashuveh [Yid.]—important

chavrusa — learning partner

Chazal — our Sages of blessed memory

chazarah — review (of studies)

chessed [pl. *chassadim*] — act(s) of kindness

chiddushei Torah — original Torah insights

Chinuch — Jewish education or upbringing

chiyuv — obligation

Chol HaMoed — the intermediate days of the Passover and Succos holidays

Chumash — the Five Books of Moses

chumrah [pl. *chumros*] — stringency

chuppah — canopy under which a Jewish marriage ceremony takes place

chushuveh balabus [Yid.] — respected layman

chutzpadik — insolent

daas Torah — Torah outlook or perspective; a determination made by Torah Sages

daven / davened [Yid.] — pray(ed)

Dayeinu — a passage from the *Haggadah* of the Passover Seder

der heim [Yid.] (lit. "in the home") — the way things were done in the "old country"

derech eretz — proper conduct

din — law, justice

din Torah — a case brought to a Rabbinic court for adjudication

dinar — coin used in Talmudic times

divrei chachmah — words of wisdom

divrei Torah — words of Torah

dugma — example

eineklach [Yid.] — grandchildren

emunah — faith

ephod — one of the garments of the High Priest

Eretz Yisrael — the Land of Israel

erev — the day before (i.e., Shabbos or a Festival)

esrog — citron; one of the Four Species taken on the holiday of Succos

fargin [Yid.] — to take joy in the success of others

Gan Eden — the Garden of Eden

gartel [Yid.] — belt (a long, sash-like belt customarily worn by some Jewish men when praying)

gedolei Yisrael — great Rabbis

Gemara kop [Yid.] — a good head for understanding Gemara

gemilus chessed [pl. *gemilus chassadim*] — performing/bestowing an act/acts of kindness

get — certificate of Jewish divorce

Geulah — the Future Redemption

hachnassas orchim — (the mitzvah of) hospitality

hadlakas neiros — lighting candles

Haftarah — weekly portion of Prophets/Writings read after the weekly Torah Portion in the synagogue

Hagaddah — prayer book for the Seder Night

HaKadosh Baruch Hu — the Holy One, Blessed is He

hakaras hatov — gratitude

Halachah — Jewish law

Hashgachah Pratis — Divine Providence

hashgachah — supervision; Providence

hatavah — kindness; an act done for the benefit of another

Havdalah — prayer recited at the conclusion of the Sabbath and Festivals

hiddur mitzvah — enhancing/beautifying a mitzvah

hilchos lashon harah — the laws of proper speech

hishtadlus — effort

ikar — the main thing/the thing of primary importance

ima — mother

imi morasi —my mother, my teacher

ir eineklach [Yid.] — great-grandchildren

Kabbalas Shabbos — the traditional prayer recited at the beginning of the Sabbath service on Friday evening

kabbed es avicha v'es imecha — honor your father and your mother (the Fifth Commandment)

Kaddish — the Mourner's Prayer

kallah — bride

kasher — to make kosher

kashrus — kosher status of a food

kavod — honor

kavod veyiras av va'eim — honor and deference for a father and mother

kavod veyiras Hashem — honor and awe of the Almighty

kedoshim — holy ones, martyrs

kedushah — holiness

kehillah — community

kibbud (pl. *kibbudim*) — honor(s)

kibbud av — honoring one's father

kibbud av va'eim — honoring one's father and mother

kibbud eim — honoring one's mother

kibbud horim — honoring one's parents

kimpeturin — a woman who recently gave birth

kinderlach [Yid.] — children

Kisei HaKavod — the Heavenly Throne

kittel [Yid.] — a white coat-like garment worn on certain solemn occasions/Jewish holidays

kivrei tzaddikim — the graves of righteous individuals

Klal Yisrael — the Jewish People

Kodesh Kedoshim — Holy of Holies (in the Temple)

Kohanim — members of the Priestly family of the tribe of Levi

korban [pl. *korbanos*] — sacrificial offering(s)

krechtzing [Yid.] — sighing

krias haTorah — reading of the Torah (in the synagogue)

kvell / kvelled [Yid.] — to delight in

l'chaim — "to life" — given as a blessing

l'ilui nishmas — for the elevation of the soul

l'ilui nishmaso — for the elevation of his soul

l'sheim Shamayim — for the sake of Heaven

landsman [Yid.] — fellow countryman

lashon hara — derogatory, damaging speech

lashon hara l'toeles — negative information spoken for a constructive purpose (according to halachic parameters)

lechatchilah — the preferable manner of doing something; a priori

leibedige [Yid.] — lively

Leil HaSeder — the Seder Night

Leil Shabbos — Friday night

leining — Torah reading (in the synagogue)

lekavod Shabbos — in honor of the Sabbath

levayah — funeral

licht bentching [Yid.] — lighting the Sabbath lights

limud zechus — judging favorably

luchos — The Tablets of the Covenant on which the Ten Commandments were inscribed

lulav — palm branch, one of the Four Species taken on the holiday of Succos

maalos — virtues

Maariv — the Evening Prayer

maasim tovim — good deeds

machateneste [Yid.] — the mother-in-law of your child

machlokes — argument

machnisei orchim — inviting guests

machshavah — thought

Maftir — concluding section of the Torah reading

maggid shiur — Torah teacher

makpid — strict; particular

mara d'asra — Rabbi; leader of a community

mashal — parable

matzeivah — tombstone

mazel tov — congratulations

mazhinka [Yid.] — youngest child

mechabed — honor

mechilah — forgiveness

mechubadig — honorable

mekayem — fulfill

melachah [pl. melachos] — (39 types of) work done during construction of the Tabernacle, which are the basis for the types of work prohibited to the Jewish People on the Sabbath

melamed — teacher of Torah subjects

menachem avel — comforting a mourner

mentchen [Yid.] — people

mesiras nefesh — self-sacrifce

mesorah — heritage

metza'er — pain

michshol — stumbling block

middah [pl. middos] — character trait

middas chassidus — a commendable approach, but beyond the minimum requirement

Midrash — the Sages' homiletical teachings

milchig [Yid.] — dairy

minhag [pl. minhagim]—custom(s)

minyan — quorum of ten men necessary for conducting a prayer service

Mishnah (pl. Mishnayos) — teachings of the Tannaim that form the basis of the Talmud

mitzvah [pl. mitzvos] — commandment; good deed

mitzvah d'Oraisa — a Biblical commandment

mitzvah tantz [Yid.] — a special dance performed at a wedding's conclusion

Modeh ani — prayer recited upon awakening in the morning, expressing gratitude for life

Moreinu — our Teacher

mosdos — institutions

Motza'ei Shabbos — the evening following Shabbos (Saturday night)

Mussaf tefillah — additional prayer recited after Shacharis on the Sabbath, Rosh Chodesh, and Festivals

mussar — ethical teachings aimed at self-refinement

nachas / *nachat* — pleasure

Navi — prophet

neshamah [pl. *neshamos*]—soul

nisyonos — tests, challenges

Oma — grandmother

Opa — grandfather

ona'ah — afflicting

ona'as devarim — causing pain with words

ona'as mamon — monetary fraud

parashah — the weekly Torah reading

pasken — to render a halachic decision

pasuk — Torah verse

pekalach [Yid.] — small packages (in context: packages of troubles/hardships)

petirah — demise

Pirkei Avos — Ethics of the Fathers

pirkei Tehillim — chapters of *Psalms*

poseik (pl. *poskim*) — halachic authority (authorities)

potch [Yid.] — slap

pushka [Yid.] — box (for charity donations)

Rabbanim — Rabbis

rachamei Shamayim — Heavenly compassion

rachamim — compassion

rachmanus — mercy

rasha — evil person

ratzon — will

ratzon Hashem — Will of G-d

rechilus — telling A what B said or did to him, thereby causing ill will between them for no halachically condoned reason

redifas shalom — pusuing peace

refuah sheleimah — a complete recovery

Ribbono shel Olam — Master of the World, i.e., G-d

rocheil — one who speaks *rechilus*

Rosh Chodesh — first day of the Jewish lunar month

Rosh Yeshivah — dean of a Torah institution

ruach hakodesh — Divine Inspiration

ruchniyus — spirituality

saba — grandfather

sandak — the honor of holding the baby during a circumcision

savta — grandmother

schlemiel [Yid.] — a clumsy person

sechel — intelligence

sefer [pl. *sefarim*]— book (Jewish topic)

Sefer Torah — handwritten scroll of the Five Books of Moses

segulah — spiritual remedy; auspicious omen

seudah — meal, especially on festive occasions

Shabbasos — pl. Sabbath

shadchan — matchmaker

sheifaleh [Yid.] — an endearing term (lit., little lamb)

shailos — questions on Jewish law

shaliach tzibbur — leader of the prayers; cantor

shalom — peace

Shalom Aleichem — "Peace be upon you"—a greeting; hymn song before the meal on Friday night

shalom bayis — domestic harmony

Shalosh Regalim — The 3 Festivals (Passover, Shavuos, Succos)

shamash — attendant

Shamayim — Heaven

Shas — the Talmud as a whole

Shavuos — the festival celebrating the giving of the Torah on Mt. Sinai

Shechinah — Divine Presence

Sheloshim — the 30-day period of mourning for a close family member

Shema — recitation of "Hear O Israel, the L-rd our G-d, the L-rd is One"

shemiras halashon — watching one's

tongue (from forbidden speech)

shep nachas [Yid.] — have pleasure

sheva berachos / sheva brachot — festive meals honoring the bride and groom during the week after the wedding

shidduch [pl. *shidduchim*] — marital match

shiluach hakan — the mitzvah of sending away the mother bird before taking the eggs from the nest

shiur [pl. *shiurim*] — lecture(s)

shiurei Torah — Torah lectures

shivah — seven-day period of mourning

shlita — acronym — may he live long

shoichet — ritual slaughterer

shomer nafsho — one who guards his soul (from sin)

shtick [Yid.] — fun/amusing things (done at a wedding, to enhance the joy of the bride and groom)

Shulchan Aruch — Code of Jewish Law

shver [Yid.] — father-in-law

siddur (pl. *siddurim*) — prayer book(s)

simanim — the indicative foods listed in the Gemara (*Kerisus* 6a, *Horayos* 12a) that should be eaten on Rosh Hashanah as an auspicious sign for a good year

simchah — joyous celebration

simchah shel mitzvah — the joy of performing a mitzvah

Simchas Torah — Festival of Rejoicing with the Torah

sinas chinam — baseless, unwarranted hatred

siyata d'Shmaya — Heavenly assistance

siyum — completion of a portion of Torah or Talmud; a celebration marking this completion

tachlis hamitzvah — the purpose of the mitzvah

tafkid — task

talmid chacham [pl. *talmidei chachamim*] — Torah scholar

talmud Torah — Torah learning

tefillah [pl. *tefillos*] — prayer(s)

tefillin — phylacteries

Tehillim — Book of *Psalms*

teshuvah — (1) answer; (2) repentance

tikkun — rectification

to'eles — purpose

Torah tzivah lanu Moshe — "Moses commanded the Torah to us" — the first verse that is customarily taught to young children

tza'ar — distress

tza'ar gidul banim — difficulties in raising children

tza'ar rav — great distress

tzedakah — charity

tzibbur — congregation

tznius — modesty

upsherin — the customary first cutting of a boy's hair, upon reaching three years of age

v'ahavta l'reiacha kamocha — "Love thy neighbor as thyself"—a Torah commandment

Yahadus — Judaism

Yamim Tovim — festivals

yehi ratzon — "May it be Your Will..."

yeshivah bachur [pl. *yeshivah bachurim*] — a young man/young men learning in a school where Torah is studied

yetzer hara — evil inclination

Yiddishkeit [Yid.] — Judaism

yirah — reverence; awe

yiras av va'eim — reverence to parents

Yiras Shamayim — Fear of Heaven

yirei shamayim — those who fear Heaven

Yizkor — Memorial Prayer

Yom Hadin — Day of Judgment

yoshon — refers to products of the five grains from the previous year's crop

zechus / zechut — merit (n); privilege

zeidy [pl. *zeides*] [*Yid.*] — grandfather(s)

zemiros — songs for the Sabbath or Festivals

zerizus — alacrity

zilzul — demeaning

zocheh — merit (v)

zt"l / ztz"l — acronym — *zecher tzaddik l'berachah* — the memory of the righteous person should be a blessing

Endnotes

Chapter 1: Honoring In Deed

1. *Sefer Meah Shearim, Shaar* 15: אלו ששנו חכמים (מאכיל ומשקה וכו') אינם אלא אבות ושרשים, ומהם מסתעפים תולדות וענפים לאלפים ולרבבות ולאין מספר וחקר, והכל לפי מקומו ושעתו ויוליד תולדות מלבו ודעתו

2. This principle is found in *Yevamos* 6a and explained in *Otzar Kibbud Av Va'eim* 126

3. *Mitzvos HaTeshuvah*, quoted in *Kibbud Av Va'eim* (Rav Y.P. Feldman): וראוי לבן להטעים לאביו ואמו מטעמים כאשר אהב

4. *Otzar Kibbud Av Va'eim* 125: וכל שימוש ושימוש שעושה מקיים מצות עשה בפני עצמו

5. *Otzar Kibbud Av Va'eim* 128: אפילו אחרים ישמשוהו ואם כן אינו חסר דבר מכל מקום עליו המצוה לכבד

6. *Mechilta, Parashas Yisro:* לכבדו בכסות נקיה
   Vayevarech Dovid, p. 71: שעל הבן להשתדל שכסות הורים יהיו נקיים

7. *Yerushalmi Peah* 1:3, *Kiddushin* 1:7

8. *Mora Horim V'Kibbudam* 1:15: ובכלל זה שידאג להם לחימום חורף

9. *Kiddushin* 31b

10. *Sefer HaMussar* of Rabbeinu Yehuda Kaltz, Chapter 5: חייב לתת או לשכור להם בית דירה הראויה

11. *Vayevarech Dovid*, p. 73: כסות נקיה ומסתבר שבכלל זה לנקות ולסדר ביתם גם הוא בכלל עשית צרכיהם דאם הוא לא יעשום יתאמצו הם לעשותו

12. *Vayevarech Dovid*, p. 79

13. *Otzar Kibbud Av Va'eim* 141

14. *Appreciating Parents*, Rav Moshe Goldberger, p. 12

15. *Sefer Chareidim* 12:1: חייב לכבדם בגופו... ובממונו ולהאכילם ולהשקותם ולעשות כל צרכיהם כעבד...

16. *Rambam, Peirush on Mishnayos, Kiddushin* 29: מצות הבן על האב הרבה מלהביאם בכאן. והענין ארוך מאד, אבל כולל אותן שני עקרים מורא וכבוד, ומסרו לנו מהם דוגמא ואמרו מורא לא ישב במקומו ולא עמד במקומו ולא סותר דבריו. כבוד מאכיל משקה מלביש מכסה מכניס ומוציא. ואלו כולם והנגרר אחריהם מחוייב על הבנים ועל הבנקות כולם שיעשו אותם לאביהם

17. *Vayevarech Dovid, She'eilos U'Teshuvos, Siman* 55

18. *Sefer Chassidim* 338: דמחויב הבן לעשות כל מלאכה במקום אביו
   Vayevarech Dovid, p. 74: כשיש לאביו חנות או עסק ונזדמן שרבתה עליו המעמסה מחויב הבן לסייע לו בעסקיו להקל עליו הטרחה

19. *Meiri, Kiddushin* 31: שחייב לכבדם כל מיני כבוד... וזהו מן הדברים שאין שיעור למעלה

20. *Chofetz Chaim Al HaTorah, Shemos* 20:12: בכלל כבוד הורים הוא גם לכבד את אלו שההורים מכבדים אותם

21. *Vayevarech Dovid*, p. 80: לכבדם בכניסה שהם יכנסו תחילה

22. *Shemos* 18:7, see verse וישק: Moshe kissed his father-in-law. How much more so a father.

23. *Melachim* 1:19: Elisha was departing to follow Eliyahu HaNavi when he asked permission to return to take leave of his parents and kiss them.

24. *Kibbud Horim* (Rav Peniri), p. 67

25. *Pele Yo'etz, Berachah*: לא יתרשל מלילך בכל ליל שבת ויומו ובחגים לנשק ידיהם ולקבל ברכתם

26. *Otzar Kibbud Av Va'eim* 150, in the name of the Chida

27. *Kibbud Horim* (Rav Peniri), p. 68

28. *Sing You Righteous* §643

Chapter 2:
When It's *Their* Will, *That's* the Way!

1. *Yerushalmi Peah* 1

Chapter 3: Whether Near or Far

1. *Otzar Kibbud Av Va'eim* 130

2. *Sefer Chassidim, Se'if* 575

Chapter 4: Hosting

1. *Menoras HaMaor, Perek Kibbud Av Va'eim*, p. 15

2. Quoted in *Otzar Kibbud Av Va'eim* 136

3. *Kovetz Mevakshei Torah* 21, p. 278, Harav Yosef Shalom Elyashiv: דיש להושיב את אביו (ואמו) במקום היותר מכובד שיש בבית הדין בחמיו, ומכל מקום, אין חיוב בדבר

4. *Vayevarech Dovid*, p. 77

5. Ibid., *She'eilos U'Teshuvos, Siman* 55

6. *Menoras HaMaor, Perek Kibbud Av Va'eim*, p. 15: מוציא כיצד. חייב הבן ללוות לאביו ולאמו ולא יחזור עד שירחקו ממנו כמלוא עיניו

7. *Mora Horim V'Kibbudam* 1:42: מצוה להביאם לביתו ולטפל בהם ועל ידי זה מקיים מצות כבוד אב ואם בכל רגע ורגע (מפי מרן רבינו יוסף שלום אלישיב) והוסיף—שאין חייב בדבר ואינו נקרא עובר על מצות כאו"א אלא מפסיד מצוה שיכול לקיימה בכל רגע ורגע, וזאת בתנאי שימצא להם פתרונות אחרים כפי המבואר

Chapter 5: Visiting Days

1. *Zohar HaKadosh, Parashas Yisro:* כבד את אביך ואת אמך - כבדם בכל מיני כיבוד, שמחם במעשים טובים שנא' יגיל גיל אבי צדיק...

2. *She'eilos U'Teshuvos, Hisorerus HaTeshuvah, Chelek* 4, *Yoreh Deah, Se'if* 9: דממה שמעינו שחייב אדם להקביל פני רבו ברגל משמע שביקור הוא בכלל כיבוד

It is proper for a talmid to visit his primary Rebbe/Rav on a Yom Tov. This is one way to show him honor. From this, we understand that visiting is a way to express *kavod*.

Otzar Kibbud Av Va'eim 135: אבל גבי... אביו ואמו אין לנו מקור מפורש לחייב אלא שיש בזה מצוה קיומית....

Harav Yosef Shalom Elyashiv, *Kovetz Mevakshei Torah* quoted in *Otzar Kibbud Av Va'eim* 471: הורים הרוצים שבניהם יבקרום ונהנים מזה צריך לבקרם משום כבוד אב ואם אפילו אם יש בזה ביטול תורה

3. *Rashi, Bereishis* 46:29: וירא אליו: יוסף נראה אל אביו

4. *Eved HaMelech*, R' Shmuel Houminer, *Shemos* 20:12: שמחה גדולה היא לאב ואם בראותם את בניהם ובפרט אם עבר איזה זמן שלא ראו אותם. ולכן, מן הראוי לבנים בעת שהולכים לראות ולקבל פני אביהם ואמם שיכוונו בזה להתראות לפניהם שיתענגו מהם ולמלא רצונם וחפצם כראוי

5. *Kibbud Av Va'eim* 112, Rav Feldman, quoting Rav M. M. Prag: יש מצוה לקבל פני אביו בכל יום ובכלל מצות כיבוד הוא. זה משום דעצם קבלת הפנים הוי כיבוד אפילו בלי שום שימוש. ואפילו אין אביו מצוווהו על זה, הוא מצוווהו על זה נמי איכא

6. This topic is dealt with in more detail later in this chapter.

7. *Otzar Kibbud Av Va'eim* 135: מ"מ אף שכתבנו שאין חייב קבוע לבקר את הורי מ"מ כתבו הפוסקים שיש חייב ללכת לפרקים לבקר הוריו

8. *Kibbud Horim* (Rav Peniri) 5:6, quoting Harav Yosef Shalom Elyashiv: ובגדר הפעמים שצריך לבקרם איני רואה לדון משום שהכל תלוי לפי הענין. שיש הורים שרוצים בזה יותר ומרגישים פגיעה בכבודם אם לא יבוא בנם לבקרם תדיר. ועוד שהדבר תלוי במעמדו של הבן וכל כך כמה אחים ואחיות הם וכו' ומי שנקודה זו רגישה אצלו יעשה שאלת חכם

9. *Mora Horim V'Kibbudam* 1:38 (heard from Harav Yosef Shalom Elyashiv and Harav Ben Zion Abba Shaul: הורים זקנים או חולים ויש צורך לטפל בהם. חייב הבן לבקרם ולשמשם בכל יום, ואפילו אם הוא גר מחוץ לעיר, או שיעשה הסדר עם אחיו, או שישכיר אדם שיטפל בהם, או שימצא עבורם הסדר הולם, ואסור לו בשום אופן לעזוב אותם מבלי טיפול

10. Ibid

11. *Vayevarech Dovid*, p. 91: אם הוריו זקנים וצריכים לבלות כדי שלא ישתוממו, מצוה על הבן להמצא אצלם ולשוחח עמם אפילו על הא ודא ובכל מילה מקיים מצוה

12. *Vayevarech Dovid, She'eilos U'Teshuvos, Siman* 2: נראה שאם אביו או אמו בודדים בבית ואין להם עם מי לדבר שמצוה על הבן ליל ך בכל יום לביתם לדבר עמהם שזה גם כן בכלל צרכיהם

13. *Piskei Rav Yitzchak Zilberstein* in *Sefer Avnei Zikaron:* אברך העוסק בתורה ואביו מאושפז בבית חולים ואביו רוצה שיבוא אליו כל יום וישהה אצלו חצי יום, אם הבן נמצא באותה העיר, חייב הבן לבא לשמשו

14. *Avos D'Rebbi Nosson, Perek 3, Halachah* 6: טוב פעם אחת בצער ממאה פעמים שלא בצער

15. *Orchos Rabbeinu*, Vol. 3, p. 108

16. *Teshuvos V'Hanhagos* 2:448: דאף באב המחוסר הכרה ואינו מרגיש כלום, דנראה שחייבים בניו בכבודו, דמאחר והוקש כבוד הורים לכבוד המקום, אף שאינו מגיב ומרגיש מאומה כיון שהמקום ציוה לכבדו זהו כבודו ומתקיים בכך רצון ה' לכבד הורים. ולכן חייבים הבנים לבקרו במיטת חליו אף שאינו מרגיש מאומה

Chapter 6: Who Pays?

1. *Shulchan Aruch* 240:5

2. *Shulchan Aruch*, ibid.

3. *Pele Yo'etz:* ואם הבן חננו ה' עושר ואביו איש עני, מוטל עליו לפרנסו ולהספיק לו כל צרכו בסבר פנים יפות

4. *Rema:* מ"מ אם ידו משגת תבוא מארה למי שמפרנס אביו ממעות צדקה שלו; A prosperous son should not use *tzedakah* money to support his parents. It is demeaning to treat parents like all other needy people. *Mora Horim V'Kibbudam* 1:15, *Se'if Katan* 23 (1)

Another reason is that if we use *tzedakah* funds for parents instead of taking from our own money, then the *tzedakah* isn't available for other needy people.

5. *Yoreh Deah* 251:3, *Hilchos Tzedakah:* פרנסת עצמו קודמת לכל אדם, ואינו חייב לתת צדקה עד שיהיה לו פרנסתו. ואח"כ יקדים פרנסת אביו ואמו אם הם עניים, והם קודמים לפרנסת בניו. ואח"כ בניו, והם קודמים לאחיו, והם קודמין לשאר קרובים. והקרובים קודמים לשכיניו, ושכיניו לאנשי עירו, ואנשי עירו לעיר אחרת, ויושבי ארץ ישראל קודמין ליושבי חוצה לארץ

6. *Chayei Adam* 67:12: אסור לבן ליתן צדקה לעני אחר דאביו קודם לכל אדם

7. *She'eilos U'Teshuvos Chasam Sofer, Yoreh Deah, Siman* 229: דאע"ג דקי"ל בהלכות צדקה סי' רנ"ז ס"ט שלא יתן האדם כל צדקותיו לעני אחד בלבד וכתב הש"ך שהוא הדין שלא יתן לקרוב אחד בלבד וינה שאר הקרובים, מכל מקום באביו צריך ליתן לו את הכל

8. *Teshuvos V'Hanhagos*, 3:286: דאם האב זקוק לעזרה, אזי אפילו יש לפני הבן מקרי צדקה חמורים יותר, חייב לתת כל כספי צדקה שלו לעזור לאביו מכח המ"ע דכיבוד אב

9. *She'eilos U'Teshuvos Chasam Sofer, Yoreh Deah, Siman* 229

10. *Mora Horim V'Kibbudam* 1:17

11. *Yeshayahu* 58: ומבשרך לא תתעלם

12. See priorities in charity contribution

13. *Mora Horim V'Kibbudam* 1:20

14. *Sefer Chassidim, Se'if* 582

15. *Teshuvos V'Hanhagos Harav Sternbuch, shlita*, 3:286: הוצאות הטלפון ומשלוח מכתבים להורים הוא משל בן והוסיף בסברא דהנמנע מלהתקשר או לשלוח מכתבים לאביו מראה שאין אביו חשוב לו ומבזהו בכך, ולהמנע ממקלה אביו ואמו צריך להוציא ממון רב, ועוד נראה שגם מדין כיבוד לא גרע כיבוד אב מכל מצות עשה, דאם בגופו חייב, כ"ש מעט כסף. ורק לחייבו לפרנסו משלו אינו חייב מדינא

16. Based on a survey by the United States Department of Agriculture for 2011

17. Rav Dessler brings a source in halachah to prove that if the father has lost his money, the son should be obliged to return to his father the money his father spent on him when raising him.

18. *Michtav MeEliyahu* V, p. 503

Chapter 7: Rise to the Occasion

1. *Kiddushin* 31b

2. *Chayei Adam* 67:7

See *Sefer Kimah V'Hiddur*, Harav Y. E. Stesman for a full discussion on the obligation to stand for parents

3. Some say, as soon as the parent passes you

4. *Sefer Kimah V'Hiddur* 10:4: If they've already passed you and then you notice, you can still stand up.

5. *Rema* 242:16 *rabo muvhak*

6. If people (strangers) are present who do not know that the son or daughter has already fulfilled his requirement to stand two times, he/she should stand once again so that he/she does not appear to be remiss in honoring his parent(!)

7. See *Mora Horim V'Kibbudam* p. 60 concerning a waiver for home or business when father and son are together all day (requiring a son to stand numerous times)

8. *Kibbud Horim* (Rav Peniri) 4:15: ובמקום שנהגו לעמוד כל זמן שהאב קורא בתורה חייב הבן לעמוד כפי המנהג ואם אינו עושה כן הרי זה מזלזל בכבוד אביו — When this is the custom, to refrain is considered a dishonor to his father.

9. *Teshuvos V'Hanhagos* quoted in *Sefer Kimah V'Hiddur* 10:34

10. *Sefer Kimah V'Hiddur* 10:30,34: שאף...

שמחל האב לבניו שלא יקומו מפניו מכל מקום יש
להם לעשות היהדור
11. *Midrash Rabbah, Bamidbar* 15:13
12. *Kibbud Horim* (Rav Peniri) 4:17: אין ראוי
שהבן יבכש מחילת אביו בקבע שנמצא מזלזל
ממש במצוה ועוד מראה בכך שקשה עליו לכבדם
ולא גרע מהנמאכילו פסיוני...
13. *Teshuvos V'Hanhagos* 3:276 and 5:274
quoted in *Sefer Kimah V'Hiddur* 10:33
14. *Sefer Kimah V'Hiddur* 10:7: הובא בשם
הגרי"ש אלישיב שליט"א וכמו"כ אם ההורים
זקנים וחולים במחלת השכחה ואינם מכירים כלל
את בניהם, חייב הבן לקום מפניהם, וכמו שחייב
לקום מפני אביו הסומא. ובדומה לזה כתב הרב
חיים קניבסקי שלי"טא לגבי זקן חולה שאינו יודע
כלום מהכבוד שמכבדים אותו ומכל מקום צריך
לכבדו
15. *Teshuvos V'Hanhagos* 2:448 quoted in
Otzar Kibbud Av Va'eim 259

Chapter 8:
Married Children's Obligations

1. *Shach, Shulchan Aruch* 240:19: ונראה דאם
אין בעלה מקפיד חייבת בכל דבר שאפשר כמו
האיש עכ"ל
   Sefer HaChinuch: ונוהגת בכל מקום ובכל
זמן בזכרים ובנקבות. ובנקבות כל זמן שאפשר להן
כלומר בכל עת שלא ימנעו אותן בעליהן
2. *Sefer Kimah V'Hiddur* 10:18: בטור ושו"ע
[סימן רמ סעיף יז] דאיש ואשה שוין בכבוד ובמורא
אב ואם. ומבואר שם דאשה נשואה כיון שאין בידה
לעשות שהיא משועבדת לבעלה, הרי היא פטורה
מכבוד אב ואם בעודה נשואה וממילא בקימה
שבידה לעשות, הרי היא חייבת [וכמו שהעירו
פוסקי זמננו]
3. *Sefer Chassidim* 335: ומטעם זה האב שבתו
נשואה ועוסקת בצרכי בעלה והאב צריך זה לא
יצווה לבתו לעשות צרכיו כל זמן שעוסקת בצרכי
בעלה ואם הבעל טוב יאמר לה לעשות צרכי האב
קודם

Chapter 9: A Winning Presentation

1. *Sefer Chareidim*, Ch. 4: גם מכל מצוותיו
שיעשה יעלה ריח טוב כתפוחים ושושנים וכל מיני
בשמים
2. Eight conditions are taken from *Sefer
Chareidim, Hakdamah* 4 (Rav Elazar Azkari, 16th century), דרך כבוד is taken from
Pele Yo'etz, Kibbud Horim, and כשמש לרבו
is Rambam (*Hilchos Mamrim, Perek* 6, Halachah 3)
3. Rav Yaakov Pinchas Feldman in *Kibbud
Av Va'eim*, p. 36, explains these conditions
in light of this mitzvah.

4. *Sefer Eved HaMelech, Parashas Yisro*
   Sefer Chareidim 9:26: כתב איש אמו ואביו
תיראו מפני צווי ה' ידמה אותם בעיניו מלך ומלכה
5. *Yerushalmi, Kiddushin Perek* 1, Halachah
7: R' Shimon ben Yochai says: גדול הוא כבוד
אב ואם שהעדיפו הקב"ה יותר מכבודו
6. *Sefer Chareidim, Hakdamah* 4: לפי רב
השמחה יגדל שכרו
7. *Bereishis* 46:29: וַיֶּאְסֹר יוֹסֵף מֶרְכַּבְתּוֹ וַיַּעַל
לִקְרַאת יִשְׂרָאֵל אָבִיו גֹּשְׁנָה וַיֵּרָא אֵלָיו
8. *Rashi*: הוא בעצמו אסר את הסוסים למרכבה
להזדרז לכבוד אביו
9. *Kiddushin* 31b
10. *Mesillas Yesharim, Perek* 18
11. *Aruch HaShulchan* 240:2: כבוד אב ואם
היא מהמצוות השכליות, ונתפשטה בכל אומה
ולשון, וגם הכופרים בתורה נזהרים בה מפני השכל
והטבע. ואנחנו עם בית ישראל נצטוינו על כל
מצוה שכלית שלא לעשותה מפני השכל, אלא
מפני צווי הקדוש ברוך הוא בתורתו הקדושה, וזה
הוא עיקר גדול במצוות התורה
12. *Rambam, Hilchos Mamrim* 6:3, quoted
by the *Rema, Shulchan Aruch* 240:4: וישמשנו
בשאר דברים שהשמש משמש רבו

Chapter 10:
Opening a "Thank Account"

1. *Sefer HaChinuch* 33
2. *Alei Shur, Chelek Sheni, Shaar Sheni, Vaad
Sheni*
3. Ibid., *Vaad Shlishi*
4. *Michtav MeEliyahu*, III, p. 95
5. *Daas Chochmah U'Mussar*, p. 174: אין
הכוונה מגרעת את המעשה...וכן מנין לנו שאסור
לעשות חסד לתועלת עצמו
6. Of course, if a worker or supplier has
the intention of being מתחסד עם הבריות,
that is the ideal combination.
7. *Career of Happiness* by Rav Avigdor
Miller, p. 164
8. *Midrash HaGadol, Shemos* 8: וכל הכופר
בטובתו של חברו לבסוף כופר בטובתו של הקב"ה

Chapter 11: The Gift of Life

1. *Sefer HaChinuch* 33: משרשי מצוה זו שראוי לו
לאדם שיכיר ויגמול חסד למי שעשה עמו טובה,
ולא יהיה נבל ומתנכר וכפוי טובה שזו מידה רעה
ומאוסה בתכלית לפני אלקים ואנשים. וישית אל
לבו כי האב והאם הם סיבת היותו בעולם, ועל כן
באמת ראוי לו לעשות להם כל כבוד וכל תועלת
שיוכל כי הם הביאוהו לעולם...
2. *Devarim* 5:16
3. *Sanhedrin* 56b: עשר מצוות נצטוו ישראל
במרה שבע מצוות בני נח והוסיפו עליהן דינים

שבת וכבוד אב ואם — Ten mitzvos were given at Marah: seven mitzvos Bnei Noach, *dinim*, Shabbos, and *kibbud av va'eim*

4. Even *chinuch* was not given by parents at that time. It was Hashem, through Moshe, who was *mechanech Klal Yisrael*.

5. *Meshech Chochmah* (*Devarim* 5:16): שנים לא היה טורח גדול על האבות בגידול בניהם

6. Ibid. and *Ksav Sofer*

7. *Aruch HaShulchan* 240:2

Chapter 12:
It's What You Say *and* How You Say It

1. *Mechilta, Parashas Yisro, Perek* 8 and *Chareidim, Perek* 12

2. *Rashi Kiddushin* 31b.

3. Ibid.

4. Ibid.: שמכבדו בדבורו, דברים טובים וניחומים ומלאכה מטיל עליו בלשון רכה, ומודה לו צורך השעה שאינן יכולים להתפרנס אלא ביגיעה זו

5. *Meiri, Kiddushin* 31a: חייב לכבדם הרבה בדברים, ולא עוד אלא שאם עושה להם כל מיני כבוד שבעולם והיה מקלה אותם בדברים יצא שכרו בהפסדו, וכל המכבד ולא כבד במעשה אלא מעט מצד מיעוט היכולת או אף שהטריחו המלאכה דרך כבוד ותועלת, שכרו כפול לו עכ"ל

6. *Shulchan Aruch* 240:6, based on *Kiddushin* 31b

7. Rambam, *Hilchos Mamrim* 6:4: The Rambam quotes the halachah from *Kiddushin* 31b and adds: וכן כל כיוצא בזה לעולם יכלול בכלל דבריו שהוא חושש בכבוד אביו ומתירא ממנו

8. *Chareidim, Perek* 12: שידבר להם בנחת בלשון רכה וכבוד ואדנות

9. *Reishis Chochmah, Perek Derech Eretz*: שיהיה דיבורו עמו בבושת ובצניעות ולא ידבר עמו אלא בנחת ובתחנונים

10. *Pele Yo'etz, Kibbud Chachamim*: ולכן יהיו כל דבריו לפניהם בקול נמוך ובדרך כבוד, בדרך ארץ, ולא זו להם אלא אף לאחרים בפניהם

11. Ibid.

12. *Vayevarech Dovid*, p. 82: בכלל כיבוד בדיבור לספר להם דברים המשמחים ובשורות טובות

13. *Chareidim, Perek* 12: דברי פיוס, צוף דבש, אמרי נועם

14. *Vayevarech Dovid*, p. 82

15. *I Kings* 19:20

16. *Ralbag*: תוילעות 22:31 ויעזב את הבקר וירץ אחרי אליהו ויאמר אשקה נא לאבי ולאמי ואלכה אחריך, ויאמר לו לך שוב וגי' (מלכים א' י"ט:כ). אין ראוי לאדם שיפרד מבית אביו ואמו בזולת ידיעתם, כדי שלא יכאיב לבם כשלא ידעו איפה

הוא, ולזה תמצא שעם רב החשק שהיה לאלישע ללכת אחרי אליהו, הנה התעורר ללכת לאביו ולאמו לנשק אותם ולהודיעם הפרדו מהם

17. *Bereishis* 27:34

Zohar: כשמוע עשו את דברי אביו ויצעק צעקה גדולה ומרה עד מאד ויאמר לאביו ברכני גם אני אבי... אמר ר' חייא כמה רעות גרמו אלו הדמעות שבכה עשו לפני אביו כדי שיתברך ממנו, משום שהיה חשוב מאד בעיניו ברכת אביו

18. *Pele Yo'etz, Berachos*: שהברכה היא קרובה להתקיים על שהם מברכים אותו מלב ומנפש בלב שלם כרחם אב על בנים

19. *Mateh Efraim*: כתוב בספה"ק דצריך האדם להתאמץ מאד ולהשתדל לקבל ברכת אביו ואמו, ואפילו בכל ימות השנה ומכל שכן בערב יוה"כ

20. Harav Yosef Shalom Elyashiv quoted in *Otzar Kibbud Av Va'eim* 693

21. *Kiddushin* 45b: לא חציף איניש לשווי לאבוה שליח

22. *Bereishis* 34:25: ויהי ביום השלישי בהיותם כאבים ויקחו שני בני יעקב שמעון ולוי אחי דינה איש חרבו ויבאו על העיר בטח ויהרגו כל זכר שני בני יעקב. בניו היו ואף על פי נהגו *Rashi*: עצמן שמעון ולוי כשאר אנשים שאינם בניו נטלו עצה הימנו

Chapter 13:
"And His Name Shall Be Called..."

1. *Midrash Tanchuma, Parashas Ha'azinu*

2. *Sefer Chassidim, Se'if* 244

3. *Sefer Veyikarei Shemo B'Yisrael*, pp. 1-3

4. *Midrash Rabbah Bereishis, Parashah* 37, *Se'if* 10: א"ר יוסי הראשונים שהיו מכירים יחוסיהם היו מוציאים שמם ע"ש המאורע, אבל אנו שאין אנו מכירים יחוסינו, אנו מוציאים לשם אבותינו וכו' ע"ש

5. *Mora Horim V'Kibbudam* 3:46

6. Ibid. עונג, כבוד ותפארת

7. See endnote 5 above

8. Harav Binyamin Zilber, *Az Nidberu, Chelek* 13:72 quoted in *Veyikarei Shemo B'Yisrael* 119:

שאע"פ שכתבו האחרונים שיש שם ע"ש הצדיק או ע"ש רבו שלימדו תורה או מופלג ומפורסם בדור, מ"מ אין לדחות בגלל זה לקרוא הילד ע"ש ההורים שהם כשרים אפילו שיש צדיקים יותר מהם, שהוא בכלל מכבדו במותו, וכ"ש אם ההורים בעצמם מבקשים מהבן ליתן שם ההורים שלהם שלא להיות חסיד שוטה לסרב, כי זה נוגע לדאורייתא של קיום מצות כיבוד אביו ואמו. ועצם קיום המצוה של כבוד אביו ואמו כיון שהתהורה הבטיחה מתן שכרה בצידה, זה כולל גם הצלחת יוצאי חלציו בעניינים הרוחניים. וא"כ

ממילא ההורים קודמין לכל

Also see Harav Mordechai Gross, *Kuntres Shemo Gorim* on the importance of naming for parents

9. See sources in *Veyikarei Shemo B'Yisrael*, p. 12

10. *Veyikarei Shemo B'Yisrael*, p. 65, quoting *Sefer Yosef Ometz*: ודע אם יש מריבה בבית היולדת על השם אז חס ושלום הוא סכנה לתינוק ע"כ טוב להתייעץ עם האם כדי שלא יהא מריבה [ובסעיף קטן י"ב: וכך כתב החיד"א בספר עבודת הקודש]

11. *Rambam, Tzava'ah*: נביאים נבאו וחכמים חכמו ויוסיפו לספר ברעת המחלוקת ולא הגיעו לתכליתה

12. *Veyikarei Shemo B'Yisroel* p. 4.

Chapter 14:
Getting to the Heart of the Matter

1. *Chayei Adam* 67:3: הכיבוד הוא במחשבה במעשה ובדיבור...דאין לומר שבלבו ובעיניו הם נבזים רק שמכבד אותם בדברים...אלא...שמכבדם בלבו שהם חשובים בעיניו ובלבו...אף שבעיני שאר בני אדם אינם חשובים כלל וזהו עיקר כיבוד

2. Brought in *Sefer Simchas Naftali*, p. 49, quoting *Sefer Givas Pinchas, Parashas Vayishlach*, in the name of the *Zohar HaKadosh*: רמ"ח מצוות עשה מכוונים נגד רמ"ח אברים שבאדם ומצות כיבוד ומורא אב ואם מכוונים נגד העינים

3. *Rabbeinu Yonah, Shaarei Teshuvah* 217: כי דרך הישרים לכסות על כל פשעים ולשבח האדם כי נמצא בו דבר טוב

4. *Avos* 1:6: עשה לך רב וקנה לך חבר והוי דן את כל האדם לכף זכות

5. *Vayevarech Dovid* p. 83: ואם נראה להבן טענות ומענות על התנהגות של א' מהוריו צריך הוא להתאמץ בכל כוחו ללמוד זכות עליהם, כדי שלא למעט מחשיבותם, ומה דבאנשים דעלמא מבואר בחז"ל הוי דן את כל האדם לכף זכות, כל שכן הורים שהוא מצווה להחשיבם

6. *Yesod VeShoresh HaAvodah, Shaar HaGadol, Shaar 1, Perek 8*

7. *Avos* 2:5: אל תדין את חברך עד שתגיע למקומו

Chapter 15:
Must We Love Our Parents?

1. *Sifra, Kedoshim:* אמר רבי עקיבא ואהבת לרעך כמוך זה כלל גדול בתורה

2. *Hilchos Dei'os* 6:3: מצוה על כל אחד לאהוב את כל אחד ואחד מישראל כגופו. לפיכך צריך לספר בשבחו ולחוס על ממונו כאשר הוא חס על ממון עצמו ורוצה בכבוד עצמו

3. *Sefer HaChinuch* 243: לא לחברך סני דעלך

תעביד

4. *Gemara Shabbos* 31a: ויהיה רוצה כבוד חברו ככבוד עצמו, ואהבתו וחמלתו על חברו כאהבתו וחמלתו על עצמו, ומבקש תועלתו, ושמח בטובתו, ומצר בצרתו

5. *Chayei Adam, Hilchos Kibbud Av Va'eim* 67:1 based on *Sefer Chareidim, Mitzvos Asei HaTeluyos BaLev*, Perek 9, 37-38

6. The *Chayei Adam* is quoting the *Sefer Chareidim*, who bases this on the *Zohar HaKadosh, Parashas Ki Seitzei*

Chapter 16:
Imperfect Parents
Who Are Perfect for Us

1. *Kiddushin* 31b

2. *Yerushalmi Peah* 1:1

3. *Devarim Rabbah* 1:15: והיתה אמו חסרת דעת

4. *Kiddushin* 31a

5. *Devarim Rabbah* 1:15: לא היה אומר לה אלא דייך אמי

6. *Sefer Tochachas Chaim, Parashas Toldos*

7. *Shulchan Aruch* 240:8

8. *Rambam Hilchos Mamrim* 6:7: לא יכלימם ולא יצער בפניהם ולא יכעוס כנגדם אלא יקבל גזרת הכתוב וישתוק... ויירא ויפחד ממלך מלכי המלכים שציוהו בכך

9. *Vayevarech Dovid, She'eilos U'Teshuvos Siman* 44: לא יזמין את אביו לדין תורה אלא יסדרו לילך ליחיד מומחה שישמע טענותיהם ויפשר ביניהם

10. Heard from Rav Ezriel Tauber

11. *Shulchan Aruch* 240:10

12. *Otzar Kibbud Av Va'eim* 138, quoting Rambam, *Hilchos Dei'os, Perek* 4: ...ומעתה נלמד ג"כ שמותר לבטל מצוה בשב ואל תעשה כדי שלא יחלה גופו ויפול למשכב. ע"כ...

Otzar Kibbud Av Va'eim: נלמד ומינה... לעניינו דאם כרוך כבוד ההורים בסכנה לבריאותו פטור מלקיים המצוה

13. See *Otzar Kibbud Av Va'eim* 138 for sources

14. *Mishnah Berurah, Siman* 622, *Shaar HaTziyun* 6

"Honor — A Final Thought"

15. *Shulchan Aruch* 240:1: צריך להזהר מאוד בכבוד אביו ואמו שהשווהו בכבודם לכבוד המקום

16. *Kiddushin* 30b: שלושה שותפים הם באדם, הקב"ה ואביו ואמו

17. *Kiddushin* 30b: בזמן שאדם מכבד את אביו ואת אמו, אומר הקב"ה מעלה אני עליהם כאילו דרתי ביניהם וכבדוני

Chapter 17:
Are We "Tripping" Our Children?

1. *Shelah HaKadosh* on the *pasuk* איש אמו ואביו תיראו:

פתח בלשון יחיד וסיים בלשון רבים "איש" אלא בא הכתוב לרמוז ולכלול גם את "תיראו" אביו ואמו של האיש שלא יהיו הם גורמים לבן שיעבור על מצוה זו

2. *Sefer Chassidim* 567: לא יצוה האב לבנו דברים הקשים וכבדים עליו לעשותם...פן ימנע מלעשות ונמצא מחטיאו

3. *Kiddushin* 32a: אמר ר' יצחק בר שילא אמר רב מתנה אמר רב חסדא: הא ב שמחל על כבודו כבודו מחול

4. *Pele Yo'etz, Ahavas HaBanim VeHabanos*: והכלל הוא לפי דעתו ומדותיו של הבן...ולא ידקדק כל כך עמהם ולפעמים יעשה עצמו כחרש לא ישמע וכאילו אינו רואה. ולפעמים יבטל רצונו מפני רצונם, וזה כלל גדול הרוצה לזכות את נפשו ונפשו בניו אחריו

5. *Otzar Kibbud Av Va'eim* 604: קודם המחילה יש עליו מצוה חיובית ואחר המחילה יש עליו מצוה קיומית

6. *Sefer Kibbud Horim*, Rav Peniri 85 quoting the *Sefer HaChinuch* and *Igros Moshe*

7. *Otzar Kibbud Av Va'eim* 599, *She'iltos*: האב שמחל על כבודו כבודו מחול אבל הכאתו וקללתו לא

8. *Minchas Chinuch* in the name of the *Ran*: דעל צערו ובזיונו לא מהני מחילה

9. *Sefer Chassidim* 570: אדם שיש לו בנים ומתחקוטטים יחדיו...לא יאמר להם תקללו אותו או אותי על מנת כן שלא תכו ולא תקללו אחיכם ואחיותיכם. אף על פי שיותר היה שמח האב שיקללו אותו אינו רשאי לומר להם כן ואינם רשאים לעשות לאביהם ולאמם כן עכ"ל

10. Ibid.

11. *Teshuvos V'Hanhagos*: תלוי בסוג הבזיון ובזיון ממש לא מועיל מחילה מה שאין כן בזלזול שאינו גדול

12. *Pele Yo'etz, Ahavas HaBanim VeHabanos*: וכבר כתבתי לעיל שראוי לאב למחול לבנים כדי להקל מעליהם עונשם...שאם אמרו חכמים (יבמות ס"ה) כשם שמצוה לומר דבר הנשמע, כך מצוה שלא לומר דבר שאינו נשמע, על אחת כמה וכמה שראוי לאב להזהיר שלא להכביד ולצוות על בניו דבר שחושש שמא לא ישמעו לו ונמצא עובר על לפני עור לא תתן מכשול (ויקרא י"ט:י"ד)...נמצא גורם צער למעלה על ידי העון של בנו...ולכן כל ערום יעשה בדעת לפי דעתו של בן ולפי מדתו...

13. ולכן טוב הוא לכל יראי ה' שימחלו לבניהם את כבודם אף בלא ידיעתם כדי שלא להענישם

Chapter 18: Awe-some Examples

1. Gemara *Kiddushin* 31:2

2. *Shulchan Aruch* 240:2: איזה 'מורא' לא יעמוד במקומו (במקום שעומד בסוד זקנים שנמצא שמשווה שמצמו לאביו) ולא ישב (ולא יעמוד) במקומו (המיוחד לו) – ולא סותר את דבריו – ולא מכריע את דבריו בפניו (אבל שלא בפניו מותר. לבוש), ולא יקראנו בשמו לא בחייו ולא במותו, אלא אומר 'אבא – מארי – אדוני – אבי'

3. *Sefer HaChinuch* 212: כתוב לירא מהאבות כלומר שיתנהג אדם עם אמו ואביו הנהגה שאדם נוהג עם מי שירא ממנו

4. *Mesillas Yesharim, Perek* 7, *Zerizus*: שהזריזות הוא תולדת ההתלהטות הפנימי כן מן הזריזות יולד ההתלהטות...כי התנועה החיצונה מעוררת הפנימית ובודאי שיותר מסורה בידה היא החיצונה מהפנימית. אך אם ישתמש ממה שבידו, יקנה גם מה שאינו בידו בהמשך שבמעשיו הוא משווה את עצמו לאביו

Otzar Kibbud Av Va'eim 29: ויש בזה משום חסרון מורא אביו בלבו...

6. *Shulchan Aruch* 240:2

7. Ibid.: One may stand in a place where his parents usually sit (וכן פסקו האחרונים)

Ben Yechabed Av, p. 89: מותר לעמוד במקום המיוחד לישיבה, אבל אסור לעמוד במקום המיוחד לעמידה

8. *Mora Horim V'Kibbudam* 2:17: Most opinions say that after a parent has passed away, it is permissible to sit in his seat

9,10. See discussion in *Otzar Kibbud Av Va'eim* 29.

11. *Yerushalmi Peah, Perek* 1, Halachah 1. *Yerushalmi Kiddushin*

12. *Mora Horim V'Kibbudam* 2:19, Se'if Katan 18

13. In some communities, the third person is preferred. For example, a child, asking his mother about her health, would say, "How is Mommy feeling?"

14. *Rambam, Hilchos Mamrim* 5:6: לא יקרא לו בשמו...אלא אומר אבא מורי *Shulchan Aruch* 240:2

15. *Kibbud Horim* (Rav Peniri), 9:18: ראוי להחמיר במקום שאפשר

16. *Otzar Kibbud Av Va'eim* 666 in the name of Harav Yosef Shalom Elyashiv

Chapter 19:
Learning to Speak a New Language

1. *Sefer Chareidim* 9:26: ולא סותר דבריו אף על פי שהוא יודע שאינו כן ולא יאמר לא כן היה

2. *Rambam, Hilchos Mamrim* 6:11: כאילו הוא שואל ממנו ולא מזהירו...

3. *Otzar Kibbud Av Va'eim* 49: ולא סותר את דבריו - אב המוכיח את בנו על טעות שעשה, אזי בנו הרוצה להצדיק את עצמו לא יאמר לאביו בלשון הסותר, כגון "זה לא אמת" או "לא נכון", אלא יאמר בלשון מתונה כמו: יש לי לומר דברים המצדיקים אותי, ויעמיד האמת על בוריה (בן יכבד אב עמ' 91)

4. וכמ"ש בפת"ש (ס"ק א') בשם ספר עצמות יוסף (קידושין ל':) דהבן עם האב יכולין להקשות ולתרץ ולהסיק מסקנות ההלכה ואין בזה משום סותר את דבריו

5. *Otzar Kibbud Av Va'eim* 48

Chapter 20: In the Public Eye

1. *Sefer HaYirah*: ואם אתה אצל בני אדם שאתה חייב בכבודם כגון אביך ואמך כבדם ותירא מהם וכו' ולא תסתור את דבריהם אם אמרו דבר אפילו ידעת כי אינו כן אל תאמר לא כן היה

2. *Shulchan Aruch* 240:8

3. *Aruch HaShulchan* 240:16: How far do we have to take *yirah*? The answer is: If we would suffer a public embarrassment by our parents, we may defend ourselves. Though we may defend ourselves at the moment and do what we can to prevent future occurrences, nonetheless we may not respond disrespectfully (בדרך בזיון).

4. *Shulchan Aruch* 240:2: אפילו לומר נראין דברי אבא

5. *Levush*: וטעם הדבר שזה זלותא לאביו מפני שנראה שדעתו מכרעת יותר מדעת אביו

6. *Aruch HaShulchan* 240:13: אם האב אומר לבן שברצונו לשמוע מה דעתו מותר לבן לומר את דעתו אפילו כאשר היא הפוכה מדברי אביו

7. *Rema*: אפילו נראין לו דברי אביו אין לו לומר נראין דברי אבא שנראה כמכריע דברי אביו אלא אם יש לו תשובה להשיב על החולקים ישיב

8. *Rashi, Kiddushin* 31b: אם היה חולק עם אחר בדבר הלכה לא יאמר נראידברי פלוני

9. *Chayei Adam*: שלא בפני אביו מותר לומר נראין דברי אבא ואדרבה יש בך כבוד לאביו

10. *Peirush Mishnayos, Kiddushin* 29

11. *Sefer Meah Shearim, Shaar* 15

12. חכם אינו נכנס בתוך דברי חברו

13. *Rabbeinu Yonah, Sefer HaYirah*: One should not interrupt a parent, because even if we interrupt a friend, we are called a *golem*

14. *Yerushalmi Peah* 1:1: איזהו מורא ... לא ידבר במקומו

15. *Rashi, Vayikra* 19:3

16. *Rashi, Bereishis* 24:50: ויען לבן לבתואל: רשע היה וקפץ להשיב לפני אביו

17. *Otzar Kibbud Av Va'eim* 55

18. *Vayevarech Dovid*, p. 59

19. *Otzar Kibbud Av Va'eim* 432

20. ibid. 438.

Chapter 21: We Aim to Please: Parents' requests and children's responses

1. *Otzar Kibbud Av Va'eim* 122: The above are *bitul mitzva*s *kavod* and some are, in addition, *lashon zilzul*. Some say that if a parent asks a child to do one of the things mentioned above and he doesn't, in addition to חוסר כבוד it is also a חוסר יראה.

2. See *Otzar Kibbud Av Va'eim* 548

3. Ibid. ס אות ד, וע"ע: באר משה (שטרן) ח"א סי' ס וכו' בשו"ת בצל החכמה ח"ב סי' נה, וכ"פ הגר"ש ואזנר שליט"א שם וכן שמעתי מהגרי"ש אלישיב שליט"א. שיש לנהוג כדעת הפוסקים המחייבים בזה

4. *Kibbud Horim* (Rav Peniri), p. 15: Since we are dealing with a *safek d'Oraisa*... ומכיון שנתבאר שדעת רוב הפוסקים ראשונים ואחרונים לחייב בזה ושרבים מפוסקי הדור הסכימו לזה, נראה שצריך לשמוע בקול אביו ואמו אף על פי שאין הדבר נוגע להם ממש ומכל מקום ישנו מקום לחלק בזה, שאף על פי שצריך לציית לאביו ואמו בדבר שאינו נוגע לגופם, הני מילי בפניהם אבל שלא בפניהם באופן שלא יגרם להם עגמת נפש, אין מחוייב לשמוע בקולם וכפי ששמעתי מהגרי"ש אלישיב שליט"א

5. *Vayevarech Dovid*, p. 410

6. Our Sages tell us: אפילו רק פתח לו הפתח את נפשו חייב לו — Even if a person did a small favor for us, we should feel indebted. How much more so a parent who sacrificed day and night for years and took care of all your needs. They tell us further, "Don't throw a stone into a well from which you drank," meaning don't pay back good with bad! [We know that if we had to fill in the rest, the ink in our pen would finish before the list.]

7. *Chofetz Chaim, Be'er Mayim Chaim, Asin* 11: וכן איתא בסמ"ק לירא פירוש שלא יעבור על דעת קונו ממה שצייוהו, וכן מוכח מהגמרא דזהו עיקרו של יראה וז"ל הגמרא בקדושין (דף לא:) לענין מורא אב ת"ר איזהו מורא לא יסתור את דבריו וכו' עי"ש

8. *Iggeres HaTeshuvah* 3:70

Chapter 22:
Less Distress, More Success

1. *Vayevarech Dovid*, p. 70: דמכלל מצות יראה
שלא לגרום שום צער לאביו

2. *Kiddushin* 30b: בזמן שאדם מכבד את אביו
ואת אמו, אומר הקב"ה מעלה אני עליהם כאילו
דרתי ביניהם וכבדוני

3. *Kiddushin* 31b: ובזמן שמצער אביו ואמו אומר
הקב"ה יפה עשיתי שלא דרתי ביניהם שאלמלא
דרתי ביניהם ציערוני

4. *Sefer Vayevarech Dovid*, p. 48: ועל כן יוותרו
זה לזה כדי למנוע צער מאביהם

5. *Reishis Chochmah*: ואם יצטרך האב לבנו,
יעשה לו כל צרכו בטוב לב ולא יזכיר לפני אביו
הטובה שהטיב לו וידבר על לבו תמיד כדי לישב
דעתו

6. *Bereishis* 30:15: ותאמר רחל אל לאה תני נא
לי מדודאי בנך, ותאמר לאה המעט קחתך את
אישי ולקחת גם את דודאי בני

7. *Sifsei Tzaddik* on *Chumash*

8. *Vayikra* 19:16

9. *Sefer Chassidim*, *Se'if* 336

10. *Hilchos Rechilus* 1:5 & 1:8

11. Ibid. *Be'er Mayim Chaim* 14

12. Ibid. 1:3

13. Ibid. 3:3

14. *Pesachim* 54b: שבעה דברים מכוסין מבני
אדם – אין אדם יודע מה בלבו של חברו

15. *Otzar Kibbud Av Va'eim* 300

16. *Sefer Tzeidah LaDerech* quoted in *Vayevarech Dovid* p. 71

17. *Vayevarech Dovid*, p. 82: בכלל כיבוד
בדיבור לספר להם דברים המשמחים, ובשורות
טובות, ולהיפך שלא לספר להם דברים של צער,
ודברים המעציבים, או בשורות רעות (אם לא
שיש הכרח לההורים לדעת אותם) [ובס' תוכחת
חיים שם שזה הטעם שנהוג העולם שאם יודע
הבן שיהיה להורי צער כאשר יודע לו שמועה
לא טובה שהבן נמנע מלספר זאת לאביו] וממילא
שאם יש הכרח יראה לאביו יספרוהו לו

18. *Sefer Chassidim*, *Se'if* 575

Chapter 23: Damah ben Nesinah

1. *Kiddushin* 31a

2. *Chayei Adam*, *Se'if* 67:11: מצוה להקיצו
מאחר שאביו שמח על זה

3. *Aruch HaShulchan* 240:40: ומכל מקום טוב
יותר להקיצו על ידי אחרים ולא על ידי עצמו
לעשות המנהג שכן וכמדומני Quoted
in *Otzar Kibbud Av Va'eim* 312 in the name
of Harav Yosef Shalom Elyashiv: לכתחילה
עדיף להעירו על ידי אחר ורק אם אי אפשר על ידי
אחר יעירו אותו בעצמו

4. Refer to *Sefer Mora Horim V'Kibbudam*,

p. 10, *Se'if* 27 for further clarification on
waking parents: לצורך מצוה מכין שכולם
חייבים בכבוד המקום"

5. *Dibros Moshe*, *Kiddushin* on this *Gemara*:
מחויב הבן להקיצו כיון שהנאתו מריווח הבן עדיף
לו מהנאת השינה. מוכרח מזה הדין שאם הוא בן
דעת הרי אין טעם לאסור להקיץ לאביו

6. The *Aruch HaShulchan* 240:40 concludes
similarly. Against all logic, it appears that
the father, Nesina, would not have appreciated being woken. אולי הכל לפי מה שהוא
אדם

7. In the text, these mitzvos are enumerated.

8. *Otzar Kibbud Av Va'eim* 310

Chapter 24: Slights, Stings, and Slurs

1. *Rambam*, *Hilchos Mamrim* 5:2: ולא על
קללה בלבד הקפידה תורה אלא אף על בזיון שכל
המבזה אביו או אמו אפילו בדברים ואפילו ברמיזה
הרי זה ארור מפי הגבורה

2. *Chofetz Chaim*, *Ahavas Chessed* (*Chelek
2*, *Perek* 11): צריך האדם להתנהג בעניני התורה
והמצוה כמו בעניני העסק: כשמחזיק חנות וכיוצא,
אינו מתעצל לישב אף בקור ולשקל לאחד, וכן
לחזר לשקל לשני וכן לשלישי. אף שמכל אחד
ואחד לא נשאר לו רוח כי אם מעט מן המעט,
ויושב ומצפה מתי יבואו אצלו סוחרים, וכשבאים,
מרב השמחה אינו מרגיש הקור. והכל מטעם שהוא
חושב שזהו סבה לחייו.... על אחת כמה וכמה
בעניני התורה והמצוה, שהוא חיי עולם, כמה צריך
האדם להיות זריז לרדף אחריהן ולהשיגן......ולא
יכבד עליו הטרחה בזה.

3. *Vayevarech Dovid*, p. 43

4. *Chofetz Chaim*, *Asin* 10: [המספר] על אביו
ואמו בודאי עובר על מצות עשה דכיבוד אב ואם.
מלבד כל זה עובר גם כן על ארור מקלה אביו ואמו,
ה' ישמרנו

5. *Hilchos Lashon Hara*, *Klal* 8

6. לא תשא שמע שוא (*Shemos* 23:1). *Chofetz
Chaim*, *Hilchos Lashon Hara*, *Klal* 6, *Se'if* 1

7. Refer to details of the halachos for listening to *lashon hara*, *Klal* 6

8. *Hilchos Lashon Hara*, *Klal* 10, *Se'if* 14:
ואפשר דהוא הדין אם כוונתו בסיפורו להפג את
דאגתו מלבו הוי כמכוון לתועלת על להבא...

9. Ibid. 3:6, *Se'if Katan* 7

10. *Shaarei Teshuvah*: 3:217 ואמר שלמה (משלי
י"ד) "אֱוִלִים יָלִיץ אָשָׁם," כי יחפש מומי בני אדם
ואשמתם ויתן בהם דופי ולא ידבר לעולם בשבח
ודבר טוב הנמצא בם, "וּבֵין יְשָׁרִים רָצוֹן," כי דרך
הישרים לכסות על כל פשעים ולשבח האדם כי
נמצא בו דבר טוב

Chapter 25:
When Following Orders
Is Against the Law

1. *Rashi* comments on the words "keep my Shabbos":

סמך שבת למורא אב ואם לומר, אף על פי שהזהרתיך על מורא אב ואם, אם יאמר לך חלל את השבת אל תשמע לו, וכן בשאר כל המצוות.

Rashi continues with the second half of the *pasuk*, אני ה' אלוקיכם:

אתה ואביך חייבים בכבודי לפיכך לא תשמע לו לבטל דברי — Both you and your parents are obligated in My honor. Therefore, do not obey your parents if it results in nullifying My words (based on the *Sifra* there, *Kiddushin* 32:1).

2. *Otzar Kibbud Av Va'eim* 546. אם הורי מוחים בו לבטל מנהג שנהגו בו ישראל, see *Vayevarech Dovid*, p. 104, for a full discussion

3. *Chofetz Chaim, Hilchos Lashon Hara* 1:5

4. *Midrash Tanchuma, Parashas Eikev*

5. *Vayevarech Dovid, She'eilos U'Teshuvos, Siman* 213: שהרי אביו עובר על איסור של ונשמרתם מאד לנפשותיכם ואסור לאדם לשמוע לאביו לעבור על איסור

6. *Otzar Kibbud Av Va'eim* 552

7. *Otzar Kibbud Av Va'eim* 556

8. *Otzar Kibbud Av Va'eim* 557

9. *Otzar Kibbud Av Va'eim* 554: If it can be avoided, its is preferable that the husband not tell his wife about his father's request

10. *Sefer Chut HaShani*, p. 265

11. *Otzar Kibbud Av Va'eim* quoting *Teshuvos V'Hanhagos Chelek* 1, *Se'if* 526: דאם הבן רוצה לקיים מילי דחסידות ואביו רוצה למונעו מחמת שחושש לכבודו דע"י הנהגת המילי דחסידות מרגיש בהתנשאות הבן עליו וכדומה, בכה"ג אסור לבן לזלזל ח"ו ברצון אביו ולפיכך נראה שאם יסבול מזה, וכ"ש שלא יצער אותו ואל יענה לו או יתנהג עמו בעזות, שבשביל מילי דחסידות עלול הוא לקבל ח"ו קללה דארור מקלה אביו ואמו ותמורת הברכה למילי דחסידות יצא שכרו בהפסדו." עכ"ל

12. *Kibbud Horim* (Rav Peniri), 11:20, in the name of Harav Yosef Shalom Elyashiv: דאם מבקשים ממנו הוריו לערוך מילת בנו לאחר חצות היום, אע"פ שמבואר בשו"ע שזריזין מקדימין למצוה ומלין מיד בבוקר, מ"מ מכיון שכל היום כשר למצוה כמבואר שם חייב לשמוע להם, אלא שישתדל להרבות עליהם רעים וידידים

שיעתירו בעדו לפניהם ואם אעפ"כ לא נתרצו ישמע בקולם. עכ"ל

13. Harav Avigdor Miller

14. *Kovetz Mevakshei Torah, Chelek* 1, *Se'if* 261, *Hanhagos and Teshuvos* of Rav Shlomo Zalman Auerbach: נכנסתי פעם למרן זצוק"ל נבחור שעמד לגמור שידוך, אך שאלתו בפיו, היות ואביו מתנגד לשידוך והוא כבר גמר אומר עם המדוברת לגמור הענין, אם יכול לעשות השידוך בלא הסכמת אביו, עפ"יד הרמ"א שבזה א"צ לקבל דעת אביו, מרן הרצין פניו ואמר לבחור בתוקף: אמנם יש כזו הלכה, אך אני בשום אופן לא אתן את ידי לזה. לא עושים דבר כזה! וכך הדגיש כמדומה פעמים מספר, ולענין מעשה אני מייעץ לדבר עם האבא בדברי חכמה. ויעץ בפרוטרוט איך לדבר עם האבא. ואכן ממש כך היה. כשעשינו כדברי מרן שינה האב מיד דעתו ואפילו השתתף

15. *Shulchan Aruch* 240:13

16. *Sefer Meah Shearim, Shaar* 16: שלא יניח הבן אב ואם וילך לו לארץ אחרת ואפילו כשהולך ללמוד תורה דרשאי מכל מקום יהיה תמיד עיניו ולבו על אבותיו...אלא ישאל שלום וידרוש ויחקור בשלומם

17. *Kovetz Mevakshei Torah*, Volume VIII, *Kovetz* 20, HaGaon Rav Avrohom Pam: דלמעשה יש להזהר בזה טובא, והחכם עיניו בראשו לראות שאם יבא ח"ו לידי קטטה ומריבה, יכשל בודאי באיסורים חמורים ויצא שכרו בהפסדו, וע"ז וכיו"ב נאמר "אוי לזה שסניגורו נעשה קטיגורו." ע"ע יתאמץ למצוא עצה למלאת רצון אביו ולצאת גם התפילה וקה"ת והבא ליטהר מסייעין אותו. עכ"ל

"Reverence — A Final Thought"

18. *Vayikra* 19:1-2

19. Rav Shamshon Raphael Hirsch: הטעם שצותה התורה בפרשת קדושים על יראת אם ואב, ולא על כבודם, כי כידוע "פרא אדם יולד" והיראה אשר ירא הילד מאבותיו בטל ילדותו, היא תשרש בו את הכח והאמונ'ה להתרגל למשל על רצונו, שיהיה ביכלתו לבטל את רצונו מפני רצון אחרים. בבטלו את רצונו בילדותו מפני רצון אבותיו, הוא יבוא למדרגת בטול רצונו בבואו לכלל כל איש, מפני רצון ה' יתברך, יראת אב ואם היא ההתחנכות הראשונה לבוא על ידה לכלל קדושה

Chapter 27: Sunset

1. *Hilchos Lashon Hora, Asin* 2

2. *Vayevarech Dovid*, p. 193. He quotes Rav Shneur Zalman Berenblatt, *ztz"l*: שלפעמים טובה להוריו הזקנים שלא לעשות להם כל צורכיהם כדי שלא יהא נדמה להם כאילו עוד אינם ראויים לכלום וכאילו עברו ובטלו מן העולם

3. *Meah Shearim, Shaar* 32:

לפיכך החכם עיניו בראשו להתנהג עם אבותיו הזקנים כדרך שהאב מתנהג עם בניו הקטנים, שמקדים ונותן להם טרם שישאלו, ומכוין את דעתם עד שלא יבכו. וכמו שנתנהגו אבותיו עמו בקטנותו ובילדותו, כן יתנהג הוא עצמו עמהם, ישיב גמולם להם.

4. Rav Kaltz: מפסיד שכרו ונטרד מן העולם

Meiri: יצא שכרו בהפסדו וקפחו

According to some opinions, the son is credited for what he does to honor his father, but punished for the shame.

5. *Shulchan Aruch* 240:4: והראה לו פנים זועפות נענש עליו, *Kiddushin* 31a and *Yerushalmi, Peah* 1

6. *Sefer Mussar* by Rav Y. Kaltz: כל המנהג עם אביו בדברים אלו וכיוצא בהן אע"פ שמאכילו ומשקהו כל מעדני מלך ומלבישו שיש ומשי ורקמה נטרד מן חיי עולם הבא

7. אם נתן אדם לחברו כל מתנות טובות שבעולם ופניו כבושים, מעלה עליו הכתוב כאילו לא נתן כלום, אבל מקבל את חברו בסבר פנים יפות אפילו לא נתן לו כלום, מעלה עליו הכתוב כאילו נתן לו כל מתנות טובות שבעולם

8. *Vayevarech Dovid*, p. 91

Chapter 28: Stepparents

1. *Chofetz Chaim, Asin* 10; *Otzar Kibbud Av Va'eim* 403

Kesubos 103a: "את אביך" לרבות אשת אביך – Here, ואת means "את אמך" לרבות בעל אמך "to include"

2. *Otzar Kibbud Av Va'eim* 634

3. *Shulchan Aruch* 240:21: אבל אחר מיתה אינו חייב בכבודם ומכל מקום דבר הגון לכבדם אף לאחר מיתה...

4. *Mora Horim V'Kibbudam* 8:43, *Se'if Katan* 46 in the name of Harav Yosef Shalom Elyashiv: The obligation to honor stepparents is the same as the obligation to honor parents.

5. *Mora Horim V'Kibbudam* 8:43: ידבר אליהם בלשון כבוד וענה באכילה ושתיה וכן שמעתי מפי הרה"ג י"ש אלישיב ומפי הרב רה"ג ב"א שאול

Sefer Chareidim 16:3-12: חייב כל אלה בעניין כבוד התלוי בדברים ונראה דהוא הדין לעניין כבוד התלוי במעשה דאין לחלק

6. *Otzar Kibbud Av Va'eim* 625: אפילו בדבר שאינו נוגע לעצם הכבוד אלא שיש בו הכשר מצוה, גם כן חייב בהם כשם שחייב לכבד אביו ואמו ובהכשר מצוה

Kibbud Horim, Rav Peniri, 15:3 in the name of Harav Yosef Shalom Elyashiv

7. *Bamidbar Rabbah* 15:13: שלושה עשר דברים חיבבם הקב"ה וקראם לי...

8. *Kesubos* 103a: כבד את אביך ואת אמך. ו' יתרה לרבות את אחיך הגדול

9. *Otzar Kibbud Av Va'eim* 641: ולעניין דינא לבני ספרד פשוט שיש לנהוג כדעת הפוסקים שחייב לכבד כל אחיו הגדולים ממנו והגרי"א שליט"א פסק שגם בני אשכנז צריכים לנהוג כן (כיבוד הורים פרק טז הערה ו, מורא הורים וכיבודם פרק ח סעיף טו)

10. *Mora Horim V'Kibbudam*, 8:43: וכן יכבד בדברים וידבר אליהם בלשון כבוד וענה באכילה ושתיה

11. *Chofetz Chaim, Asin* 10

12. *Sefer Chassidim* 345: מי שלא ראה אביו ואמו בעומדו על דעתו, היכן [יקיים] כיבוד אב ואם, ויש לו זקן וזקנה, הרי זה יקיים עליהם מצות כיבוד כאילו הוא בניהם. וכן אם לא ראם, ויש לו אחים גדולים ממנו, יכבדם...הרי מעלין עליו כאילו קיים כיבוד ומורא.

Chapter 29: In-Laws

1. *Bamidbar* 17:5: לא יהיה כקרח וכעדתו

2. *Vayikra* 19:17: לא תשנא את אחיך בלבבך

3. *Ibid.* 19:18: ואהבת לרעך כמוך

4. *Ibid.* 19:15: בצדק תשפט עמיתך

5. *Pele Yo'etz, Chamiv VaChamoso:* ולכן אם ארע שאשת הבן היא אשה רעה קשת רוח, חייבא רמיא על הזקנים לסבל עולה ולנהלה בנחת בנעם שיח ולא יכבידו עלם עליה, ואם עושה דברים שלא כהגן ייסרוה בינם לבינה בסתר ולא יגלו את נבלותה לבריות, רק ישבחוה ויחשיבוה בפני הבריות, וכל שכן שלא יגלו ולא יעשו קטטה עם אביה ואמה. וכל שכן וקל וחמר שישמרו את נפשם שלא יגלו נבלותה לבעלה, שמא יכנס טינא בלבו ויבוא לשנאתה. ואוי להם אם אם יהיו גורמים כך, שהרי השם הקדוש שנכתב בקדושה צוה הקדוש ברוך הוא למחקו על המים בשביל לשים שלום בין איש לאשתו. ויותר טוב שיסבלו אב ואם אלף דעות ולא ישימו מחלוקת בין איש לאשתו

6. See *Otzar Kibbud Av Va'eim* 667 for a review of sources

7. *Vayevarech Dovid*, p. 151: אשה נשואה חייבת לכבד חמיה וחמותה. דחייבת גם מטעם כבוד בעלה וכבוד הוריו הוא כבודי

8. *Parashas Yisro* 18:7: ויצא משה לקראת חתנו וישתחו ויישק לו וישאלו איש לרעהו לשלום ויבאו האהלה

9. *Mechilta, Parashas Yisro:* ומכאן אמרו שיהא אדם מוכן לכבוד חמיו (נוהג כבוד בחמיו)

Midrash Shochar Tov (Shmuel 24:12): "ואבי ראה גם ראה", מכאן שחיב אדם בכבוד חמיו כאביו. וכן מובא במדרש תלפיות: חיב אדם בכבוד חמיו כאביו

10. *Sefer Kibbud Av Va'eim*, p. 21, quoting the *Bach* and the *Shach*

11. *Mora Horim V'Kibbudam,* 8:57: ...ולשון
כבוד ואדנות
12. *Mora Horim V'Kibbudam* 8:57: יכבדם
באכילה ושתיה (בשם פוסקי הדור)
13. *Otzar Kibbud Av Va'eim* 671: כשהורי
הבעל מתארחים בביתו ומסיבים כולם על השלחן,
תגיש האשה תחילה את המנות הראשונות לחמיה
ולחמותה ורק אחר כך תגיש לבעלה ואין רשות
לבעלה להקפיד שנתנו לו תחילה דהלא מחוייב
הוא לראות שהמנות הראשונות ילכו לאביו ולאמו
(בשם הרב פסח א. פאלק) — At a meal, a husband's parents should be served before the husband, since it is improper for him to eat before his parents.
14. *Sefer Kibbud Av Va'eim,* p. 21, quoting *Sefer She'eilos U'Teshuvos Binyan Olam, Yoreh Deah, Siman* 47: מהדרים אותו בדברים ונותנים לו יד לסמכו
15. *Sefer Kimah V'Hiddur* 10:22: יש שכתב
שצריך לקום מלא קומתו מפני חמיו וחמותיו
בשיעור ד' אמות וכן האשה צריכה לקום מפני
חמיה וחמותה – Either standing up completely or just rising a little bit — both sons-in-law and daughters-in-law
16. *Kovetz Mevakshei Torah* 21, p. 278, in the name of Harav Yosef Shalom Elyashiv: ויש
להושיב את אביו ואמו במקום היותר מכובד שיש
בבית וכן הדין בחמיו וחמותו ומכל מקום אין חיוב בדבר
17. *Otzar Kibbud Av Va'eim* 663
18. *Aruch HaShulchan* 240:38: אם אין לאב,
וגם אין לו בנים שיזונו, וחתנו הוא עשיר, כופין
אותו לזונו במעות צדקה שלו שהרי לא גרע
מקרובו. ועד שהרי חייב בכבוד חמיו
19. *Otzar Kibbud Av Va'eim* 666, psak of Rav Yosef Shalom Elyashiv: דאע"פ שבחמיו
יש רק דיני כבוד ואין דיני מורא, מ"מ אסור לקרוא
להם בשמם משום דשלו לקרוא להם בשמם
הוא גם כבוד להם וחייב בכבודם. וכן לא ישב על
מקומם דג"כ כבוד הוא להם שלא ישב על מקומם
וחייב בכבודם (מבקשי תורה כ"א עמ' שי"ד)
20. *Otzar Kibbud Av Va'eim* 672: אסור לו
לצערם ולבזותם וישתדל לנהוג עמהם בדרך שלא
תעורר מחלוקת
21. *Sefer Cheshbon Pirtei HaMitzvos,* Rav Tzvi Aryeh Goldman 1904, p. 23, quoted in *Sefer Kibbud Av Va'eim* (Rav Feldman): ועוד כמה יגיעות וטרחות ימים ולילות והוצאות
יגעו וטרחו והוציאו חמיו וחמותו, עד שגדלו את
הבן או הבת והשיאום אותם, נמצא שבכלל כבוד
חמיו וחמותו יש ג"כ חיוב פרעון החוב כמו בכבוד
אב ואם כנזכר בשם המדרש, ואם ח"ו אינם
מכבדים אותם רק עוד מצערים אותם, לבד שעובר
על דברי חז"ל ועובר על כמה לאוין ועשין, עוד
הוא בכלל משלם רעה תחת טובה רח"ל, לכן חייב

רמיא על החתן להיות מכבד אותם בכל מיני כבוד
בחייהם ובמותם. וביותר צריך לזרז את האשה
שתהא זהירה בכבוד חמיה וחמותה
22. *Kiddushin* 81b
Shulchan Aruch 22, Se'if 10
23. *Shaar HaTevunah, Perek* 15: ומה שאמרו
חז"ל וכלם בלשון הרע, הלא סימן על זה תכף,
בלשון הרע סלקא דעתך, אלא אימא באבק לשון
הרע. ואף באבק שם המהרש"א דמה שאמרו
כלם, היינו רק שאם האדם לא יתן עיניו ולבו על
דבורו, ויניח אותו על טבעו, בודאי כלם יכשלו בו...
אבל לא כונו חז"ל חס ושלום לומר שהאדם לא
יוכל להנצל כלל מאבק לשון הרע
24. *Bava Basra* 165a
25. *Mishlei* 27:19: כמים הפנים לפנים כך לב אדם
לאדם, heard from Rav Dovid Weinberger in the name of the Belzer Rebbe
26. *Vayikra* 19:17 — commentators ad loc.
27. *Sefer HaChinuch* 238: היא קשה מכל
השנאה הגלויה ועליה הזהירה התורה ביותר
Sefer HaMitzvos L'Rambam, Mitzvah Lo Sa'aseh 302: שנאת הלב היא חטא חזק יותר מן
הכל
28. *Rambam, Hilchos Deios Perek* 6, Halachah 6: כשיחטא איש לאיש לא ישטמנו
וישתוק אלא מצוה עליו להודיע ולומר למה עשית
לי כך וכך שנא' הוכח תוכיח את עמיתך...
29. *Chofetz Chaim, Klal* 10, *Se'if* 14
30. *Pele Yo'etz, Chamiv VaChamoso*
31. Ibid.: כמה יגיעות אדם יגע וכמה סובל צער
גידול בנים עד שמגיעם לפרק נישואין ומקום
לטובה ולהשיאם ולמצוא מרגוע לנפשם ואחר כך
כלה קמה בחמותה ומתרבה המחלוקת והקטטה
בבית ועושה שגם הבן יעשה מחלוקת וקטטה עם
אביו ואמו
32. Ibid.: אישה יראת ה' היא תתהלל, שתכבד
את חמיה ואת חמותה יותר ויותר וכל מגמתה
תהיה להשיג ולדעת את רצונם ולעשות רצונם
כרצונה
33. *Sefer Chareidim* 12:3-10: וכן האיש חייב
בכבוד חמיו וחמותו, וטעמא משום דאיש ואשתו
כחד גופא חשיבי ואב של זה כאב ואם של זה

Chapter 30: Mending the Fifth

1. *Rambam, Hilchos Teshuvah* 2:9: אבל עבירות
שבין אדם לחבירו...אינו נמחל לו לעולם עד שיתן
לחבירו מה שהוא חייב לו וירצהו. אע"פ שהחזיר
לו ממון שהוא חייב לו צריך לרצותו ולשאול
ממנו שימחל לו. אפילו לא הקניט את חבירו אלא
בדברים צריך לפייסו ולפגוע בו עד שימחל לו
2. *Mitzvos HaLevavos,* p. 19: אף אם נתן לו דמי
בושתו אינו נמחל לו, עד שיבקש ממנו למחול לו
3. Ibid.: וזמן בקשת המחילה הוא מחוייב בכל
עת. וקץ המחילה הוא בעי"כ

4. *Minchas Chinuch, Mitzvah* 33: ולא מהני
תשובה אם לא ירצה את אב ואם

5. *Sefer HaTeshuvah*, HaRav Yosef Cohen:
יזהר מאד שכאשר יבוא אל חברו לבקש סליחתו
אל יתנצל עליו בתירוצים שונים ולפעמים התירוץ
עלול יותר להכעיסו ויכל להרוס כל הענין.

והעיקר כשיבוא לבקש סליחתו יהיה בהכנעה
גדולה, ולהכיר ולהודות בחטאו, יבקש שימחול
לו על אשמתו, כי יש לו חרטה גמורה על
העולה הגדולה שעשה...

6. Even if the son or daughter feels provoked, he should at least apologize for his
part in the contention.

7. *Rambam, Hilchos Teshuvah:* החוטא צריך
לפרט החטא וחברך יכיר שמתחרט באמת ובלב
שלם. ובודאי ימחול לו

8. *Mitzvos HaLevavos, Hilchos Nekimah
U'Netirah*, p. 34: לא ישלח תחילה שליח
לפייסו רק ילך מעצמו לפייסו. אם קשה לו לילך
בעצמו תחילה או שידוע שיותר קרוב הפיוס ע״י
איש אמצעי שיעשה שלום ביניהם יכול לעשות
ע״י אמצעי

9. *Rambam, Hilchos Teshuvah:* אפילו לא
הקניט את חבירו אלא בדברים צריך לפייסו ולפגע
בו עד שימחל לו

Chapter 31:
Seizing the Power from Eisav

1. *Sefer Chassidim, Siman* 339: "ויאמר
עשו הנה אנכי הולך למות, ולמה זה לי בכורה"
(בראשית כה, לב). למה כתוב מה שחשב עשו?
אלא שלא תתמה, למה נתן הקדוש ברוך הוא
ממשלה לבני עשו? לומר, שתדיר בשביל אביו
הלך למקום סכנה, למקום החיות, כדי לצוד ציד
להביא לאביו

Chapter 32: The Reward

1. *Midrash Tanchuma, Parashas Eikev*: תני
רשב״י שתי מצוות גילה הקב״ה מתן שכרן, אחת
קלה שבקלות ואחד חמורה שבחמורות ואלו הן:
שילוח הקן וכבוד אב ואם, הרי הן שוין במתן שכרן
בעוה״ז

2. *Kiddushin* 39:2: שכר מצוה בהאי עלמא ליכא

3. *Eiruvin* 22: היום לעשותם ולמחר לקבל שכרם

4. *Baal HaTurim, Parashas Yisro*: חסר יוד
שאין אריכת ימים בעוה״ז

5. *Yerushalmi Peah* 1:1

6. *Sefer Kad HaKemach L'Rabbeinu Bachya*
(Kibbud Av Va'eim): גדול כח מצות כבוד אב
ואם והיא מצוה נכבדת כזהב והבריות רואין לעין
כי יש בשכרה פירות בעוה״ז או בשלוה והצלחה
שיוסיף לו השי״ת בכל מעשיו או באריכת ימים
והוא השכר הקבוע במצוה זו

7. Translated with permission from *Mar-*

veh L'Tzameh*, 1995 כ״ט אדר תשע״ב גליון ,
"Yeled B'Matanah"

8. *Ramban, Shemos* 20:12: למען יאריכן ימיך
על האדמה, יבטיח כי במצוה הזאת יהיו כל ימותנו
ארוכים

9. *Ohr HaChaim HaKadosh, Parashas Yisro:* למען יאריכן ימיך, אומר "יאריכו" שמשמע
בעצמם ולא אמר אאריך ימיך

10. *Mishnah Sotah* 1:7

11. *Chasam Sofer, Sefer Toras Moshe, Devarim* 28:11: והותירך ה' לטובה בפרי בטנך

Chapter 33:
It's Not Over When It's Over

1. According to most opinions, this is con-
sidered a Torah obligation. See sources in
Vayevarech Dovid p. 156 and *Mora Horim
V'Kibbudam* p. 145

2. *Rambam, 13 Ikarim*: אני מאמין באמונה
שלימה שהבורא יתברך שמו גומל טוב לשומרי
מצוותיו ומעניש לעוברי מצוותיו

3. *Shemiras HaLashon Shaar HaTevunah* 8

4. *Ahavas Chessed, Chelek 2, Perek* 15, footnote:

ויצייר האדם בנפשו: אלו היה הוא בעצמו, חס
ושלום משלך באש או בשאר יסורים קשים – כמה
היה חפצו ותשוקתו שבניו יכנסו בעבי הקורה
בעבורו, באיזה עצה שיוכלו, להצילו מזה העונש
הנורא. כזה וכזה יראה הוא בעצמו לעשות עבור
נשמת אביו ואמו, שעמלו בכל כחותיהם עליו
עד שעשאוהו לאיש, להצילם בכח מעשיו הטובים
מענש עוונותיהם המר, כי בודאי אדם אין צדיק
בארץ וגו'. ובפרט בתוך שבעה ושלשים, שאז כח
הדין מתוח יותר, כידוע...

5. *Sanhedrin* 104a

6. ברא כרעא דאבוה *Ahavas Chessed, Chelek
2, Perek* 15; *Pachad Yitzchak Igros V'Ksavim*
242:

...ברא כרעא דאבוה. ולמה דוקא רגל? ולמה
אין הבן נחשב לידו של אביו? - רק בני אדם בהאי
עלמא נחשבים ל"מהלכים". ואלו נשמות ומלאכים
עומדים הם נקראים...כיון שאדם מת, נעשה חפשי
מן המצוות, ובלי מצוות אין הילוך של עליה. ישנה
רק עמידה במדרגה אחת. הרגל היא האבר אשר
על ידו נעשה האדם למהלך. והיינו ברא כרעא
דאבוה. כלומר, שאם האב נמצא מצד עצמו במצב
של עמידה, מ"מ הניח אחריו בן הגון, הרי הבן
עושה את אביו ל"מהלכים", אפילו במקום שהאב
מצד עצמו הוא במצב של עמידה...

7. *Iggeres HaTeshuvah* 79

8. רמב״ן:
[ד' אמר לאברהם בברית בין הבתרים] "ואתה
תבוא אל אבותיך בשלום" בשרו שיש לאביו חלק
לעולם הבא (בראשית רבה)... לשון רש״י: למדך

שעשה תרח תשובה בשעת מיתה או שמא יש לו
חלק לעולם הבא שאמרו חז"ל (סנהדרין קד) ברא
מזכי אבא - בזכות בנו

9. *Kibbud Horim* (Rav Greenwald), p. 177, quoting the *Zohar, Bechukosai*:

רבי אלעזר הרבה את זכויותיו של אביו רבי
שמעון בר יוחי בעולם הבא בזכות מעשיו הטובים

From here we learn that even if a parent was a *tzaddik gamur*, a child can increase this parent's merit in the next world

10. *Ahavas Chessed, Chelek 2, Perek 15*: כמו
שכתב בספר "יש נוחלין", דזכויות ומצוות שעושה
הבן אחר מיתת אביו – הוא כפרה לנפש אביו, אף
על פי דמנפשה קעבד. וכתב על זה בנו, בעל השל"ה,
וזה לשונו: ולא זו בלבד שמציל את אביו מדינה של
גיהנם ומוציא אותו מן היסורין, אלא אף זו שמכניסו
אחר-כך לגן עדן, ונותנו במחיצת הצדיקים...

11. *Vayevarech Dovid*, p. 156… דזהו מזון רוחני
וצרכיו הרוחניים שלו...

12. *Pele Yo'etz, Kibbud Av Va'eim:* ידמה כאילו
נותן לו מטעמים כאשר אהב אביו

13. *Arizal, Likutei Torah, Parashas Yisro*:
שיראה לחדש חידושי תורה בכל שבת ושבת
ומועיל לנשמת אבותיו ובגין כך מעטירין לאביו
ואמו בגן עדן

14. *Otzar Kibbud Av Va'eim* 435:
ולדינא נקטו אחרוני הפוסקים וגדולי ההוראה
דכל שמזכיר אביו או אמו בכל ענין הוא אומר הכ"מ
(כ"מ מדברי הבא"ח שופטים ש"ע ס"ר שכתב:
"כשמזכיר שם אביו יאמר וכו' כ"ב בקצוש"ע סי'
קמ"ג ס"ח ובשו"ת עמק הלכה ז"ב סי' ג"ב וכ"כ
בספר מורא הו"כ עמ' קמ"ז בשם הגרפ"ץ א"ש
זצ"ל ובעמ' קץ"ד בשם הגרי"ש שליט"א). ולפי"ז
פשוט דגם בת צריכה לומר על אביה או אמה הריני
כפרת משכבו או משכבה.

15. *Teshuvos V'Hanhagos* 4:272

16. *Zohar, Bechukosai:* זוהר בחוקותי קט"ו
ע"ב: כבד את אביך ואת אמך. מצוה זו בחייו
מתחייב בה. לאחר מיתה אפשר שתאמר שפטור
ממנה. לא כן הוא. ואע"ג שמת, מחויב בכבודם
עוד יותר מבחייהם.

17. *Vayevarech Dovid*, p. 160, based on *Shulchan Aruch* 340

18. *Mora Horim VeKibbudam* 12:19, *Se'if Katan* 19

19. *Ahavas Chessed, Chelek 2, Perek 15:* בודאי
הוא עושה הצלה גדולה ונחת רוח לנשמתו, the *Shelah HaKadosh* quoted in *Ahavas Chessed* p. 180

20. *Rema* 376: כשהבן מתפלל ומקדש ברבים,
פודה אביו ואמו מן הגהינם

21. *Morah Horim VeKibbudam* 13:7

22. *Mourning in Halachah* 39:21, footnote 36

23. *Kitzur Shulchan Aruch* 26:22: אף על פי

שאמירת הקדיש והתפילות מועילות להאבות
מכל מקום אין אלו אלו העקר. אלא העקר שהבנים
ילכו באורך מישור כי בזה הם מזכים האבות...ויש
לו לאדם לצוות את בניו להחזיק באיזה מצוה ואם
מקיימין נחשב יותר מן הקדיש והוא תקנה טובה
גם למי שאין לו בנים אלא בנות

24. *Rema, Shulchan Aruch, Yoreh Deah* 376

25. צור כל העולמים צדיק בכל הדורות הקל
הנאמן...שכל דבריו אמת וצדיק נאמן אתה ה'
ונאמנים דבריך

26. *Rema, Shulchan Aruch, Yoreh Deah* 376

27. *Teshuvas Chasam Sofer, Yoreh Deah* 345
שכל מי שאומר קדיש שמגיע לחברו לא
הועיל לעצמו ולא הפסיד לחברו דמכל מקום עולה
לנשמת מי ששייך לו

28. *Mourning in Halachah*, p. 406

29. *Ahavas Chessed, Chelek 2, Perek 15*

30. *Mishnah Berurah, Hilchos Yom Kippur* 521, *Se'if Katan* 19

ומסתברא דאם הבן נותן [צדקה] בעד אביו
בכל גווני מועיל להקל דינו דברא מזכה אבא

31. *Pele Yo'etz: Kavod*:
לכן לא יגרע אפילו יום אחד כל ימי חייו ליתן
צדקה עבור נפש הוריו

32. *Rabbi Avigdor Miller Speaks*, p. 109

33. *Kesubos* 50a. It says in *Tehillim*, וצדקתו
עומדת לעד, on which the Gemara says, "One who writes Torah, *Nevi'im*, and *Kesuvim* and lends them to others, it is an everlasting memorial.

34. *Sefer Chassidim* 571:
... והיו לו אחים ואחיות והיו מתקוטטים עמו,
והיה מקללן ומכעיסן, והיה לאביו ולאמו צער...
ועשו אמר (שם כז מא) יקרבו ימי אבל אבי ואהרגה
את יעקב אחי, ובחייו לא רצה להרוג שלא יצטער
אביו לכך אל תצער אביך לקלל זרעו בחייו. וגם
לאחר מותו יש לו לאדם לחשוב אלו היה אבי
חי היה מצטער אבי גם אחרי מותו לא אקלל,
כי הנשמה רוח האדם, לאחר מותו יודעת כל מה
שבזה העולם

35. *Vayevarech Dovid*, p. 171: בעוה"ר מצוי
מאוד שבפטירת האב נעשה מחלוקת בין הבנים
אודות חלוקת הירושה וכדומה, ומבואר בספרים
דנשמת המת אין לו מנוחה בזמן שיש מחלוקת בין
בניו...וכשיש איזה סכסוכים (בין האחים והאחיות
או האלמנה) יקבלו על עצמן לסדר הכל ע"י
תלמיד חכם הבקי בדינים אלו, והכל על מקומו
יבא בשלום.)

36. *Zohar, Bechukosai*:
שאם הבן הולך בדרך רע ודאי מבזה לאביו
ועושה לו קלון, ואם הבן הולך בדרך הישר ומתקן
מעשיו, אז ודאי מכבד לאביו, מכבדים בעולם הזה
נגד בני אדם (דהיינו שמזכירים את אבותיהם
לטוב ואומרים אשרי יולדתו). ומכבדו בעולם

הבא נגד הקב"ה, והקב"ה חס על אביו ומושיבו
בכסא כבוד

37. *Ahavas Chessed, Chelek 2, Perek* 15

והנה באמת על ידי כל מצוה שהבן עושה מועיל
להנפטר, כמו שהובא שם בספר "יש נוחלין". בשם
הראשונים. וכל שכן במצוה זו של חסד שנתעורר
למעלה על ידי זה מדת החסד, כמה יועיל זה
למעלה לנפש הנפטר, שיתנהג השם יתברך עמו
בכל עניניו גם כן במדת החסד. גם שעל ידי זה
נזכר שם של אבותיו לעיני הכל לטובה. שאומרים:
אשרי שזה ילד, אשרי שזה גדל! וממילא נתעורר
עליהם זכות ורחמים גם כן מלמעלה.

38. Besides the mitzvah of *chessed* —
והלכת בדרכיו — providing loans is a fulfillment of the mitzvah את כסף תלוה אם
עמי. This is the only type of *chessed* that
has an added mitzvah over and above the
general admonition to do kindness. The
chessed of a loan is greater than *tzedakah*,
because it involves less embarrassment
for the recipient; a loan is more dignified
than taking charity. *Tzedakah* is a one-time
gift vs. a lending fund whose loans are
continual.

39. *Chofetz Chaim* (ibid.): לעשות גמ"ח קבוע
לזכר נשמת אבותיהם ובזה היה מתעלה נפשם
מאד למעלה כי מכל הלוואה והלוואה שנתוסף
להם מצות עשה דאורייתא ממילא נתוסף זכות
אבותיהם גם כן.

40. *Pele Yo'etz, Chessed*:

אשרי אנוש יעשה זאת יקנה כלים הצריכים
לרבים וישאיל להם בזה יכול אדם לקנות חיי
עולם הבא

41. *Midrash Tanchuma, Parashas Noach*

42. *Arizal, Likutei Torah, Parashas Yisro*:

שיראה לחדש חידושי תורה בכל שבת ושבת
ומועיל לנשמת אבותיו ובגין כך מעטירין לאביו
ואמו בגן עדן

43. *Kibbud Horim* (Rav Greenwald), p. 187:

זוהר פרשת נשא: שהחתן בלימודו תורתו
ומעשיו הטובים גורם לעילוי רוחני לחותנו בעולם
העליון

44. *Yesod V'Shoresh HaAvodah, Shaar* 8,
Perek 12: וגם נראה לי ברור, אם חושב אדם איזה
שעה ביום שבת קדש לחדש בשכלו איזה הנהגה
טובה בעבודת יוצרנו ובוראנו יתברך שמו ויתעלה,
שיתנהג בהנהגה ישרה זו כל ימי השבוע ולתת
בהנהגה זו נחת רוח ליוצרנו ברוך הוא וברוך שמו, הן

בהנהגת טהרת המחשבה, הן בהנהגת הדבור למעט
בכל יכלתו, הן בהנהגות התמדת למודו יותר
מימים שחלפו ועברו, הן בהנהגות כונת התפלה. או
בברכת הנהנין וכיוצא, אף בהנהגת אכילה ומשגל,
גם במשא ומתן שלו לעסוק בה על צד ההתר,
זה ברור שמלאכת מחשבת ישרה כתורה יחשב,
והבורא יתברך שמו ויתעלה ישתעשע בחדוש
זה בפמליא שלו, גם יתעטר הוא יתברך שמו
וכל פמליא שלו וכל נשמות הצדיקים שבגן עדן,
כמבואר בזהר הקדוש הנזכר לעיל, וחשב עם קונהו
כאלו חדש סתרי תורה על דרך האמת
הנשמה נהנית מהדלקת

45. *Rabbeinu Bechaye*:
הנר

46. *Vayevarech Dovid*, p. 170

47. *Mora Horim V'Kibbudam* 12:39,59

See "The Neshama Should Have an
Aliyah" by Rabbi Tzvi Hebel, p. 128, for
extended discussion

48. *Mourning in Halachah*, 44:2

49. *Sefer Panim Yafos, Behaaloscha*

50. *Kitzur Shulchan Aruch* 143:21:

מי שהוא רוצה באמת לכבד את אביו ואת
אמו, יעסוק בתורה ובמעשים טובים, שזהו הכבוד
הגדול להאבות שאומרים הבריות אשרי לאב ואם
שגדלו בן כזה...

51. *Pele Yo'etz, Kibbud Av Va'eim*

Epilogue

1. אלא במזלא תליא מילתא — Rav Hai Gaon
Bereishis (*Mashal Rav Hai Gaon, Siman* 13,
quoted in *Yalkut Lekach Tov, Parashas Korach*; also *Michtav MeEliyahu*, 4th volume, p.
303). The exact wording of *Chazal* is, "It depends on *mazal*." But since we know מזל אין
לישראל — the Jewish lot is not decided by
mazal, *Chazal* tell us that this is not referring
to *mazal kochavim* but *Hashgachah Pratis*.

2. Why don't we find a special prayer for
our children's success in the *Shemoneh
Esrei*? Because then we might think that
davening for children three times a day is
enough!

3. *Sefer Ruach Chaim* on *Pirkei Avos* 5:3:

עשרה נסיונות נתנסה אברהם אבינו ע"ה ועמד
בכולם

משלי: מתהלך בתומו צדיק אשרי בניו אחריו:
כי כמה מידות שהצדיק טרח ויגע להשיג לבניו
אחריו המה בטבע מוטבע ובקצת יגיעה יגיעו לזה